English and Korean in Contrast

English and Korean in Contrast

A Linguistic Introduction

Jong-Bok Kim
Kyung Hee University, Seoul, Korea

WILEY Blackwell

Library of Congress Cataloging-in-Publication Data:

Names: Kim, Jong-Bok, 1966- author.
Title: English and Korean in contrast : a linguistic introduction /
    Jong-Bok Kim, Kyung Hee University, Seoul, Korea.
Description: Hoboken, New Jersey : Wiley-Blackwell, 2024. | Includes
    bibliographical references and index.
Identifiers: LCCN 2023024907 (print) | LCCN 2023024908 (ebook) | ISBN
    9781394157372 (cloth) | ISBN 9781394157389 (adobe pdf) | ISBN
    9781394157396 (epub)
Subjects: LCSH: English language–Grammar, Comparative–Korean. | Korean
    language–Grammar, Comparative–English. | Contrastive linguistics.
Classification: LCC PE1099 .K48 2024 (print) | LCC PE1099 (ebook) | DDC
    495.7–dc23/eng/20231204
LC record available at https://lccn.loc.gov/2023024907
LC ebook record available at https://lccn.loc.gov/2023024908

Cover Design: Wiley
Cover Image: 'Emotion of Color' © Cho Jaeman 2015

Set in 9.5/12.5pt STIXTwoText by Straive, Chennai, India

SKY10063775_010524

Contents

Preface

This book presents a comprehensive analysis of the major contrasts between Korean and English. Contrastive descriptions of languages occur at many different levels of linguistic structure: speech sounds (phonetics and phonology), word formation (morphology), phrase and sentence structure (syntax), word and clause meaning (semantics), language uses (pragmatics and discourse), and so forth. It is well known that the two typologically unrelated languages English and Korean show many contrasts with respect to these linguistic factors. This book offers an introductory, systematic comparison of these factors from a linguistic perspective.

The contrastive analysis of these two typologically distinctive languages can provide strong foundations for the understanding of English from the perspective of Korean, and that of Korean from the perspective of English. This in particular will help language learners (L1 as well as L2) identify major sources of difficulty or ease in learning or understanding the structure of the two languages. The book, based on previous contrastive studies and an exploration of the relevant literature on the two languages as well as linguistic typology in general, is expected to achieve at least the following goals:

- Provide a better understanding of the linguistic structures of the two target languages
- Develop insights into some major mistakes that are frequently made by L2 learners irrespective of their L1
- Account for observed errors and offer a way to outline the differences between the two languages, which can serve as guideposts for second-language teaching and learning
- Help students apply the contrastive knowledge of the two target languages to related fields such as language acquisition, language pedagogy, psycholinguistics, bilingualism, language therapy, translation, and so forth.

This book grew out of my teaching the undergraduate course "English and Korean: A Contrastive Analysis" for several years. The book, developed from several manuscripts I used in the course with the title of "Understanding Grammatical Contrasts between English and Korean" (Pagijong Press), relies on a variety of published sources on Korean and English, including my own. I tried to include in the bibliography all the references from which I have learned a great deal about English and Korean linguistics over more than a decade, but I may have missed some sources. The students who have used the manuscript of this book in its early stages deserve my special gratitude for their questions, comments, and suggestions. They helped me understand what students need to better understand the structure of the two languages from a contrastive perspective. Many linguists helped or influenced me in developing and refining the materials discussed in this book, including Anne Abeillé, Gabriela Bîlbîie, Bob Borsley, Rui Chaves, Hee-Rahk Chae, Suk-Jin Chang, Sae-Youn Cho, Sungdai Cho, Incheol Choi, Jae-Woong Choi, Chan Chung, Mark Davies, Adle Goldberg, Javier Perez Guerra, Yasunari Harada, Martin Hilpert, Chu-Ren Huang, Sea-Eun Jhang, Paul Kay, Nayoung Kwon, Taeho Kim, Chungmin Lee, Hanjung Lee, Juwon Lee, Kiyong Lee, Laura Michaelis, Philip Miller, Yunju Nam, Joanna Nykiel, Byungsoo Park, Chongwon Park, Dongwoo Park, Sanghee Park, Byong-Rae Ryu, Peter Sells, Sanghoun Song, Frank Van Eynde, James Yoon, Eun-jung Yoo, and others whose names I may have omitted here. My (former) graduate students studying English as well as Korean linguistics also helped me develop this textbook. In particular, I thank Jihye Kim, Jungsoo Kim, Hee-Yeon Kim, Okgi Kim, Geonhee Lee, Seulkee Park, Youn-Gyu Park, and Sim Rok for their feedback and editorial assistance. I also thank the anonymous reviewers of the book manuscript for their constructive suggestions. The editorial team at Wiley, including Rachel Greenberg, Ed Robinson, Radhika Raheja Sharma, and Tiffany Taylor, also deserve many thanks for helping this project reach completion. This work was supported by the Ministry of Education of the Republic of Korea and the National Research Foundation of Korea (NRF-2021S1A6A4046103).

I dedicate this book to all of my family members who have constantly supported me, regardless of where I am and what I am doing.

Abbreviations

ACC	accusative
AGT	agentive
AGR	agreement
ARG	argument
ARG-ST	argument-structure
AUX	auxiliary
AVM	attribute-value matrix
BAKGR	background
CAUS	causative
C-CONT	constructional content
CL	classifier
CONTRA	contrastive
COMIT	comitative
COMP	complementizer
COMPS	complements
CONJ	conjunctive
CONN	connective
COORD	coordination
COP	copula
DAT	dative
DECL	declarative
DEL	delimiter
FIN	finitive
FML	formal
FOC	focus
FUT	future
GEN	genitive
HON	honorific
IMP	imperative

IND	index
INST	instrument
LFN	long-form negation
LOC	locative
MOD	modified
NMLZ	nominalizer
NOM	nominative
NONFIN	nonfinite
NPI	negative polarity item
PAST	past
PASS	passive
PL	plural
PNE	prenominal ending
POS	parts of speech
PROM	promissive
PRES	present
PRED	predicate
PROP	propositive
PST	past
QUE	question
REL	relativizer
SFN	short-form negation
SRC	source
SUBJ	subject
SUG	suggestive
TENSE	tense
TOP	topic

1

Linguistic Differences: Where Do They Come From?

Learning a second or foreign language (L2) has a variety of cognitive benefits, including improving memory, problem-solving and critical-thinking skills, the ability to multitask, and so forth. However, it is at the same time a formidable task. When we try to learn a foreign language whose sound or grammatical structure is quite different from that of our mother tongue, the process can be long and painstaking. When learning Korean as a second or foreign language, English speakers typically have more difficulty than native speakers of Japanese, whose linguistic structure is similar to that of Korean. Meanwhile, Korean speakers spend much more time learning English than Germans or French people do learning the typologically similar English. What is the reason? Many factors can cause this kind of difference in learning, but linguistic and cultural dissimilarities may be prime ones.

1.1 Linguistic Differences

Korean is the native language of about 80 million people in South and North Korea and more in expatriate communities across the world. In terms of typology, it is often said to belong to the Altaic language family (although some controversies remain). In terms of grammatical structures, Korean is similar to languages like Japanese in that it has an SOV (subject-object-verb) order. In terms of vocabulary, it is heavily influenced by classical Chinese. A large proportion of Korean words are either coined in Korean using Chinese characters or borrowed from the Chinese language directly.

On the other hand, English belongs to the Indo-European language group, which includes French, German, Spanish, Portuguese, and so forth. The earliest forms of English were related to a group of West Germanic dialects brought to

Great Britain by Anglo-Saxon settlers in the fifth century and developed over more than 1,500 years. Modern English has been spreading since the seventeenth century, due to the worldwide influence of Great Britain and the United States, and it now serves as a global lingua franca. In terms of structure, it has an SVO (subject-verb-object) order, and the vocabulary of English is characterized by at times massive influences from other languages like Latin, Greek, French, and so forth.

Many English-speaking language learners feel that Korean is one of the most difficult languages to learn. It is often said that it requires three times more effort for native speakers of English to learn Korean than another Indo-European language like French. This, in turn, implies that English is one of the most difficult languages for Koreans to study. A primary reason for this has to do with the substantial linguistic differences between Korean and English. For example, (1) illustrates major structural differences between Korean and English:

(1) 선생-님-이   학생-들-을   사랑하-시-었-습니-다.
    sensayng-nim-i haksayng-tul-ul salangha-si-ess-supni-ta
    teacher-HON-NOM student-PL-ACC   love-HON-PST-FRML-DECL
    'The teacher loved students.'

The first line represents the Korean alphabet system Hangul and the second line the Yale Romanization system.[1] The third line shows the glosses for each expression, and the fourth is the English translation. As seen in the example, Korean places the verb *salangha-si-ess-supni-ta* 'love-HON-PST-FRML-DECL' in the sentential final position. The Korean verb also has a rather complex inflectional system. While the English verb *love* has only the past tense suffix *-ed*, the Korean counterpart *salangha-* 'love' occurs with four suffixes *si-ess-supni-ta* 'HON-PST-FRML-DECL,' and each of these has its own grammatical function (see Chapter 3).[2] The subject *sensayng-nim-i* 'teacher-HON-NOM' and the object *haksayng-tul-ul* 'students-PL-ACC' are also marked with an overt case marker: nominative (NOM) *-i* and accusative (ACC) *-ul*. The nominative marker is usually attached to the subject of a sentence, whereas the accusative marker goes with an object (see Chapter 3 for details).

---

1 The Yale system differs from the Revised Romanization of Korean proposed by the Ministry of Culture, which is most widely and officially used in Korea. In the Korean writing system, there is no hyphen within words. The hyphens given in this textbook are to help understand how each word is coined with nominal particles or verbal suffixes. Refer to Chapter 2 for a complete table of the Korean Romanization system.

2 The meanings of the abbreviations are given in parentheses: NOM (nominative), HON (honorific), PST (past), FRML (formal), and DECL (declarative). As we proceed, details of these abbreviations will be discussed.

In addition to such differences between English and Korean, the two languages differ in their sound systems. For example, unlike English, Korean has no voiced consonants among its basic sounds (called phonemes). That is why Koreans have difficulty distinguishing between voiceless consonants like [f] and voiced ones like [v]. For example, if speakers are not conscious of or have not learned them, they would have trouble differentiating or producing English pairs like the following:

(2) a. pin vs. bin
    b. tin vs. din
    c. fine vs. vine

However, this does not mean the phonetic system of Korean is simpler than that of English. Unlike English, Korean has triplets for many consonants. For instance, the basic sound [k] or [t] in Korean has three different variants of each consonant sound that are not easy for English speakers to identify (the Korean writing system, Hangul, is a phonemic alphabet, and the Yale Romanization is given immediately after each Korean word here):

(3) a. [k]: 가 ka, 카 kha, 까 kka
    b. [t]: 다 ta, 타 tha, 따 tta

As just illusrated, in learning English or Korean, we need to appreciate the key linguistic differences of the two languages to reach the desired level of linguistic competence within a limited time. It is important to understand why Koreans or foreigners have difficulties pronouncing some sounds or producing certain constructions in their target language. Language learning requires patience and tireless effort, but recognizing the linguistic reasons for these difficulties will help language learners greatly.

1.2 Cultural Differences

In addition to these linguistic difficulties, language learners also encounter cultural differences in their target languages. It is often noted that learning a target language cannot be done without understanding the culture imbued in the language. Without understanding the life, culture, history, and society of America or England, it is hard for Korean students to master English. The same goes for English speakers trying to learn Korean. For example, if students are not accustomed to American culture, they will have trouble figuring out the meaning of *paper or plastic, for here or to go, any cash back*, etc. Korean or Japanese people often ask English-speaking people personal questions like *How old are you? Where are you going? Are you married?* and so forth, since such expressions are used daily in the mother languages. However, these personal questions often embarrass foreigners, including native speakers of English, since such questions are considered impolite in Western culture.

Cultural differences are often reflected in languages. An intriguing example can be found in the uses of the pronoun *wuli* 'we' in Korean. Consider the following dialogue occurring between a greeter and a greetee with his wife:

(4) A: 만나서   반갑습니다.
      manna-se pankap-supni-ta
      meet-CONN glad-FRML-DECL
      'Glad to meet you.'
    B: 저도   반갑습니다.
      ce-to   pankap-supni-ta
      me-too glad-FRML-DECL
      'Glad to meet you too.'
    A: 우리 집사람입니다.
      wuli cipsalam-i-pni-ta
      our   housewife-COP-FRML-DECL
      (literally) 'This is our wife.'

This conversation demonstrates one striking difference in the usage of the pronoun 우리 wuli 'we/our' in Korean. In English, the correct pronoun here is the first person, 'my.' It is often observed that Korean speakers use the first person pronoun 'our' in place of the first-person pronoun 'my,' as illustrated by the following:

(5) a. 우리 아들에게 전화해   줘.
      wuli atul-eykey cenhwahay cwu-e
      our son-to   call   give-SUG
      '(lit.) Please call our son.'

    b. 이 것   우리 집-으로 보내 줘.
      i   kes   wuli cip-ulo ponay cwu-e
      this thing our home-to send give-SUG
      'Please send this to our house.'

One possible account for the distinctive use of the pronoun 우리 wuli 'we' in Korean is that English-using societies have a "me-orientation" culture, while Korean has a "we-orientation" culture. That is, Korean places more emphasis on "we" (our group) than "me" (personal): the groups one belongs to are more important than the individual self. This cultural difference seems to be reflected in the usage of personal pronouns.

This is one simple case showing that language is, in a sense, a reflection of society, culture, life, and history. Without understanding these reflections in language, we end up learning just the surface of the target language and miss the depth of the language, which may eventually hinder our communication skills.

1.3   Why Contrastive Analyses?

Contrastive analyses compare languages to investigate their grammatical similarities and differences. These help us understand how the compared languages work in terms of linguistic structures. In addition, a linguistic comparison between two or more languages can help us understand where recurrent errors come from and what we need to focus on for language learning or teaching. The reason for grammatical errors made by L2 langauge learners is sometimes hard to identify, but contrastive studies between their L1 and L2 often allow us to pin down the underlying sources for the errors in a simple and clear way. By doing so, we also can understand why it is much easier or more difficult for us to learn a certain target language.

The properties shared by most natural languages are often called *Universal Grammar*. For instance, every language has a way to ask a question, make a negative sentence, or express a situation in the past or future. There are also general rules, often called *principles*, that most languages follow. For instance, in general, reflexive pronouns like *herself* in English and 자기자신 cakicasin 'self' in Korean need to have their antecedent (referring to the same individual) in the same clause (the symbol * means ungrammatical):

(6) a. Mimi$_i$ loves herself$_i$/*himself$_i$.
    b. 모모가$_i$ 자기자신$_{i/*j}$을 사랑한다.
       Momo-ka   caki.casin-ul   salangha-n-ta
       Momo-NOM self-ACC   love-PRES-DECL
       'Momo loves herself.'

The reflexive nouns *herself* in (6a) and 자기자신 cakicasin 'self' in (6b) both need to be coindexed (marked by subscript indexes) by their antecedent: *Mimi* and *Momo*, respectively. This kind of property is observed in most human languages and is often taken to be part of the general principles in natural languages.

Note that in addition to general principles, there are also values that distinguish languages, which are called *parameters*. The SVO language English is head-initial, while the SOV language Korean is head-final. Given that V is the head of a VP (verb phrase), V is in the initial position in English (VO), but it is in the final position (OV) in Korean (see Chapter 4):

(7) a. head-initial: SVO (subject-verb-object)
    b. head-final: SOV (subject-object-verb)

The first step in finding such a parametric value is to do a contrastive analysis of the two languages. Identifying parametric differences thus helps us understand key differences among the languages in question and further enhances the understanding of their grammar.

There are other advantages to studying languages from a contrastive perspective. The knowledge of contrasting grammatical properties of the two languages in question can be applied in many applied disciplines, such as second language teaching and learning, sociolinguistics and psycholinguistics, translation, and even historical linguistics. For instance, the proper Korean translation of the simple English sentence *I love you* does not include the corresponding Korean pronouns *I* and *you*. It is simply 사랑해 salanghay 'love' since in daily language use, Korean does not express pronouns as long as the given context tells us who is uttering the sentence to whom (see Chapter 5).

1.4 What This Book Is About

With the aim of better understanding English and Korean, two typologically different languages, this book focuses on linguistic similarities and differences between them.

The book starts with a discussion of sound systems in the two languages: that is, the kinds of basic sounds these languages have. We then examine the types of lexical (word) categories in each language. The differences in the sound systems and lexical categories differentiate the two languages. The book also discusses the formation of phrases projected from the lexical categories in English and Korean. These languages have different lexical categories, but we will observe that their combinatorial rules for forming well-formed phrases and sentences are quite similar. Using the basic combinatorial rules for forming phrases and sentences in the two languages, we will discuss several key syntactic constructions, including auxiliary, tense/aspect, relative clause, passive, interrogative, and comparative constructions. The book also discusses topic and focus constructions as well as agreement phenomena in which we observe how English and Korean behave differently in expressing discourse-related factors. We will also briefly review how the languages behave alike and differently in terms of figurative speeches including metaphors.

This book thus studies key grammatical properties (sound, word, syntax, semantics, and pragmatics) of English and Korean from a contrastive perspective. Its goal is to help students develop keen insights into the linguistic structures of the two languages.

Exercises

1   Try to think of at least three more linguistic differences between Korean and English. The differences can be anything about sound, grammar, meaning, or usage.

2   Visit a website for a Hangul to Yale Romanization converter (e.g. http://asaokitan.net/tools/hangul2yale), and analyze the following Korean sentences in the format of examples like (1) in this chapter (Korean sentence, Yale Romanization, gloss, and translation). Following the style given in (1), try to segment each of the Korean words by its root (or stem) and suffix(es), as far as you can.

    (i) a. 눈이 왔다.
          'It snowed.'
       b. 미미가 달렸다.
          'Mimi ran.'
       c. 장미가 예쁘게 피었다.
          'Roses bloomed pretty.'
       d. 나는 학생이다.
          'I am a student.'
       e. 모모가 그 책을 읽었다.
          'Momo read the book.'
       f. 학생들 모두가 서울로 갔다.
          'All of the students went to Seoul.'
       g. 아버지가 피아노를 치고 어머니가 노래를 한다.
          'Father plays the piano, and mother sings.'
       h. 친구가 동생에게 선물을 주었다.
          'The friend gave a present to the brother.'
       i. 아이가 그 책을 매일 읽었다.
          'The child read the book every day.'
       j. 영어와 한국어의 차이를 공부하였다.
          'We studied differences between English and Korean.'

3   Each language has different onomatopoeic and mimetic words, as given in (i). Provide three additional pairs of English and Korean examples, and discuss what this difference implies about the relationship between sound and meaning.

    (i) a. oink vs. 꿀꿀 kkwulkkwul
       b. meow vs. 야옹 yaong
       c. twinkle twinkle vs. 반짝반짝 panccakpanccak

4   Kinship terminology is heavily influenced by culture. Look at your family tree, including at least five different relatives (excluding parents and siblings), and compare the kin terms in English and Korean.

5   Discuss how to express the following English expressions in Korean. In addition, discuss what causes such differences between the two languages.
   (i) a. wearing a hat/clothes/shoes/gloves/a scarf
        b. putting on a hat/clothes/shoes/gloves/a scarf
   (ii) a. playing the violin/the trumpet/the cello
        b. looking at the sky/watching a movie/seeing pictures

2

Sounds and Writing Systems: How to Speak and Write

2.1 Introduction

Every language has basic sounds called *phonemes*. Phonemes are *distinctive* sounds in a given language that allow us to distinguish one word from another. Two sounds are distinctive from each other if the sound differences cause a distinction in meaning, like the sounds /p/ and /b/ in *pat* and *bat*.

One way to determine whether two sounds in a language are distinctive is to identify a *minimal pair* (a pair of words) that differ in only one phonological element but have distinct meanings. For example, the sounds /b/ and /t/ in the English words *bin* and *tin* are distinctive sounds and form a minimal pair because they vary by only a single sound but have different meanings. The same goes for the Korean sounds /p/ and /t/, as given in (1b). The aspirated [p^h] in (2b) is not a phoneme in English; but the same sound in Korean is a phoneme because it induces a meaning difference, as seen from (2b)[1]:

(1) a. bin, tin
    b. 본 pon 'base,' 돈 ton 'money'
(2) a. spin[spin] vs. spin[sp^hin]
    b. 반 pan 'half' vs. 판 p^han 'board'

In recognizing the set of sounds in each language, we thus need to identify the phonemes in each language. These phonemes are classified as *consonants* (자음 *caum* in Korean)' and *vowels* (모음 *moum* in Korean), depending on how the air stream is blocked in pronouncing the sounds. In producing consonants, the flow of breath is temporarily obstructed or blocked. Vowels are produced with a relatively free outward flow of breath. Every language has consonants and vowels but a different set of these sounds. In what follows, we will see what kinds of consonant and vowel sounds English and Korean have.

---

1 Basic sounds (phonemes) are represented in slashes / /, and the realization of these sounds (phones) are in square brackets [ ].

English and Korean in Contrast: A Linguistic Introduction, First Edition. Jong-Bok Kim.
© 2024 John Wiley & Sons, Inc. Published 2024 by John Wiley & Sons, Inc.

2.2   English Sound Systems

Both English and Korean sounds are produced when air is exiting (egressive) the lungs (pulmonic). The air in the lung travels up to the windpipe (trachea) and through the *larynx* (often called the Adam's apple or voice box). Across the larynx are two muscles called *vocal folds* or cords that open during normal breathing but close during eating. The space between the cords is known as the *glottis*. The sound made in this area is glottal. The vocal cords can be relaxed so the flow of air from the lungs passes through freely (voiceless) or held close together so they vibrate as air passes through (voiced); see Figure 2.1.

Sounds made in these ways can be further divided into two main categories: consonants and vowels. As noted earlier, *consonants* are produced when the airflow is partially or completely stopped, while*vowels* are are made with the air flowing freely.

2.2.1   English Consonants

In describing English consonants, we need to refer to three qualities:

- *Voiced vs. voiceless*: Whether the vocal cords are vibrating
- *Place of articulation*: Where the sound is produced (i.e. where in the vocal tract a constriction is made or where the vocal tract is more narrow)
- *Manner of articulation*: How the vocal tract modifies the air stream to produce the sound

These qualities tell us how and where English consonants are produced. Table 2.1 classifies English consonants: the first column represents how they are made (manner of articulation), and the top line indicates where they are made (place of articulation).

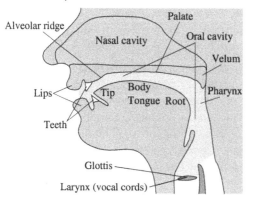

Figure 2.1   Anatomical structure of the human vocal system.

Table 2.1 English consonant sounds.

Manner/Place		Bilabial	Labio-dental	Inter-dental	Alveolar	Palatal	Velar	Glottal
Stops	[−voice]	/p/			/t/		/k/	/ʔ/
	[+voice]	/b/			/d/		/g/	
Fricatives	[−voice]		/f/	/θ/	/s/	/ʃ/		/h/
	[+voice]		/v/	/ð/	/z/	/ʒ/		
Affricates	[−voice]					/ʧ/		
	[+voice]					/ʤ/		
Nasals	[+voice]	/m/			/n/		/ŋ/	
Liquids	[+voice]				/l/, /r/			
Glides	[+voice]	/w/				/j/		

Voiced vs. Voiceless

Voiced and voiceless sounds can be distinguished as follows: "Are the vocal cords vibrating (voiced) or not vibrating (voiceless)?" By touching our Adam's apple when we produce consonants, we can tell voiceless and voiced sounds apart. Voiced sounds cause a vibration, buy voiceless sounds do not. In Table 2.1, all the obstruent sounds (stops, fricatives, and affricates) have a voiced/voiceless pair, whereas sonorant sounds (nasals, liquids, and glides) have only voiced sounds. Obstruent sounds are thus made with a significant air obstruction, and sonorant sounds are made with relatively little air obstruction.

Place of Articulation

This quality concerns where the sound is made. The following list summarizes the classification of English consonants based on place of articulation:

- *Bilabial*: Sounds made by bringing both lips closer together. English sounds: [p], [b], [m], and [w]. Examples: *pat, bat, mat, with.*
- *Labio-dental*: Sounds made with the lower lip against the upper front teeth. English sounds: [f], [v]. Examples: *fat, vat.*
- *(Inter)dental*: Sounds made with the tip of the tongue between the front teeth. English sounds: [θ], [ð]. Examples: *thigh, thy.*
- *Alveolar*: Sounds made with the tongue tip at or near the alveolar ridge. English sounds: [t], [d], [s], [z], [n], [l], [r]. Examples: *tab, dab, sip, zip, nose, loose, red.*
- *Palatal*: Sounds made with the tongue near the hard palate (the hard part of the roof of the mouth). These are often called post-alveolar or palatal-alveolar sounds because they are made in the area between the alveolar ridge and the

hard palate. English sounds: [ʃ], [ʒ], [ʧ], [ʤ], [j]. Examples: *leash, measure, church, judge, yes.*

- *Velar*: Sounds made with the tongue near the velum. English sounds: [k], [g], [ŋ]. Examples: *kill, gill, sing.*
- *Glottal*: Sounds made at the larynx (the space between the vocal cords is the glottis). English sounds: [h], [ʔ]. Examples: *high, uh-oh.*

Manner of Articulation

This quality refers to how the sound is made. The following is a summary:

- *Stop*: Sounds made by obstructing the air stream completely in the oral cavity. English sounds: [p], [b], [t], [d], [k], [g], [ʔ]. Examples: *pen, boy, cat, go, top, do, king, gang, kitten (*[t] *as a glottal stop).*
- *Fricative*: Sounds made by stopping the air stream almost completely. English sounds: [f], [v], [θ], [ð], [s], [z], [ʃ], [ʒ], [h]. Examples: *five, vine, thing, this, sip, zip, ship, azure, hot.*
- *Affricate*: Sounds made by briefly stopping the air stream completely and then releasing the articulators slightly so that friction is produced (a combination of stop and fricative). English sounds: [ʧ], [ʤ]. Examples: *choose, orange.*
- *Nasal*: Sounds made with the air stream escaping through the nasal cavity when the velum is lowered. English sounds: [m], [n], [ŋ]. Examples: *mango, noon, sing.*
- *Liquid*: Sounds made with little obstruction of air. [l] and [r] are both liquid sounds but differ in that [l] is produced while resting the tongue on the alveolar ridge, with the air stream escaping around the sides of the tongue (lateral). In producing [r], there are many variations among speakers, but the sound is usually voiced and articulated in the alveolar region by curling the tip of the tongue behind the alveolar ridge (retroflex). Examples: *liquid, radio.*
- *Glide*: Sounds made with only a slight closure of the articulators. If the vocal tract were any more open, the result would be a vowel sound. (Glides are sometimes referred to as "semi-vowels" because they are midway between consonants and vowels, but they are classified as consonants.) English sounds: [w], [j]. Examples: *west, yes.*

2.2.2 English Vowels

English vowels are the most sonorant (sounds that permit the relatively unrestricted flow of air) and audible sounds and are produced with the vocal tract open. Vowels can be classified based on four main qualities:

(3) a. *Tongue height*: Raising or lowering the body of the tongue
b. *Tongue advancement*: Advancing or retracting the body of the tongue
c. *Lip rounding*: Rounding or not rounding the lips
d. *Tenseness*: Making these movements with a tense or lax gesture

Table 2.2 English vowel sounds.

		Front	Central	Back
High	[+tense]	/i/ (s<u>ea</u>t)		/u/ (s<u>ui</u>t)
	[−tense]	/ɪ/ (s<u>i</u>t)		/ʊ/ (p<u>u</u>t)
Mid	[+tense]	/e/ (s<u>ay</u>)	/ɚ/ (b<u>ir</u>d)	/o/ (b<u>oa</u>t)
	[−tense]	/ɛ/ (s<u>e</u>t)	/ʌ/ (c<u>u</u>t), /ə/ (sof<u>a</u>)	/ɔ/ (c<u>au</u>ght)
Low	[+tense]			
	[−tense]	/æ/ (s<u>a</u>t)		/ɑ/ (s<u>o</u>ck)

Given these four vowel qualities, English vowels can be represented as shown in Table 2.2.

In producing vowels, there is no obstruction of the airflow. The air stream is modified by the positioning of the tongue, lips, and jaw, which results in different vowel qualities. With vowels, the placement of the tongue (from front to back and from the bottom to roof of the mouth) and the amount of lip rounding are important in defining and classifying the sound. Following are more detailed descriptions:

- *Front/central/back*: The position of the tongue from front to back in the mouth during the production of the sound. Front: *sit, sea, left, mad*. Central: *about, utter*. Back: *book, caught, bought*.
- *High/mid/low*: The placement of the tongue from the roof to the floor (bottom) of the mouth when making the sound. High: *machine, rule*. Mid: *bet, cat*. Low: *had, father*.
- *Lip rounding*: Whether the lips are rounded ([u], [ʊ], [o], [ɔ]) or unrounded (all the other vowels) when the sound is made. Rounded: *note, look, rule, boot*.
- *Tense vs. lax*: The relative tenseness of the vocal muscles. /i, e, u, o/ are tense; all others are lax. Tense: *repeat, treat, hat, steel, lap, kneel, great, hair*. Lax: *sit, live, rat, bet, boy, swap, mat, hit*.

2.3 Korean Hangul Alphabet and Romanization

Before we discuss the phonemic sounds in Korean, it is important to understand the Korean writing system, Hangul. A key feature of this writing system is a "phonemic" alphabet directly mapped to each sound. Hangul, widely considered one of the most scientific writing systems, consists of 40 letters: 10 pure

Table 2.3 Korean Hangul alphabet for consonants.

Consonants	Phonemic	Yale	Sample sounds in English
ㄱ	k	k	*g* as in *god, guess*
ㄴ	n	n	*n* as in *noon, name*
ㄷ	t	t	*d* as in *day*
ㄹ	l	l	*l* as in *lock, ill*
ㅁ	m	m	*m* as in *mom*
ㅂ	p	p	*b* as in *bad*
ㅅ	s	s	*s* as in *sigh*
ㅇ	ŋ	ng	*ng* as in *sing*
ㅈ	ʧ	c	*j* as in *jail*
ㅊ	ʧʰ	ch	*ch* as in *charge, church*
ㅋ	kʰ	kh	*k* as in *key*
ㅌ	tʰ	th	*t* as in *tea*
ㅍ	pʰ	ph	*p* as in *pool, pizza*
ㅎ	h	h	*h* as in *hat*
ㄲ	k'	kk	
ㄸ	t'	tt	
ㅃ	p'	pp	No matching sounds in English
ㅆ	s'	ss	
ㅉ	ʧ'	cc	

vowels, 11 compound vowels, 14 basic consonants, and 5 double consonants. These are shown in Table 2.3, and each consonant character in Hangul is linked to the corresponding phonemic sound. For each letter, the table also includes the matching Yale Romanization.

In addition to these consonant characters, Hangul has the vowel characters shown in Table 2.4. They are grouped as simple and complex vowels.[2] Note that the Yale Romanization is just for this textbook (or linguistic texts). The phonemic values are related to sounds, whereas the Yale system converts the Hangul characters into an alphabet system that does not reflect their exact pronunciation.

---

2 The Korean phonetic or International Phonetic Association (IPA) system is adopted from Sohn (1999).

Table 2.4 Korean Hangul alphabet for vowels.

Vowels	Phonemic	Yale	Sample sounds
ㅏ	a	a	Similar to *ah, father*
ㅑ	ja	ya	Similar to *yard, yacht*
ㅓ	ə	e	Similar to *cut, lawn*
ㅕ	jə	ye	Similar to *just, yawn*
ㅗ	o	o	Similar to *order, home*
ㅛ	jo	yo	Similar to *Yoda, yolk*
ㅜ	u	wu	Similar to *Ungaro, moon*
ㅠ	ju	yu	Similar to *you*
ㅡ	ɨ	u	Similar to *good, put*
ㅣ	i	i	Similar to *easy, meet*
ㅐ	ɛ	ay	Similar to *pan*
ㅒ	jɛ	yay	Similar to *said*
ㅔ	e	ey	Similar to *egg*
ㅖ	je	yey	Similar to *yeah*
ㅘ	wa	wa	Similar to *wa*
ㅚ	we	oy	Similar to *weight*
ㅙ	wɛ	way	Similar to *wagon, wear*
ㅝ	wə	we	Similar to *one, water*
ㅟ	y, wi	wi	Similar to *we*
ㅞ	we	wey	Similar to *wear*
ㅢ	ɨi	uy	No matching sound in English

2.4 Korean Sound Systems

2.4.1 Korean Consonants

Korean consonants are slightly different from their English counterparts in that they are classified with respect to two qualities: place and manner of articulation. Table 2.5 represents Korean consonants based on these two criteria.

Only Voiceless Consonant Phonemes
As noted in Table 2.5, one significant difference between Korean and English is that Korean has no voice vs. voiceless pairs as its consonant phonemes.

Table 2.5 Korean consonant chart.

	Bilabial	Alveolar	Palato-Alveolar	Velar	Glottal
Stop	p pʰ p' ㅂ ㅍ ㅃ	t tʰ t' ㄷ ㅌ ㄸ		k kʰ k' ㄱ ㅋ ㄲ	
Affricate			ʧ ʧʰ ʧ' ㅈ ㅊ ㅉ		
Fricative		s s' ㅅ ㅆ			h ㅎ
Nasal	m ㅁ	n ㄴ		ŋ ㅇ	
Liquid		l ㄹ			

Korean consonants are all voiceless, although they can be voiced depending on the context. This is why the table does not include the voiceless and voiced distinction. Unlike English, Korean has three distinctive voiceless sounds in the stop and affricate categories: plain voiceless consonants (/p,t,k, ʧ/), aspirated voiceless consonants (/pʰ, tʰ, kʰ, ʧʰ/, and unaspirated fortis consonants (p', t', k', ʧ').

Place of Articulation
Korean consonants are not different from those in English or other languages in terms of where they are produced. Just like English consonants, Korean consonants are produced by the lips and tongue. In represening Korean consonants, it is a traditional practice in Korean to add the vowel sound ㅏ[a] to each consonant. Note that in represening Korean phonemic sounds, we could use the phonemic Hangul characters, instead of the IPA symbols.

- *Bilabial*: Sounds like 바 pa, 마 ma, 파 pha, and 빠 ppa are articulated with both lips.

  (4) 밥 pap 'meal,' 맛 mas 'taste,' 파 pha 'green onion,' 빵 ppang 'bread'
- *Alveolar*: Sounds like 나 na, 타 tha, 따 tta, 사 sa, 싸 ssa, and 라 la are articulated with the tongue against or close to the superior alveolar ridge.

  (5) 나무 namwu 'tree,' 타잔 thacan 'tarzan,' 따로 ttalo 'separately,' 사자 saca 'tiger,' 싸움 ssawum 'fight,' 라면 lamyen 'ramen'
- *Palatal*: Sounds like 자 ca, 차 cha, and 짜 cca are consonants articulated with the body of the tongue raised against the hard palate (the middle part of the roof of the mouth).

  (6) 잔 can 'glass,' 차 cha 'tea,' 짝 ccak 'mate'

- *Velar*: Sounds like 강 kang, 카 kha, and 까 kka are produced with the back of the tongue against the velum.

  (7) 강 kang 'river,' 칼 khal 'knife,' 까마득 kkamatuk 'far off'
- *Glottal*: The sound 하 ha is produced with an open glottis.

  (8) 힘 him 'power,' 호수 hoswu 'lake,' 허리 heli 'waist'

Manner of Articulation

The second property that distinguishes consonants is how they are pronounced or articulated:

- *Stop*: Sounds that involve, first, a stricture of the mouth that allows no air to escape from the vocal tract and, second, the compression and release of the air. Unlike English which has only plain stops (though they can be aspirated in most cases), Korean has three different stops (plosives): plain, aspirated, and tense (fortis). Plain stops are 바 pa, 다 ta, 가 ka. These sounds can be aspirated like 파 pha, 타 tha, 카 kha, or tensed like 빠 ppa, 따 tta, 까 kka.

  (9) 파도 phato 'wave,' 타도 thato 'overthrow,' 카페 khaphe 'coffee shop,' 빠름 ppalum 'fast,' 따름 ttalum 'following,' 까메오 ccameyo 'cameo'
- *Affricate*: Sounds that begin as stops and end as fricatives. Korean has one affricate consonant: 자 ca. When it is aspirated, we have 차 cha, and when it is tensed, we have 짜 cca.

  (10) 자기 caki 'self,' 차기 chaki 'next,' 짜기 ccaki 'knitting'
- *Fricative*: 'Hissing' sounds produced by the air escaping through a small passage in the mouth. Plain fricatives are 사 sa, 하 ha, but the former can be tensed, producing 싸 ssa.

  (11) 사기 saki 'cheating,' 하기 haki 'doing,' 싸기 ssaki 'wrapping'
- *Nasal*: Sounds like 마 ma, 나 na, 앙 ng (the final sound) are made with the air escaping through the nasal cavity. All the other consonants are made in the oral cavity.

  (12) 마지막 macimak 'last,' 나지막 nacimak 'low,' 양지 yangci 'sunny side'
- *Liquid (lateral)*: The sounds 라 la is produced by the air escaping from the mouth along the sides of the tongue.

  (13) 라디오 latio 'radio'

2.4.2 Korean Vowels

As shown in Table 2.6, Korean vowels can be phonetically classified by three properties: (i) whether they are produced in the front, center, or back of the mouth; (ii) whether they are produced with the tongue in a high, middle, or low position; and (iii) whether they are rounded or not (in writing Korean vowels, the

Table 2.6   Korean vowel chart.

	Front	Central	Back
High	i (ㅣ)	ɨ (ㅡ)	u (ㅜ)
Middle	e (ㅔ)	ə (ㅓ)	o (ㅗ)
Low	ɛ (ㅐ)		a (ㅏ)

unpronounced symbol ' ㅇ ' is added in front of each vowel). For example, 이 i and
에 e are front vowels, whereas 아 a, 오 o, 우 u are back vowels.

Of these eight vowels, we have five basic vowels and three nonbasic ones:

(14) a. ㅣ i, ㅔ e, ㅏ a, ㅗ o, ㅜ u:
      기름 kilum 'oil,' 셈 seym 'count,' 아름 alum 'armful,' 오름 olum 'climbing-
      up,' 우산 wusan 'umbrella'
    b. ㅓ ə, ㅐ ɛ, ㅡ ɨ:
      어머니 emeni 'mom,' 샘 saym 'envy,' 금 kum 'gold'

Of these, ㅐ ɛ is a double vowel, a combination of the vowels ㅏ and ㅣ. There
are several more double vowels with the matching Hangul, combining a glide and
a vowel. The following are some examples:

(15)   ㅑ ya, ㅕ ye, ㅛ yo, ㅠ yu:
      야구 yakwu 'baseball,' 여유 yeyu 'relaxing,' 요지 yoci 'main point,' 유지 yuci
      'maintain'

It is often assumed that the eight key vowels and these four vowels form key vowels
in Korean. Double vowels like the following also have matching Korean characters:

(16) ㅘ wa, ㅚ oe, ㅙ wae, ㅝ wo, ㅟ wi, ㅞ we, ㅢ ui:
      와전 wacen 'misinform,' 외로움 oylowum 'loneliness,' 왜 way 'why,' 워낙
      wenak 'quite,' 위로 wilo 'console,' 웨이트 weyithe 'waiter,' 의뢰 uyloy
      'request'

2.5   Syllable Structures

2.5.1   English Syllable Structures

The phoneme sounds in each language are combined to form *syllables* that make
meaningful words or parts of words. The sound combinations are not random but
follow certain rules. For instance, English does not have words beginning with a
consonant sequence like [tʃj] or [zbf].

The essential part of a syllable is a vowel sound (V), which is called nucleus. This vowel nucleus can be preceded by a consont (C) or a cluster of consonants (CC or CCC), which is called onset. The nucleus can be also followed by the coda consonant(s). The following is a syllable template in English.

(17) (CCC)   + V   + (CCC)
     Initial consonant   Vowel   Final consonant

For instance, words like *oh* [o] have just one vowel V as its syllable component, *try* [trai] has a CCV syllable structure, and *text* [tekst] uses CVCCC.

A syllable is typically represented using a tree structure, such as the following for the word *plant*:

(18)

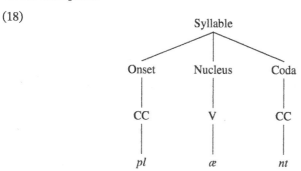

As illustrated here, the syllable has three key members: onset, nucleus, and coda. As noted, the nucleus is the core of the syllable, the onset is a consonant or consonant cluster preceding the vowel nucleus, and the coda is any consonant following the vowel. The onset and coda sounds are optional, but the nucleus is mandatory. Note that a vowel-like consonant such as [m], [l], or [n] can function as a nucleus, as in *film*, and *bottle*, and *hidden*, respectively since these sounds are sonorant like vowel sounds.

Syllables are thus phonological blocks for a given word and influence the stress patterns and prosodic patterns in English:

(19) a. phOtograph
     b. photOgraphy
     c. photogrAphic

Notice that the stress in each word (marked with the capital letter) is placed on a different syllable. Every English word with more than one syllable or word part has a defined stress pattern. The stress pattern in English plays a vital role in achieving accurate pronunciation. Placing the stress of a given word on the wrong syllable makes the word hard to decipher.

2.5.2 Korean Syllable Structures

Each language has a slightly different syllable structure, depending on the possible onset and coda sounds. Korean syllable structure is simpler than that of English, as seen from the following Korean syllable template:

(20) (C)   + V   + (C)
      Initial consonant   Vowel   Final consonant

Each syllable can be written either horizontally from left to right or vertically from top to bottom in columns from right to left, depending on the property of the vowel. If the vowel has a flat form (ㅗ, ㅜ, ㅡ), representing the earth, the letters are horizontal. If the vowel has a vertical form (ㅏ, ㅓ, ㅣ), representing a standing human, the letters are vertical. Consider the following examples:

(21) a. ㅇ + ㅏ = 아 a
     b. ㄴ + ㅏ = 나 na
     c. ㄱ + ㅏ + ㅁ = 감 kam
     d. ㄲ + ㅜ + ㅁ = 꿈 kkwum
     e. ㄲ + ㅗ + ㅊ = 꽃 kkoch

As noted here, vowels like ㅏ, ㅑ, ㅓ, ㅕ, and ㅣ are placed on the right side of the initial consonant, whereas vowels like ㅗ, ㅛ, ㅜ, ㅠ, and ㅡ are placed under the initial consonant. In addition, notice that the final Hangul version can include consonant clusters:

(22) a. ㄱ + ㅏ + ㅄ = 값 kaps 'price'
     b. ㄴ + ㅓ + ㄳ = 넋 neks 'soul'
     c. ㅎ + ㅡ + ㄺ = 흙 hulk 'soil'
     d. ㅅ + ㅏ + ㄻ = 삶 salm 'a living'

Of the two consonants, one is not pronounced. When a vowel follows a word that ends with a consonant cluster, the second consonant of the cluster is pronounced, as in the following:

(23) a. 삶 salm + 이 i 'life-NOM' = 살미
     b. 값 kaps + 을 ul 'price-ACC' = 갑슬

When there is no first consonant, the symbol ㅇ is placed to the left of or on top of the vowel, as in 아 a or 오 o.

Another point to note is that the onset can have a glide sound like [y] or [w]:

(24) a. 교사 kyosa 'teacher'
     b. 과거 kwake 'past'

Thus the Korean syllable structure is as follows:

(25) (C)(G) + V + (C)

These examples show some variations in the syllable structures we can find in Korean.

(26) a. V: 이 'this'
　　 b. GV: 요 yo 'blanket'
　　 c. CGV: 표 myo 'grave'
　　 d. VC: 입 ip 'mouth'
　　 e. CVC: 집 cip 'house'
　　 f. CGVC: 병 pyeng 'bottle'

As we have seen so far, the Korean writing system Hangul is an alphabet, a syllabary, and logographs all at once. Each word is made from alphabet letters linked to the syllable structure.

2.6 Suprasegmental Features

We have discussed the phonetic properties of each segmental sound in English and Korean and analyzed each consonant or vowel sound based on its phonetic properties. For example, we can understand consonants depending on the place and manner of their articulation, whereas vowels are analyzed according to their height, frontness, and roundness. This approach classifies each sound or segment based on *segmental* features. Sounds can have additional features, especially when combined. These are called *suprasegmental* features such as *stress/accents, intonations*, and *length*.

2.6.1 English Suprasegmental Features

In English, stress and intonation play crucial roles in recognizing words. Stressed vowels are enunciated clearly and prominently, whereas unstressed vowels are blurred or pronounced faintly. Unstressed vowels in English are typically reduced to a schwa (ə). For instance, the final syllable of *intonation* and the second syllable of *emphasize* are unstressed and reduced to a schwa.

Note that derivational suffixes may change the stress pattern in English (see Chapter 3 for more discussion):

(27) a. analyze, analysis, analytical
　　 b. diplomat, diplomacy, diplomatic
　　 c. politic, politician, political

In contrast, there is no distinction in Korean between stressed and unstressed vowels because every vowel in an utterance receives about the same amount of stress. Consequently, every vowel is uttered clearly and prominently. Because of this native-language background, Korean learners often fail to blur (or reduce to the barred i [ɨ] or schwa [ə]) an unstressed vowel when they speak English.

Recognizing where to put the accent is an essential part of learning English. Even the categorical difference causes different stress patterns:

(28) a. insUlt (verb) vs. Insult (noun)
    b. recOrd (verb) vs. rEcord (noun)

Further examples of the importance of accents can be found in words like *platoon* and *manipulation*. These words are read as *platOOn* and *manipulAtion*: if we place a little more stress on the accented syllable, the unaccented syllable can be hard to hear.

Just like this word-level stress, phrasal-level or sentence-level stress plays an important role in English. Consider the following two accents:[3]

(29) WHITE house vs. white HOUSE

When we have the accent on *white*, it means a house whose color is white but at the same time can have a special meaning: the residence of the US president. When the accent is on *house*, it means a regular house whose color is white. As such, a different accent can result in a different meaning. English places an accent on a vowel in every word.

Sentence-level stress, called *intonation*, makes a big difference in English. For instance, there are three different ways to say this simple sentence:

(30) a. He got an A on the test ↘.
    b. He got an A on the test ↗.
    c. He got AN A on the test. ↘

A declarative statement has a lowering intonation, as in (30a). However, a rising intonation at the end of a sentence becomes a type of question, as in (30b). We can even place a rising intonation on a phrase to express surprise, as in (30c).

2.6.2 Korean Suprasegmental Features

Unlike English, Korean does not have an accent – or if it does, the canonical accent always comes on the first syllable. Foreigners thus do not need to worry about where to place an accent in a Korean word. However, the suprasegmental feature *length* plays a certain role, although most young people do not use this distinction:[4]

(31) a. 말 mal 'horse' vs. 말 mal: 'talk'

---

3 The accented word is in all capital letters.
4 A colon indicates long length for a vowel.

b. 눈 nwun 'eyes' vs. 눈 nwun: 'snow'

c. 배 pay 'belly' vs. 배 pay: 'ship'

The length of a vowel makes a completely different word. However, we can usually recognize which one a speaker means given clues from the context:

(32) a. In the context that Mimi talks a lot:

미미가   말이   참   많다.

Mimi-ka   mal-i   cham manh-ta

Mimi-NOM speech-NOM very   many-DECL

'Mimi is very talkative.'

b. In the context referring to Mimi's eyes:

눈이   참   예쁘다.

nwun-i   cham   yeppu-ta

eye-NOM very   pretty-DECL

'(Your) eyes are very pretty.'

Such data shows us that, unlike in English, the length of vowels in Korean functions as a suprasegmental feature; however, language learners usually do not need to worry about this because context can provide clues about the meaning of the word in question.

2.7 Contrastive Notes

2.7.1 Consonants

Voiced and Voiceless

A key feature of Korean consonants is that there are no voiced consonants as phonemes. English consonants generally have voiced and voiced pairs, but Korean consonants have voiceless, aspirated, and tensed triplet consonants. As noted earlier, English consonants, except for nasals and liquids, are called obstruents because they are made by obstructing the airflow. The English obstruents come in pairs, each consisting of a voiceless obstruent and its voiced counterpart. Thus English has such pairs as /p/ and /b/, /t/ and /d/, /k/ and /g/, /θ// and /ð/, /s/ and /z/, and /ʃ// and /ʒ/. On the other hand, Korean does not have corresponding obstruent pairs. Instead, Korean has triads or triplets of voiceless obstruents, each consisting of a lenis (soft) voiceless obstruent, its aspirated counterpart, and its fortis (hard or tensed) "glottalized" counterpart. Thus Korean has such triplets as /p/ (ㅂ), /pʰ/ (ㅍ), /p'/ (ㅃ). The only exception is the pair /s/ (ㅅ), /s'/ (ㅆ), where there is no aspirated version of the obstruent.

Labio-Dental and Interdental

Unlike English, Korean has no labio-dental and interdental consonants as phonemes. That is, Korean phonemes do not include /f/ and /v/, and /ð/ and /θ/. This important property leads to the following differences.

- English distinguishes between /p/ and /b/ or /p/ and /f/, but Korean does not. Consequently, Koreans often have difficulty hearing the difference between the two English sounds in each pair. Thus they often find it hard to discriminate between *pine* and *fine, pile* and *file, leap* and *leaf*, *cup* and *cuff*, and so on.
- Because Korean does not have /v/, and the Korean /p/ happens to be the closest sound to the English /v/, Koreans often use /p/ for /v/. In addition, because Korean does not have /b/, and /p/ is the closest consonant, people say 'pan' for 'ban,' 'pack' for 'back,' 'prick' for 'brick,' and so on.
- Because the English voiced /ð/ and voiceless /θ/ consonants are nonexistent in Korean, language learners often use /s/ for these, making mistakes by saying *sin* for *thin*, *sing* for *thing*, and so on.

Retroflex

Another notable difference between the two languages involves the lateral and retrospect sounds. That is, English has the /l/ vs. /r/ contrast, but Korean does not. As a result, Koreans often have difficulty distinguishing between these two English sounds. Koreans who are learning English often find it difficult to distinguish *light* from *right*, *load* from *road*, and so on.

2.7.2 Different Vowel Sets

We have seen that except for the five basic vowels like /a, i, e, o, u/, English and Korean have different vowel sets. There is no English vowel corresponding to the Korean sound [ɨ] in ㅗ, and there is no Korean vowel corresponding to the English vowel [æ] in *sat*.

2.7.3 Syllable and Consonant Clusters

As we have noted, the maximal syllable structure for English is CCCVCCC or CGVCC, whereas Korean has the CGVC syllable structure. This means the English onset and coda allow consonant clusters while the Korean onset and coda do not. A Korean syllable cannot start with two or three consecutive consonants: there must always be a vowel after the first consonant. The sound of *good* can be a Korean word, but when pronouncing words like *stay* or *example*, Korean speakers often add one additional syllable.

Similarly, a syllable can never end with two consonants in Korean. Korean learners often restructure English consonant clusters to make them conform to the Korean syllable structure by adding a weak sound schwa like [ɨ] between two consonants.. For instance, *strike, skunk* and *mist* are often pronounced as two syllable words with the insertion of a barred "i" (or ɨ) between the consonants in the cluster.

Another common error concerns the unpronounced final "e." Except for a few words like *recipe* and *fiance*, the "e" at the end of words in English is usually not pronounced: *type, snake, make*, and so forth. Korean speakers often make these two-syllable words, incorrectly adding the barred "i" (or ɨ).

2.7.4 Stress vs. Nonstress

One clear difference between Korean and English is the stress suprasegmental feature. We have seen that English is a stress-timed language where individual word stress is significant, but Korean is a syllable-timed language where stress is not crucial. In Korean, rhythm and intonation are based on the syllable, whereas in English, they are based on stress.

We have noted that differences in stress can lead to differences in meaning (noun vs. verb):

(33) a. Addict, addIct
b. Attribute, attrIbute
c. cOnduct, condUct
d. Increase, incrEAse

Derivational suffixes like *-ful, -less, -ment* do not change the stress, but those like *-ic(al), -ious, -ity* place the stress on the syllable just before the suffix:

(34) a. color vs. colorful, effort vs. effortless, amuse vs. amusement
b. economy vs. economical, courage vs. courageous, curious vs. curiosity

To have such phonetic competence is a key to learning English.

2.8 Conclusion

As we have seen so far, there are many differences between the phonetic and phonological properties of English and Korean. Understanding these differences will help both ESL (English as a second language) Korean learners and KSL (Korean as a second language) English-speaking learners.

The set members of English phonemic consonants and vowels differ from those of Korean sounds. Recognizing these differences is the first step to understanding the two languages. For instance, we need to realize the voiced vs.

voiceless distinction for English consonants; but for Korean consonants, we must understand the triple set of each consonant sound: plain, aspirated, and tensed. When these phonemic sounds are combined, the languages add suprasegmental features, contributing to the language peculiarities. Accents (stresses) are crucial in English but not in Korean. This accompanies the key difference: English is a stress-timed language in which individual word stress is significant, whereas Korean is a syllable-timed language where each consonant has a vowel attached (often causing English speakers of Korean to add an extra syllable).

Exercises

1   Referring to what we discussed in this chapter, try to write out the English and Korean consonant charts with one example word for each sound.

2   As studied in this chapter, draw English and Korean vowel charts, and give one word for each vowel in the charts.

3   Give the Yale Romanization, glosses, and translations of the following Korean words. In addition, give the phonetic symbol of the first sound and provide its phonetic descriptions (i.e. voiced/voiceless, place of articulation, and manner of articulation).

   (i) a. 불, 풀, 뿔
      b. 덜다, 털다, 떨다
      c. 자다, 차다, 짜다
      d. 근, 큰, 끈
      e. 사다, 싸다, 회다
      f. 마음, 나이, 앙증 (final sound)
      g. 라디오, 노래

4   Identify the syllable structure of the following Korean words:

   (i) a. 차 cha:
      b. 앙 ang:
      c. 앎 alm:
      d. 책 chayk:

5   Provide the syllable structures of the following English words in a tree structure (see (18)). Then write how Korean people would pronounce each of these words and give its syllable structure. State the differences, and discuss what may cause them.

(i) a. each, window, tomato

    b. text, test, street, skirt, experiment

    c. type, make, debate, celebrate

6 Convert the following Hangul to Yale Romanization and glosses. Refer to the Yale Romanization table or http://asaokitan.net/tools/hangul2yale/.

(i) a. 말과 글자는 다르다.
    'Language and writing systems are different.'

    b. 소리와 의미의 관계는 임의적이다.
    'The relationship between sound and meaning is arbitrary.'

    c. 알파벳의 기원은 그리스 문자이지만, 한글은 세종대왕이 만들었다.
    'The origin of the alphabet is Greek letters, while Hangul was invented by King Sejong.'

    d. 언어는 소리 기호와 의미의 연결망이다.
    'Language is a semantic web between sound symbols and meanings.'

    e. 한 언어를 안다는 것은 그 언어의 소리를 안다는 것이다.
    'Knowing a language means knowing the sounds of that language.'

    f. 철자는 언어의 소리를 정확하게 반영하지 않는다.
    'Spelling does not consistently represent the sounds of language.'

    g. 수화에서는 손모양, 손과 팔의 움직임, 손의 위치가 말소리의 변별적 자질 역할을 한다.
    In sign languages, the configuration of the hand,the movement of the hand and arm, and the location of the hand function as the segmental features in speech sounds.

7 This chapter discussed how the basic sounds (phonemes) in English and Korean can be classified and produced. When these sounds are combined to form words, phrases, and sentences, they sometimes also affect neighboring sounds. In the following English and Korean examples, identify the phonological rules.

(i) a. What did you do together?

    b. 같이   무엇을   했니?
    kath-i   mwues-ul ha-yess-ni?
    together what-ACC do-PST-QUE
    'What did you do together?'

3

Words: Where Every Sentence Begins

3.1 Introduction

Every language speaker understands or recognizes many words in their mother tongue. It is often said that people use more than 10,000 words in daily life. The words in each language can be classified into subgroups, often called *parts of speech*, or 품사 *phwumsa* in Korean, based on their shared grammatical properties. For example, English and Korean are said to have the following parts of speech or lexical categories:

(1) a. *English parts of speech*: noun, verb, adjective, adverb, preposition, conjunction, particle, determiner, …
   b. *Korean parts of speech*: nominal, verbal, adnominal, adverbial, conjunction, …

At first glance, the two languages seem to have different parts of speech, but in this chapter, we will see their similarities as well as distinctive properties.

3.2 English Parts of Speech

When given a (new) word, we can identify its part of speech or lexical category based on several tests, including its morphological and positional possibilities. Consider the lexical category of *email* in each of the following sentences:

(2) a. Feel free to email me.
   b. They used to send me multiple emails.

The syntactic position of *email* indicates the category. In (2a), *email* is a verb occurring after the infinitival marker *to* and combines with the following object *me*, while *email* in (2b) is used as a noun with the plural marking *-s* after the adjective *multiple*. As such, the morphological and distributional cues tell us

English and Korean in Contrast: A Linguistic Introduction, First Edition. Jong-Bok Kim.
© 2024 John Wiley & Sons, Inc. Published 2024 by John Wiley & Sons, Inc.

the lexical category of the word *email*. In this section, we consider the English lexical categories.

3.2.1 Nouns

One crucial feature of English nouns is that they are classified as countable or uncountable (or mass) nouns. For example, consider the differences between the countable noun *book* and the uncountable noun *evidence* (the symbol * means ungrammatical):

   (3) a. He gave *book/a book/this book/those books to Bill.
       b. He gave evidence/*an evidence/the evidence/*evidences to Bill.

As illustrated in (3), countable nouns combine with an article (like *a*) or can be used as plural forms, whereas uncountable nouns can occur only with the definite article *the*. When learning English, this distinction is important. What makes it difficult for English learners is that the distinction between countable and uncountable nouns does not depend on their meaning:

   (4) a. furniture: *a furniture, *furnitures
       b. difficulty: a difficulty, difficulties

In terms of meaning, *furniture* refers to a concrete object which we may be able to count, whereas *difficulty* denotes an abstract property. However, the former is used as uncountable while the latter is used as countable.

A further complication arises from the fact that many words can be used as either countable or uncountable:

   (5) a. Caffeine is the active constituent of drinks such as coffee.
       b. She came in for a coffee and then talked about her friend.

Thus English nouns can be countable, uncountable, or both. Of course, the countable and uncountable uses of nouns like *coffee, cake, beer*, and so forth depend on the context.

In addition to these common nouns (countable and uncountable), there are other types of nouns:

   (6) a. Pronouns: he, she, it, who, what, ...
       b. Proper nouns: Seoul, Korean, Kim, Lee, ...

Pronouns referring to people, places, or things are classified as personal pronouns (*he, she*), relative pronouns (*which, who*), indefinite pronouns (*none, several*), interrogative pronouns (*which, who*), and so forth. Meanwhile, proper nouns refer to specific people or things.

3.2.2 Verbs: Main and Auxiliary

There are two types of verbs in English, main and auxiliary, both of which can express tense (present, past) information.

Main Verbs

English main verbs are classified at least into five types depending on their *complementhood*, which specifies what a verb can combine with. That is, each verb in the following examples is different in terms of what it can combine with to form a complete VP (verb phrase):

(7) a. Intransitive: Kim disappeared. vs. *Kim disappeared the city.
   b. Linking verb: Kim remained really calm. vs. *Kim remained.
   c. Transitive: Kim liked Korean. vs. *Kim liked.
   d. Ditransitive: Kim taught Mimi Korean. vs. *Kim taught calm.
   e. Complex transitive: Kim found Korean interesting. vs. *Kim found.

As the examples show, the intransitive *disappear* requires no object or complement. It only requires a subject. Put differently, such an intransitive verb "subcategorizes" or "selects" no complement but one subject argument. There is only one required participant in the event of disappearing, which is linked to the subject. On the other hand, *remain* requires a predicative complement AP (adjective phrase) like *really calm*. The transitive verb *like* combines with its object NP (noun phrase) *Korean*. Meanwhile, the transitive verb *teach* has two different objects: an indirect object (*Mimi*) and a direct object (*Korean*). Finally, the complex transitive verb *find* requires two complements: an object (*Korean*) and a predicative complement (*interesting*), which describes the property of the object *Korean*. The complementhood (often called subcategorization) properties therefore determine what kinds of element(s) each verb combines with.

Auxiliary Verbs

Auxiliary verbs are helping main verbs in represening information such as *tense* (past and present) and *modality* (e.g., possibility, ability, and obligation):

(8) a. Judging by the clouds, it might rain today.
   b. He can speak three languages, but none of them well.
   c. You must wash your hands before cooking.

The auxiliary *might* represents a possibility in the past, *can* the ability of the subject, and *must* the obiligation the hearer needs to perform. Based on their semantic and pragmatic functions, the auxiliary verbs in English can be classified into four types, as given in the following with illustrative examples:

(9) Modal auxiliary: *can/could*, *will/would*, *must*, *shall/should*, must, *may/might*.
   a. We could access the internet.
   b. We would access the internet.
   c. We may access the internet.

(10) Aspectual auxiliary: *have/be*
   a. We have accessed the internet.
   b. We are accessing the internet.

(11) Dummy auxiliary: *do*
    We do not want to access the internet.

(12) Infinitival marker auxiliary: *to*
    We want to access the internet.

Modal auxiliaries express the ideas of possibility, futurity, or necessity, while the auxiliary verbs *have* and *be* denote an aspect of the situation: completion or ongoing. The auxiliary *do*, peculiar in English, has no meaning but marks tense information. It typically occurs with negation. The infinitival marker *to* can also be considered an auxiliary verb because it has no meaning but marks nonfinite tense information. Chapter 7 discusses the detailed properties of these auxiliary verbs in English.

3.2.3 Adjectives

English adjectives are classified into two groups: attributive and predicative. For example, the attributive *happy* in (13a) is modifying the noun *man*, whereas the predicative *happy* in (13b) is describing the property of the subject *he*:

(13) a. He is a happy man.
    b. He is happy.

Canonically, most adjectives can be used as both types. But adjectives with the prefix *a-* can only be used as predicative, and a handful of adjectives can only be used as attributive:

(14) a. Predicative use only: alive, asleep, afraid, alone, …
    b. Attributive use only: mere, utter, former, …

These lexical properties determine whether adjectives can be used as modifiers or predicates:

(15) a. This is the main problem. vs. *This problem is main.
    b. This is the former president. vs. *This president is former.

(16) a. This man is alone. vs. *This is an alone man.
    b. The fish is alive. vs. *This is an alive fish.

The examples tell us that *main* and *former* are used only as attributive adjectives, whereas *alone* and *alive* function only as predicative adjectives. Except for these limited sets of predicative and attributive adjectives, English adjectives can be used as either attributive or predicative.

3.2.4 Adverbs

Whereas adjectives tell us something about the properties of an individual (person or thing), adverbs describe the way an individual does something.

Adverbs typically refer to the manner, location, time, or frequency of an action:

(17) a. Kim gets up [early] even on weekends.
    b. Drive the car [carefully].
    c. The tickets sold out [fast].
    d. Kim [frequently] swims in the morning.

Adverbs, either in irregular forms like *well, fast, hard* or in *-ly* forms like *quickly, early*, modify verbs, adjectives, or adverbs:

(18) a. The team played [badly] last night.
    b. It was [clearly] a bad match.
    c. The team played [extremely] badly last night.

3.2.5 Determiners

In English, nouns are often preceded by determiners such as *a, an, the, this, that, any*, and so forth. These determiners indicate what a noun is referring to:

(19) a. the taxi, the taxis, this paper, that paper, those apples, …
    b. a taxi, any taxi, each taxi, every taxi, …

The determiners in (19a) are generally used as definite, while those in (19b) are indefinite, referring to specific or nonspecific individuals, respectively.

    A simple rule in using determiners in English is that they cannot be repeated: there can be only one determiner in an NP. Thus, English does not allow two consecutive determiners:

(20) a. *this a taxi
    b. *my the book

The distributional test indicates that the interrogative *which* or *whose* is also a determiner:

(21) a. whose book/*whose the book/the book
    b. which book/*which my book/my book

3.2.6 Prepositions

There are about 150 prepositions in English, expressing various relationships such as time, space, direction, possession, and cause. Following are some examples of English prepositions with their meanings:

(22) a. I have been working [since] this morning. (temporal)
    b. The rabbit ran [under] the gate. (direction)

    c. He was fired [for] the offense. (cause)
    d. We traveled [by] air. (means)
    e. I would like my gardenburger [with] lettuce. (accompaniment)
    f. We're [for/against] the idea. (support)
    g. That dog [of] Mary's ate my homework. (possession)
    h. They came [despite] the weather. (concession)
    i. We cut the cheesecake [with] a knife. (instrument)
    j. I baked cookies [for] Mary. (benefactive)

The basic combinatorial property of the preposition is that it combines with a nominal (NP) expression:

(23) a. across town, after class, at home, on fire, to school, …
      b. after the storm, on their white horses, between the gaps, …

Prepositions are important words, but even advanced language learners have difficulty using them correctly. The complication arises partially because many prepositions have more than one meaning. For example, the prepositions *by* and *in* can have many different uses, as seen in the following examples:

(24) a. by accident, by air, by the river, by the way, by the weekend
      b. in the morning, in the car, in an hour, in my own words

In these examples, each use of *by* or *in* has a different meaning. This again indicates that there is no one-to-one mapping relation between form and meaning.

3.2.7 Particles

One peculiar part of speech in English is particle. A limited number of English prepositions function as particles. In terms of form, particles are a subset of prepositions. An obvious difference from prepositions is that particles can occur either immediately after the verb or after the object. Compare the following contrast between particles and prepositions:

(25) Particles:
      a. She took *down* the suitcase.
      b. She took the suitcase *down*.

(26) Prepositions:
      a. She ran *down* the street.
      a. *She ran the street *down*.

What we can observe here is that the particle *down* can in a sense move around from the verb-particle position to the object-particle one. But the preposition has no such mobility, as seen from (26). Mobility is thus a key feature that distinguishes particles from prepositions. Let us consider more examples:

(27) a. Kim ran up the hill.
 b. Kim ran down the street.
(28) a. Kim ran up the bill.
 b. Kim broke down the door.

We can see the difference in the mobility of *up* and *down* here:

(29) a. *Kim ran the hill up.
 b. *Kim ran the street down.

(30) a. Kim ran the bill up.
 b. Kim broke the door down.

The difference indicates that *up* and *down* in (27) are prepositions, while those in (28) are particles.

Another distinctive property of the two parts of speech is that particles form a strong cohesion with the preceding verb, but prepositions do not. No adverbial element intervenes between the verb and the particle:

(31) Particles:
 a. I will put on my trousers.
 b. *I will put carefully on my trousers.

(32) Prepositions:
 a. I will look after my children.
 b. I will look carefully after my children.

3.2.8 Conjunctions

English has two types of conjunctions that conjoin two expressions: coordinating and subordinating.

(33) a. Coordinating conjunctions: for, and, nor, but, or, yet, so, ; (semicolon) (FANBOYS;)
 b. Subordinating conjunctions: when, if, since, while, although, because, ...

In English, there are only eight coordinating conjunctions that link two sentences. These can be remembered using the acronym FANBOYS; (including the semicolon). Each is illustrated here:

(34) a. She could not go to the show, for she did not have enough money.
 b. Julie bought her mom a sweater, and her mother loved it.
 c. Maria didn't finish her essay, nor did she finish her math.
 d. I wanted to backpack through Europe last summer, but my mom told me I couldn't.
 e. You can take a cruise to Greece, or you can travel to Mexico.

   f. Jill spent all her money at the Banana Republic sale, yet she went back the next day for more bargains.

   g. Ted didn't have enough money to fly to Boston, so he took the train.

   h. Jane already came to the party; the others will join her soon.

We can see that the coordinating conjunctions, as the name indicates, conjoin two "equal" expressions: two sentences or two phrases. Meanwhile, subordinating conjunctions introduce a subordinate clause that can appear in either the sentential initial or final position:

(35) a. Although the water was warm, I didn't swim.
     b. I didn't swim, although the water was warm.

(36) a. When Kim started teaching English, he was quite young.
     b. Kim was quite young when he started teaching English.

Note that the subordinating clause is optional. It modifies the main clause but cannot form a sentence by itself because its existence is subordinate to the main clause.

(37) a. (Although I do not always like being taught), I'm always ready to learn.
     b. *Although I do not always like being taught.

3.2.9 Complementizers

Expressions that can occur in the following contexts form a different lexical group:

(38) a. She didn't think __ she could stand on her own.
     b. I doubt __ he would listen to any moderate voice.
     c. I'm anxious __ him to give us the names of the people.

The words that can occur in these particular slots in (38) are strictly limited:

(39) a. She didn't think *that* [she could stand on her own].
     b. I doubt *if* [he would listen to any moderate voice].
     c. I'm anxious *for* [him to give us the names of the people].

The italicized words here differ from the other lexical categories we have seen so far. They introduce a complement clause (marked here by square brackets) and are sensitive to the tense of that clause. A tensed clause is known as a *finite* clause instead of an infinitive clause (see Chapter 5). For example, *that* and *if* introduce or combine with a tensed sentence (present or past tense), whereas *for* requires an infinitival clause marked with *to*. We cannot disturb these relationships:

(40) a. *She didn't think *that* [her to stand on her own].
     b. *I doubt *if* [him listening to any moderate voice].
     c. *I'm anxious *for* [he gave us the names of the people].

The term *complement*, as noted earlier, refers to an obligatory dependent clause or phrase relative to a lexical head like the verb. The italicized elements in (40) introduce a clausal complement and are consequently known as *complementizers* (abbreviated C). There are only a few complementizers in English (*that, for, if*, and *whether*), but nevertheless they have their own lexical category.

3.3 Korean Parts of Speech

Korean parts of speech are slightly different from their English counterparts. They are traditionally grouped into four main categories:

(41)

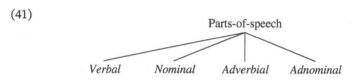

These categories seem quite different from the English ones. However, if we look at their subtypes, the categories in the two languages are similar. For example, the category *verbal* includes *verb*, *adjective*, and *auxiliary*, whereas *nominal* includes *noun*, *pronoun*, *numeral*, and *verbal noun*. The category *adnominal*, as the name indicates, modifies a *nominal* expression, whereas the category *adverbial* modifies a *verbal* category.

3.3.1 Nominals

Traditionally, nominals are subclassified as following:

(42) a. Common nouns: 학생 haksayng 'student,' 책상 chakysang 'desk,' 사과 sakwa 'apple,' ...
b. Proper nouns: 서울 Seoul, 미아 Mia, 김 Kim, 미미 Mimi, ...
c. Pronouns: 나 na 'I,' 너 ne 'you,' 그녀 kunye 'she,' ...
d. Verbal nouns: 공부 kongpwu 'study,' 수출 swuchwul 'export,' 수입 swuip 'import,' 연구 yenkwu 'research,' 노래 nolay 'song,' ...
e. Bound nouns: 것 kes 'thing,' 수 swu 'possibility,' 척 chek 'pretend,' 줄 cwul 'expect,' ...
f. Classifiers: 명 myeng 'person,' 개 kay 'thing,' 권 kwon 'book,' 병 pyeng 'bottle,' 장 cang 'piece,' ...

A large body of Korean common nouns stem from Chinese characters, such as 산 *san* 'mountain,' 역 *yek* 'station,' and 문화 *mwunhwa* 'culture.' Others are native to the Korean language (e.g. 나라 *nara* 'country,' 날 *nal* 'day'). Because Korean nouns have no number distinction, Korean common nouns can be either singular or plural, depending on the context:

(43) a. 책(들)이   많다
      chayk-tul-i   manh-ta
      book-PL-NOM   many-DECL
      'There are many books.'

     b. 책이   한   권이다
      chayk-i   han kwon-i-ta
      book-NOM one CL-COP-DECL
      'There is one book.'

The plural marking in (43a) is optional: the context can tell us whether the noun refers to more than one book or not. When required to be specific about a quantity, the language often uses the numeral classifier, as in (43b).

Just like English, Korean has pronouns and proper nouns. Korean pronouns are highly influenced by the honorifics in the language. Pronouns change form depending on the social status of the person or people spoken to (e.g. for the first person singular pronouns corresponding to the English 'I,' there are both the informal 나 *na* 'I' and the honorific/humble 저 *ce* 'I'). The following examples include typical personal pronouns in the language:

(44) a. 나 na 'I,' 너 ne 'you,' 그 ku 'he,' 그녀 kunye 'she,' 우리 wuli 'we'
     b. 당신 tangsin 'you,' 그분 kupwun 'he/she'

Bound pronouns are a unique subtype of nominals in Korean. Bound nouns (BNs) exhibit various peculiar properties not found in common nouns in Korean. For example, unlike canonical common nouns, bound nouns like *kes* cannot occur independently: they must combine with a determiner or a preceding clause. This is unusual, considering that Korean allows most core arguments (subject or object) to be freely omitted with a proper context:

(45) a. 이   것
      *(i)   kes
      this   thing

     b. 우리가   모두   놀랐던   것
      *(wuli-ka motwu nollass-ten)   kes
      we-NOM   all   surprise-MOD thing
      'the thing that we are all surprised at'

BNs also place restrictions on the types of their complements. For example, unlike 것 kes in (45), bound nouns like 수 swu and 바 pa select only a sentential complement: determiners or simple adjectival elements cannot serve as their complements:

(46) 모모는   잠을   잘   수가   없었다.
     Momo-nun cam-ul   ca-l   swu-ka eps-ess-ta
     Momo-TOP sleep-ACC sleep-MOD BN-NOM not.exist-PST-DECL
     'Momo couldn't sleep.'

BNs are also peculiar in their restrictions on the types of predicates following them. For example, the BN 수 *swu* can combine only with the predicate 있다 iss-ta 'exist' or 없다 eps-ta 'not exist,' whereas the BN 리 li requires only *eps-*. In addition, BNs like 듯 tes, 뻔 ppen, and 적 cek occur only with 하-다 *ha-* 'do,' whereas the BN 것 kes occurs with the copula verb 이다 i-ta 'is-DECL' or 같다 kath-ta 'seem-DECL.'

(47) a. 모모가   올   리가   없다/있다.
      Momo-ka o-l   li-ka   epsta/*issta
      Momo-NOM come-MOD BN-NOM not.exist/exist
      'It is unlikely that Momo will come.'

   b. 선생님이   오실   것 같다/있다.
      sesayngnim-i o-si-l   kes kath-ta/*issta
      teacher-NOM come-HON-MOD BN seem-DECL/exist.
      'It seems that the teacher will come.'

Another important subgroup of nouns is verbal nouns (VNs), which have both verbal and nominal properties. VNs combine with the light verb 하다 ha-ta 'do-DECL' and function as main verbs:

(48) a. 미아는   한국어를   공부(를)   하였다.
      Mia-nun hankwuke-lul kongpwu(-lul) ha-yess-ta
      Mia-TOP Korean-ACC   study-ACC   do-PST-DECL
      'Mia studied Korean.'

   b. 현대는   자동차를   미국에   수출(을)   한다.
      Hyundai-nun catongcha-lul mikwuk-ey swuchwul(-ul) ha-n-ta
      Hyundai-TOP car-ACC   America-to export-ACC   do-PRES-DECL
      'Hyundai exports cars to America.'

Unlike common nouns, VNs act like verbs, requiring complements. They can function as predicates by themselves but often combine with the light verb 하다 ha-ta 'do-DECL.' This light verb is often taken to have no semantic meaning because its existence is optional.

A further distinguishing property of nominals in Korean is that the language employs classifiers (CLs) and numerals in naming and counting objects in the world. Syntactically, numeral classifiers are a subclass of nouns. However, unlike

Table 3.1 Ten most frequently used classifiers in Korean.

CL type	Referents classified	Examples
개 kay	general objects	사과 한 개 sakwa han kay 'apple one CL'
번 pen	events	노래 한 번 nolay han pen 'song one CL'
명 myeng	person	학생 한 명 haksayng han myeng 'student one CL'
방울 pangwul	liquid	눈물 한 방울 nwunmwul han pangwul 'tear one CL' '
장 cang	flat objects	종이 한 장 congi han cang 'paper one CL'
대 tay	machinery	자전거 한 대 cacenke han tay 'bike one CL'
건 ken	incidents	계약 한 건 kyeyak han ken 'contract one CL'
마리 mali	animals	사자 한 마리 saca han mali 'lion one CL'
자 ca	length	옷감 한 자 oskam han ca 'cloth one CL'

common nouns, they cannot stand alone and must combine with a numeral or a limited set of determiners, as in *(두 twu) 개 kay 'two CLs' (numeral), or *(여러/몇 yeleo/myech) 개 kay 'several CLs' (quantifier). Semantic constraints on the 10 most frequently used classifiers are given in Table 3.1.

The uses of numeral classifiers also indicate another difference between English and Korean. For instance, English has expressions like *two glasses of water* (but not *two waters*), and Korean uses 물 두 잔 *mwul twu can* 'water two classifier.' The classifiers can occur in varied syntactic environments, as seen from the following illustrations for the classifier 명 *myeng*:

(49) a. Genitive case (GC) type:

세　　명의　　　범인이　　　정말　　　있었다.
sey　myeng-uy pemin-i　　cengmal iss-ess-ta
three CL-GEN　criminal-NOM really　exist-PST-DECL
'There were really three criminals.'

  b. Noun initial (NI) type:

범인　　세　　명이　　정말　　있었다.
pemin　sey　myeng-i cengmal iss-ess-ta
criminals three CL-NOM　really　exist-PST-DECL

  c. Floated quantifier (FQ) type:

범인이　　　정말　　세　　명　　있었다.
pemin-i　　cengmal sey　myeng iss-ess-ta
criminals-NOM really　there CL　exist-PST-DECL

In the GC type, NUM-CL appears with the genitive case marking, preceding the head noun 범인 pemin 'criminal,' whereas in the NI, the NUM-CL sequence follows the head noun.[1] Meanwhile, in the FQ type, the head noun is case-marked, followed by NUM-CL.

3.3.2 Adnominals

Expressions belonging to this lexical group can modify a nominal element. There are three main types of adnominals: determiners, possessive nominals, and relative clauses. Let us consider determiners first:

(50) a. Attributive determiners: 새 say 'new,' 헌 hen 'old,' 옛 yeys 'old,' …
   b. Indicative determiners: 이 i 'this,' 그 ku 'that,' 저 ce 'that,' 이런 ilen 'this kind of,' 저런 celen 'that kind of,' …
   c. Interrogative determiners: 어느 enu 'which,' 무슨 mwusun 'what,' 어떤 etten 'which,' …
   d. Numeral determiners: 모든 motun 'all,' 여러 yele 'several,' 한 han 'one,' 두 twu 'two,' 셋 seys 'three,' …

These determiners function as adnominals modifying a nominal in the prenominal position:

(51) a. 새   책을   읽었니?
      say   chayk-ul   ilk-ess-ni?
      new book-ACC read-PST-QUE
      'Did you read new books?'
   b. 무슨   책을   읽었니?
      mwusun chayk-ul   ilk-ess-ni?
      which   book-ACC read-PST-QUE
      'Which book did you read?'

The nominal expression modified by an adnominal can be either lexical (simple word) or non-lexical one (phrasal element):

(52) a. 그 [학생] ku haksayng 'the student,' 어떤 [학생] etten haksayng 'a certain student'
   b. 그 [착한 학생] ku chakha-n haksayng 'the honest student,' 어떤 [착한 학생] etten chakha-n haksayng 'a certain honest student'

However, the attributive determiner can modify only a lexical expression:

(53) a. 그 새 책 ku say chayk 'the new book'
   b. *새 그 책 *say ku chayk 'new the book'

---

1 There are two types of numerals in the language: native origin (하나 hana 'one,' 둘 twul 'two,' 세 seys 'three,' …) and Chinese origin (일 il 'one,' 이 i 'two,' 삼 sam 'three,' …).

The second type of adnominals is genitive-marked possessive adnominals:

(54) 이 아이는 미아의 동생이다.
　　 i　 ai-nun　 Mia-uy　 tongsayng-i-ta
　　 this child-TOP Mia-GEN sister-COP-DECL
　　 'This is Mia's sister.'

The genitive nominal 미아의 mia-uy 'Mia-GEN' functions as an adnominal expression.

The third type of adnominal is a relative-like expression:

(55) 이 아이는 [정말　 착한]　　 동생이다.
　　 i　 ai-nun　 cengmal chakha-n　 tongsayng-i-ta
　　 this child-TOP really　 honest-MOD sister-COP-DECL
　　 'The child is a really honest brother.'

The adjectival predicate 착한 chakha-n 'honest-MOD' together with the adverbial expression 정말 cengmal 'really' is in the adnominal position. These bracketed expressions form a relative clause modifying the head nominal 동생 tongsaying 'sister' (see Chapter 10 for a detailed discussion of relative clauses in Korean).

Note that these three adnominal types can occur together with no restriction in their ordering:

(56) a. 그 착한　　 미미의　 동생이　　 떠났다.
　　　　 ku chakha-n　 Mimi-uy　 tongsayng-i ttena-ss-ta
　　　　 this honest-MOD Mimi-GEN sister-NOM　 leave-PST-DECL
　　　　 '(lit.) The honest Mimi's sister left.'

　　 b. 착한　　　 그 미미의　 동생이　　 떠났다.
　　　　 chakha-n　 ku Mimi-uy　 tongsayng-i ttena-ss-ta
　　　　 honest-MOD the Mimi-GEN sister-NOM　 leave-PST-DECL
　　　　 '(lit.) The honest Mimi's sister left.'

　　 c. 미미의　 그 착한　　 동생이　　 떠났다.
　　　　 Mimi-uy　 ku chakha-n　 tongsayng-i ttena-ss-ta
　　　　 Mimi-GEN this honest-MOD sister-NOM　 leave-PST-DECL
　　　　 '(lit.) The honest Mimi's sister left.'

The flexible ordering of adnominals is thus another key property of nominal structure in the language (see Chapter 5 for more about ordering flexibility).

3.3.3 Verbals: Adjective and Verb Together

A distinctive property of Korean parts of speech is that the language makes no distinction between verbs and adjectives. They behave alike in many syntactic ways and differ in only a few respects. This is why the language has the category *verbal* (or 용언 'yongen' in traditional Korean grammar), which includes not only *verb* but also *adjective*. As seen from the following examples, both can be used as predicates:

(57) a. 하하가　빨리　달렸다.
　　　Haha-ka　ppalli talli-ess-ta
　　　Haha-NOM fast　run-PST-DECL
　　　'Haha ran fast.'

　　 b. 하하가　　많이　　아팠다.
　　　Haha-ka　　manhi　aphu-ass-ta
　　　Haha-NOM very　　sick-PST-DECL
　　　'Haha was very sick.'

As seen here, both include past tense and declarative suffixes and function as the finite predicate of the sentence.

One grammatical difference between the two is that unlike verbs, adjectives cannot have the present tense marking, *(nu)n*:

(58) a. 미미가　　달린다.
　　　Mimi-ka　　talli-n-ta
　　　Mimi-NOM run-PRES-DECL
　　　'Mimi runs.'

　　 b. 미미가　　아프다/아팠다/*아픈다.
　　　Mimi-ka　　aphu-ta/aph-ass-ta/*aphu-n-ta
　　　Mimi-NOM sick-DECL/sick-PST-DECL/*sick-PRES-DECL
　　　'Mimi is/was sick.'

The main distinction between verbs and adjectives is semantic: adjectives describe a stative situation, whereas verbs denote a nonstative situation. That is, the verb 달리다 *talli-ta* 'run' in (58a) describes an action performed by the subject, whereas 아프다 *aphu-ta* 'sick' in (58b) denotes the stative situation of the subject. A traditional way to distinguish these is to use the feature STATIVE:

(59) a. Verbal predicates or verbs: [STATIVE +] verbs
　　 b. Adjectival predicates or adjectives: [STATIVE −] verbs

Reflecting this distinction, we often use the term *nonstative verbs* to refer to adjectival predicates (adjectives in English).

Other than these semantic and morphological differences, the two behave alike in most environments. Just as in English, adjectives and verbs in Korean are subclassified according to what they combine with – that is, what kind of complement they select:

(60) a. Intransitive adjectives: 푸르다 phwulu-ta 'blue,' 아름답다 alumtap-ta 'beautiful,' 높다 noph-ta 'high,' ...

   b. Transitive adjectives: 무섭다 mwusep-ta 'afraid,' 좋다 coh-ta 'fond,' ...

(61) a. Intransitive verbs: 가다 ka-ta 'go,' 자다 ca-ta 'sleep,' 놀다 nol-ta 'play,' ...

   b. Complex intransitive verbs: 되다 toy-ta 'become,' 처신하다 chesinha-ta 'behave,' 승진하다 sungcinha-ta 'promote,' ...

   c. Transitive verbs: 먹다 mek-ta 'eat,' 차다 cha-ta 'kick,' 빌리다 pilli-ta 'borrow,' ...

   d. Ditransitive verbs: 보내다 ponay-ta 'send,' 주다 cwu-ta 'give,' ...

Following is an example sentence for each type of adjective and verb:

(62) a. 저 꽃이   참   아름답다.
ce kkoch-i   cham alumtap-ta
the flower-NOM really pretty-DECL
'The flowers are really pretty.'

   b. 미아는 책이   참   좋다.
Mia-nun chayk-i   cham coh-ta
Mia-TOP book-NOM really fond-DECL
'Mia is really fond of books.'

(63) a. 미아가   잔다.
Mia-ka ca-n-ta
Mia-NOM sleep-PRES-DECL
'Mia sleeps.'

   b. 미미가   사장이   되었다.
Mimi-ka   sacang-i   toy-ess-ta
Mimi-NOM chairman-NOM become-PST-DECL
'Mimi became CEO.'

   c. 미미가   사과를   먹었다.
Mimi-ka   sakwa-lul mek-ess-ta
Mimi-NOM apple-ACC eat-PST-DECL
'Mimi ate an apple.'

   d. 미미가   사과를   동생에게   주었다.
Mimi-ka   sakwa-lul tongsayng-eykey   cwu-ess-ta
Mimi-NOM apple-ACC younger.brother-DAT give-PST-DECL
'Mimi gave an apple to her younger brother.'

The examples show that the intransitive adjective and verb do not require a complement, whereas transitive ones combine with a complement.

The Korean *verbal* category can also be divided into *main* and *auxiliary* verbs:

(64) a. Auxiliary verbs: 싶다 siph-ta 'would like to,' 지다 ci-ta 'become,' 되다 toy-ta 'become,' …

b. Main verbs: 먹다 mek-ta 'eat,' 가다 ka-ta 'go,' 보내다 ponay-ta 'send,' …

These auxiliary verbs play a role in 'helping' the main verbs by extending their meaning, as illustrated in the following:

(65) a. 미아는   사과를   먹고   싶었다.
Mia-nun sakwa-lul mek-ko siph-ess-ta
Mia-TOP   apple-ACC eat-CONN would.like-PST-DECL
'Mia would like to eat an apple.'

b. 방이   밝아   지었다.
pang-i   palk-a   ci-ess-ta
room-NOM bright-CONN become-PST-DECL
'(lit.) The room became brightened.'

c. 그 일이   잘   되어   간다.
ku il-i   cal toy-e   ka-n-ta
the work-NOM well become-CONN go-PRES-DECL
'The work is under way smoothly.'

Auxiliary verbs in Korean cannot stand alone, even in elliptical environments. They must occur with the preceding main verbs:

(66) *미아는 싶었다.
Mia-nun siph-ess-ta
Mia-TOP would.like-PST-DECL
'(lit.) Mia would like to.'

One thing worth noting is that many auxiliary verb forms can also be used as main verbs. For instance, the verb form *ka-ta* 'go-DECL' in (65c) can be used both as a main verb and as an auxiliary verb. When used as an auxiliary verb, it conveys the sense of continuation of the action denoted by the main verb, whereas its main verb simply means 'go.'

In English, the copula verb *be* behaves like an auxiliary verb in many respects (see Chapter 7). Similarly, Korean has the positive copula verb 이다 i-ta 'is-DECL' and the negative 아니다 ani-ta 'not-DECL':

(67) a. 김은   학생이다.
Kim-un haksayng-i-ta
Kim-TOP student-COP-DECL
'Kim is a student.'

b. 김은   학생이   아니다.
   Kim-un haksayng-i ani-ta
   Kim-TOP student-NOM not.COP-DECL
   'Kim is not a student.'

Like the other auxiliary verbs, but unlike main verbs, copula verbs cannot be used alone. In particular, the positive one must occur with a predicative expression like 학생 haksayng 'student' in (67a).

3.3.4 Adverbials

Adverbials can be classified into two groups, depending on their origin. The pure adverbs are root lexemes, whereas derived adverbs are formed with the combination of a verb and a special suffix like -이 -i, -히 -hi, 리 -li, or 게 -key:

(68) a. Pure adverbs:
        아주 acwu 'very,' 자주 cacwu 'often,' 꼭 kkok 'surely,' 너무 nemwu 'too much,' 종종 congcong 'often,' …
     b. Derived adverbs:
        많이 manh-i 'many,' 조용히 coyong-hi 'quietly,' 멀리 mel-li 'far away,' 빠르게 ppalu-key, …

Adverbials can also be classified according to their meaning, just like English adverbs:

(69) a. Temporal: 이미 imi 'already,' 방금 pangkum 'just,' …
     b. Frequency: 가끔 kakkum 'sometimes,' 또 tto 'again,' 항상 hangsang 'always,' …
     c. General: 모두 motwu 'all,' 같이 kathi 'together,' 잘 cal 'well,' …
     d. Interrogative: 왜 way 'why,' 언제 encey 'when,' 어떻게 ettehkey 'how,' …
     e. Degree: 아주 acwu 'very,' 더 te 'more,' 매우 maywu 'very,' …
     f. Conjunctive: 즉 cuk 'that is,' 그래서 kulayse 'so,' 그러나 kulena 'but,' …

In terms of grammar, the more important distinction comes from their position. For example, even though most adverbs, including *pangkum* 'just,' can appear in any location, a few adverbials like *cal* 'well' appear only in the preverbal position:

(70) a. (방금)   원빈은   (방금)
        (pangkum) Wonbin-un   (pangkum)
        just   Wonbin-TOP   just

수영을   (방금)   하였다.
swuyeng-ul   (pangkum)   ha-yess-ta
swimming-ACC   just   do-PST-DECL
'Wonbin just swam.'

b. (*잘) 원빈은   (*잘) 수영을   (잘) 하였다.
(*cal) Wonbin-un (*cal) swuyeng-ul   (cal) ha-yess-ta
well Wonbin-TOP well swimming-ACC well do-PST-DECL
'Wonbin swam well.'

3.4 Expanding Verbals and Nominals

3.4.1 Verbal and Nominal Derivations and Inflections in English

There are two main morphemes (meaningful morphological unit) that can expand the lexical base (citation or lexeme entries) in languages: *inflectional* and *derivational* suffixes (morphemes). Inflectional morphemes are affixes that carry grammatical meaning but do not change the part of speech or meaning of the word. For example, the past form -*ed*, the present form -*s*, and the participle form -*ing* are inflectional morphemes attached to the base form:

(71) a. play: played, plays, playing
     b. change: changed, changes, changing

The attachment of these morphemes does not change the lexical category and basic meaning of the base form or its lexical category. In this sense, the following suffixes are all taken to be inflectional:

(72) a. Inflectional suffixes: -es, -ed, -en, -er (comparative), -est
     b. Examples: writes, chases, written, happier, happiest

Meanwhile, derivational morphemes are suffixes or morphemes added to a lexeme to change its meaning or lexical category. They are used to make a new, different lexeme.

(73) a. sad vs. sadly, drink vs. drinkable, promote vs. promotion, …
     b. happy vs. unhappy, moral vs. amoral, possible vs. impossible, …

Derivational morphemes can be either suffixes or prefixes and typically change the lexical category of the base they attach to.

(74) a. Derivational morphemes in English: -ful, -able, im-, un-, -er (person), …
     b. Examples: fearful, lovable, impossible, unlucky, undo, driver, …

Because derivational morphemes change the meaning of base (e.g. *lucky* vs. *unlucky*), they produce a new word, whereas inflectional morphemes produce grammatical variants of the same word.

As such, English has a simple inflectional system, but Korean has a much more complex morphological system that most non-native speakers have great difficulty acquiring.

3.4.2 Verbal Inflections in Korean

Basic Suffixes

Korean, a fundamentally agglutinative language, uses affixation as the major mechanism for word formation. A fully inflected Korean verb consists of an obligatory mood suffix and a variety of intervening optional ones, as illustrated by the following example:

(75) 읽히시었다고만   하셨다.
      ilk-hi-si-ess-ta-ko-man   ha-si-ess-ta
      read-CAUS-HON-PST-DECL-COMP-only say-HON-PST-DECL
      '(The teacher) said he/she just made them read.'

Here, the verb root *read* is followed by the suffixes for causative, honorific, past tense, declarative, complementizer (similar to English *that*), and delimiter marker (only), in order. Most are optional except the declarative ending suffix. The root cannot occur alone in a sentence. That is, the verb in Korean cannot be an independent word without inflectional suffixes. However, the suffixes cannot be freely attached to a stem or word: they have a regular fixed order, as reflected in the traditional template in (76).

(76) V-root + (Pass/Caus) + (Hon) + (Tense) + Mood

As seen in (76), the suffixes marking passive/causative, honorific, tense, and mood information are strictly ordered. The mood suffix is obligatory, while the other suffixes are optional. A short inventory of these suffixes is given in (77).

(77) a. Passive/Cause: -이 i, -히 hi, -리 li, -기 ki (-우 wu, -구 kwu, 추 chwu)
      b. Honorific: -(으)시 -(u)si
      c. Tense: -었/-았 -ess/-ass (Past), -겠 -keyss (future)
      d. Mood: -다 -ta (declarative), -까 -kka (question), -(어)라 -(e) (imperative),
         -(읍)시다 -(u)psita (formal propositive), -자 -ca (informal propositive),
         -습니다 -supnita (formal declarative), -습니까 -supnikka (formal question, …

The passive and causative suffixes (all seven types) are different from the other three in that they can change the type of the main verb they attach to. For example, the active verb 먹다 mek-ta 'eat' has two arguments (subject and object), agent subject and patient object. In contrast, its passive counterpart 먹히다 mek-hi-ta 'eat-PASS-DECL' has just one patient subject. In this sense, they function as derivational suffixes. The remaining verbal suffixes are inflectional, adding honoring, tense, or mood information. Morphologically, the inflectional suffixes preceding mood are optional, but a mood suffix must be attached to a verb stem in simple sentences. Thus the verbal stem and the mood suffix are mutually bound: the bare verb root or stem cannot be used uninflected in any syntactic context, and it should be inflected at least with the mood suffix, as shown in (78).

(78) a. 읽(었)다 ilk-(ess)-ta 'read-(PST)-DECL'
b. *읽었 *ilk-ess 'read-PST'

The template, for instance, allows all the following:

(79) a. 달리-다 talli-ta 'run-DECL'
b. 달리-시-었-다 talli-si-ess-ta 'run-HON-PST-DECL'
c. 잡-히-었-다 cap-hi-ess-ta 'catch-PASS-PST-DECL'
d. 마치-었-습니-까? machi-ess-supni-kka 'finish-PST-FRML-QUE'

At a glance, the template given in (77) appears to capture the ordering generalizations and combinatory possibilities of verbal suffixes. But note that the template alone may allow us to generate ill-formed combinations such as those in (80).

(80) a. 가-(*었)-자 ka-(*ess)-ca 'go-PST-PROP'
b. 가-(*었)-라 ka-(*ess)-la 'go-PST-IMPER'

The propositive mood suffix -자 -ca and imperative mood suffix -라 -la in (80a,b) cannot combine semantically with the tense suffix. Such suffixes, mainly due to their meaning, have selectional or co-occurrence restrictions in addition to their position in the mood slot.

Connectives

There is another group of verbal suffixes. They are attached not to the final verb in matrix clauses but to the governed or dependent main verb, which cannot stand alone. For example, when a main verb precedes an auxiliary verb, the main verb needs to have a special connective suffix:

(81) 미아는   사과를   먹어   보았다.
Mia-nun sakwa-lul mek-e   po-ass-ta
Mia-TOP   apple-ACC   eat-CONN try-PST-DECL
'Mia tried to eat an apple.'

The connective -어 -e here must be combined with the auxiliary verb. It cannot host a tense suffix like the following:

(82) *사과를   먹었어   보았다.
     sakwa-lul mek-ess-e   po-ass-ta
     apple-ACC eat-PST-CONN try-PST-DECL
     '(int) tried to eat an apple.'

Because such connective suffixes differ from suffixes like declarative endings, they form a different *connective suffix* group. These connective suffixes can be divided into four groups according to the kind of root or stem they can co-occur with, as shown in (83).

(83) a. CONN1: -아/-어 -a/-e
     b. CONN2: -지/-게/-고 -ci/-key/-ko
     c. CONN3: -어야/-나 -eya/-na
     d. CONN4: -고 -ko

CONN suffixes exclusively occupy the end of a verb form (i.e. no two CONN suffixes can co-occur). These connective markers allow words like the following:

(84) a. CONN1: 읽-어 ilk-e 'read-CONN1'
     b. CONN2: 읽-지 ilk-ci 'read-CONN2'
     c. CONN3: 읽-어야 ilk-eya 'read-CONN3'
     d. CONN4: 읽-었-다-고 ilk-ess-ta-ko 'read-PST-MOOD-CONN4'

Verbs ending with such connective markers occur with a limited set of expressions like an auxiliary. For instance, those with V-어야 V-eya are followed by the auxiliary type 하다 ha-ta, yielding a meaning of obligation:

(85) 우리는   책을   읽어야   한다.
     wuli-nun   chayk-ul   ilk-eya   ha-n-ta
     we-TOP   book-ACC   read-CONN   do-PRES-DECL
     'We must read books.'

As such, we need to distinguish connectives belonging to at least four different groups but will use CONN as a cover term except for the complementizer (COMP) -ko. In Chapter 7, we will see detailed combinational restrictions of verbs marked with connective suffixes.

Category-Changing Suffixes

The verbal suffixes we have seen so far do not change the category information of the stem to which they are attached. Let us use some category-changing suffixes. There are at least two classes of nominalizers in Korean: lexical (or derivational) nominalizers, -이 -i and -기 -ki, and sentential (or gerundive/inflectional) nominalizers, -음 -um and -기 -ki.

(86) a. 놀기 nol-ki, 쓰기 ssu-ki 'writing,' 'playing,' 놀이 nol-i 'play' 높이 noph-i 'height'

 b. 놀았음 nol-ass-um 'write-PST-NMLZ,' 놀았기 nol-ass-ki 'play-PST-NMLZ'

In (86a), -기 ki and -이 i are attached to the verb stem and form new words. In this sense, they are lexical nominalizers functioning as derivational ones. In the meantime, -음 um and -기 ki in (86b) function as inflectional nominalizers, attached to the past-tense stem. Unlike lexical nominalizers, the sentential and inflectional nominalizers -음 -um and -기 -ki are productive in that (i) there is virtually no restriction on the morphological host, (ii) there is no crucial change in the meaning (semantically compositional), and (iii) the internal structure of the clause headed by the nominalized element is fully transparent to other syntactic processes such as scrambling and intervening elements:

(87) a. 우리는   김이   학교에   갔음을   알았다.
  wuli-nun [Kim-i   hakkyo-ey   ka-ss]-um-ul   al-ass-ta
  we-TOP   Kim-NOM school-LOC go-PST-NMLZ-ACC know-PST-DECL
  'We knew that Kim went to school.'

 b. 남자가   여자를   사랑하기가   어렵다.
  [namca-ka yeca-lul   salangha]-ki-ka elyep-ta
  man-NOM   woman-ACC   love-NMLZ-NOM   difficult-DECL
  'It is difficult for men to love women.'

The nominalizers -음 -um and -기 -ki in (87a,b) are attached to the tensed stem and underived verb root, respectively. They nominalize the embedded clause, as can be seen from the NOM and ACC case markings.

Category-Neutral Suffixes
The suffixes we have seen so far restrict the category information of the host they are attached to. However, suffixes like delimiters do not restrict the category information of their morphological host.

(88) a. 잘-만 cal-man 'well-only'
 b. 먹어-만 mek-e-man 'eat-CONN-only'
 c. 남자-만 namca-man 'man-only'

As in (88), the delimiter -man 'only' can attach to an adverb, verb, or noun stem. (89) shows two main classes (X-delimiter and Z-delimiter) of such delimiters with respect to their ordering.

(89) a. X-delimiters: -만 -man 'only,' -까지 -kkaci 'even,' 마저 -mace 'even,' -조차 -cocha 'even,' ...
 b. Z-delimiters: -은/-는 -(n)un 'TOP/FOCUS,' -도 -to 'also,' -(이)라도 -(i)lato 'even,' ...

These two groups have strict ordering restrictions, as given in template (90).

(90) V-stem + X-delimiter + Z-delimiter

The cases in (91) show that these ordering restrictions cannot be violated.

(91) a. *먹-어-은-만 *mek-e-un-man 'eat-CONN-ZDEL-XDEL'
　　 b. *먹-어-라도-만 *mek-e-lato-man 'eat-CONN-ZDEL-XDEL'

As we said, these delimiters can be attached to verbs marked with a connective suffix:

(92) a. 읽-지-만-은 (않았다) ilk-ci-man-un (anhassta) 'read-CONN-XDEL-ZDEL (did not)'
　　 b. 잡-아-만-은 (보았다) cap-a-man-un (poassta) 'catch-CONN-XDEL-ZDEL (tried)'

　Thus, delimiters are another case that employs rigid suffix ordering and combinatory restrictions with respect to other verb suffixes and stems. To capture the behavior of these delimiters with respect to other verbal suffixes, a purely templatic view needs either strict subcategorization information for each suffix or additional templates or mechanisms.

3.4.3 Nominal Expansion in Korean

Suffixes can be attached to nominal (noun) expressions, but they behave quite differently. One property that distinguishes nominal suffixes from verbal suffixes in Korean is that the nominal suffixes, traditionally called 조사 *cosa*, are all optional, as shown in the following example:

(93) 선생 + (님) + (들) + (에게) + (만) + (은)
　　 sensayng + (nim) + (tul) + (eykey) + (man) + (un)
　　 teacher + Hon + Pl + Postp + X-Del + Z-Del
　　 'to the (honorable) teachers only'

All the nominal suffixes are optional except for the noun root 선생 *sensayng*. The following template reflects the ordering possibilities of the nominal suffixes and the optionality:

(94) N-base – (Hon) – (Pl) – (Postp) – (Conj) – (X-Delim) – (Z-Delim)

All the suffixes decode various grammatical functions but need not be realized. The following list gives the nominal particles or suffixes belonging to each slot.

(95) a. Honorific: 께서 kkeyse 'HON.NOM'
　　 b. Plural: 들 tul 'PL'

   c. Postposition: 에게 eykey 'DAT,' 한테 hanthey 'DAT,' 에서 eyse 'LOC,' 에 ey 'LOC,' (으)로 (u)lo 'instrument,' 까지 kkaci 'GOAL'

   d. Conjunctive: 하고 hako 'with,' 보다 pota 'than,' 부터 pwuthe 'from,' 처럼 chelem 'like'

   e. X-delimiter: 만 man 'only,' 까지 kkaci 'even,' 조차 cocha 'even,' 밖에 pakkey 'only'

   f. Z-delimiter: 은/는 (n)un 'Topic/Focus,' 도 to 'also,' 이/가 i/ka 'NOM,' 을/를 l(ul) 'ACC,' 의 uy 'GEN'

Traditionally, nominal suffixes are treated as independent lexical categories, even though they act more like suffixes because they cannot appear alone. As the template indicates, the nominal suffixes have ordering restrictions. For instance, examples like the following are allowed:

(96) a. 선생-님-이 sensayng-nim-i 'teacher-HON-NOM'

   b. 선생-님-들-과 sensayng-nim-tul-kwa 'teacher-HON-PL-CONJ'

   c. 선생-님-들-에게-만-은 sensayng-nim-tul-eykey-man-un 'teacher-HON-PL-DAT-DEL-TOP'

However, the template blocks examples like the following that violate the ordering of the nominal suffixes:

(97) a. *선생-님-들-은-에게 *sensayng-nim-tul-un-eykey 'teacher-HON-PL-DEL-DAT'

   b. *선생-님-들-과-에게 *sensayng-nim-tul-kwa-eykey 'teacher-HON-PL-CONJ-DAT'

   c. *선생-님-들-은-이 *sensayng-nim-tul-un-i 'teacher-HON-PL-TOP-NOM'

In summary, Korean morphology is much more complex than English morphology. Verbal and nominal words contain a variety of morphemes linked to their own meanings and grammatical functions. This is why Korean is considered an agglutinative language. In this type of language, words may contain different morphemes to determine their meanings, but all morphemes (including stems and suffixes) tend to remain unchanged after being combined.

3.5 Contrastive Notes

3.5.1 Different Sets of Lexical Categories

We have seen that English and Korean employ different sets of lexical categories:

(98) a. English: noun, verb, adjective, preposition, adverb, determiner, particle, conjunction, complementizer

   b. Korean: nominal, verbal, adnominal, adverbial

These categories are determined by the groups of words that share distributional properties in the language.

It is important to note that Korean lexical categories (nominal, verbal, adnominal, and adverbial) are more general than those in English. For instance, the verbal category includes not only verbs but also adjectives. Considering their wider distributional properties and similarities with categories in English, we can posit the following hierarchy for both languages. We will discuss the rationale for this hierarchy in due course.

(99)

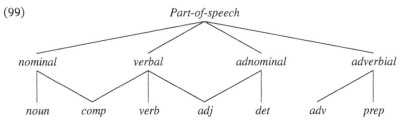

In this hierarchy, the upper-level categories correspond to Korean and the lower-level categories to English. Note that *comp* (complementizer) and *adj* are cross-classified: for instance, *comp* is a subtype of *nominal* as well as *verbal*, addressing its dual properties:

(100) a. I believe [that the president has to do better].
       b. [That he had run away] didn't make sense.

The CP, projected from the complementizer *comp*, is used as a nominal, functioning as the object and subject, respectively. The hierarchy also shows that *nominal* has two subtypes, *noun* and *comp*, implying that they may behave similarly. This can be easily seen in the following:

(101) a. Cohen proved [$_{NP}$ the independence of the continuum hypothesis].
       b. Cohen proved [$_{CP}$ that the continuum hypothesis was independent].

We can observe here that the NP and CP function as the object of the verb, which is a canonical property of nominals. In Korean, the category *verbal* has two subtypes, *verb* and *adj*. This reflects the fact that *verbal* includes not only nonstative verb expressions but also stative adjectival expressions, as we have discussed in this chapter.

There are also some clear differences between the two languages with respect to the members of lexical categories.

- *Particles*: There is no corresponding lexical category in Korean. The particle category is a distinctive feature of English.

- *Prepositions*: Korean has no English-style prepositions. In many cases, English prepositions are realized as nominal suffixes. The following example illustrates this:

(102) a. Mimi went to school with her friends by bike.

    b. 미미는   학교에   친구와   자전거로   갔다.
       Mimi-nun hakkyo-ey chinkwu-wa cacenke-lo ka-ss-ta
       Mimi-TOP school-at   friend-with   bike-by   go-PST-DECL

One might suggest that *-ey*, *-wa*, and *lo* are postpositions. But they are more like suffixes in that they cannot stand alone, unlike English, as in *Whom did Mimi go to school with?*

- *Determiners*: In Korean, determiners are taken as adnominals and loose in their ordering, as seen in the following:

(103) a. 어려운   그 책
       elyewu-n   ku chayk
       difficult-MOD the book

    b. 그 어려운   책
       ku elyewu-n   chayk
       the difficult-MOD book

- *Verbs and adjectives*: Korean makes no distinction between verbs and adjectives. They all serve as verbals and differ only with respect to semantic features like stative vs. nonstative.

3.5.2 Simple vs. Rich Verbal Inflection Systems

Korean verbs can be inflected with a variety of suffixes. We have seen that even the sentence type is marked by the verb inflection; no syntactic operations (moving the auxiliary to the front) are necessary to mark sentence mood. For instance, consider the following:

(104) a. Mia met Momo in the school.
    b. Will Mia meet Momo in school?
    c. Whom did Mia meet in the school?

Sentence (104a) is declarative, making a statement. To have a corresponding polar question, English requires an auxiliary verb at the beginning of the sentence, as in (104b). For a *wh*-question, it also needs a *wh*-expression in front of the sentence. Korean is quite different – it marks such a sentence type (mood) on the verb with a suffix:

(105) a. 미아는 학교에   갔다.
　　　　 Mia-nun hakkyo-ey ka-ss-ta
　　　　 Mia-TOP school-to go-PST-DECL
　　　　 'Mia went to school.'

　　　 b. 미아는 학교에   갔니?
　　　　 Mia-nun hakkyo-ey ka-ss-ni?
　　　　 Mia-TOP school-to go-PST-QUE?
　　　　 'Did Mia go to school?'

　　　 c. 누가   학교에   갔니?
　　　　 nwu-ka   hakkyo-ey ka-ss-ni?
　　　　 who-NOM school-to go-PST-QUE
　　　　 'Who went to school?'

3.5.3 Simple vs. Rich Nominal Inflections

We have seen that Korean nominals can be extended in various ways with nominal suffixes or particles. These suffixes include case markings like NOM (nominative) and ACC (accusative), as well as locative or temporal markings like -에/-에서 -ey/-eyse, which correspond to English prepositions. This implies that English prepositions are realized as nominal suffixes (called 조사 cosa) in Korean.

3.6 Conclusion

In this chapter, we have discussed lexical (word) categories in English and Korean that form the basic units of a given sentence. The two languages have different sets of lexical categories: English has nouns, verbs, adjectives, adverbs, prepositions, determiners, particles, conjunctions, and complementizers, while Korean has nominals, verbals, adnominals, and adverbials. At first glance, these English and Korean lexical categories seem quite different; but if we consider their subcategories, particularly those of Korean lexical categories, we have seen that the two share many lexical properties. Apart from those shared properties, each language has its own unique lexical categories. We have also noted that lexical expressions in both languages can undergo derivational and inflectional processes. The inflectional processes in English are simple, while in Korean, they are complex due to the rich inflection and derivation system. All these differences can act as starting points where the two languages behave differently in many respects.

Exercises

1 Provide the lexical category of each word in the following English sentences:

   (i) a. The frog sat in his yard with a friend.
      b. My friend could speak English fluently, but her friend may not.
      c. The baby turned a light off.
      d. I wondered if I made the right decision to make this change.
      e. The argument is that if people don't have incentives to get rich, everyone will stop trying.

2 Identify whether the underlined word is a particle or a preposition in English. In doing so, try to use the mobility test.

   (i) a. I looked <u>up</u> the stairs.
      b. I looked <u>up</u> a word in the dictionary.
      c. Kim cheers <u>up</u> his students.
      d. The children ran <u>down</u> the hall.
      e. Kim let <u>down</u> his friend for a long time.
      f. Lee took <u>off</u> her hat.
      g. Lee fell <u>off</u> the table.

3 Provide the lexical category of each word in the following Korean sentences:

   (i) a. 미미는　　교실에서　　　공부하는　　　　것이　　　싫다.
        Mimi-nun kyosil-eyse　　kongpwuha-nun kes-i　　silh-ta
        Mimi-TOP classroom-LOC study-TOP　　　　thing-NOM not.fond.of-DECL
        'Mimi is not fond of studying in the classroom.'

      b. 미미가　　사과를　　아주 빨리　먹었다.
        Mimi-ka　　sakwa-lul acwu ppalli mek-ess-ta
        Mimi-NOM apple-ACC very fast　eat-PST-DECL
        'Mimi ate the apple very fast.'

      c. 하늘은　푸르고　　내 마음은　즐겁다.
        hanul-un phwulu-ko nay maum-un culkep-ta
        sky-TOP　blue-and　my heart-TOP joyful-DECL
        'The sky is blue, and my heart is joyful.'

      d. 여섯 명의　　　학생들이　　　축구를　　　시작했다.
        yeses myeng-uy haksayng-tul-i chwukkwu-lul sicakha-yess-ta
        six　CL-GEN　student-PL-NOM soccer-ACC　start-PST-DECL
        'Six students started soccer.'

e. 서울의　　지하철이　　매우　　깨끗하다.
Seoul-uy　cihachel-i　maywu　kkaykkusha-ta
Seoul-GEN　subway-NOM　very　clean-DECL
'The subway at Seoul is very clean.'

f. 미미가　새　책을　한　권　　주었다.
Mimi-ka　say　chayk-ul　han　kwon　cwu-ess-ta
Mimi-NOM　new　book-ACC　one　volume　give-PST-DECL

그　책을　　내일　　읽고　　싶다.
ku　chakyk-ul　nayil　ilk-ko　siph-ta
the　book-ACC　tomorrow　read-CONN　would.like DECL
'Mimi gave me a new book. I would like to read that book soon.'

4　We have seen that in Korean verbal and nominal suffixes can be attached to the verb and noun stem. Provide at least five extended examples for each case that can be extended from the following noun and verb stem.

(i) a. 학생 haksayng 'student'
　　b. 친구 chinkwu 'friend'
　　c. 교실 kyosil 'classroom'
　　d. 부모 pwumo 'parents'
　　e. 정직 cengcik 'honest'

(ii) a. 마시- masi- 'drink'
　　b. 배우- paywu- 'learn'
　　c. 놀- nol- 'play'
　　d. 공부하- kongpwuha- 'study'
　　e. 아프- aphu- 'sick'

5　Verbs in English and Korean do not necessarily behave similarly. As exemplified here, a transitive verb in English sometimes corresponds to an intransitive verb in Korean and vice versa.

(i) a. Kim discussed this matter with Mimi.
　　b. *Kim discussed about this matter with Mimi.

(ii) a. 김은　이　문제에　　대해　미미와　　토론하였다.
Kim-un　i　mwuncey-ey　tayhay　Mimi-wa　tholonha-yess-ta
Kim-TOP　this matter-DAT　about　Mimi-with　discuss-PAST-DECL

　　b. 김은　이　문제를　　미미와　　토론하였다.
Kim-un　i　mwuncey-lul　Mimi-wa　tholonha-yess-ta
Kim-TOP　this matter-ACC　Mimi-with　discuss-PAST-DECL

Provide more than three English-Korean pairs that show such a mismatch (e.g. discuss vs. 토론하다 *tholonha-ta*).

6 The English copula verb *be* has several different uses;
  (i) a. Kim is the student. (identificational)
     b. Kim is happy/a student. (predicative)
     c. Kim is in Seoul. (locative)
Each of these three uses can be translated into Korean with the verb *i-* or as *iss-*:
  (ii) a. 김이   그 학생이다
        Kim-i   ku haksayng-i-ta
        Kim-NOM the student-COP-DECL

     b. 김이   행복하다
        Kim-i   hayngpokha-ta
        Kim-NOM happy-DECL

     c. 김이   서울에   있다
        Kim-i   Seoul-ey iss-ta
        Kim-NOM Seoul-LOC exist-DECL

What generalizations can you make from these facts? Discuss the difference in the uses of the copula verbs in the two languages.

7 We have seen that expressions like 연구 *yenkwu* 'research' are verbal nouns in the sense that they can be used as nouns while behaving like verbs. They typically combine with the light verb 하다 *ha-ta*, as in 연구하다 *yenkwu-ha-ta*. Find at least five Korean sentences that include a verbal noun from real-life data (e.g. newspaper articles, magazines, blogs), and identify the 'complement' type. For instance, for 연구하다 *yenkwu-ha-ta*, select an NP like 영어를 *yenge-lul* 'English' as its complement.

8 Provide Yale Romanizations/glosses for the following Korean examples. While doing the Romanization, including hyphens for all the particles and suffixes.
  (i) a. 선생님께서만이 우리를 이해하신다.
        'Only the teacher understands us.'
     b. 그 토끼도 불행하게도 사냥꾼에게 잡히었다.
        'Unfortunately, the rabbit was also caught by the hunter.'
     c. 미미는 공부만 하고 싶었다.
        '(lit.) Mimi likes to do study only.'
     d. 학생들이 두 언어의 차이점을 많이 배우게 되었다.
        '(lit.) Students became to learn the differences of the two language a lot.'
     e. 어려움들이 여기 저기에 있었지만, 잘 이겨냈다.
        'Difficulties were here and there, but we overcame them well.'

4

Phrases: Combining Words and Building Larger Expressions

4.1 Introduction

In the previous chapter, we learned that words are the basic units of a sentence and are further classified into lexical categories or parts of speech based on their shared grammatical properties. These words combine with other expressions to form bigger expressions called *phrases*. Phrases are *constituents* that we can identify from their elements. In this sense, phrases are said to be projections of lexical categories. The following examples in the brackets include basic phrases in English:

(1) a. [$_{NP}$ New <u>books</u> on linguistics] are very interesting. (NP = noun phrase)
   b. Kim is [$_{AP}$ very <u>happy</u> with the new job]. (AP = adjective phrase)
   c. She drives [$_{AdvP}$ much more <u>carefully</u> than her sister]. (AdvP = adverb phrase)
   d. Kim darted [$_{PP}$ <u>from</u> the room]. (PP = prepositional phrase)

Note that all these phrases are projected from the underlined *head* lexical expression (N, A, Adv, P), which is the essential expression in the phrase.

Korean is not different in this respect. Korean lexical expressions are also projected into phrasal expressions by themselves or by combining with other expressions:

(2) a. [$_{NP}$ 이　문법책이]　　재미있다.
   　　i　mwunpep.chayk-i　caymi-iss-ta
   　　this grammar.book-NOM interesting-exist-DECL
   　'This grammar book is interesting.'
   b. 미미가　　[$_{VP}$ 빨리　돌아왔다].
   　Mimi-ka　　ppalli　tola-o-ass-ta
   　Mimi-NOM　quickly　come.back-PST-DECL
   　'Mimi came back quickly.'

English and Korean in Contrast: A Linguistic Introduction, First Edition. Jong-Bok Kim.
© 2024 John Wiley & Sons, Inc. Published 2024 by John Wiley & Sons, Inc.

c. [$_{AdvP}$ 너무   빨라서] 잡지   못했다.
nemwu ppallase cap-ci   mosha-yess-ta
too   fast   catch-CONN not-PST-DECL
'I couldn't catch it because it was too fast.'

Just like English phrases, phrases in Korean are projected from the underlined lexical head. In this chapter, we will consider how phrases are formed in each language.

4.2 Main Phrases in English

4.2.1 Noun Phrases

A primary feature of English noun phrases (NPs) is that they can contain a determiner:

(3) a/the/this/that/any/some/his honest friend

The determiner can be indefinite (*a, some*) or definite (*the, this, that*). But an important constraint of English determiners is that multiple determiners cannot be used together:

(4) a. *every the book
    b. *my the book

The NP can have a prenominal modifier as well as a postnominal modifier, forming a larger NP:

(5) a. that [tall] boy
    b. a [criminal] court
    c. his [very tall] son

(6) a. the student [in the class]
    b. the student [with a hat]
    c. the student [to finish the project]
    d. the student [who is reading the book]

The bracketed expressions in (5) modify the following noun, and the bracketed expressions in (6) modify the preceding noun. The difference is that the prenominal modifier is only a simple adjectival phrase (AP), whereas the postnominal modifier can be various types ranging from a PP or VP to a relative clause.

A reliable way to figure out what kind of expression can function as an NP is to do a distributional test. For instance, given that a sentence consists of an NP followed by a VP, any expression that fills the following underlined position and forms a sentence can be considered an NP:

(7) _____ [ran 5 miles in an hour].

Among the numerous possibilities, the following could fill in the blank and make a grammatical sentence:

(8) a. Friends (N)
   b. The friend (Det N)
   c. The new friend (Det Adj N)
   d. The new friend [$_{PP}$ at school] (Det Adj N PP)
   e. The new friend [$_{VP}$ jogging every day] (Det Adj N VP)
   f. The friend [$_S$ who can speak Korean] (Det N S-rel)

The combinatorial possibilities projecting NPs that we have seen so far can be represented by the following PS (phrase structure) rules:

(9) NP → (Det) (Adj) N (PP|VP|S)

The PS rules say that an NP can consist of Det, Adj, N, and PP|VP|S (the symbol | means a disjunction). All expressions are optional except the pivotal expression N, which we call the *head* of the NP. That is, in forming an NP, the obligatory expression is the head N. The vertical line (|) indicates different options for the same place in the linear order. These options in the NP rule can then be represented in a tree structure:

(10)

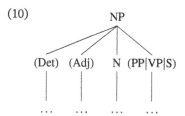

Note that an NP can perform various grammatical functions (subject, object, complement, or modifier), as discussed in detail in the next chapter. Consider the following examples:

(11) a. [The student] failed his driving test. (subject)
   b. Shall we plant [some rose bushes] in the corner? (object)
   c. Jim is [the best student in his class]. (predicative complement)
   d. They consider this [a very grave error of judgment]. (predicative complement)
   e. He suddenly turned up [last week]. (modifier)

The grammatical functions of these NPs range from subject to object or predicative complement. However, NPs like *last week* are adverbial in that they describe a temporal point.

4.2.2 Verb Phrases

As is the case for NPs, a reliable way to identify VPs is through distributional tests. For example, anything that can fill the following underlined position and complete a sentence is a VP:

(12) Mimi _____.

Here are some examples:

(13) a. Mimi [fell]. (V)
　　b. Mimi [feels [grateful to the guy]]. (V AP)
　　c. Mimi [lost [the race]]. (V NP)
　　d. Mimi [passed [the ball] [to her friend]]. (V NP PP)
　　e. Mimi [offered [her sister] [the best seats]]. (V NP NP)
　　f. Mimi [made [him] [angry]]. (V NP AP)

All the bracketed expressions here are VPs. Their PS rules are as follows:

(14) a. VP → V
　　b. VP → V AP
　　c. VP → V NP
　　d. VP → V NP PP
　　e. VP → V NP NP
　　f. VP → V NP AP

We can see that each verb type in (13) participates in different VP rules. That is, the PS rule for an intransitive verb like *fell* is (14a), whereas the rule for a ditransitive verb like *offered* is (14e). These PS rules generate a tree structure like the following:[1]

(15)

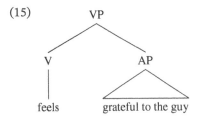

Note that the VPs in (13) are all finite, in that the *head* verbs are marked with tense information. Unlike these finite VPs, we can also have non-finite

---

1 The triangle for a phrase is used when we are not concerned about its internal structure.

(non-tensed) VPs. Consider the following:

(16) a. The Republicans [nominate Newt].
    b. The Republicans might [nominate Newt].
    c. The Republicans want to [nominate Newt].

In (16a), the VP *nominate Newt* is a finite one in which the verb *nominate* marks present tense information. However, in (16b) and (16c), the verb is nonfinite in that it does not bear any tense information. In the former, it is embedded in the bigger finite VP *might nominate Newt*, which is allowed by the following VP rule:

(17) VP → V[AUX +] VP

The rule means a VP can consist of a (finite) auxiliary and a VP, allowing the following VP structure:

(18)

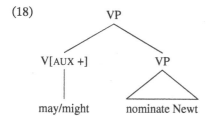

The modal auxiliary *may/might* marks the tense information of the VP, but the following VP includes no tense information. As such, VPs are finite or non-finite, depending on the tense information on the verb. Note that VPs can also be marked with *aspectual information* describing an ongoing or completed situation:

(19) a. Kim [has written a letter].
    b. Kim [is writing a letter].

The VP in (19a) describes a completed situation, and the one in (19b) represents an ongoing writing situation (see Chapter 6 for a detailed discussion of aspectual properties). These VPs are all allowed by the PS rule in (17).

4.2.3 Adjective Phrases

APs (adjective phrase) also have a core element (adjective) and occur in various positions with other elements:

(20) a. Mimi is [happy]. (A)
    b. Mimi is [happy with the class]. (A PP)
    c. Kim felt [doubtful about the outcome of the experiment]. (A PP)

    d. Kim considered him [loyal to the company.] (A PP)
    e. Kim is [proud that the team won the gold medal]. (A CP)
    f. Kim is [happy to meet his old friend]. (A VP)

Such possibilities are allowed by PS rules like the following:

(21) AP → A (PP|S|VP)

Once again, the head of an AP is A (adjective), from which the phrase is projected with the optional expressions PP, or S, or VP. With these possibilities, (20b) has a structure like the following:

(22)

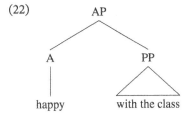

APs, as discussed in the previous chapter, occur in either attributive or predicative uses like *a [really happy] person* or *The person is [really happy]*.

4.2.4 Adverbial Phrases

Adverbial phrases (AdvPs) including an adverb represent a group of two or more words functioning as a modifier to a verbal expression:

(23) a. Tim's sister hardly behaved [less foolishly].
     b. You were driving [faster than 100 km/h].
     c. He turns up [suspiciously often].

As the examples show, AdvPs can include a modifier. This means AdvPs have the following general PS rule:

(24) AdvP → (Adv(P)) Adv

The PS rule can be represented with the following tree structure:

(25)

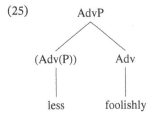

Remember that the term *adverbial* differs from the form value *adverb*. Adverbial phrases, referring to their grammatical function, not their grammatical form or category, include all phrases that act like an adverb that modifies a verbal expression. Consider the following examples:

(26) a. I will go to bed [AdvP very soon].
    b. I will go to bed [PP in an hour].
    c. I will go to bed now [VP to wake up early].
    d. I will go to bed [Conj-S when I've finished my book].

The bracketed expressions are different types of phrases: AdvP, PP, VP, and Conj-S (subordinating clause; see section 4.2.5). However, they all function as an adverbial expression or a modifier. The form values are different, but they all have an adverbial function.

4.2.5 Prepositional Phrases

The bracketed phrases in the following sentences are examples of prepositional phrases (PPs) in English:

(27) a. She walked [around his desk].
    b. Ryan could see her [in the room].
    c. David walked [on top of the building].
    d. They walked [up the stairs].
    e. Philip ate [in the kitchen].

All these PPs have a preposition as the central element of the phrase (i.e. as the head of the phrase). The remainder of the phrase, usually an NP, is called the prepositional *complement* or *prepositional object*. This explains why we need an accusative pronoun as the prepositional complement, not a nominative one:

(28) a. I went to the cinema [with them/*they].
    b. [Against whom/*who] did you protest if there was nobody present?

   These PPs can be represented by the following simple PS rule:

(29) PP → P NP

This rule states that a PP has the head P and its object NP. The rule can be represented in a tree structure:

(30)

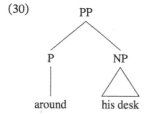

Note that PPs can be modified by an intensifying adverb:

(31) a. right [behind the house]
      b. partly [because of his teacher]
      c. exactly [like your father]
      d. reasonably [near the office]

For such examples, we can introduce a PP rule like the following:

(32) PP → Adv PP

4.2.6   Complementizer Phrases and Subordinating S (Conj-S)

Embedded clauses headed by a complementizer like *that, whether*, or *if* are called CPs:

(33) a. Lee believed [that [Kim left]].
      b. Lee wondered [whether [Kim left or not].
      c. Lee wondered [if [Kim left]].

To allow such combinations, we can introduce a PS rule like the following, where C means the complementizer category:

(34) CP → C S

This allows a structure like the following:

(35)

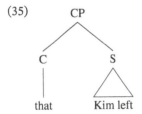

Subordinating conjuncts like *because, after, since, although, if, when* and so forth also introduce a subordinating clause:

(36) a. Kim studied grammar [because [it was required]].
      b. Kim left [after [Lee arrived]].
      c. Kim left [although [Lee arrived]].

A key difference between the clause introduced by a subordinating marker and the one marked by a complementizer is that the former clause is optional but the latter is obligatory:

(37) a. Kim believed *(that Kim left).
    b. Kim studied grammar (because it was required).

Unlike the subordinating marker, the complementizer thus introduces a required complement clause. One way to represent this difference is to have a PS rule like the following for a subordinating clause:

(38) Conj-S → Conj S

This rule allows the following structure:

(39)

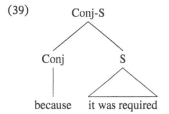

4.3 Phrases in Korean

In the previous chapter, we saw that Korean has four main lexical categories: nominal, verbal, adnominal, and adverbial. Because phrases are projected from these categories, we have nominal, verbal, adnominal, and adverbial phrases, which are slightly different from English. However, we call them NPs, VPs, Adnominal Phrases, and AdvPs to match phrases in English.

4.3.1 Nominal Phrases

A key property of Korean nominal phrases is that the determiner is optional, and even a countable noun requires no determiner:

(40) a. 그 학생들이   달리었다.
    ku haksayng-tul-i talli-ess-ta
    the student-PL-NOM run-PST-DECL
    'The students ran.'

   b. 학생들이   달리었다.
      haksayng-tul-i talli-ess-ta
      student-PL-NOM run-PST-DECL
      '(The) students ran.'

   c. 학생이   달리었다.
      haksayng-i   talli-ess-ta
      student-NOM   run-PST-DECL
      '(The/A) student(s) ran.'

Unlike English, Korean does not require the countable singular noun to combine with an adnominal expression like determiner. This means the NP has the following PS rule (taking Det as a subtype of adnominal for convenience):

(41) Nominal-P → (Det) N (to be revised)

This rule allows the following structure:

(42)   Nominal Phrase = NP

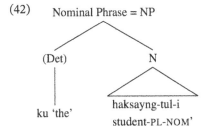

    (Det)   N

                  haksayng-tul-i
    ku 'the'   student-PL-NOM'

The rule in (41) is similar to the English PS rule for NPs. However, notice that prenominal expressions in Korean have a great deal of flexibility in their distributional possibilities. For example, the prenominal expression "honest" in Korean can either precede or follow the determiner:

(43) a. 그 착한   학생
     ku chakha-n haksayng
     the honest-MOD student
     'the honest student'

   b. 착한   그 학생
     chakha-n ku haksayng
     honest-MOD the student
     'the honest student'

This flexibility in the position of adnominal expressions implies the following structures:

(44) a.

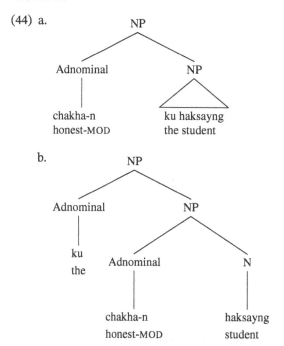

These two structures illustrate that, unlike the English NP rule, the head of an NP in Korean can be either an N or an NP.

Adnominal and prenominal expressions, including English-type determiners, can largely be classified as deterministic or phrasal prenominal. Deterministic prenominals, which we call *determinants*, roughly correspond to determiners in English. As noted in the previous chapter, these lexical determinants include the following:

(45) a. characteristic: 새 *say* 'new,' 헌 *hen* 'old,' 옛 *yeys* 'old,' 딴 *ttan* 'other,' …
   b. indicative: 이 *i* 'this,' 그 *ku* 'the,' 저 *ce* 'that,' …
   c. interrogative: 어느 *enu* 'which,' 무슨 *mwusn* 'what,' 어떤 *etten* 'which,' …
   d. quantificational: 모든 *motun* 'all,' 몇 *myech* 'some,' 여러 *yele* 'several,' …
   e. numeral: 한 *han* 'one,' 두 *twu* 'two,' 세 *sey* 'three,' …

Unlike these lexical determinants, as discussed in Chapter 3, there are also phrasal prenominal expressions such as adjectival (relative-clause) elements, verbal relative clauses, and genitive-marked possessive NPs:

(46) a. Adjectival predicate:

　　[아주 비싼]　　　(그) 책
　　acwu pissa-n　　　ku chayk
　　very expensive-MOD the book
　　'(the) very expensive book'

b. Relative clause:

　　[미아가 읽은]　　그 책
　　[Mia-ka ilk-un]　　ku chayk
　　Mia-NOM read-MOD the book
　　'the book that Mia read'

c. Genitive:

　　[미아의] 그 책
　　[Mia-uy] ku chayk
　　Mia-GEN the book
　　'Mia's book'

As seen in these examples, the adjectival expression *pissa-n* 'expensive-MOD' or *chakha-n* 'honest-MOD' is derived from the adjectival predicate *pissa-ta* 'expensive' *chakha-ta* 'honest.' Attaching the prenominal suffix -*(u)n* makes it modify a nominal expression (see Chapter 10 for the treatment of such an expression as a relative clause). The relative clause in (46b), projected from the verb marked with the prenominal modifying suffix -*(u)n*, can also function as an adnominal expression. The genitive NP in (46c) is marked with -*uy* and also functions as an adnominal expression. These are all adnominal phrasal expressions modifying a nominal expression which we mark as NP to make the Korean nominal structure parallel to the English NP structure.

To reflect such possibilities in forming NPs, the PS rule in (41) is revised as follows:

(47) NP → AdnominalP, N(P)
　　(adnominal: Det, XP[MOD], or NP[*poss*])

An NP (nominal phrase) in Korean can thus consist of an adnominal expression (marked AdnominalP as a cover term) followed by a nominal (which can be either a simple N or an NP). The adnominal expression, as discussed earlier, includes not only a determiner but also an adjectival or relative clause marked with the modifying suffix (MOD) or a possessive (*poss*) NP. This rule then allows the following structures:

(48) a.

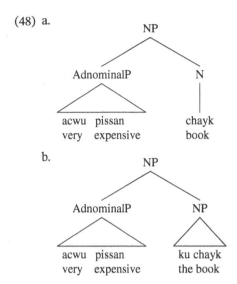

b.

The expression *pissa-n* 'expensive-MOD' is an adjectival or stative verb but serves as a prenominal modifier.[2] This adjectival expression can function as an adnominal expression to the simple noun *chayk* 'book' in (48a) and to the NP *ku chayk* 'the book' in (48b). (46b) and (46c) have structures like the following (MOD means modifier):[3]

(49) a.

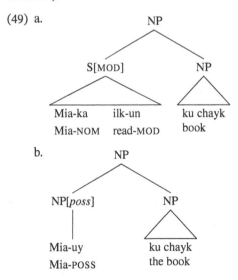

b.

---

2 As we will see, Korean does not have the category "adjective" because adjectives and verbs differ only in terms of meaning.
3 For the detailed structure of relative clauses in Korean, refer to Chapter 10.

As we also discussed in the previous chapter, the ordering of these phrasal prenominal elements is much more flexible than that of the lexical determinants. Consider these illustrative examples:

(50) a. 미아가   읽은   비싼   그 책
      Mia-ka   ilk-un   pissa-n   ku chayk
      Mia-NOM read-MOD expensive-MOD the book
      'the expensive book that Mia read'

   b. 그 비싼   미아가   읽은   책
      ku pissa-n   Mia-ka   ilk-un   chayk
      the expensive-MOD Mia-NOM read-MOD book
      'the expensive book that Mia read'

   c. 그 미아가   읽은   비싼   책
      ku Mia-ka   ilk-un   pissa-n   chayk
      the Mia-NOM read-MOD expensive-MOD book
      'the expensive book that Mia read'

As shown here, the relative clause *Mia-ka ilk-un* 'Mia-NOM read-MOD' can precede or follow the indicative determinant *ku* 'the.' Its position is also flexible relative to the adjectival modifier *pissa-n* 'expensive-MOD.' The structure of (50a) can be represented as follows:

(51)

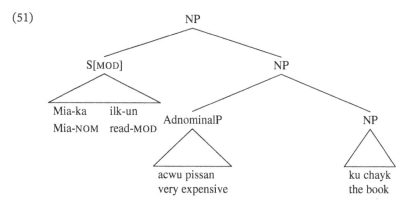

These ordering differences among adnominal expressions may accompany subtle differences in meaning, but they all are well-formed.

4.3.2 Verbal Phrases: Stative and Nonstative VPs

In Chapter 3, we saw that predicates in Korean can be classified as statives (adjective in English) and nonstatives (verb in English). We repeat the data here:

(52) a. Intransitive adjectives: 푸르다 phwulu-ta 'blue,' 아름답다 alumtap-ta 'beautiful,' 높다 noph-ta 'high,' …

b. Transitive adjectives: 무섭다 mwusep-ta 'afraid,' 좋다 coh-ta 'fond,' …

(53) a. Intransitive verbs: 가다 ka-ta 'go,' 자다 ca-ta 'sleep,' 놀다 nol-ta 'play,' …

b. Complex intransitive verbs: 되다 toy-ta 'become,' 처신하다 chesinha-ta 'behave,' 승진하다 sungcinha-ta 'promote,' …

c. Transitive verbs: 먹다 mek-ta 'eat,' 차다 cha-ta 'kick,' 빌리다 pilli-ta 'borrow,' …

d. Ditransitive verbs: 보내다 ponay-ta 'send,' 주다 cwu-ta 'give,' …

We have also seen that each of these predicates combines with different complement types, some of which are repeated here:

(54) a. 저 꽃이 [아름답다].
ce kkoch-i [alumtap-ta]
the flower-NOM pretty-DECL
'The flowers are pretty.'

b. 미미가 [사과를 먹었다].
Mimi-ka [sakwa-lul mek-ess-ta]
Mimi-NOM apple-ACC eat-PST-DECL
'Mimi ate an apple.'

c. 미미가 [사과를 동생에게 주었다].
Mimi-ka [sakwa-lul tongsayng-eykey cwu-ess-ta]
Mimi-NOM apple-ACC younger.brother-DAT give-PST-DECL
'Mimi gave an apple to her younger brother.'

The bracketed expressions here are all VPs that combine with the subject and form a complete sentence. These (stative and nonstative) VPs can be formed from the following PS rules:

(55) a. VP → V
b. VP → NP V
c. VP → NP NP V (where V means verbal and NP means nominal phrase)

One difference from English, as we can observe here, is that the verb in the VP rules is in the final position. These PS rules allow well-formed VPs in the language. For instance, (54b) has the following structure allowed by (55b):

(56)

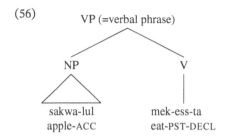

Note that the PS rules in (55) do not distinguish between stative and nonstative verbal predicates. Even though there are such differences between stative VPs and nonstative VPs, they are identical in many respects. That is, statives behave exactly like nonstatives in serving as a predicate, marking honorific, tense, and mood information:

(57) a. 저 꽃이   참   아름다웠다.
ce kkoch-i   cham alumtaw-ess-ta
the flower-NOM really pretty-PST-DECL
'The flowers were really pretty.'

b. 선생님이   참   아름다우시다.
sensayng-nim-i   cham alumtawu-si-ta
teacher-HON-NOM really pretty-HON-DECL
'The teacher is really pretty.'

c. 선생님이   참   아름다워지시었다.
sensayng-nim-i   cham alumtawe-ci-si-ess-ta
teacher-HON-NOM really pretty-become-HON-PST-DECL
'The teacher became really pretty.'

The two different types of predicates project VPs. However, they do so differently in several respects. First, as we saw in the previous chapter, they differ in the occurrence of the present tense suffix *(nu)-n*:

(58) a. 읽는다/달린다
ilk-nun-ta/talli-n-ta
read-PRES-DECL/run-PRES-DECL
'be reading'/'be running'
b. 푸르다/*푸른다   슬프다/*슬픈다
phwulu-ta/*phwulu-n-ta sulphu-ta/*sulphu-n-ta
blue-DECL/blue-PRES-DECL sad-DECL/sad-PRES-DECL
'be blue'/'be sad'

Only nonstative verbs project a VP with the present tense marking.

Second, as also noted in the previous chapter, stative adjectives are in general disallowed in propositives and imperatives:

(59) a. 책을 　읽자!
  chayk-ul ilk-ca!
  book-ACC read-PROPOS
  'Let's read books!'

  b. *슬프자!
  *sulphu-ca!
  sad-PROPOS
  'Let's be sad!'

Third, unlike nonstative verbs, statives cannot be progressive with -고 있다 -*ko iss-ta* 'in the process of':[4]

(60) a. 김이 　달리고 　있다.
  Kim-i talli-ko iss-ta
  Kim-NOM run-CONN exist-DECL
  'Kim is running.'

  b. *김이 　건강하고 　있다.
  *Kim-i kenkangha-ko iss-ta
  Kim-NOM healthy-CONN exist-DECL
  ' (lit.) Kim is being healthy.'

Fourth, only nonstative verbs can appear with 'intentive' and 'purposive' conjunctive suffixes such as -려고 -*lyeko* and -기 위하여 -*ki wihaye*:[5]

(61) a. 김이 　10킬로를 　달리려고 　노력하였다.
  Kim-i 10km-lul talli-lyeko nolyekha-yess-ta
  Kim-NOM 10.km-ACC run-in.order.to try-PST-DECL
  'Kim tried to run 10 km.'

  b. *김이 　기쁘려고 　노력하였다.
  *Kim-i kippu-lyeko nolyekha-yess-ta
  Kim-NOM happy-in.order.to try-PST-DECL
  'Kim tried to be happy.'

Imperative sentences also can differentiate statives and nonstatives. When a stative verb is used in an imperative form, it means exclamatory, not imperative:

(62) a. 사과를 　먹어라!
  sakwa-lul mek-ela!
  apple-ACC eat-IMP
  'Eat the apple!'

---

4 See Chapter 7 for more details of such constructions.
5 See Chapter 7 for further discussion of auxiliary verbs in Korean.

b. 추워 라!
chwu-wela!
cold-EXCL
'Oh, it's cold here!'

The verb *mek-* is nonstative, denoting an action, whereas *cwup-* 'cold' is a stative predicate.

Furthermore, the object of a nonstative verb takes accusative case, but that of an adjective or stative verb takes nominative case:

(63) a. 미아가   소설을/*이   읽었다.
　　　Mia-ka   sosel-ul/*i   ilk-ess-ta
　　　Mia-NOM novel-ACC/NOM read-PST-DECL
　　　'Mia read the novel.'

b. 미아가   모모가/*를   부럽다.
　　Mia-ka   Momo-ka/*lul pwulep-ta
　　Mia-NOM Momo-NOM/ACC envious-DECL
　　'Mia is envious of Momo.'

To reflect these similarities and differences, we can introduce the feature STA-TIVE: adjectives or stative verbs are positive, and nonstative verbs are negative. In examples like the previous ones, the subject combines with a VP whose verb bears the positive STATIVE feature, as illustrated in the following:

(64)

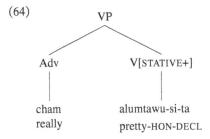

But the VP projected from a nonstative verb like *talli-ta* 'run-DECL' bears the negative STATIVE feature value.

4.3.3 Adverbial Phrases

We have seen that adverbials in Korean, just like adverbs in English, modify a verbal expression (verb or clause) or another adverbial phrase. They then project an AdvP as follows:

(65) a. [아주 많이]   먹었다.
     [acwu manhi] mek-ess-ta
     very   much   eat-PST-DECL
     '(Someone) really ate a lot.'

   b. [정말   빨리]   달리었다.
     [cengmal ppalli] talli-ess-ta
     really   fast   run-PST-DECL
     '(Someone) ran really fast.'

Because AdvPs can be projected from an adverb alone or by more than one adverb, we have the following PS rule:

(66) AdvP → (Adv) Adv

This PS rule allows the following structure:

(67)

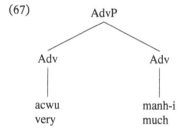

4.4 Complex Phrases: Expanding the Size of Phrases

We have seen that in both English and Korean, phrases can be more complex than a simple word. For instance, English NPs can be expanded by having either a prenominal or postnominal modifier:

(68) a. The [eager] student is usually successful.
   b. The student [who is eager to study] is usually successful.
   c. The student [with a cell phone] is not allowed in the classroom.

The prenominal expression is typically an adjective or an AP, whereas the post-nominal is a relative clause or a PP.

   VPs can also be expanded with a modifier:

(69) a. Mimi [speaks Korean [fluently]].
   b. Larry [ate breakfast [in a restaurant]].
   c. James [answered the question in English [because he had a foreign visitor]].

The VPs here are modified by an AdvP, a PP, or a subordinate clause. Even PPs can be made more complex in English with an adverb or a preposition:

(70) a. Tommy, [along [with the other students]], breathed a sigh of relief.
    b. The plane emerged [from [behind the cloud]].
    c. She threw the ball [right [into the hoop]].

Korean is no exception in this respect. As we have observed, nominal phrases (NPs) can become more complex with other expressions:

(71) a. 그녀가   [어려운   [그 일을]] 해냈다.
      kunye-ka elyewu-n   ku il-ul   haynay-ss-ta
      she-NOM   difficult-MOD the job-ACC complete-PST-DECL
      'She completed the difficult job.'
    b. 그녀가   [모두가   피하는   [그 일을]] 해냈다.
      kunye-ka motwu-ka   phiha-nun ku il-ul   haynay-ss-ta
      she-NOM   everyone-NOM avoid-MOD the job-ACC complete-PST-DECL
      'She has completed the task that everyone avoids.'

The stative predicate *elyewu-n* 'difficulty-MOD' or the relative clause (*motwu-ka phiha-nun* 'everyone-NOM avoid-MOD') modifies the nominal head, forming a larger NP. VPs can also be expanded with an adverbial expression:

(72) a. 미나가   [열심히   [독일어를   배웠다]].
      Mina-ka   yelsimhi tokile-lul   paywu-ess-ta
      Mina-NOM diligently German-ACC study-PST-DECL
      'Mina studied German diligently.'
    b. 미나가   [정말   열심히   [독일어를   배웠다]].
      Mina-ka   cengmal yelsimhi tokile-lul   paywu-ess-ta
      Mini-NOM really   diligently German-ACC study-PST-DECL
      'Mina studied German really diligently.'

Here the adverb *yelsimhi* 'diligently' or the AdvP *cengmal yelsimhi* 'really diligently' expands the VP's size.

4.5 Contrastive Notes

4.5.1 Noun Phrases vs. Nominal Phrases

We have seen that English has noun phrases, whereas Korean has more extended nominal phrases. A key reason for this difference is that Korean nominal phrases are flexible in terms of requiring determiners as well as ordering the prenominal expressions – their appearance and positions are quite flexible. In the English translation of the Korean example in (73), the noun *mailman* is preceded by the definite article *the*. This same noun could be preceded by the indefinite article *a*. This means English has distinct definite and indefinite articles.

(73) 미미가　　우편배달원을　　　만났다.
　　 Mimi-ka　 wupyenpaytalwon-ul manna-ss-ta
　　 Mimi-NOM mailman-ACC　　　meet-PST-DECL
　　 'Mimi met a/the mailman.'

However, Korean does not have articles indicating definiteness or indefiniteness. All the determiners are optional in nominal phrases. Although the definiteness of a nominal phrase (or NP) can be indicated by demonstratives like 그 *ku* 'the/that,' their presence is optional. Definiteness comes from the context:

(74) 미미가　　책을　　　읽었다
　　 Mimi-ka　 chayk-ul　 ilk-ess-ta
　　 Mimi-NOM book-ACC read-PST-DECL
　　 'Mimi read a book/the book/books.'

The object *chayk-ul* 'book-ACC' can be interpreted either as indefinite or definite, depending on the situation.

4.5.2 Verb Phrases and Verbal Phrases

Given the possible phrases in English and Korean, one question is whether Korean has an AP. We have seen that Korean does not have an adjective category to project an AP. This is because "predicative" adjectives in Korean behave like verbs in syntactic distribution. Compare the following simple examples:

(75) a. 하늘이　　정말　　　푸르다.
　　　 hanul-i　 [cengmal　 phwulu-ta]
　　　 sky-NOM really　　　 blue-DECL
　　　 'The sky is really blue.'
　　 b. 하늘이　　비를　　　내린다.
　　　 hanul-i　 [pi-lul　　 nayli-n-ta]
　　　 sky-NOM rain-ACC pour-PRES-DECL
　　　 '(lit.) The sky gives us rain.'

The expression *phwulu-ta* 'blue-DECL' in Korean corresponds to the English adjective *blue* but is used just like the verb *nayli-n-ta* 'pour-PRES-DECL.' The only differences between these two are the stative and nonstative semantic features: the former is STATIVE and the latter verb is non-STATIVE. The feature [STATIVE +/−] on the Korean verbal phrases can thus be linked to English APs and verb phrases, respectively.

4.5.3 Adnominal Phrases

Traditional Korean grammar has an adnominal category for expressions in the prenominal position. As discussed in Section 4.2, determiners and relative clauses can function as adnominal phrases. In English, a determiner phrase, genitive NP, or AP can also function as an adnominal phrase:

(76) a. [my] friend
    b. [the student's] responsibilities
    c. [really hard-working] students

The key difference concerns the ordering possibilities of these adnominal expressions. Unlike in English, the ordering of Korean adnominal phrases is relatively free:

(77) a. 나의　　그　　친구
      na-uy　ku　chinkwu
      I-GEN　the　friend
      'the friend of mine'
    b. 그　　나의　　친구
      ku　na-uy　chinkwu
      the　I-GEN　friend
      'the friend of mine'

As noted here, the determiner and the genitive phrase can occur consecutively in either order, which is impossible in English.

4.5.4 Prepositions and Case Marking

English has PPs projected from prepositions:

(78) a. Kim is [in the classroom].
    b. Kim is [with a friend].
    c. Kim came to the school [by car].

Some prepositions can even combine with a PP:

(79) a. She pulled [out of the race].
    b. [Up to that point], I had no experience with linguistics.

We have seen that the corresponding Korean postpositions are realized as nominal suffixes:

(80) a. 교실에서 kyosil-eyse 'classroom-at'
    b. 친구와 chinkwu-wa 'friend-with'
    c. 차로 cha-lo 'car-by'

These expressions are thus not PPs (prepositional phrases) but simply nominal phrases marked with a specific postposition or semantic case marking, as represented in the following:

(81)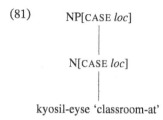

Similar projections can be seen with common nouns like *haksayng* 'student,' pronouns like *na* 'I' and *ne* 'you,' and proper nouns like *Mimi* and *Momo*. These are all nouns, but they can be projected into NPs without combining with a determiner.

4.6 Conclusion

This chapter has discussed the phrasal types in English and Korean, projected from lexical heads. In English, the main phrasal types include NPs, VPs, APs, AdvPs, PPs, etc. Each phrasal type is formed by PS (phrase structure) rules. In Korean, major phrasal types are NPs (nominal phrases), VPs (verbal phrases), AdvPs (adverbial phrases), and adnominal phrases.

The phrasal types in both languages share certain properties in their syntactic formation, but their internal features and properties are slightly different. These differences set the two languages apart.

Exercises

1   Use the words in each of the following examples to build all the possible NPs in English:
   (i) a. tall, handsome, man, that
       b. best, my, at, friend, Seoul
       c. we, the, problem, major, encounter
       d. the, a, students, in, classroom

2   From the words in each of the following examples, build all the possible nominal phrases in Korean:

(i) a. 그 ku 'the,' 부지런한 pwucilenhan 'diligent,' 학생 haksayng
'student,' 어제 만난 ecey manna-n 'yesterday meet-MOD'

b. 미미가 읽은 Mimi-ka ilk-un 'Mimi-NOM read-MOD' 그 ku 'the,'
재미있는 caymiissnun 'interesting,' 책 chayk 'book'

c. 착한 chakhan 'honest,' 모든 motun 'all,' 친구 chinkwu 'friend,'
미미의 Mimi-uy 'Mimi-GEN'

3 Draw tree structures for the following, and give PS rules for the VP in each
sentence:

(i) a. Jane covered the baby with a blanket.
  b. The window broke.
  c. John touched the cat.
  d. Bill pounded the metal flat.
  e. Kim tried to be honest.
  f. Kim placed the books in the box.
  g. John talked to Mary about the problem.
  h. The photo reminded Kim of his father.

4 Identify the stative property ([STATIVE +] or [STATIVE −]) of the Korean predicates
in (i) with a sentential example that can support your answer. For each Korean
sentence, give the glosses and English translation, as in (ii):

(i) 앉다 anc-ta 'sit,' 타다 tha-ta 'burn,' 슬프다 sulphu-ta 'sad,' 달리다 talli-ta
'run,' 발견하다 palkyenha-ta 'discover,' 무섭다 mwusep-ta 'fear,' 알다
al-ta 'know,' 깨닫다 kkaytat-ta 'recognize'

(ii) 미미가   빨리   달린다.
Mimi-ka   ppalli   talli-n-ta
Mimi-NOM   fast   run-PRES-DECL
'Mimi ran fast.'

5 Draw tree structures for the following, give the VP PS rule for each case, and
mark the value of the STATIVE for each VP.

(i) a. 미미가   노래한다.
Mimi-ka   nolayha-n-ta
Mimi-NOM   sing-PRES-DECL
'Mimi sings.'

b. 미미가   정상에   도착하였다.
Mimi-ka   cengsang-ey tochakha-yess-ta
Mimi-NOM   submit-at   arrive-PST-DECL
'Mimi arrived at the summit.'

c. 미미는 돌이가 무섭다.
Mimi-nun Toli-ka mwusep-ta
Mimi-TOP Toli-NOM afraid-DECL
'Mimi is afraid of Tori.'

d. 미미가 아름다운 집을 지었다.
Mimi-ka alumta-wun cip-ul ci-ess-ta
Mimi-NOM pretty-MOD house-ACC build-PST-DECL
'Mimi built a pretty house.'

e. 미미는 정답을 알았다.
Mimi-nun cengtap-ul al-ass-ta
Mimi-TOP answer-ACC know-PST-DECL
'Mimi knew the answer.'

6 English has a particle category, as shown in the following examples:

(i) a. Mary turned down the offer.
 b. Mary turned the offer down.
(ii) a. Mary turned off the light.
 b. Mary turned the light off.

Give a tree structure for each sentence, and then identify the PS rule that generates each VP. In addition, give tree structures and VP-forming PS rules for the following two sentences.

(iii) a. Mary looked up the word.
 b. Mary looked up the newspaper.

7 Draw tree structures for the following English and corresponding Korean sentences and discuss how the two languages differ with respect to the complementizer and conjunction categories.

(i) a. Kim thought that Mimi left early.
 b. Kim ran one mile, although the weather was bad.
(ii) a. 모모는 미미가 일찍 떠났다고 생각하였다
 Momo-nun Mimi-ka ilccik ttena-ss-ta-ko sayngkakha-yess-ta
 Momo-TOP Mimi-NOM early leave-PST-DECL-COMP think-PST-DECL
 'Momo thought Mimi left early.'

 b. 날씨가 나빴지만 김은 열심히 달렸다
 nalssi-ka nappu-ass-ciman Kim-un yelsimhi talli-ess-ta
 weather-NOM bad-PST-although Kim-TOP hard run-PST-DECL
 'Although the weather was bad, Kim ran hard.'

5

Grammar Rules: Constructing Sentences

5.1 Form and Function

In analyzing sentences, we can refer to at least two dimensions: form and function. For example, each English sentence can be analyzed using syntactic categories like NPs and VPs, or it can be analyzed using grammatical functions like subject and object:

(1) a. Syntactic categories: N, A, V, P, NP, VP, AP, PP …
    b. Grammatical functions: SUBJ (subject), OBJ (object), MOD (modifier), PRED (predicate), …

Notions like *NP*, *VP*, and *AP* are "form" (categorial) values of each phrase, whereas concepts such as *subject*, *object*, *predicate*, and *modifier* represent the grammatical "function" that each phrasal constituent plays in a given sentence. For example, consider the following simple sentence:

(2) The monkey scratched a boy on Monday.

This sentence can be structurally represented in terms of either syntactic categories or grammatical functions:

(3) a. $[_S [_{NP}$ The monkey$] [_{VP}$ scratched $[_{NP}$ a boy$] [_{PP}$ on Monday$]]]$.
    b. $[_S [_{SUBJ}$ The monkey$] [_{PRED}$ scratched $[_{OBJ}$ a boy$] [_{MOD}$ on Monday$]]]$.

As shown here, *the monkey* is an NP in terms of its syntactic form but is the subject (SUBJ) of the sentence in terms of its grammatical function. The NP *a boy* is the OBJ (object), and the verb *scratched* functions as a predicator. The entire VP can be considered a PRED (predicate), which describes a property of the subject. *On Monday* is a PP in terms of its syntactic category but serves as a modifier (MOD) to the VP. This chapter discusses how these two notions, form and function, interact with each other in the organization of a sentence.

English and Korean in Contrast: A Linguistic Introduction, First Edition. Jong-Bok Kim.

5.2 Grammatical Functions

To make sentences, first we need to form phrases from words or other phrases. In building up any phrase, there is one obligatory element, the *head*:

(4) a. NP b. VP c. AP

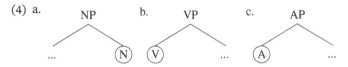

The circled element is essential within the given phrase. This essential head is the pivot of any phrase: the head of an NP is an N, the head of a VP is a V, and the head of an AP is an A. The head of each phrase thus determines its "projection" into a larger phrasal constituent.

The notion of *headedness* is important in grammar because the head dictates what it must combine with. For example, consider the following:

(5) a. We all looked at the building.
   b. *We all looked the building.

(6) a. The defendant denied the accusation.
   b. *The defendant denied at the accusation.

(7) a. The teacher placed the books on the table.
   b. *The teacher placed the books.

In each of these sentences, the head of its VP is the main verb. The verb *looked* is an intransitive verb combining with a PP, but not with an object NP. The verb *denied* here requires an NP object, whereas *placed* requires an object and a locative PP. All these combinatorial properties come from the head verb: the verb itself determines what kind of element(s) it combines with.

In a similar manner, the head of an AP is an adjective:

(8) a. Phil is fearful of spiders and sinkholes.
   b. *Phil is fearful spiders and sinkholes.

(9) a. This printer is compatible with most PCs.
   b. *This printer is compatible for most PCs.

The adjective *fearful*, as the head of an AP, requires a PP[*of*] as its complement, whereas *compatible* needs to combine with a PP[*with*].

We can observe the same phenomenon in Korean:

(10) a. 학생들이   미아를 반장으로   뽑았다.
      haksayng-tul-i Mia-lul pancang-ulo   ppop-ass-ta
      student-PL-NOM Mia-ACC class.president-as select-PST-DECL
      'The students selected Mia as the class president.'
   b. *학생들이   미아를 반장을   뽑았다.
      haksayng-tul-i Mia-lul pancang-ul   ppop-ass-ta
      student-PL-NOM Mia-ACC class.president-ACC select-PST-DECL
   c. *학생들이   미아를 반장에게   뽑았다.
      haksayng-tul-i Mia-lul pancang-ekey ppop-ass-ta
      student-PL-NOM Mia-ACC class.president-DAT select-PST-DECL

The verb 뽑다 *ppop-ta* 'select' takes three arguments, but the third argument must represent a "status" with the case marking -으로 *-ulo*. Again, the head determines what it needs to combine with.

Note that this *subcategorization* requirement for what a verb needs to combine with differs between languages. For instance, the verb *po-ta* 'look-DECL' in Korean can combine with an object NP, unlike the corresponding English verb:

(11) 우리는   큰   빌딩을/*에   보았다.
     wuli-nun khu-n pilting-ul/ey   po-ass-ta
     we-TOP   big-MOD building-ACC/at see-PST-DECL
     'We saw a big building.'

This example tells us that the verb cannot combine with a nominal expression with the locative marker *-ey*. Instead, it must combine with the accusative NP object.

The (phrasal) expressions that a head (e.g. verb, adjective, noun, or preposition) should combine with are called *complements*. The complements include direct objects, indirect objects, predicative complements, and oblique complements, all of which may be required by a lexical head. Consider the following examples:

(12) a. The book emphasizes [the danger of climate change]. (direct object)
   b. He taught [me] how to drive. (indirect object)
   c. Pat will always remain [a good friend]. (predicative complement)
   d. The school has to rely [on the goodwill of the parents]. (oblique complement)

The bracketed phrases here are required by the verbs *emphasizes, taught, remain*, and *rely* and thus function as complements of these verbs.

Each verbal predicate (stative or nonstative) in Korean also has a complement requirement:

(13) a. 미미가   [사장이]   되었다. (predicative complement)
      Mimi-ka   sacang-i   toy-ess-ta
      Mimi-NOM chairman-NOM become-PST-DECL
      'Mimi became CEO.'
   b. 미미가   [사과를] 먹었다. (direct object)
      Mimi-ka   sakwa-lul mek-ess-ta
      Mimi-NOM apple-ACC eat-PST-DECL
      'Mimi ate an apple.'
   c. 미미가   사과를   [동생에게]   주었다. (indirect object)
      Mimi-ka   sakwa-lul tongsayng-eykey   cwu-ess-ta
      Mimi-NOM apple-ACC younger.brother-DAT give-PST-DECL
      'Mimi gave an apple to her younger brother.'

The bracketed phrases function as complements of the verbs. The only difference from English is that the complements in Korean can be unexpressed if the context provides their information.

In addition to the complements of a head, a phrase may also contain *modifiers* (also called adjuncts or adverbials):

(14) a. Momo [$_{VP}$ [$_{VP}$ offered advice to his students] *in his office*].
   b. Momo [$_{VP}$ [$_{VP}$ offered advice to his students] *with love*].

The PPs *in his office* and *with love* here provide further information about the action described by the verb but are not required by the main verb. These phrases are optional and function as modifiers, and they serve to augment the minimal phrase projected from the head verb *offered*.

Again, Korean is no different from English in this respect. The VP can also have an optional modifier:

(15) a. 학생들이   어제   미아를 반장으로   뽑았다.
      haksayng-tul-i ecey   Mia-lul pancang-ulo   ppop-ass-ta
      student-PL-NOM yesterday Mia-ACC class.president-as select-PST-DECL
      'Yesterday, the students selected Mia as the class president.'
   b. 미아가   교실에서   노래를   불렀다.
      Mia-ka   kyosil-eyse   nolay-lul pwule-ss-ta
      Mia-NOM classroom-LOC song-ACC sing-PST-DECL
      'Mia sang a song in the classroom.'

In these examples, the expressions 어제 *ecey* 'yesterday' and 교실에서 *kyosil-eyse* 'classroom-LOC' are modifiers: they are not used by the main verb *ppop-ass-ta* 'select-PST-DECL' or *pwule-ss-ta* 'sing-PST-DECL,' respectively.

What we have seen so far can be summarized as follows:

(16) a. *Head*: A lexical or phrasal element essential in determining a larger phrase's category and internal structure.

　　b. *Complement*: A phrasal element that a head must combine with – that is, it is selected by the head. Complements include direct objects, indirect objects, predicative complements, and oblique complements.

　　c. *Modifier*: A lexical or phrasal expression not selected by a head that functions as an adjunct to the head phrase.

In addition to these, there are two more grammatical functions: subject and specifier. The grammatical concept of a subject is clear:

(17) a. [Elvis] [sang softly].

　　b. [The furious dog] [chased me].

　　c. [They] [made the problem more difficult].

These examples have two subparts, subject and predicate, as indicated by the square brackets. The subject of an active sentence is typically a doer who performs the action described by the verb or causes the action. The subject of a sentence agrees with the main verb:

(18) a. With his friends, he never sings/*sing.

　　b. The events of the last month *saddens/sadden me.

　　c. The student with flowers takes/*take her mother out to lunch.

In (18a), the subject is not the plural NP *his friends*, but the singular pronoun *he*, and the main verb agrees with respect to the number value. The same is true in Korean: the subject agrees with the main verb with respect to the honorific:

(19) 학생들과　　　　함께　　　선생님이　　　오신다.
　　 haksang-tul-kwa hamkkey sensayng-nim-i o-si-n-ta
　　 student-PL-with together teach-HON-NOM come-HON-PRES-DECL
　　 'The teacher is coming with the students.'

The subject in Korean is typically marked with the marker -*i/ka* and can further agree with the main verb in terms of the honorific marking. In (19), the subject is *sensayng-nim-i* 'teacher-HON-NOM,' and it agrees with the main verb with the suffix marking *si*.

Now for the grammatical notion of a specifier, consider the following examples:

(20) a. *a* little dog, *the* little dogs (indefinite or definite article)

　　b. *this* little dog, *those* little dogs (demonstrative)

　　c. *my* little dogs, *their* little dog (possessive adjective)

　　d. *every* little dog, *each* little dog, *some* little dog, *either* dog, *no* dog (quantifier)

　　e. *my friend's* little dog, *the Queen of England's* little dog (possessive phrase)

The italicized expressions here are neither subjects nor complements. Most are determiners; some consist of several words, as in (20e) (*my friend's, the Queen of England's*). In terms of semantics, these expressions "specify" the properties of the following nominal expressions and thus are called specifiers. Following this tradition, this book adopts the concept of a specifier referring to a determiner or a determiner phrase like *my friend's* in English.

5.3 Mapping between Grammatical Function and Form

In most cases, subjects and objects are NPs. But note that not only NPs but also other categories (e.g. CPs, VPs) can function as subjects or objects:

(21) a. [$_{NP}$ The termites] destroyed the sand castle.
   b. [$_{VP}$ Being honest] is not an easy task.
   c. [$_{CP}$ That John passed away] surprised her.
   d. [$_S$ What John said] is questionable.
   e. [$_{VP}$ To finish this work] is beyond his ability.

(22) a. I sent [$_{NP}$ a surprise present] to John.
   b. They wondered [$_S$ what she did yesterday].
   c. They believed [$_{CP}$ that everybody would pass the test].
   d. They tried [$_{VP}$ to block the passage].

Similarly, adverbs/AdvPs and PPs are typical modifiers, but NPs, Ss, VPs, and PPs can also function as modifiers:

(23) a. John left [$_{AdvP}$ very early].
   b. John has been at Stanford [$_{PP}$ for four years].
   c. John studied hard [$_{VP}$ to pass the exam].
   d. She disappeared [$_{Conj-S}$ when the main party arrived].
   e. I ate too much at supper [$_{NP}$ last night].

Korean is no exception in this respect. The object is typically an accusative-marked NP as in (24a), but it can also be a sentence, as in (24b):

(24) a. 미미가   친구를   믿었다.
   Mimi-ka   chinkwu-lul mit-ess-ta
   Mimi-NOM friend-ACC   believe-PST-DECL
   'Mimi believed the friend.'
   b. 미미가   [친구가   착하다고]   믿었다.
   Mimi-ka   chinkwu-ka chakha-ta-ko   mit-ess-ta
   Mimi-NOM friend-NOM   honest-DECL-COMP believe-PST-DECL
   'Mimi believed that the friend was honest.'

A modifier is typically an adverb, but a sentential expression can also serve as a modifier:

(25) a. 미미가   [빨리] 달렸다.
　　　Mimi-ka   ppalli talli-ess-ta
　　　Mimi-NOM fast   run-PST-DECL
　　　'Mimi ran fast.'

　　b. 미미가   [아무도 모르게] 달렸다.
　　　Mimi-ka   amwuto molukey talli-ess-ta
　　　Mimi-NOM anybody not.know run-PST-DECL
　　　'Mimi run without anybody recognizing her.'

In (25), the adverb *ppalli* 'fast' is a modifier, but in (25b), the full sentential clause functions as a modifier.

The English and Korean data here indicate that there is no one-to-one correspondence between categories (form) and grammatical function. For instance, an NP can be a subject, an object, a predicate, or a modifier. Subjects can be marked by a variety of categories like NPs, VPs, and even CPs. There can thus be one-to-many or many-to-one mapping relations between (grammatical) form and function.

5.4 English Grammar Rules

5.4.1 Forming English Sentences

We have seen that PS rules allow us to form well-formed phrases in English. For instance, as we saw in the previous chapter, the following are some VP PS rules in English:

(26) a. VP → V
　　b. VP → V AP
　　c. VP → V NP
　　d. VP → V NP PP
　　e. VP → V NP NP
　　f. VP → V NP CP

Such VP rules allow VPs like the following in English:

(27) a. Lee ran.
　　b. Lee remained calm.
　　c. Lee rejected the help.
　　d. Lee reminded Kim of Christmas parties.
　　e. Lee refused him permission to enter the room.
　　f. Lee warned him that there would be a demonstration.

Note that the VP rules that generate each example here depend on the subcategorization properties of the verb. That is, the verb *ran* in (27a) has no complement, whereas the verb *remain* (27b) has an AP complement, as represented with the feature COMPS (complements) in the following:

(28) a. run: [COMPS < >]
     b. remain: [COMPS <AP>]

Note that the verb run has no complement as in (28a), and the matching PS rule (VP → V) reflects this. The verb *remain* selects an AP ast its complement, and the PS rule (VP → V AP) applicable to the verb also repeat this information redundantly. We can thus observe that the COMPS value indicates what kind of PS rules we need to apply. This redundance is clearly observed as follows:

(29) a. rejected: [COMPS < NP >] (matching PS rule: VP → V NP)
     b. reminded: [COMPS < NP, PP >] (matching PS rule: VP → V NP PP)
     c. refused: [COMPS < NP, NP >] (matching PS rule: VP → V NP NP)
     d. warned: [COMPS < NP, CP >] (matching PS rule: VP → V NP CP)

The COMPS value of each verb is the same as the sister values of the corresponding PS rule in (26). There are thus redundancies between the COMPS information of each verb and the PS rule the verb is linked to.

    The optimal way to remove such redundancies is to collapse all the PS rules into the so-called X-bar (or X′) grammar rules. For instance, all the VP PS rules can be schematized as the following Head-Complement Rule:

(30) Head-Complement Rule:
     XP → Head, Complement(s)

This rule, in which the variable X represents any head lexical expression such as an A or a P, also covers other PS rules like the following:

(31) a. AP → A PP
     b. PP → P NP

The simple grammar rule in (30) thus allows us to replace all the PS rules headed by a lexical element, those in (26) as well as those in (28).

    As we saw earlier, each phrase can be more complex when modified. This complexity can be captured by the following grammar rule:

(32) Head-Modifier Rule:
     XP → Head, Modifier

This rule replaces modifier PS rules like these:

(33) a. VP → VP PP
     b. VP → VP Adv(P)
     c. VP → VP VP

Note that we allow the modifier to be a lexical category like A or Adj or a phrase like AdvP and PP.

These grammar rules, traditionally called X-bar rules, can be represented in a tree structure:

(34)

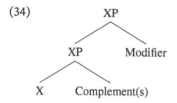

As given here, the head X combines with its complement(s), resulting in an XP. This phrase can then combine with another modifier. The following example illustrates these two rules:

(35)

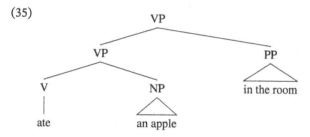

The Head-Complement Rule allows phrases consisting of a lexical head with any number of complements. In (35), the head verb *ate* combines with the complement NP *an apple*. There can be more than one complement:

(36)

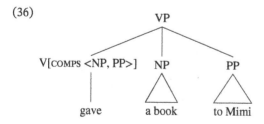

The lexical head *gave* combines with two complements (NP and PP), making a well-formed head-complement phrase.

The Head-Modifier Rule is for the combination of a modifier and its head. The lexical or phrasal modifier can be in either the beginning or end position.

(37) a.

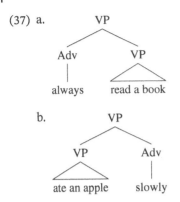

b.

These structures tell us that the adverbs *always* and *slowly* modify the VP, allowing a well-formed head-modifier phrase.

We need another grammar rule for the following PS rule:

(38) S → NP VP

This PS rule can be captured by the following X-bar or grammar rule:

(39) Head-Subject Rule:
    XP → Subject, Head

The Head-Subject Rule ensures that the subject combines with the head VP, generating structures like the following:

(40)

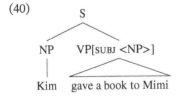

The final rule we need to introduce allows the combination of a noun head with a specifier (determiner or determiner phrase), as in the following:

(41)

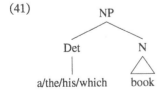

The combination of these two expressions is allowed by the following rule:[1]

(42) Head-Specifier Rule:
XP → Specifier, Head

This rule could be applied to other phrases, but it is used only for NP structures to assign a special status to determiners.

5.4.2 Simple English Sentences

Let us consider how the (X-bar) grammar rules we have discussed so far allow simple English sentences. In doing so, note what kind of COMPS value each verb has and how it is satisfied or becomes empty (is discharged) after the verb combines with its COMPS value.

Intransitive verbs: This type of verb does not have a complement:

(43) a. Kim disappeared.
b. *Kim disappeared Bill.

(44) a. Kim sneezed.
b. *Kim sneezed the money.

These verbs have no complement. Such intransitive verbs are projected into VPs with no complement and then combined with the subject, forming a sentence:

(45)

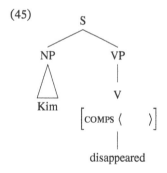

This is a type of head-complement construction with no complements.
Linking verbs: Verbs such as *look*, *seem*, *remain*, and *feel* require a complement, which is typically from the AP category:

(46) a. The president looked [weary].
b. The teacher became [tired of the students].
c. The lasagna tasted [scrumptious].

---

1 As in the literature, if the subject is a type of specifier, the Head-Specifier Rule can also include the Head-Subject Rule.

    d. Kim remained [somewhat calm].
    e. The jury seemed [ready to leave].

These verbs also can use phrases like NPs as complements:

(47) a. Kim became a success.
    b. Kim seemed a fool.
    c. Kim remained a student.

This kind of linking verb has two arguments: subject and complement. The subject is typically an NP, and the complement functions as a predicative expression ([PRD +]):

(48)

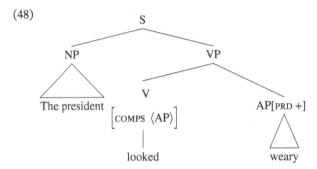

Transitive verbs: Unlike linking verbs, pure transitive verbs use a referential, non-predicative NP as their complement, functioning as direct objects:

(49) a. Kim saw Fred.
    b. Alice typed the letter.
    c. Clinton supported the health care bill.
    d. Raccoons destroyed the garden.

The transitive verb projects a structure as in (50), where the verb combines with its referential NP object as its complement:

(50)

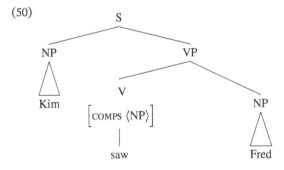

Ditransitive verbs: Similar to such monotransitive verbs as *destroy*, English also has what are called ditransitive verbs. These verbs take an IO (indirect object) followed by a DO (direct object):

(51) a. The school board leader asked the students a question.
 b. The parents bought the children nonfiction novels.
 c. Kim taught new students English syntax.

Such verbs have three arguments: the subject and two complement NPs, which function as indirect and direct objects, respectively. The resulting structure with such verbs as *give, bring, tell, show*, and *offer* is typically called a "double object" construction. The ditransitive verb may project a structure like the following, where the verb combines with two object complements:

(52)

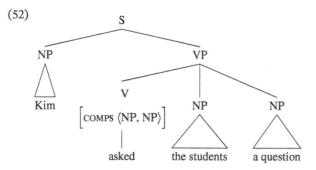

Complex transitive verbs: There is another type of transitive verb that has two complements, one functioning as a direct object and the other as a predicative phrase (NP, AP, PP, or VP) describing a property of the object:

(53) a. Kim regards Bill as a good friend.
 b. The sexual revolution makes some people uncomfortable.
 c. Ad agencies call young people Generation X-ers.
 d. Historians believe FDR to be our most effective president.

In (53a), the predicative PP *as a good friend* follows the object *Bill*; in (53b), the AP *uncomfortable* serves as a predicate phrase of the preceding object *some people*. In (53c), the NP *Generation X-ers* is the predicative phrase. In (53d), the predicative phrase is an infinitive VP. Like linking verbs, these verbs require a predicative ([PRD +]) XP as one of their complements.

(54)

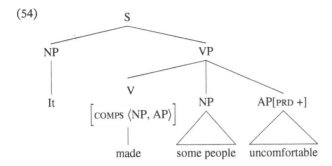

The structure shows that the verb *made* combines with an object NP and an XP that functions as a predicate, in accordance with the Head-Complement Rule.

The five types of verbs we have seen so far represent typical examples, but there are verbs that do not fit into any of these classes:

(55) a. *Kim carried to the door.
     b. Kim carried her on his back.

(56) a. Kim reminded her of the last time they met.
     b. They warned me that the item was expensive.

The complement (COMPS) value of these values is as follows:

(57) a. carry: [COMPS <NP, PP[*to*]>]
     b. remind: [COMPS <NP, PP[*of*]>]
     c. warn: [COMPS <NP, NP, CP>]

As seen from their COMPS value, these verbs do not belong to the five typical verb types but allow the sentences in (56). Sentence (56b) would have a structure like the following:

(58)

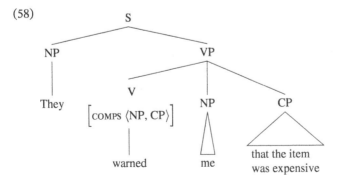

5.5 Korean Grammar Rules

5.5.1 Forming Korean Sentences

Just as in English, all the PS rules required for Korean can be replaced by the following three (X-bar) grammar

(59) a. Head-Subject Rule
   XP → Subject, Head
  b. Head-Modifier Rule
   XP → Modifier, Head
  c. Head-Complement Rule
   XP → Complement, Head

The only difference is that the head is in the final position in a head-final language (SOV), and there is only one complement in the Head-Complement Rule. Let us consider how these grammar rules allow basic Korean sentences.

First, consider the Head-Subject Rule, which is the same as in English. The rule allows the combination of a subject and its predicate VP. For instance, consider the following simple sentence with its structure:

(60) a. 미아가   달리었다
   Mia-ka   talli-ess-ta
   Mia-NOM   run-PST-DECL
   'Mia ran.'

  b.

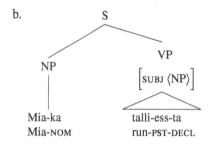

As illustrated in the structure, the verb 달리었다 *talli-ess-ta*, without requiring an object, forms a VP and then combines with the subject 미아가 *Mia-ka*. The result is a well-formed head-subject phrase that is a sentence.

The Head-Complement Rule is for the combination of a head and its complement. For instance, as in (61), the transitive verb *mek-ess-ta* combines with its NP complement functioning as the direct object:

(61)

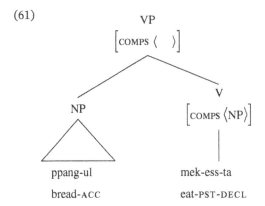

Once the verb combines with its COMPS value, its COMPS value is satisfied or discharged (combined with the head). The mother VP then requires no further COMPS value, as indicated by its empty value.

Note that when a verb has more than one argument, the structure is different than in English. Compare the English and Korean Head-Complement Rules:

(62) a. Head-Complement Rule (English)
      XP → *Complement(s)*, Head
  b. Head-Complement Rule (Korean)
      XP → *Complement*, Head

The difference lies in the number of complement(s). In English, there can be one or more complements, whereas in Korean, there is only one complement. Thus we have the following "binary" structure for Korean (its English counterpart has a "ternary" structure):

(63)

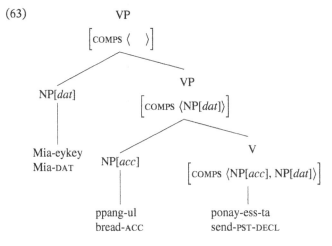

The structure tells us that the head verb 보내었다 *ponay-ess-ta* combines with the NP object 빵을 *ppang-ul*, forming a VP. This resulting VP will then combine with its remaining complement NP 미아에게 *Mia-eykey*. Note that the ordering of the two complements can be changed, too:

(64)

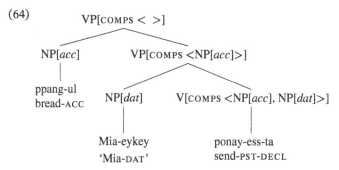

In this case, the verb combines with its dative-marked NP complement first, and the resulting VP combines with the object NP. Note that the verb's COMPS value is empty after combining with all these complements. The generalization we see here is that the phrasal complement in Korean can be discharged at any projection level:

(65) Complement Discharge Rule:
   Korean discharges a phrasal complement or the subject at any projection level, whereas English discharges all the complements before the subject.

This parametric difference between English and Korean explains why Korean word order is rather free, whereas in English it is fixed. Thus all the following possibilities are allowed as long as the verb is in the final position:

(66) a. 미아가   준에게   책을   보냈다.
      Mia-ka   Joon-eykey chayk-ul ponay-ess-ta
      Mia-NOM Joon-DAT   book-ACC send-PST-DECL
      'Mia sent Joon the book.'

   b. 미아가 책을   준에게   보냈다.
      Mia-ka chayk-ul Joon-eykey ponay-ess-ta

   c. 준에게   미아가 책을   보냈다.
      Joon-eykey Mia-ka chayk-ul ponay-ess-ta

   d. 책을   미아가 준에게   보냈다.
      chayk-ul Mia-ka Joon-eykey ponay-ess-ta

   e. 준에게   책을   미아가 보냈다.
      Joon-eykey chayk-ul Mia-ka ponay-ess-ta

All these sentences have the same meaning, but the subject and complements are scrambled. Note that, as in these examples, the subject need not be in the initial position. It can appear any place, yielding a structure like the following:

(67)

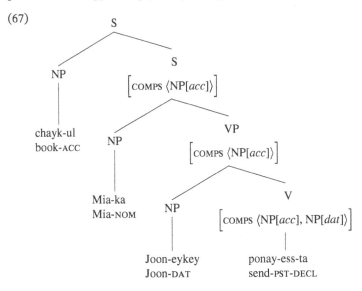

In this structure, the verb first combines with the dative NP complement *Joon-eykey*, and the resulting phrase combines with the subject NP *Mia-ka* 'Mia-NOM.' This resulting VP then combines with the object NP[*acc*] *chayk-ul* 'book-ACC.' The object is thus discharged after the subject is saturated. This is possible because the complement and the subject can be discharged at any level.

In addition to these two grammar rules, we have further freedom if we add the Head-Modifier Rule. The Head-Modifier Rule allows a modifier expression like an adverbial element to combine with its head:

(68)

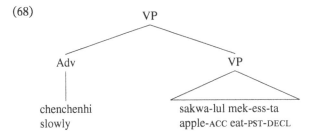

The modifier can be either a lexical expression or a phrasal expression.

5.5.2 Simple Korean Sentences

Just as in English, the complement (COMPS) requirement for each verb in Korean decides the VP structure. Consider the different verb types in the following:

(69) a. 비가　　왔다.
　　　pi-ka　　o-ass-ta
　　　rain-NOM　come-PST-DECL
　　　'It rained.'

　b. 준이　　사장이　　　되었다.
　　　Joon-i　　sacang-i　　　toy-ess-ta
　　　Joon-NOM　president-NOM　become-PST-DECL
　　　'Joon became the president.'

　c. 도둑이　　잡혔다.
　　　totwuk-i　cap-hi-ess-ta
　　　thief-NOM　catch-PASS-PST-DECL
　　　'The thief was caught.'

　d. 준이　　감기에　　걸렸다.
　　　Joon-i　　kamki-ey　kel-li-ess-ta
　　　Joon-NOM　cold-at　　catch-PASS-PST-DECL
　　　'Joon caught a cold.'

　e. 준이　　그　책을　　읽었다.
　　　Joon-i　ku　chayk-ul　ilk-ess-ta
　　　Joon-NOM　the　book-ACC　read-PST-DECL
　　　'Joon read the book.'

　f. 준이　　선생님에게　　　칭찬을　　받았다.
　　　Joon-i　　sensayng-nim-eykey　chingchan-ul　pat-ass-ta
　　　Joon-NOM　teacher-HON-DAT　　praise-ACC　　receive-PST-DECL
　　　'Joon won praise from the teacher.'

　g. 준이　　그　책을　　미미에게　　주었다.
　　　Joon-i　ku　chayk-ul　Mimi-eykey　cwu-ess-ta
　　　Joon-NOM　the　book-ACC　Mimi-DAT　　give-PST-DECL
　　　'Joon gave the book to Mimi.'

All these verbs require different complements, and the combinations are allowed by the Head-Complement Rule, as illustrated by the following structure:

(70)

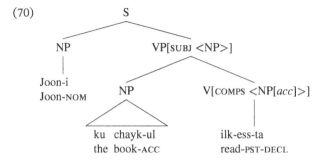

The verb combines with its object complement, and then the resulting VP combines with its subject. Each combination is allowed by the Head-Complement and Head-Subject Rules, respectively.

Note that we could apply these two rules in a different order:

(71)

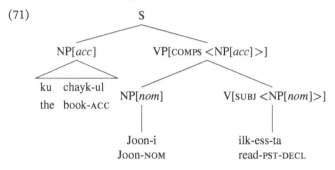

This example differs from (70) in that the verb combines with its subject and then the resulting phrase combines with the object. In the present system, a complete sentence implies that all the subject (SUBJ) and complement (COMP) values are discharged. Allowing the head verb to combine with the subject at any phrasal level makes the grammar flexible regarding word order. This is also a key difference between English and Korean.

5.5.3 Grammar Rule for Auxiliary Constructions

Before discussing auxiliary constructions in English and Korean in Chapter 7, let us see one simple difference between English and Korean auxiliary verbs.

(72) a. Mimi would eat apples.
  b. 미미는   사과를   먹고   싶었다.
     Mimi-nun sakwa-lul mek-ko siph-ess-ta
     Mimi-TOP   apple-ACC eat-CONN wish-PST-DECL
     'Mimi wanted to eat apples.'

(73) a. Mimi would quickly eat apples.

b. *미미는   사과를   먹고   빨리 싶었다.
   Mimi-nun sakwa-lul mek-ko ppali siph-ess-ta
   Mimi-TOP apple-ACC eat-CONN fast wish-PST-DECL
   'Mimi wanted to eat apples fast.'

As seen from the contrast here, an adverb can intervene between an auxiliary verb and a main verb in English. However, this is not possible in Korean. The English facts require no additional mechanism, as seen from the following bracketed structures:

(74) Mimi [$_{VP}$ would [$_{VP}$ quickly [$_{VP}$ eat apples]]].

As Chapter 7 discusses in detail, the Korean auxiliary verb forms a tight syntactic unit with the preceding verb, as given in the following structure. To allow such syntactic cohesion or such a syntactic combination, we can introduce one more grammar rule for Korean:

(75) Head-LEX Rule:
   V → [LEX +], Head[AUX +]

This rule allows an auxiliary verb to combine with a main verb, yielding another verb complex (see Chapter 7 for further details). This grammar rule then allow a structure like the following for (73a):

(76)

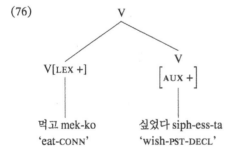

The resulting verb complex combines with the object 사과를 *sakwa-lul* 'apple-ACC' to form a VP:

(77)

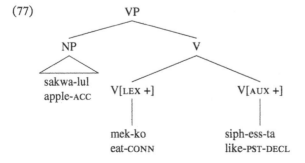

5.6   Contrastive Notes

5.6.1   SVO vs. SOV

One of the most frequently cited features of Korean syntax is its word order. Korean is an SOV language, meaning the basic word order of transitive sentences is subject-object-verb.

(78) a. Kim ate the apple.
 b. 김이   사과를   먹었다
   Kim-i   sawka-lul mek-ess-ta
   Kim-NOM apple-ACC eat-PST-DECL
   'Kim ate the apple.'

The structures of these two sentences clearly represent this difference:

(79) a.

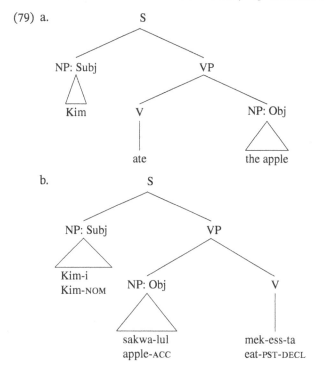

b.

5.6.2   Head-Initial vs. Head-Final

Reflected in the SOV vs. SVO types is headedness. Korean is a head-final language, whereas English is a head-initial language, as represented in the following:

(80) a. English: Head initial

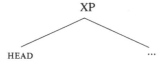

b. Korean: Head final

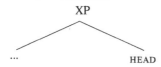

This parameter implies the verb-object order in English and the object-verb order in Korean:

(81) a. [$_{VP}$ [$_V$ ate] [$_{NP}$ the apple]]

    b. [$_{VP}$ [$_{NP}$ 사과를]   [$_V$ 먹었다]]
      [$_{VP}$ [$_{NP}$ sakwa-lul] [$_V$ mek-ess-ta]]
      apple-ACC   eat-PST-DECL
      'ate the apple'

5.6.3 Fixed vs. Free Word Order

As we have noted, English follows stringent word order restrictions:

(82) a. Mimi ate an apple in the morning.
    b. *Mimi ate in the morning an apple.

However, in Korean, word ordering is flexible. The only strong constraint for word order is that each sentence ends with a tensed verb. Otherwise, permutations of the major constituents in a sentence are flexible, as noted earlier and illustrated by the following:

(83) a. 김이   메리에게   책을   주었다.
      Kim-i   Mary-eykey chayk-ul cwu-ess-ta
      Kim-NOM Mary-DAT   book-ACC give-PST-DECL
      'Kim gave a book to Mary.'
    b. Kim-i chayk-ul Mary-eykey cwu-ess-ta
    c. Mary-eykey Kim-i chayk-ul cwu-ess-ta
    d. chayk-ul Mary-eykey Kim-i cwu-ess-ta
    e. chayk-ul Kim-i Mary-eykey cwu-ess-ta
    f. Mary-ekey chayk-ul Kim-i cwu-ess-ta

5.6.4 Pro-Drop Languages

There are two types of languages in terms of the possibility of omitting pronouns. Consider the following dialogue:

(84) A: This cake is quite delicious.
  B: Who baked *it*?
  A: I don't know. Do you want to eat *it* more?

The italicized expressions are pronouns, and they cannot be omitted. However, in languages like Korean, these pronouns can be omitted because they can be inferred from the context:

(85) A: 이 케이크 맛있네.
  i kheikhu masiss-ney
  this cake delicious-DECL
  'This cake is quite delicious.'
  B: 누가 구웠지?
  nwu-ka kwu-wess-ci
  who-NOM bake-PST-QUE
  'Who baked *it*?'
  A: 모르겠어. 더 먹을래?
  molukeyss-e te mek-ul-lay?
  not.know-DECL more eat-FUT-QUE
  '*I* don't know. Do you want *it* more?'

As illustrated here, the pronouns are omitted but can be inferred from the context. Languages with such a property are often called *pro-drop* languages. Korean is thus a pro-drop language, but English is not.

An important condition of omitting a pronoun is its recoverability from the context. Deletion of the first-person and second-person pronominal subjects in Korean is especially free:

(86) a. (제가) 그 책을 사겠습니다.
  (cey-ka) ku chayk-ul sa-keyss-supnita
  (I-NOM) the book-ACC buy-FUT-FRML.DECL
  'I will buy the book.'
  b. (당신은) 언제 떠나세요?
  (tangsin-un) encey ttena-seyyo?
  (You-TOP) when leave-QUE?
  'When do you leave?'

In the first sentence, the first-person subject is not expressed, and in the second, the second-person subject is unexpressed, because these subjects are recoverable in a discourse context.

5.6.5 Complement Omission

In English, the complements required by a verb must be satisfied either internally or externally:

(87) a. *He [placed his hand].
　　b. *He [placed under the comforter].
　　c. *He [placed his hand warm].
　　d. He [placed his hand under the comforter].

(88) a. This is the comforter under which he [placed his hand].
　　b. This is his hand that he [placed under the comforter].
　　c. *This is the comforter that he placed his hand under it.

The verb *placed* requires two complements: NP and PP. These complements need to be satisfied within the internal VP, as in (87), or externally, as in (88).

Note that, unlike in English, all the complements are optional in Korean as long as they are cued by the given context:

(89) (미미가)　(사과를)　먹었다.
　　(Mimi-ka)　(sakwa-lul)　mek-ess-ta
　　Mimi-NOM　apple-ACC　eat-PST-DECL
　　'Mimi ate an apple.'

When the context provides information about the person who ate an apple, we can remove the subject. The object can also be dropped when we can conjecture what Mimi ate. In Korean, both the subject and the object thus need not be realized: both are understood from the context. However, this is impossible in English: sentences like *Ate an apple* are not allowed. In this sense, we often say Korean is a discourse-oriented language.

5.7　Conclusion

We have seen that to form phrases in English and Korean, we could employ PS (phrase structure) rules, but the application of PS rules is tightly connected to the complement(s) (COMPS) value of each lexical head (V, A, P). Given these lexical properties, all the PS rules can be merged into three simple grammar rules: the Head-Complement Rule, Head-Subject Rule, and Head-Modifier Rule. Both languages adopt these key rules. The differences have to do with how to discharge the required COMPS value of each lexical category. English requires discharging all the COMPS values simultaneously, whereas Korean allows them to be discharged one by one. In addition, Korean can discharge the SUBJ value at any stage, implying that the subject can be combined with a head at any level. This leads to the key difference in word order: English is a fixed-word-order language, and whereas Korean is a free-word-order language.

Exercises

1   Draw trees for the following sentences, and identify which grammar rule (e.g. Head-Subject, Head-Complement, Head-Modifier) allows each phrase.

    (i) a. Kim is in the park.
       b. Kim is fond of apples.
       c. Kim gives Sandy a book.
       d. That Kim sleeps surprises Sandy.
       e. Sandy believes that Kim sleeps.
       f. Kim told Sandy that Pat slept.
       g. Kim tries to sleep.
       h. Kim made Lee clean the room.
       i. Kim persuaded Sandy to leave.

2   Draw tree structures for the following sentences, and state what kind of complement type each verb combines with. In doing so, remember that the discharge of complement(s) differs from English.

    (i) a. 미미가　달린다.
        Mimi-ka　talli-n-ta
        Mimi-NOM run-PRES-DECL
        'Mimi is running.'
      b. 미아가　감기에　걸리었다.
        Mia-ka　kamki-ey kel-li-ess-ta
        Mia-NOM cold-at　catch-PASS-PST-DECL
        'Mia caught a cold.'
      c. 그 그림이　마음에　들어요.
        ku kulim-i　maum-ey tul-eyo
        the painting-NOM heart-at　enter-DECL
        'I like the painting.'
      d. 사람들이　미미가　착하다고　생각하였다.
        salam-tul-i　Mimi-ka chakhata-ko sayngkakha-yess-ta
        people-PL-NOM Mimi-NOM kind-CONN　think-PST-DECL
        'People thought that Mimi was kind.'

e. 김은　　메리를　　떠나도록　　　　설득하였다.
   Kim-un Mary-lul ttena-tolok   seltukha-yess-ta
   Kim-TOP Mary-ACC leave-in.order.to persuade-PST-DECL
   'Kim persuaded Mary to leave.'

(ii) a. 미미는　　여전히　젊다.
    Mimi-nun yecenhi celm-ta
    Mimi-TOP still   young-DECL
    'Mimi is still young.'

   b. 그에게　　책이　　　많다.
    ku-eykey chayk-i   manh-ta
    he-DAT   book-NOM many-DECL
    'He has many books.'

   c. 미미는　　개가　　무섭다.
    Mimi-nun kay-ka   mwusep-ta
    Mimi-TOP dog-NOM afraid-DECL
    'Mimi is afraid of dogs.'

   d. 미미는　　십분을　　　　걸었다.
    Mimi-nun sippwun-ul   kel-ess-ta
    Mimi-TOP ten.minutes-ACC walk-PST-DECL
    'Mimi walked for 10 minutes.'

3 Transliterate each sentence using Yale Romanization, and then draw a tree structure for each sentence.

   (i) a. 미미가 몸이 아프다.
       '(lit.) Mimi has her body sick.'
    b. 미미가 영어를 공부하기가 어렵다.
       'It is hard for Mimi to study English.'
    c. 미미가 메리가 건강하다고 생각한다.
       'Mimi thinks that Mary is healthy.'
    d. 미미가 재빨리 맥주를 상자에 숨겼다.
       'Mimi quickly hid the beer in the box.'
    e. 미미가 메리에게 영어가 어렵다고 말했다.
       'Mimi told Mary that English is difficult.'

4 We have seen that, unlike English, Korean is a scrambling language in which each constituent except the final verb can be freely moved around. Give all the possible word orders in the following sentence, and draw a tree structure for each.

(i) a. 메리가　　학교에　　정말　　일찍　갔다.
　　　Mimi-ka　hakkyo-ey　cengmal　ilccik　ka-ss-ta
　　　Mimi-NOM　school-to　really　　early　go-PST-DECL
　　　'Mimi really went to school.'

　b. 선생님이　　　　공부를　　　　열심히
　　　sensayng-nim-i　kongpwu-lul　yelsimhi
　　　teacher-HON-NOM　study-ACC　　diligently

　　하는　　학생을　　　사랑한다.
　　ha-nun　haksayng-ul　salangha-n-ta
　　do-MOD　student-ACC　love-PRES-DECL
　　'The teacher loves the students who study diligently.'

5　Discuss the possible readings of the following English and Korean sentences, and then offer a syntactic structure for each reading.

　(i) a. John saw a man with a telescope.
　　　b. I saw that gas could explode.
　(ii) a. 미미가　　만난　　친구의　　　아들이　서울로　갔다.
　　　　Mimi-ka　manna-n　chinkwu-uy　atul-i　Seoul-lo　ka-ss-ta
　　　　Mimi-NOM　meet-MOD　friend-GEN　son-NOM　Seoul-to　go-PST-DECL
　　　b. 미미는　　웃으면서　　　노래하는　　친구를　　　보았다.
　　　　Mimi-nun　wus-umyense　nolayha-nun　chinkwu-lul　po-ass-ta
　　　　Mimi-TOP　smile-whereas　sing-MOD　　friend-ACC　see-PST-DECL

6　Many sentences have matching nominalizations, as seen from the following English and Korean examples. Draw tree structures for these, and discuss any similarities between the sentences and nominalizations. In doing this, refer to the grammatical notion of specifiers discussed in the chapter.

　(i) a. The enemy destroyed the city.
　　　b. the enemy's destruction of the city
　(ii) a. 적들이 도시를 파괴하였다.
　　　b. 적들의 도시 파괴

7　Draw trees for the following English and Korean genitive phrases. In addition, identify what kind of grammar rules are involved in forming the phrases.

　(i) a. my friend's sister's desk
　　　b. 내 친구의 동생의 책상

6

Tense and Aspect: Describing When and How a Situation Happens

6.1 Ways to Describe an Event

Describing a situation or event involves at least three dimensions: tense, aspect, and mood (TAM). These three concepts are grammatical categories realized in the verbal structure, either morphologically or syntactically. Semantically, they all have something to do with time. Tense tells us when a situation occurs, and aspect tells us how it occurs or how the speaker views it in terms of its continuity (ongoing) or completeness. Mood refers to the attitude about the situation expressed by a given sentence. It tells us whether the stiuation is actually happening, possibly happening, or being commanded to happen.

We can interpret tense as referring to a temporal point when an event takes place or a state holds, as represented on a linear timeline:

(1) Three points of tense:

As represented here, three reference points for tense indicate when a situation happens or holds. Each language has a different way of describing these three temporal points. For instance, to describe an event that happened earlier, English typically uses the suffix -ed, and Korean uses the suffix -ess/ass:

(2) a. It rained yesterday.
     b. 어제   비가   왔다.
       ecey   pi-ka   o-ass-ta
       yesterday rain-NOM come-PST-DECL
       'It rained yesterday.'

English and Korean in Contrast: A Linguistic Introduction, First Edition. Jong-Bok Kim.
© 2024 John Wiley & Sons, Inc. Published 2024 by John Wiley & Sons, Inc.

Aspect, unlike tense, refers to how an event is happening from the speaker's point of view. It describes the internal temporal constituency of a situation. That is, aspect describes whether a situation is ongoing or completed. An ongoing situation can have three different points, represented with circles on the linear timeline:

(3) Three types of ongoing processes:

| PAST | PRESENT | FUTURE |
| PROGRESSIVE | PROGRESSIVE | PROGRESSIVE |

Again, languages adopt different grammatical apparatus to describe these three types of ongoing situations. In English, the most typical way is to use the *be* + V-*ing* construction:

(4) a. Mimi was singing the song at 9:00 am yesterday.
   b. Mimi is singing the song now.
   c. Mimi will be singing the song at 9:00 tomorrow.

In a similar manner, Korean uses V-고 있다 'V-*ko iss-ta*' to express an ongoing situation:

(5) 미미가   노래를   부르고   있다.
   Mimi-ka   nolay-lul   pwulu-ko   iss-ta
   Mimi-NOM   song-ACC   sing-CONN   exist-DECL
   'Mimi is singing a song.'

As in this example, the present progressive event is expressed with the main verb marked with the verb form *-ko* and the following auxiliary verb *iss-* 'exist.'

In addition to these ongoing processes, a situation can start from a certain point but be completed at a temporal point in the past, present, or future. This "perfect" aspect also has three different classes, each represented by an arrow and an endpoint bar:

(6) Three types of completion processes:

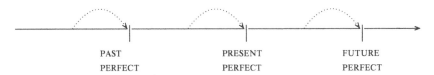

| PAST | PRESENT | FUTURE |
| PERFECT | PERFECT | PERFECT |

In English, these cases are often described using the construction *have* + V[*en*]:

(7) a. Mimi had finished the homework at 11:00 pm last night.
b. Mimi has finished the homework just now.
c. Mimi will have finished the homework by 10:00 am tomorrow morning.

A peculiar property of Korean is that it has no overt marker to express the aspectual situation of completion. For instance, as in (8), the perfect is simply expressed by the past tense suffix *-ess*:

(8) 미미가 11 시에 숙제를 마쳤다.
mimi-ka yelhan si-ey swukcey-lul machi-ess-ta
Mimi-NOM 11 hour-at homework-ACC finish-PST-DECL
'Mimi (had) finished the homework at 11.'

As shown in the English translation, the past suffix *-ess* can be interpreted as referring either to the past tense or to the past perfect.

Note that the ongoing and completion aspects can be combined to describe a situation that started earlier but is still ongoing:

(9) Three types of completion-ongoing processes:

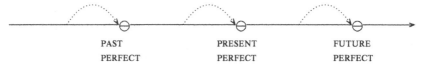

| | PAST | PRESENT | FUTURE |
| PERFECT | PERFECT | PERFECT |

To describe such a situation, English uses the combination of an ongoing (be + V-ing) and a perfect construction (have + V[*en*]):

(10) a. Past perfect progressive: Mimi had been running for an hour.
b. Present perfect progressive: Mimi has been running for an hour.
c. Future perfect progressive: Mimi will have been running for an hour.

Korean can also express such situations, as follows:

(11) 미미가 한 시간 동안 달리고 있다.
Mimi-ka han sikan tongan talli-ko iss-ta
Mimi-NOM one hour for run-CONN exist-PST-DECL
'Mimi has been running for an hour.'

The example includes a construction for the progressive (V-*ko iss-ta*) but has no expression to indicate a perfect situation. The context allows such an interpretation.

In sum, there are 12 different ways to refer to the absolute location of an event or action in time (tense) and how an event or action is to be viewed with respect to time (aspect). Each language employs its own way of describing these reference points and views, which will be discussed in more detail in this chapter.

6.2 How to Describe an Event in English

6.2.1 Tense and Verb Inflection Form

As noted, tense represents when the event in question takes place and refers to the absolute location of an event or action in time: present, past, or future. In English, tense is typically marked by the verbal inflection marker *-ed* or *-es*:

(12) a. Kim kicked the ball. (Past)
 b. Kim kicks the ball. (Present)

However, it has no suffix marker for future tense. The futurity of an event can be expressed through the use of an auxiliary verb like *will* or *shall*:

(13) a. Kim will kick the ball.
 b. Kim shall kick the ball.

Let us consider verb forms in English in more detail. Intuitively, English verbs have six grammatical forms. For example, the verb *drive* can take the following forms:

(14) DRIVE: drives, drove, drive, driving, driven, to drive

The present- and past-tense forms are usually classified together as finite (*fin*), and the rest are nonfinite (*nonfin*) in some way. Using this division, we might lay out the verb forms as in (15):

(15) Types of English verb forms:

Finiteness	Verb forms	Example
fin	*pres*	He *drives* a car.
	pst	He *drove* a car.
	pln	They *drive* a car.
nonfin	*bse*	He wants to *drive* a car.
	ing	*Driving* a car, he sang a song.
		He was *driving*.
		He is proud of *driving* a car.
	en	*Driven* by hunger, he kept hunting.
		The car was *driven* by him.
		He has *driven* the car.
	inf	He has *to drive*.

The finite (*fin*) forms have three subtypes: (*pres*), past (*past*), and plain (*pln*). The first two forms are typically marked with *-es* and *-ed*, but the third has no morphological marking, as in *They call me Kim*. The plain form, although identical to the citation form, is used for present tense when the subject is anything other than third-person singular.

Notice that there may be discrepancies between form and function: the *past* verb canonically describes a past event, as in (16a), and the present (*pres*) and plain (*pln*) verbs represent a present event, as in (16b). However, this is not always true. For example, the *pres* in (16c) describes a future event:

(16) a. Kim called me yesterday.
     b. Kim smiles a lot because of his two sons.
     c. Kim leaves town tomorrow.

The nonfinite (*nonfin*) forms include base (*bse*), present participle (*ing*), past participle (*en*), and infinitive (*inf*). In terms of the morphological form, the plain and base forms are identical to the lexical base (or citation) or the lexeme form. The lexeme is the basic, representative lexical unit. For instance, *drive, drives, driving, drove, drive* are forms of the same lexeme: DRIVE. In this sense, we can consider a lexicon as consisting of lexemes as headwords. Even though the two forms are identical in most cases, substitution tests by the past form or by the verb *be* show a clear difference:

(17) a. They write/wrote to her.
     b. They are/*be kind to her.

(18) a. They want to write/*wrote to her.
     b. They want to be/*are kind to her.

The verbs in (17) are plain forms; those in (18) are base forms with no tense information.

The infinitive form is only for the auxiliary verb *to*. This infinitival marker takes as its complement a verb or VP in the *bse* form. Certain verbs like *try* and *hope* require an infinitival VP as a complement:

(19) a. They tried to write to her/*writing to her.
     b. They hoped to write to her/*writing to her.

With these classifications, we can have the following hierarchy for the values of the attribute vform (verb inflection form):

(20)

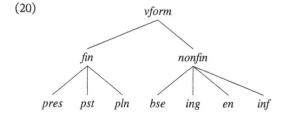

Remember that the two nonfinite values *ing* and *en* have their own subvalues based on the different uses given in (15):

(21) Usages of the present participle (*ing*) form:
    a. He is <u>writing</u> another long book about beavers.
       (part of the progressive aspect construction)
    b. <u>Feeling hungry</u>, I opened the fridge and found a sandwich.
       (used as a present participle to mark it as a sentence modifier)
    c. He is proud of his son's <u>passing</u> the bar exam.
       (used in a gerundive construction)

(22) Usages of the past participle (*en*) form:
    a. The chicken has <u>eaten</u>.
       (part of the perfect aspect construction)
    b. The chicken was <u>eaten</u>.
       (part of the passive voice construction)
    c. <u>Seen</u> from this perspective, there is no easy solution.
       (used as a past participle to mark a sentence modifier function)

Each of these examples has a unique constructional usage with a different function. To reflect this fact, we can assign a VFORM value to each use, as given in the following:

(23) Usages of *ing* and *en* forms:

VFORM	Subvalue	Example
ing	prp	*Singing* a song, he played.
	prog	He was *singing*.
	ger	He is proud of *singing* the song.
en	psp	*Sung* by the singer, it became popular.
	pass	The song was *sung* by the singer.
	perf	The singer has *sung* the song.

The need to distinguish between *fin* and *nonfin* is easily determined. Every declarative sentence in English must have a finite verb with tense information:

(24) a. The student [learns the differences].
    b. The student [learned the differences].
    c. The students [learn the differences].

(25) a. *The student [learning the answers].
    b. *The student [to learn the answers].

The examples in (25) are unacceptable because *learning* and *to learn* have no expression of tense – i.e. they are not finite. This in turn shows us that only finite verb forms can be used as the head of the highest VP in a declarative sentence, satisfying a basic requirement placed on English declarative sentences:

(26) Declarative Sentence Rule:
For a declarative sentence to be well-formed, its verb form value (VFORM) must be finite.

This simple rule explains the contrast in the following:

(27) a.

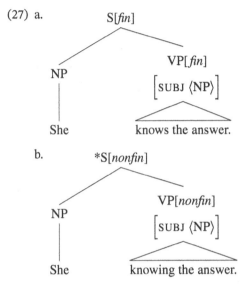

b.

This contrast means every sentence must have a finite verb to be a well-formed declarative sentence.

6.2.2 Aspects: Ongoing and Completion

Unlike tense, aspect describes an action's completion, duration, or repetition. The two primary aspects of English are perfect (completion) and progressive (ongoing). The two auxiliary verbs employed for the aspectual information are *be* and *have*:

(28) a. David has fallen in love.
   b. David is falling in love.

In (28a), the action took place in the past, but it is implied that it took place recently and that the situation is still relevant up to the present. This represents a "completed (perfect)" event. Meanwhile, in (28b), the action of falling in love is still "ongoing (progressive)." The following illustrates the uses of aspect describing a completed or ongoing situation:

(29) a. Progressive: was writing, is writing, will be writing
  b. Perfect: had written, have written, will have written
  c. Perfect progressive: had been writing, has been writing, will have been writing

Tense and aspect are thus different in terms of meaning. Tense refers to the time point when an event occurs (past, present, future), and aspect describes how an action is viewed in relation to the discourse, representing either a completed or an ongoing event. Tense is thus more concerned with an event's absolute time (one point), whereas aspect is concerned with duration. Tense is typically marked by a verbal suffix, and aspect is marked by an auxiliary verb.

The progressive aspect usually describes an event that occurs during a limited time period. This aspectual information is expressed with the construction *be* + VP[*ing*]:

(30) a. We are studying now.
  b. She was building a garage.
  c. He will be taking a test at 8:00 am tomorrow.

The progressive aspect can combine only with a dynamic or nonstative verb. It cannot combine with a stative verb:

(31) a. *She is believing in God.
  b. *She is knowing algebra.
  c. *I am owning a sailboat.

When a stative verb is used in the progressive form, it describes an ongoing action:

(32) a. I am craving spaghetti.
  b. He is having an asthma attack.
  c. He is being obnoxious.

The perfect aspect focuses on the completion of an event, marked with the auxiliary *have* and the perfect form (*-en*) of the verb. It expresses that the action in question had, has, or will have been completed by a specific point in time. This point of time could be defined by a time expression (e.g. *by 5 o'clock*) or a clause (*by the time you get home, when I arrived*). The following are examples of the perfect aspect:

(33) a. I've lived here for 10 years. (from 10 years ago until now)
  b. By 5 o'clock, he had finished the letter. (at some time before 5 o'clock)
  c. When I arrived, they had already left. (at some time before I arrived)

    d. I will have done the ironing by the time you get home. (between now and when you get home)

Note that we can combine a perfect with a continuous aspect, expressing that the action at issue had, has, or will have been in progress for some time at a specific time. The following are some illustrative examples:

(34) a. I've been waiting for this moment all my life. (from when I was born until now)
    b. By 1995, Pat had been living in Scotland for 20 years. (from 1975 to 1995)
    c. When Mary gets home, Kevin will have been sleeping for hours. (Kevin's sleep lasting from some point of time before Mary gets home until she gets home)

6.2.3 Situation Types

We have seen that tense locates a situation in time (past, present, future), whereas aspect gives us information about the temporal structure of a situation, as again observed from examples like the following:

(35) a. He was drowning (but somebody saved him). [tense: past, aspect: progressive]
    b. He drowned (*but somebody saved him). [tense: past, aspect: non-progressive]

We can describe the internal properties of each situation. These properties are inherent in the lexical meaning of the verb or the meaning of a VP. Consider the following:

(36) a. I hit the sofa. [instantaneous]
    b. I beat the sofa. [lasts longer because of several hits]

The verb *hit* describes an instantaneous situation, whereas *beat* indicates a situation that lasts longer and happens repeatedly. All these are internal properties of the verb involved.

    There are two criteria for determining situation types: telicity and durativity. A situation is *telic* when it has a natural completion or endpoint. If it does not, it is *atelic*. Consider the following:

(37) a. The plane flew to London. [telic: the event stops when the plane reaches London]
    b. The plane flew. [atelic: no goal mentioned, so no obvious endpoint]
    c. She ate a bag of chips. [telic: eating stops when the bag is empty]
    d. She ate (chips/plates of chips). [atelic: there is no specific amount of chips, the consumption of which would mean the end of the eating event]

Telicity differentiates the uses of the durative *for* or *in* PPs:

(38) a. He painted a picture in/*for three hours.
 b. He painted for/*in three hours.

(39) a. He ran to the bus stop in/*for three minutes.
 b. He ran for/*in three minutes.

Atelic situations can occur with *for*-PPs, whereas telic situations can be measured by *in*-PPs.
 Another criterion depends on whether a situation is *durative* or *punctual*.

(40) a. Punctual: explode, flash, hit the wall, win the game, reach the summit, discover the answer
 b. Durative: paint (a picture), swim, work, read a book

As observed from these examples, a situation is durative if it lasts for a period of time. It is punctual if it is instantaneous.
 With these two criteria, situations are classified into four different types:

(41) a. States: static (unchanging) throughout the duration (e.g. *know the answer, own/have a car, it stinks*)
 b. Activity: durative and atelic (e.g. *eat ice cream, play the piano, push a cart*)
 c. Achievements: punctual and telic (e.g. *spot a tiger, hit the wall, win the game, reach the goal*)
 d. Accomplishments: durative and telic activity with an achievement at the end (e.g. *hammer the metal flat, paint a picture, recover from a sickness*)

The classification is summarized in the following table 6.1:
 As we saw earlier, each situation type is sensitive to certain phenomena. For example, states are not compatible with the progressive aspect:

(42) a. *He is stinking.
 b. *He is knowing the answer.

Table 6.1 Semantic features of eventuality types.

	Stativity	Durative	Telic	Examples
State	+	−	n/a	own, resemble, have, love, …
Activities	−	+	−	run, walk, write letters, …
Accomplishment	−	+	+	run a mile, write a letter, …
Achievement	−	−	+	recognize, reach, win, start, …

Unlike activities or accomplishments, states also cannot be the complement of verbs like *force* and *persuade*.

(43) a. *I forced him to know the answer.
    b. I forced him to work.

States cannot occur with adverbs like *deliberately, carefully*, either:

(44) a. *I knew the answer carefully.
    b. I worked carefully.

6.2.4 Sentence Types and Mood

Another key grammatical aspect of a situation is mood, which expresses the attitude of a situation. Grammatical mood, also known as sentence mode or type, tells us the quality or tone of the sentence in question, to make the writer's or speaker's intention clear. When considering mood in grammar, there are five basic types: indicative, interrogative, imperative, subjunctive, and conditional. Each language has its own way of expressing these mood types.

In English, mood is tightly linked with sentence type. English distinguishes a set of clause types that are characteristically used to perform different kinds of mood or speech acts:

(45) a. Declarative: John is clever.
    b. Interrogative: Is John clever? Who is clever?
    c. Exclamative: How clever you are!
    d. Imperative: Be very clever.

Each clause type has its own functions to represent a mood. For example, typically, a declarative makes a statement, an interrogative asks a question, an exclamative represents an exclamatory statement, and an imperative issues a directive (see the following table 6.2):

Table 6.2 Sentence types and functions.

Sentence types	Functions
Declarative	Makes a statement or tells something
Interrogative	Asks a question
Exclamatory	Shows surprise about a fact
Imperative	Commands something

However, these correspondences are not always one-to-one. For example, the declarative in (46a) represents not a statement but a question, whereas the interrogative sentence (46b) indicates a directive:

(46) a. I ask you if this is what you want.
  b. Would you mind taking out the garbage?

The vast majority of sentences are declarative, expressing an indicative mood that makes a statement. The subjunctive mood is another type, but it can be represented by different sentence types:

(47) Subjunctive mood:
  a. If I were there, I would. (declarative)
  b. I demand he be removed! (exclamatory)
  c. What if he were there? (interrogative)

All these sentence types express conditions that are doubtful or not factual. That is, such a sentence indicates a hypothetical state – a state contrary to reality, such as a wish, a desire, or an imaginary situation. In this sense, these sentences are considered subjunctive.

6.3 How to Describe an Event in Korean

6.3.1 Tense in Korean

In Korean, tense is also marked by verbal suffixes. Three tense forms are distinguished based on verb inflections:

(48) a. Present: -은/는 -(n)un, Ø
  b. Past: -었/았 -(e)ss, -ass, -yss
  c. Future: -젰 -keyss

Like English, Korean has a verbal suffix to represent present or past tense information. Unlike English, Korean can use a verbal suffix like *keyss* to describe a future reference point. The following are some examples:

(49) a. 미미가   노래를   부른다.
        Mimi-ka   nolay-lul pwulu-n-ta
        Mimi-NOM song-ACC sing-PRES-DECL
        'Mimi sings a song.'
  b. 미미가   노래를   불렀다.
        Mimi-ka   nolay-lul pwulu-ess-ta
        Mimi-NOM song-ACC sing-PST-DECL
        'Mimi sang a song.'

c. 미미가 　 노래를 　 부르겠다.
Mimi-ka 　 nolay-lul 　 pwulu-keyss-ta
Mimi-NOM 　 song-ACC 　 sing-FUT-DECL
'Mimi will sing a song.'

The future marking -겠 -*keyss* is similar in meaning to the English auxiliary verb *will* and can represent a volitional or conjectural meaning. For instance, (49c) can describe not a future situation but just a possible situation that could happen in the near future.

Sentences projected from a main verb inflected with such a verbal suffix are finite, marking tense information. This projection could be represented in a tree structure:

(50)

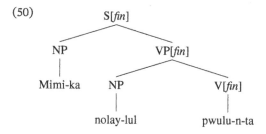

The head verb is finite, and this tense information is projected to the mother VP and then to the sentence.

Note that the present tense is formed with -은/는 *(n)un* or zero (Ø) for verbs and zero for stative verbs (adjectives):

(51) a. 하늘이 푸르다.
hanul-i 　 phwulu-Ø-ta
sky-NOM 　 blue-PRES-DECL
'The sky is blue.'

b. 미미가 　 착하다.
Mimi-ka 　 chakha-Ø-ta
Mimi-NOM 　 nice-PRES-DECL
'Mimi is nice.'

The past tense is formed by the suffix -*ess* (variants are *ss*, -*ass*).

(52) a. 사람들이 　 유성을 　 보았다.
salam-tul-i 　 yuseng-ul 　 po-ass-ta
people-PL-NOM 　 shooting.star-ACC 　 see-PST-DECL
'People saw shooting stars.'

b. 사람들이   착각을   했다.
   salam-tul-i   chakkak-ul   ha-yess-ta
   people-PL-NOM   illusion-ACC   do-PST-DECL
   'People had an illusion.'

The past tense indicates a definite and completed event or state that took place in the past and can also describe a past event or state that still has some bearing on the present time. As in the present tense, temporal (punctual, durative, or repetitive) modifiers help to clarify the meaning of the past tense together with the stative or dynamic property of the verb.

(53) a. 나는   그 때   열 살이었다.
        na-nun ku ttay yel sal-i-ess-ta
        I-TOP   the time 10 years.old-COP-PST-DECL
        'I was 10 years old then.'

     b. 그 꽃은   아름다웠다.
        ku kkoch-un alumtap-ess-ta
        the flower-TOP pretty-PST-DECL
        'The flowers were pretty.'

     c. 아침마다   수영을   했다.
        achim-mata   swuyeng-ul   ha-yess-ta
        morning-every swimming-ACC do-PST-DECL
        '(I) did swimming every morning.'

     d. 종이   십 분마다   울렸다.
        cong-i   sip pwun-mata   wulli-ess-ta
        bell-NOM 10 minute.every ring-PST-DECL
        'The bell rang every 10 minutes."

     e. 미미가   왔어.
        Mimi-ka   o-ass-e
        Mimi-NOM   come-PST-DECL
        'Mimi came."

In these examples, the verb includes the past suffix -*ess*. (53a) and (53b) represent the past state, and (53c) and (53d) describe the habitual past. Note that (53e) implies that Mimi is still here.

In addition to the suffix -*keyss*, the future tense can be expressed by a lexical-type construction. We have seen that English can use an auxiliary verb like *will* or a semi-auxiliary *be going to*. Similarly, Korean can employ the expression V-를 것이 다 *V-(u)l kes-i-ta*:

(54) 미미가   노래를   부를   것이다.
    Mimi-ka   nolay-lul   pwulu-l   kes-i-ta.
    Mimi-NOM   song-ACC   sing-FUT   KES-COP-DECL
    'Mimi will sing a song.'

The main verb is marked with the connective suffix *(u)l* and is followed by the bound noun *kes* combined with the copula verb. This pattern is used to describe a future event more frequently than the suffix *-keyss*.

A stative verb is similar to an English plain verb form, as in *They speak Korean*, where the verb *speak* has no suffix but represents the present tense. The zero and the suffixes in (53) are thus all finite verb forms (VFORM), whereas those connective suffixes are nonfinite verb forms:

(55) a. finite VFORM: -은/는 -*(n)un*, Ø, -었/았 -*(e)ss, -ass, -yss*, -겠 -*keyss*
    b. nonfinite VFORM: CONN1: -아/-어 -*a/-e*, CONN2: -지/-게/-고 -*ci/-key/-ko*
       CONN3: -어야/-나 -*eya/-na*, CONN4: -고 -*ko*, …

The nonfinite forms are on the main verb when the verb combines with the following auxiliary, as we saw in Chapter 3:

(56) a. 미미가   책을   읽어   보았다.
       Mimi-ka   chayk-ul   ilk-e   po-ass-ta
       Mimi-NOM   book-ACC   read-CONN   try-PST-DECL
       'Mimi tried to read a book.'
    b. 미미가   책을   읽게   되었다.
       Mimi-ka   chayk-ul   ilk-key   toy-ess-ta
       Mimi-NOM   book-ACC   read-CONN   become-PST-DECL
       'Mimi began to read a book.'
    c. 미미가   책을   읽어야   한다.
       Mimi-ka   chayk-ul   ilk-eya   ha-n-ta
       Mimi-NOM   book-ACC   read-CONN   do-PRES-DECL
       'Mimi must read a book.'
    d. 미미가   책을   읽었다고   생각한다.
       Mimi-ka   chayk-ul   ilk-ess-ta-ko   ha-n-ta
       Mimi-NOM   book-ACC   read-PST-DECL-COMP do-PRES-DECL
       '(I) think Mimi read the book.'

In each case, the main verb *ilk-* 'read' has a different connective marker. The type of connective marker depends on the auxiliary verb that follows the main verb (see Chapter 7 for further discussion).

In sum, the VFORM (verb inflection form) values in Korean that we have discussed here can be represented by the following simplified format:[1]

(57)

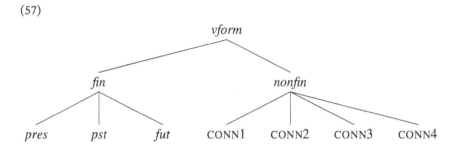

Note that similar to English, in some examples we can observe mismatching between verbal suffixes and tense information. As in the following, the present form indicates events or states pertaining not only to the present but also to the future:

(58) a. 미아가   내일   영국으로   떠난다.
      Mia-ka   nayil   yengkwuk-ulo ttena-n-ta
      Mia-NOM tomorrow England-to   leave-PRES-DECL
      'Mia leaves for England tomorrow.'

   b. 미아가   곧   학생이   된다.
      Mia-ka   kot   haksayng-i   toy-n-ta
      Mia-NOM soon   student-NOM become-PRES-DECL
      'Mia will soon become a student.'

---

1 There are other VFORM values in Korean, as given in an example like the following:

  (i) 미미가   가면   모모도   간다.
      Mimi-ka   ka-myen   Momo-to   ka-n-ta
      Mimi-NOM go-if   Momo-also   go-PRES-DECL
      'If Mimi goes, Momo also goes.'

The suffix *-myen* is equivalent to the conditional conjunction *if* in English. Because this kind of suffix is not selected by a verb, we can take conjunction markers in the language as independent verbal suffixes. See Kim (2016) for a detailed discussion.

The present form can also be interpreted as denoting the future in embedded clauses:

(59) a.

미미가	내일	온다고	들었다.
Mimi-ka	nayil	o-n-ta-ko	tul-ess-ta
Mimi-NOM	tomorrow	come-PRES-DECL-CONN	hear-PST-DECL

'(I) heard that Mimi comes tomorrow.'

b.

내일	날씨가	좋다고	들었다.
nayil	nalssi-ka	coh-ta-ko	tul-ess-ta
tomorrow	weather-NOM	fine-DECL-CONN	hear-PST-DECL

'(I) heard that tomorrow the weather will be fine.'

Just as in English, Korean declarative sentences must be finite:

(60) Declarative Sentence Rule in Korean:
For a declarative sentence to be well-formed, its verb form (VFORM) value must be finite.

A declarative sentence cannot end with a nonfinite verb. For instance, the verbs in the following end with the connective suffix -*ci* and -*na*, and thus they cannot function as the head of an independent clause.

(61) a.

*미미가	책을	읽지.
Mimi-ka	chayk-ul	ilk-ci
Mimi-NOM	book-ACC	read-CONN

b.

*미미가	책을	읽나.
Mimi-ka	chayk-ul	ilk-na
Mimi-NOM	book-ACC	read-CONN

6.3.2 Aspect in Korean

As noted earlier, aspect refers to a grammatical category that emphasizes various phases of the verbal action that occurs. In English, we have discussed the ongoing and completion aspects, which employ the auxiliary verbs *be* and *have*. Korean also has grammatical ways of representing the ongoing and completion aspects. In expressing an ongoing situation, the form V-고 있다 V-ko iss-ta 'V-ko exist-DECL' is used, as noted earlier:

(62) a.

심판이	호각을	불고	있다.
simphan-i	hokak-ul	pwul-ko	iss-ta
referee-NOM	whistle-ACC	blow-CONN	exist-DECL

'The referee is blowing the whistle.'

b. 심판이　　호각을　　불고　　있었다.
simphan-i　hokak-ul　pwul-ko　iss-ess-ta
referee-NOM　whistle-ACC　blow-CONN　exist-PST-DECL
'The referee was blowing the whistle.'

c. 심판이　　호각을　　불고　　있겠다.
simphan-i　hokak-ul　pwul-ko　iss-keyss-ta
referee-NOM　whistle-ACC　blow-CONN　exist-FUT-DECL
'The referee will be blowing the whistle.'

With the appropriate tense suffix, the auxiliary verb *iss-* 'exist' together with the *-ko* marked main verb describes an ongoing situation. In addition, the pattern V-는 중 이다 V-nun cwung-i-ta 'is in the middle of doing V' can describe an ongoing event:

(63) 심판이　　　호각을　　　부는　　　중이다.
simphan-i　　hokak-ul　　pwu-nun　　cwung-i-ta
referee-NOM　whistle-ACC　blow-CONN　middle-COP-DECL
'The referee is in the middle of blowing the whistle.'

The bound noun 중 cwung combines with the main verb 'blow' marked with the suffix *nun* and describes the ongoing situation of blowing the whistle.

As such, Korean has an overt way of expressing a progressive aspect but has no corresponding way of expressing a continuous aspect as in English. This can be observed from the following pair:

(64) a. Mimi has now finished the homework.

b. 미미가　　방금　　숙제를　　마쳤다.
Mimi-ka　pangkum　swukcey-lul　machi-ess-ta
Mimi-NOM　now　　homework-ACC　finish-PST-DECL
'Mimi has just finished the homework.'

Sentence (64b) corresponds to the English perfect sentence in (64a). Note that the Korean sentence has only the past tense suffix *-ess* and no other expression to indicate the continuous aspect.

The past perfect is often expressed by doubling the past tense suffix:

(65) a. 정원에　　꽃이　　피었다.
cengwen-ey　kkoch-i　phi-ess-ta
garden-at　flowers-NOM　bloom-PST-DECL
'Flowers bloomed in the garden.'

b. 정원에   꽃이   피었었다.
  cengwen-ey   kkoch-i   phi-ess-ess-ta
  garden-at   flowers-NOM   bloom-PST-PST-DECL
  'Flowers had bloomed in the garden.'

The single use of the past tense suffix in (65a) denotes a situation that occurred in the past, but the double use in (65b) describes a past perfect situation.

When the auxiliary verb 있다 iss-ta 'exist' combines with a main verb marked with the suffix -아 -*a* rather than -*ko*, we can also have a perfect or 'resultant' reading. Compare the following:

(66) a. 미미가   의자에   앉고   있다.
     Mimi-ka   uyca-ey   anc-ko   iss-ta
     Mimi-NOM   chair-at   sit-CONN   exist-DECL
     'Mimi is sitting on the chair.'

    b. 미미가   의자에   앉아   있다.
     Mimi-ka   uyca-ey   anc-a   iss-ta
     Mimi-NOM   chair-at   sit-CONN   exist-DECL
     'Mimi sat on the chair and existed in that state.'

The two sentences differ only in the connective markers -*ko* and -*a* on the main verb 앉다 anc-ta 'sit-DECL,' but they have different aspect readings. The *V-ko iss-ta* construction in (66a) expresses a progressive state, describing the action of Mimi's sitting down on the chair and it being in progress. Meanwhile, the *V-a iss-ta* construction in (66b) represents a consequent or resultant (or perfect) state, describing the state of Mimi's sitting in the chair and this resultant or consequent state holding at the reference time. As expected, the past perfect or future perfect can be expressed using a past tense or future marking expression:

(67) a. 미미가   의자에   앉아   있었다.
     Mimi-ka   uyca-ey   anc-a   iss-ess-ta
     Mimi-NOM   chair-at   sit-CONN   exist-PST-DECL
     'Mimi had sat on the chair.'

    b. 미미가   의자에   앉아   있을   것이다.
     Mimi-ka   uyca-ey   anc-a   iss-ul   kes-i-ta
     Mimi-NOM   chair-at   sit-CONN   exist-CONN kes-COP-DECL
     'Mimi will have sat on the chair.'

6.3.3 Situation Types in Korean

Just as in English, in Korean, situations can be classified into four types:

(68) a. State:

미미가   아프다.
Mimi-ka   aphu-ta
Mimi-NOM   sick-DECL
'Mimi is sick.'

b. Activity:

미미가   달린다.
Mimi-ka   talli-n-ta
Mimi-NOM   run-PRES-DECL
'Mimi runs.'

c. Accomplishment:

미미가   한   시간 동안   의자를   만들었다.
Mimi-ka   han sikan-tongan uyca-lul   mantul-ess-ta
Mimi-NOM one hour-for   chair-ACC make-PST-DECL
'Mimi made a chair for an hour.'

d. Achievement:

미미가   정상에   도달했다.
Mimi-ka   cengsang-ey   totalha-yess-ta
Mimi-NOM   top-LOC   reach-PST-DECL
'Mimi reached the top (of the mountain).'

As illustrated here, the state verb 아프다 aphu-ta 'sick-DECL' describes a situation that continues to exist, representing a nondynamic situation with no perceptible change. The remaining three eventuality types, often called *events*, express that something changes. However, as discussed for English, these event types have different internal structures. For example, achievements and accomplishments such as 도달하다 totalha-ta 'reach-DECL' and 만들다 mantul-ta 'make-DECL' have natural endpoints (telic) when they occur with a complement like 정상에 *cengsang-ey* or 의자 uyca 'chair,' respectively. Meanwhile, activities such as 달리다 talli-ta 'run-DECL' are homogeneous, with no natural endpoint (atelic). The distinction between accomplishments and achievements is difficult to make, but the main difference comes from the property of duration. Unlike accomplishments, achievements do not mark duration and are prevented from being modified by a *for*-PP:

(69) a. 미미는　　한　시간-{만에/*-동안}　집에　　도착했다.
　　　　Mimi-nun　han　sikan-maney/*tongan　cip-ey　　tochakha-yess-ta
　　　　Mimi-TOP　one　hour-in/*for　　　　house-at　arrive-PST-DECL
　　　　'Mimi arrived at home in/*for an hour.'

　　b. 미미는　　한　시간-{만에/-동안}　집을　　　지었다.
　　　　Mimi-nun　han　sikan-maney/tongan　cip-ul　　ci-ess-ta
　　　　Mimi-TOP　one　hour-in/for　　　　house-ACC　build-PST-DECL
　　　　'Mimi built the house in/for an hour.'

Building a house is something we can do for a period of time, but arriving at a place is not. This explains why the achievement eventuality in (69a) is incompatible with the delimited expression. As such, the four types of lexical aspects are sensitive to inherent properties such as stativity, durativity, and telicity.

One thing worth noting here concerns aspectual coercion or shift. The eventuality type is determined not purely by the lexical property of the verb involved but also by the expressions participating in the predication (e.g. VP level). For example, the internal structure of the object NP (e.g. definiteness) or the property of its dependent (modifier or complement) can shift or coerce the type of eventuality. The verb 달리다 *talli-ta* 'run' can represent either an activity or an accomplishment, depending on the type of its dependent, as in the following:

(70) a. 미미가　　　달렸다.
　　　　Mimi-ka　　talli-ess-ta
　　　　Mimi-NOM　run-PST-DECL
　　　　'Mimi ran.'

　　b. 미미가　　집까지　한　시간만에　　달렸다.
　　　　Mimi-ka　cip-kkaci　han　sikan-maney　talli-ess-ta
　　　　Mimi-NOM　home-to　one　hour-in　　run-PST-DECL
　　　　'Mimi ran to the home in an hour.'

Example (70a) represents an activity situation, but in (70b), with the addition of the PP "in an hour," the situation shifts to an accomplishment. The object property also can shift the eventuality type:

(71) a. 미미가　　편지　한통을　　읽었다.
　　　　Mimi-ka　pyenci　hanthong-ul　ilk-ess-ta
　　　　Mimi-NOM　letter　one-ACC　　read-PST-DECL
　　　　'Mimi read a letter.'

b. 미미가   편지들을   읽었다.
   Mimi-ka   pyenci-tul-ul   ilk-ess-ta
   Mimi-NOM   letter-PL-ACC   read-PST-DECL
   'Mimi read letters.'

With the singular indefinite object NP in (71a), we have an accomplishment event; but with the plural object in (71b), we have an activity event.

6.3.4 Sentence Types and Mood in Korean

As noted, the concept of sentence types is closely related to the notion of mood: a verb category or form expressing the speaker's attitude about what the sentence describes. Unlike in English, where word order represents sentence mood, Korean employs a verb suffix ending for each type of sentence mood:

(72) a. Declarative

   사과를   먹었다.
   sakwa-lul   mek-ess-ta
   apple-ACC   eat-PST-DECL
   '(He) ate an apple.'

b. Interrogative

   사과를   먹었니?
   sakwa-lul   mek-ees-ni?
   apple-ACC   eat-QUE
   'Did you eat the apple?'

c. Imperative

   사과를   먹어라!
   sakwa-lul   mek-ela!
   apple-ACC   eat-IMP
   'Eat an apple!'

d. Exclamative

   하늘이   참   푸르구나!
   hanul-i   cham   phwulu-kwuna!
   sky-NOM   really   blue-EXCL
   'The sky is really blue.'

A declarative sentence describes statements (indicative), and an interrogative sentence states a question. The imperative form is used to issue a direct command or order. Similar to English, the correspondence between sentence form and mood type (or speech act) can be overridden in Korean.

Because the verbal ending indicates a sentence mood, Korean can represent a variety of moods such as suggestive (propositive) and promissive. Each of the following examples introduces a different verbal ending:

(73) a. Suggestive

    사과를   먹자.
    sakwa-lul   mek-ca!
    apple-ACC   eat-SUG
    'Let's eat an apple.'

  b. Promissive

    사과를   먹으마.
    sakwa-lul   mek-uma
    apple-ACC   eat-PROM
    'I promise that I will eat an apple.'

Note that the mood type of each sentence can be realized in many different speech styles:

(74) a. 사과를   먹-었다/어/네/어요/습니다.
    sakwa-lul   mek-ess-ta/e/ney/eyo/supnita
    apple-ACC   eat-PST-DECL
    '(He) ate an apple.'

  b. 사과를   먹-었니/나/어요/습니까?
    sakwa-lul   mek-ess-ni/e/na/eyo/supnikka?
    apple-ACC   eat-PST-QUE
    'Did (he) eat an apple?'

  c. 사과를   먹-어라/어/게/어요/으오/으시오.
    sakwa-lul mek-ela/e/key/eyo/uo/usio
    apple-ACC eat-PST-IMP
    'Eat an apple!'

The endings here indicate whether the mood type is informal, colloquial, or formal.

6.4 Contrastive Notes

6.4.1 Tense

In representing three points of tense, English generally uses verbal suffixes for the past and present tense but an auxiliary verb like *will* for the future tense. Korean uses verbs suffixes like -*ess* and -*nun* to represent past and present, but it employs the suffix -*keyss* or the complex form -*l kes-i-ta* for future:

(75) a. Minho will come back to Seoul.

    b. 민호가   서울로   돌아올   것이다.
        Minho-ka   Seoul-lo   tolao-l   kes-i-ta
        Minho-NOM   Seoul-to   come.back-FUT   thing-COP-DECL
        'Minho will come back to Seoul.'

6.4.2 Aspect

In English, ongoing situations are expressed by the construction *be* + V-*ing*, whereas Korean uses V-고 있다 V-ko iss-ta 'V-ko exist-DECL.'

(76) a. Minho is coming back to Seoul.

    b. 민호가   서울로   돌아오고   있다.
        Minho-ka   Seoul-lo   tolao-ko   iss-ta
        Minho-NOM   Seoul-to   come.back-CONN   exist-COP-DECL
        'Minho is coming back to Seoul.'

Meanwhile, completed situations in English are described by *have* + V-en, but in Korean they are expressed by the past verbal suffix -*ess*:

(77) a. Minho has come back to Seoul.

    b. 민호가   서울로   돌아왔다.
        Minho-ka   seoul-lo   tolao-ss-ta
        Minho-NOM   seoul-to   come.back-PST-DECL
        'Minho has come back to Seoul.'

Unlike English, where the perfect aspect is typically marked by *have* + V[*en*], Korean uses the past-tense suffix to mark the present perfect. The context thus determines whether -*ess* is interpreted as past or perfect.

6.4.3 Sentence Types and Mood

In English, sentence types are determined by word order, whereas in Korean, they are marked by the verb ending marker. For instance, an interrogative sentence inverts the subject-auxiliary in English, but in Korean, the only difference is the sentence ending marker:

(78) a. Minho has come back to Seoul.

    b. Has Minho come back to Seoul?

(79) a. 민호가   서울로   돌아왔다/니?
　　 Minho-ka   seoul-lo   tolao-ss-ta/ni
　　 Minho-NOM   seoul-to   come.back-PST-DECL/QUE
　　 'Minho has come back to Seoul./Has Minho come back to Seoul?'

In English, the four different sentence types (declarative, question, imperative, and exclamative) differ with respect to word order. However, in Korean, the differences among the four and other types lie in the verbal suffix type.

6.5 Conclusion

Tense, aspect, and mood are three key grammatical categories that each sentence expresses. As discussed, the two languages have different ways of expressing these categories.

To describe the three tenses (present, past, and future), English has two overt inflectional markings, *-es*, *-ed*, that typically describe past or present situations. Future situations are described by an auxiliary verb like *will* or semi-auxiliary expressions like *be going to*. Meanwhile, Korean uses three different inflectional markings to describe the three tenses. To describe aspectual (ongoing and continuous) properties of a situation, English uses the two auxiliary verbs *have* and *be*, each of whose VP complement must be in a special VFORM value. Korean represents ongoing or continuous events using the auxiliary verb *-iss-ta* that combines with a main verb with the VFORM value *-ko* or *-a*. In English, the types of sentence mood are determined by the word order; but in Korean, sentence mood types are marked by verb endings. Proper usages of these grammatical categories are very key to express the situations involved in an appropriate manner.

Exercises

1   The situation or event of Kim's chasing a dog can be realized in 12 different ways with respect to tense (3 types) and aspect (9 types). Give all 12 ways of expressing this running situation in English, and then translate the sentences into Korean with Romanization and glosses. In addition, discuss key differences between the English and Korean tense and aspect system as much as you can.

2   Both English and Korean have finite and nonfinite VFORM values, as discussed in the chapter. Using the verbs *choose* and *lead* for English and the verbs 날다 nal-ta 'fly' and 자르다 calu-ta 'cut' for Korean, construct three sentences where these verbs are used as finite and three sentences where they are used as nonfinite.

3 Transliterate the following Korean sentences, and draw a tree for each to check which grammar rule (Head-Complement, Head-Subject, Head-Modifier) allows each phrasal combination. In addition, specify the tense/aspect, situation type, and mood of each sentence.

(i) a. 미미가 많이 운다.
   'Mimi cries a lot.'
   b. 우리는 지난 주에 테니스를 쳤다.
   'We played tennis last week.'
   c. 그 때 도둑은 사라졌었다.
   'The thief disappeared at that time.'
   d. 숙제를 시간내에 마치자.
   'Let's try to finish the homework in time.'
   e. 미미가 미아와 체스를 두고 있다.
   'Mimi is playing chess with Mia.'
   f. 미미가 운동장에서 놀고 있다.
   'Mimi is playing at the playground.'
   g. 미미가 침대에 누워 있었다.
   'Mimi was lying (or Mimi was in the state of lying in the bed).'
   h. 서울에 살았었니?
   'Have you ever lived in Seoul?'
   i. 내일 미미를 만나겠다.
   'I will see Mimi tomorrow.'
   j. 기상청이 내일 비가 온다고 한다.
   'The weather forecast says it will rain tomorrow.'

4 Identify the situation type for the predicate in each of the following English sentences.

(i) a. John works even on the weekends.
   b. I found a solution to the problem.
   c. He wrote beautiful poems.
   d. Mary drew a painting.
   e. Mary loves John.
   f. Bill died last night.
   g. Sue ran a mile this morning.
   h. Bill resembles his mother.
   i. They all recognized the mistakes.
   j. I usually drink beer on Saturday.

5 Translate the following English sentences into Korean, and discuss what grammatical mechanisms are employed in Korean to express aspects of perfection or completion. In addition, discuss differences in the aspect systems in the two languages as much as you can.

(i) a. I have finished my homework already.
   b. Jane has lived abroad for five years.
   c. Have you studied contrastive linguistics before?
(ii) a. I had been to Seoul twice by the time I was 10 years old.
   b. Had you studied linguistics before you took this class?
(iii) a. In two years, I will have saved $2,000.
   b. Kim will have taught linguistics for 20 years in 2030.

6 Korean has at least four situation types: state, activity, accomplishment, and achievement. Give two sentences for each of these situation types.

7 Consider the following examples, and identify the use of the tense suffix *ess* with respect to tense and aspect.

(i) a. 꽃이 활짝 피었네!
      'Flowers are in full bloom.'
   b. 문이 활짝 열렸네.
      'The door is wide open.'
   c. 신부가 신랑보다 늙었다.
      'The bride is older than the groom.'
   d. 우리 아내는 안경을 썼다.
      'My wife wears glasses.'
   e. 음식이 많이 남았니?
      'Is there a lot of food left?'
   f. 넌 내일 죽었다.
      'You will die tomorrow.'

Also compare the following pair, and discuss each sentence's tense and aspect.

(ii) a. 미미는 그 책을 읽었다.
      'Mimi read the book.'
   b. 미미는 그 책을 읽었었다.
      'Mimi had read the book.'
(iii) a. 미미는 축구 선수였다.
      'Mimi was a soccer player.'
   b. 미미는 축구 선수였었다.
      'Mimi had been a soccer player.'

7

Auxiliary Systems: Helping Main Verbs

7.1 Introduction

In the previous chapter, we saw that in expressing aspectual (ongoing and continuous) properties of a situation, auxiliary verbs are often employed. An auxiliary verb (also called a helping verb) helps the main verb to add further semantic information for the given sentence. For instance, auxiliary verbs can represent modality, expressing permission, ability, prediction, possibility, or necessity:

(1) a. Kim must be nearly there by now.
   b. Kim might arrive a bit later than I'd anticipated.
   c. A trip like this can take hours more than one expects.

Korean auxiliary verbs can also express possibility or necessity:

(2) a. 미미가   편지를   읽었나   보다.
      Mimi-ka   pyenci-lul ilk-ess-na   po-ta
      Mimi-NOM   letter-ACC read-PST-CONN seem-DECL
      'Mimi might have read the letter.'

   b. 미미가   편지를   읽어야   한다.
      Mimi-ka   pyenci-lul ilk-eya   ha-n-ta
      Mimi-NOM   letter-ACC read-PST-CONN must-PRES-DECL
      'Mimi must read the letter.'

In this chapter, we will discuss the grammatical properties of such modal auxiliary verbs as well as other auxiliary verbs in English and Korean.

English and Korean in Contrast: A Linguistic Introduction, First Edition. Jong-Bok Kim.
© 2024 John Wiley & Sons, Inc. Published 2024 by John Wiley & Sons, Inc.

7.2 English Auxiliary System

English auxiliary verbs can be classified into four groups:

(3) a. Modal auxiliary: *can, must, will, shall, may*
 b. Aspectual: *have, be*
 c. Dummy finite: *do*
 d. Infinitival: *to*

These auxiliary verbs behave differently from main verbs in various respects. An important difference between auxiliary and main verbs is that auxiliaries cannot occur alone in a typical (non-elliptical) sentence. For instance, we cannot remove the main verb from a sentence, leaving only the auxiliary:

(4) a. I would like a new job. vs. *I would a new job.
 b. You should buy a new car. vs. *You should a new car.
 c. He must be crazy vs. *He must crazy.

Auxiliary verbs require a VP headed by a main verb. On the other hand, main verbs can occur without an auxiliary verb.

(5) a. I bought a new car.
 b. I could buy a new car.

However, in some sentences, an auxiliary occurs alone when the following VP is elided. This is especially true in responses to questions:

(6) a. Q: Can you solve the problem?
 b. A: Yes, I surely can.

The answer is understood to mean "Yes, I surely can solve the problem." This phenomenon, known as VP ellipsis (VPE), allows the VP following the auxiliary verb to be elided.

Auxiliary verbs are different from main verbs in several other respects. In particular, they differ from main verbs with respect to the so-called NICE-Tag (Negation, Inversion, Contraction, Ellipsis, and Tag question) phenomena. See the following contrasts:

(7) Negation:
 a. Mimi will not leave.
 b. *Mimi left not.

(8) Inversion:
 a. Will Mimi leave the party now?
 b. *Left Mimi the party already?

(9) Contraction:
    a. Kim couldn't leave the party.
    b. *Kim leftn't the party early.

(10) Ellipsis:
    a. If anybody is spoiling the children, Kim will __.
    b. *If anybody keeps spoiling the children, Kim keeps __.

(11) Tag question:
    a. You will leave soon, won't you?
    b. *You will not leave soon, leave you?

These contrasts show that unlike main verbs, as in (7) finite auxiliary verbs can host a sentential negation *not* right after them and can undergo subject-auxiliary inversion, as in (8). (9) and (10) show that they can also be contracted with the sentential negation marker *not*; and the following verb phrase can even be deleted or elided. Furthermore, they can be used in the tag question, as in (11). None of this is possible with main verbs.

7.2.1 Modals

In English, modal verbs are auxiliary verbs that can be used to change the modality of a sentence. The main function of modal auxiliary verbs is to allow the speaker or writer to express their opinion of or attitude about a proposition. These attitudes can cover a wide range of possibilities, including obligation, asking for and giving permission, disapproval, advising, logical deduction, ability, possibility, necessity, absence of necessity, and so on. In addition, each modal verb can have more than one meaning, and the interpretation of a particular modal verb will depend heavily on the context in which it is being used, as in the following examples:

(12) a. It might take more than a week. (possibility)
    b. You might have told me about it! (showing disapproval)
    c. He must take his medicine three times a day. (obligation)
    d. He must be French. (logical deduction)
    e. I can't lift that suitcase by myself. (ability)
    f. That can't be the right answer. (logical deduction)
    g. May I look at the questions now? (asking for permission)
    h. They say it may snow tomorrow. (possibility)

What we can observe here is that one modal verb can have more than one meaning, and one meaning can be expressed by more than one modal verb.

One effective way to identify modal verbs is by their defectiveness (they have neither participles nor infinitives). That is, they can occur only in finite forms – not as infinitives or participles.

(13) a. *to will/*canned/*canning
      b. *Kim wants to can/will study syntax.

Further, they have no third-person inflection form (-*s/es* form):

(14) a. *Kim musts leave the party early.
      b. *Kim wills leave the party early.

In terms of their subcategorization information, modal verbs combine with a base VP as their complement:

(15) a. Kim can [kick/*kicked/*kicking/*to kick the ball].
      b. Kim will [kick/*kicked/*kicking/*to kick the ball].

(16) a. *Kim must [$_{VP[fin]}$ bakes a cake].
      b. *Kim must [$_{VP[fin]}$ baked a cake].

Consider the following structures for these sentences:

(17) a.

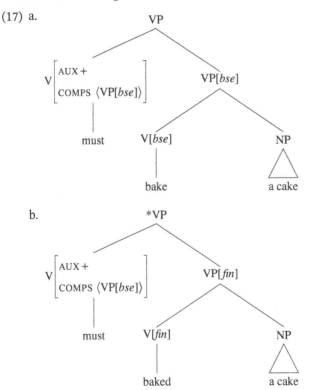

The structure in (17a) is a well-formed head-complement structure, but (17b) is not simply because the modal auxiliary *must* requires a base VP as its complement. This lexical information can be represented as a feature strucure. The following means a modal verb like *must* bears the positive value for the feature AUX, its verb-inflection form VFORM is finite, and it selects a base VP as its complement.

(18) $\begin{bmatrix} \text{AUX} + \\ \text{VFORM}\,\mathit{fin} \\ \text{COMPS}\,\langle\text{VP}[\mathit{bse}]\rangle \end{bmatrix}$

7.2.2 Aspectual Verbs: *Be* and *Have*

As discussed in the previous chapter, the auxiliary verbs *be* and *have* are used to present the aspectual information of completion and ongoing:

(19) a. Kim has finished the project.
    b. Kim is singing the song.

The auxiliary *has* in (19a) describes a situation in which Kim completed the project, whereas in (19b), *be* contributes to the description of an ongoing situation of Kim's singing the song.

Consider the progressive *be*. It is not difficult to determine that the aspectual verb *be* has all NICE properties:

(20) a. Kim is not singing a song.
    b. Is Kim singing a song?
    c. Kim isn't singing a song.
    d. Kim is singing a song, and Mary is __, too.

Note that there are three uses of *be*: copula *be*, passive *be*, and progressive *be*:

(21) a. Kim is a student.
    b. Kim is found by the student.
    c. Kim is running into the water.

The three uses of the auxiliary verb *be* here all have the auxiliary properties. However, each case has a different complement (COMPS) value:

(22) a. Copula *be*: XP[PRD +] (where XP means AP, NP, PP)
    b. Passive *be*: VP[*en*]
    c. Progressive *be*: VP[*ing*]

The structure generated from (22a) is something like the following:

(23)

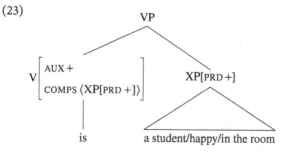

The structure tells us that the auxiliary verb *is* select a predicative XP as its complement. One thing to note is that the copula verb is the only verb in this sentence, implying that the copula *be* is also used as a main verb. In this sense, the copula *be* is a main verb with the auxiliary properties. We observe a similar fact with *have*. When *have* is used as a main verb in British English, it passes NICE properties:

(24) a. Kim has not enough money.
     b. Has Kim enough money?

Like *be*, *have* also behaves like an auxiliary verb with respect to the NICE phenomena:

(25) a. Kim has not sung a song.
     b. Has Kim sung a song?
     c. Kim hasn't been singing a song.
     d. Kim has sung a song, and Mary has __, too.

For the subcategorization, *have* requires a VP whose head verb is in the perfect form. The subcategorization information is enough to predict the ordering restrictions for auxiliary verbs:

(26) a. He has [seen his children].
     b. He will [have [been [seeing his children]]].
     c. He must [have [been [being interrogated by the police]]].

(27) a. *Americans have [paying income tax ever since 1913].
     b. *George has [went to America].

In (27a), the auxiliary *has* combines with a perfect VP. In (27b), the modal *will* combines with a base VP. In (27c), the modal *must* combines with a base VP first, and the following auxiliary verbs *have*, *been*, and *being* combine with a proper VP complement. (27a) is ungrammatical because *have* requires a past participle VP, not a progressive VP. (27b) is out because the following VP is finite.

(28)

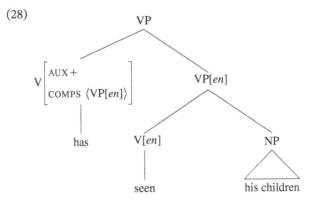

The verb *seen* combines with its object complement *his children,* forming a head-complement construction. The auxiliary verb *has* combines with this VP as its complement

7.2.3 Periphrastic *Do*

The so-called dummy *do* exhibits the NICE properties like other auxiliaries:

(29) a. Kim does not leave the town.
　　 b. In no other circumstances does Kim drink alcohol.
　　 c. They don't leave the town.
　　 d. Jane likes the apples, but Mary doesn't __.

Like other modals, *do* does not appear in infinitive clauses.

(30) a. *They expected us to do leave him.
　　 b. *They expected us to can leave him.

Unlike the auxiliaries *have* and *be*, *do* is specified to be *fin(ite)*. This property accounts for why no auxiliary element can precede *do*.

(31) a. He might [have left].
　　 b. *He might [do leave].

Note that *do* also requires a base VP in the finite environment, as represented in the following structure:

(32)

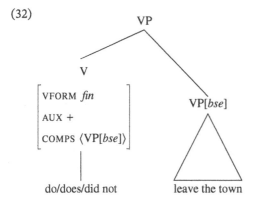

$$\left[\begin{array}{l} \text{VFORM } \textit{fin} \\ \text{AUX } + \\ \text{COMPS } \langle \text{VP}[\textit{bse}]\rangle \end{array}\right]$$

do/does/did not　　leave the town

7.2.4 Infinitival Clause Marker *To*

The auxiliary verbs *to* and *do* are similar in that they do not have a core meaning, but differ in one small way: *do* appears only in finite contexts, and *to* only in non-finite contexts.

(33) a. *Kim believed Lee to do leave here.
　　 b. Kim believes Lee to have left here.

This infinitival marker, similar to modal auxiliary verbs, must combine with a base VP:

(34) a. Kim will [leave/*leaving/*leaves the town].
     b. Kim tries to [leave/*leaving/*leaves the town].

In terms of NICE properties, the nonfinite auxiliary *to* observes the VP ellipsis criterion:

(35) a. Mimi wanted to go home, but Peter didn't want to __.
     b. Mimi voted for Bill because his father told him to __.

This means the infinitive marker *to* generates a head-complement structure like the following:

(36)

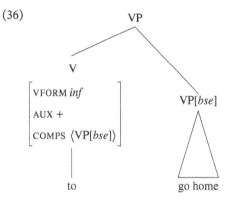

7.2.5 Auxiliary and Negation

As noted earlier, NICE (negation, inversion, contraction, ellipsis) phenomena are sensitive to the presence of auxiliary verbs. English has two types of negation. The first is constituent negation, which modifies any nonfinite VP. Observe that *not* in the following behaves like the adverb *never*:

(37) a. Kim wants never/not to leave the city.
     b. Never/not having aches and pains is not a virtue.

This constituent negation *not* modifies a nonfinite VP, as shown in the following structure:

(38)

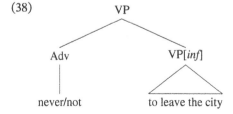

Unlike this constituent negation, the more widely used sentential negation occurs right after a finite auxiliary verb:

(39) a. Kim could/would/should not move to another city.
     b. Kim is not moving to another city.
     c. Kim has not moved to another city.

The negation here scopes over the whole sentence, as seen from a possible paraphrase:

(40) a. It is not the case that Kim will move to another city.
     b. It is not the case that Kim is moving to another city.

This negator can be contracted with the preceding finite auxiliary and can occur in a yes-no polar question:

(41) a. Couldn't/Wouldn't/Shouldn't Kim move to another city?
     b. Isn't Kim moving to another city?
     c. Hasn't Kim moved to another city?

Such examples imply that the sentential negator and the preceding auxiliary form a syntactic unit, as seen in the following structure:

(42)

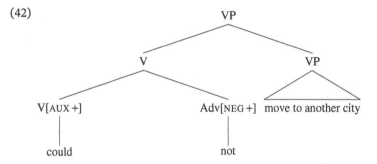

The combination of a finite auxiliary verb and sentential negation is allowed by the following grammar rule:

(43) Head-LEX Rule:
     V → V, X[LEX +]

The feature LEX is assigned to expressions like sentential negation, a particle (see Chapter 4 and 5), and a preposition (see Chapter 8). This rule allows the finite auxiliary *could* in (42) to combine with the negator *not*, yielding another complex verb.

7.3 Korean Auxiliary System

7.3.1 Types of Auxiliary Verbs and

Auxiliary verbs in Korean are traditionally subclassified based on their semantic contributions. Consider a typical classification with examples:

(44) a. Completion

풀어가다 phwul-e ka-ta 'solve-CONN gradually-DECL'

b. Service

놀아주다 nol-a cwu-ta 'play-CONN for-DECL,' 읽어주다 ilk-e cwu-ta 'read-CONN for-DECL'

c. Attempt

먹어보다 mek-e po-ta 'eat-CONN try-DECL,' 만나보다 manna-a po-ta 'meet-CONN try-DECL'

d. Conjecture

먹나보다 mek-na po-ta 'eat-CONN maybe-DECL,' 오나싶다 o-na siph-ta 'come-CONN maybe-DECL'

e. Repetition

웃어대다 wus-e tay-ta 'smile-CONN on-DECL,' 먹어대다 mek-e tay-ta 'eat-CONN on-DECL'

f. Hold

막아두다 mak-a twu-ta 'block-CONN stay-DECL,' 감아놓다 kam-a noh-ta 'wrap-CONN leave-DECL'

g. Expectation

먹고싶다 mek-ko siph-ta 'eat-CONN wish-DECL'

h. Existence

걸려있다 kelli-e iss-ta 'hang-CONN exist-DECL'

i. Obligation

먹어야한다 mek-eya han-ta 'eat-CONN must-DECL'

j. Habit

먹곤하다 mek-kon ha-ta 'eat-CONN used.to-DECL'

Auxiliary verbs often carry aspectual interpretations. One issue that arises from such a classification is that the standard of semantic classifications is not decisive or coherent enough, causing the literature to use slightly different classifications.

As noted earlier, one important constraint in auxiliary construction is that the auxiliary imposes a designated connective verb form (VFORM) value on the preceding verb it combines with.

(45) a. 미미가　　　사과를　　먹{-고/*-어}　싶다.
Mimi-ka　　sakwa-lul　mek-ko/*-e　siph-ta
Mimi-NOM　apple-ACC　eat-CONN　　wish-DECL
'Mimi would like to eat apples.'

　b. 미미가　　　사과를　　먹{*-고/-어}　보았다.
Mimi-ka　　sakwa-lul　mek-*ko/-e　po-ass-ta
Mimi-NOM　apple-ACC　eat-CONN　　try-PST-DECL
'Mimi tried to eat apples.'

As such, the preceding main verb must have a specified connective form, which cannot be violated.

The table in (46) is the classification of auxiliary verbs based on the required VFORM (connective vform) value of the preceding main verb.

(46) Types of auxiliary verbs by the VFORM value

Meaning	VFORM value	auxiliary verbs
Continue	*a/e*	가다 ka-ta 'gradually', 오다 o-ta 'gradually'
Completion	*a/e*	내다 nay-ta 'finish,' 버리다 peli-ta 'finish'
Service	*a/e*	주다 cwu-ta 'for,' 드리다 tuli-ta 'for'
Attempt	*a/e*	보다 po-ta 'try'
Repetition	*a/e*	쌓다 ssah-ta 'again,' 대다 tay-ta 'again'
Hold	*a/e*	놓다 noh-ta 'save,' 두다 twu-ta 'save'
Existence	*a/e*	있다 iss-ta 'exist'
Inchoative	*a/e*	지다 ci-ta 'become'
Conjecture	*na*	보다 po-ta 'maybe,' 싶다 siph-ta 'maybe'
Hoping	*ko*	싶다 siph-ta 'wish'
Progressive	*ko*	있다 iss-ta 'on.going'
Ended up	*ko*	말다 mal-ta 'end.up'
Obligation	*ya*	하다 ha-ta 'must'
Habit	*kon*	하다 ha-ta 'used.to'
Result	*key*	되다 toy-ta 'become'
Negation	*ci*	않다 anh-ta 'not'

Certain auxiliary verbs can have more than one semantic function. For example, 보다 *po-ta* can either mean 'attempt' or 'conjecture,' and 하다 *ha-* can add modality meanings such as obligation, habit, progressive, and so forth. The distinction comes from the main verb's VFORM value. As seen in the table, auxiliary verbs are subgrouped based on the VFORM value of the main verbs they combine with. This can be represented as a type hierarchy system:

(47)

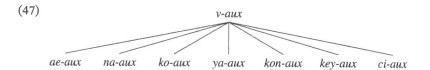

The *ae-aux* type includes most of the auxiliary verbs that combine with a main verb with *-a/e*, as illustrated by the following:

(48) a. 먹어가다 mek-e ka-ta 'eat-CONN gradually.do-DECL'
  b. 잡아내다 cap-a nay-ta 'catch-CONN finish-DECL'
  c. 도와주다 tow-a cwu-ta 'help-CONN for-DECL'
  d. 읽어보다 ilk-e po-ta 'read-CONN try-DECL'

Such auxiliary verbs cannot combine with the main verb marked with a different VFORM value:

(49) a. *먹어야 가다 *mek-eya ka-ta 'eat-CONN gradually.do-DECL'
  b. *잡곤 내다 *cap-kon nay-ta 'catch-CONN finish-DECL'
  c. *돕지 주다 *top-ci cwu-ta 'help-CONN for-DECL'
  d. *읽지 보다 *ilk-ci po-ta 'read-CONN try-DECL'

Again, the examples illustrate that each auxiliary requires a main verb with a special VFORM value.

7.3.2 Three Possible Structures

Consider a sentence including an auxiliary verb:

(50) 미미가　　책을　　읽고　　싶었다.
  Mimi-ka　chayk-ul　ilk-ko　　siph-ess-ta
  Mimi-NOM　book-ACC　read-CONN　wish-PST-DECL
  'Mimi would like to read the book.'

In terms of its structure, there are three possible analyses for such a sentence with English glosses only:

(51) a. VP-analysis:
    Mimi-NOM [[VP book-ACC　read-CONN] [V like-PST-DECL]].
  b. Morphological analysis:
    Mimi-NOM book-ACC　[V read-CONN　like-PST-DECL].
  c. Complex predicate analysis:
    Mimi-NOM book-ACC　[V [V read-CONN] [V like-PST-DECL]].

Let us consider the merits and problems of each analysis.

• *VP-analysis*: The VP-analysis as given in (51a) assumes that the auxiliary verb has a VP complement. This means the auxiliary construction is structurally similar to the control construction with a verb like *seltukha-* 'persuade.' However, there are significant differences between such control and auxiliary constructions. For example, they differ in case alternations. Unlike control verbs, auxiliary verbs can allow their object to be marked by either accusative or nominative:

(52) 미미가   사과를/가   안먹고   싶었다.
     Mimi-ka   [[sakwa-lul/ka   an-mek-ko]   siph-ess-ta]
     Mimi-NOM   apple-ACC/NOM   not-eat-CONN   like-PST-DECL
     'Mimi would like not to eat the apple.'

The object *sakwa* 'apple' can be marked both ACC and NOM due to the presence of the auxiliary verb. Given that the auxiliary verb influences this case alternation, the VP-analysis needs to posit nonlocal case assignment rules for such an example: the auxiliary verb is outside the local VP but somehow needs to be able to refer to the object.

• *Morphological analysis*: The morphological analysis given in (51b) assumes that the main verb and the following verb form one morphological word, mainly for simplicity. The analysis may capture the cohesive properties of the two verbs but does not reflect the productivity of the construction, particularly with respect to multiple occurrences of auxiliary verbs:

(53) a. 먹고   싶다
      mek-ko   siph-ta
      eat-CONN like-DECL

    b. 먹고   싶어   한다
      mek-ko   siph-e   ha-n-ta
      eat-CONN like-CONN do-PRES-DECL

    c. 먹고   싶어   하지   않다
      mek-ko   siph-e   ha-ci   anh-ta
      eat-CONN like-CONN do-CONN   not-DECL

    d. 먹고   싶어   하지   않게   되다
      mek-ko   siph-e   ha-ci   anh-key   toy-ta
      eat-CONN like-CONN do-CONN   not-CONN   become-DECL

    e. 먹고   싶어   하지   않게   되어   버렸다
      mek-ko   siph-e   ha-ci   anh-key   toy-e   peli-ess-ta
      eat-CONN like-CONN do-CONN   not-CONN   become-CONN end.up-PST-DECL

As illustrated in these examples, we can add one more auxiliary verb to each example with an appropriate connective maker on the preceding one. There is no limit to the number of auxiliary verbs we can add. This implies that we cannot list all the possible combinations in the lexicon. A more serious issue arises from the possibility of adding a delimiter or even a case marker to the non-final auxiliary verb:

(54) a. 먹고만   싶다
     mek-ko-man   siph-ta
     eat-CONN-only like-DECL
     'would like to only eat'

   b. 먹고도   싶어를   하지   않았다
     mek-ko-to   siph-e-lul   ha-ci   anh-ass-ta
     eat-CONN-also like-CONN-ACC do-CONN not-PST-DECL
     'did not want to eat'

Given that the attachment of a case marker is a syntactic phenomenon, we cannot generate such examples in the.lexicon

  • *Complex predicate approach*: The main idea of this analysis, as illustrated in (51c), is that the main verb and the following auxiliary verb are combined at the syntax level and behave like one complex predicate. This direction, which we adopt here, can account for the properties of the auxiliary construction that differ from those of the typical VP complement constructions. In what follows, we will see that phenomena including case alternation and syntactic cohesion can follow from this complex predicate analysis.

7.3.3 Complex Predicate Formation

We have seen that in English, an auxiliary verb combines with a VP headed by a proper VFORM verb. In terms of syntactic combination, Korean auxiliary verbs behave differently. Each auxiliary verb combines not with a VP but rather with a main verb alone. That is, the main verb and the following auxiliary verb are combined at the syntax level and form a complex predicate. For instance, each of the following auxiliary verbs combines with a preceding main verb, forming a cohesive unit that acts like a complex predicate.

(55) a. 먹어   가다
     mek-e   ka-ta 'eat gradually'
     eat-CONN go-DECL

   b. 먹어   보다
     mek-e   po-ta   'try to eat'
     eat-CONN try-DECL

   c. 먹어야   해요
     mek-eya hay-yo 'must eat'
     eat-CONN do-SUG

The complex predicate analysis allows the combination of an auxiliary verb with its main verb. This is represented as follows:

(56)

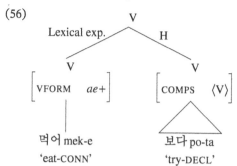

This shows that the auxiliary verb *po-ta* 'try' combines with the main verb *mek-e* 'eat-CONN', forming a complex predicate.

There are several pieces of evidence for the complex predicate properties of the construction. We have seen that the present tense marking in Korean is -은/는 *(n)un*. An observable constraint is that this tense marking cannot occur with a stative verb (or adjectival predicate):

(57) a. 먹는다
    mek-nun-ta
    eat-PRES-DECL
 b. *아름답는다
    *alumtap-nun-ta
    pretty-PRES-DECL

However, observe the following contrast:

(58) a. 먹지   않는다
    mek-ci   anh-nun-ta
    eat-CONN not-PRES-DECL
 b. *아름답지   않는다
    *alumtap-ci anh-nun-ta
    pretty-CONN not-PRES-DECL

The contrast in (58) indicates that the present tense marking in the negative auxiliary verb depends on the property of the main verb (predicate). This in turn means the negative auxiliary verb inherits the main verb's stative properties, forming a complex predicate.

Case assignments are local in Korean, indicating that the case assigner and the controlled case-marked NP are in the same local domain (clause). One intriguing fact is that the auxiliary construction allows case alternations. Observe the following:

(59) a. 미미는   그   영화{-를/*-가}   보았다.
      Mimi-nun ku yenghwa-lul/*-ka po-ass-ta
      Mimi-TOP the movie-ACC/*NOM see-PST-DECL
      'Mimi has seen the movie.'
   b. 미미는   그   영화{-를/-가}   보고   싶다.
      Mimi-nun ku yenghwa-lul/ka po-ko siph-ta
      Mimi-TOP the movie-ACC/NOM see-CONN wish -DECL
      'Mimi would like to see the movie.'

The auxiliary 싶- *siph-* allows the case alternation of the NP object 영화 *yenghwa* 'movie.' This possibility can be easily accounted for if we assume that the main and auxiliary verbs form one complex predicate, behaving like one verb.

The complex predicate property of the main and auxiliary verbs can be further seen from syntactic cohesion. The two are cohesive and behave like one unit. For example, in the auxiliary construction, the main verb cannot be omitted, and the ordering relation cannot be changed:

(60) a. 미미는   어려움을   *(견뎌)   냈다.
      Mimi-nun elyewum-ul *(kyenti-e) nay-ss-ta
      Mimi-TOP difficulty-ACC overcome-CONN end-PST-DECL
      'Mimi has overcome the difficulties.'
   b. *미미는   어려움을   내어   견뎠다.
      *Mimi-nun elyewum-ul nay-e kyenti-ess-ta
      Mimi-TOP difficulty-ACC end-CONN overcome-PST-DECL

The tight syntactic cohesion between the main verb and the following auxiliary verb can also be observed because no expression can intervene between the two.

(61) a. 미미는   마마를   (정말)   떠나도록   (정말)   설득하였다.
      Mimi-nun Mama-lul (cengmal) ttena-tolok (cengmal) seltukha-yess-ta
      Mimi-TOP Mama-ACC really leave-CONN really persuade-PST-DECL
      'Mimi (really) persuaded Mary to (really) leave.'
   b. 미미는   사과를   (정말)   먹고   (*정말)   싶었다.
      Mimi-nun sakwa-lul (cengmal) mek-ko (*cengmal) siph-ess-ta
      Mimi-TOP apple-ACC really eat-CONN really like-PST-DECL
      'Mimi wants to really eat an apple.'

As such, unlike the typical VP complement construction in (61a), the auxiliary construction in (61b) displays tight syntactic cohesion.

To form complex predicates, languages like Korean allow the combination of two lexical verbs. This kind of combination is allowed by the Head-LEX (lexical) Rule:

(62) Head-LEX Rule:
     V → V, V[AUX +]

The construction rule specifies that the head V combines with another lexical expression. This rule, interacting with appropriate lexical entries for auxiliary verbs, allows the following structure:

(63)

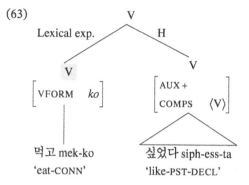

Note that the resulting combination forms a complex predicate and inherits the complement requirement of the main verb, as represented in the following general rule:

(64) Complex predicate formation constraint:
The complex predicate inherits the main verb's complement requirement.

This constraint allows the sentence in (65) to have the structure in (66):

(65) 미미가   사과를   [먹고   싶었다].
Mimi-ka   sakwa-lul   mek-ko   siph-ess-ta
Mimi-NOM apple-ACC eat-CONN would.like-PST-DECL
'Mimi always would like to eat apples.'

(66)

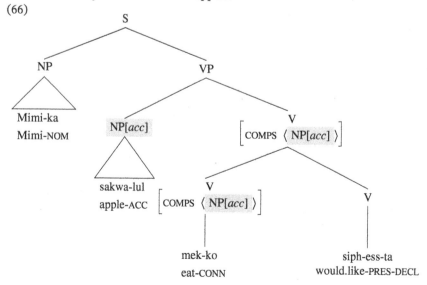

The auxiliary verb *siph-ess-ta* first combines with the main verb *mek-ko*, forming a complex predicate. This complex predicate inherits the complement requirement of the main verb *mek-ko*, which is why the resulting complex predicate can combine with the object *sakwa-lul*. This analysis also predicts that, as we saw in (57), there is no limit to the number of auxiliary verbs in Korean, as long as each auxiliary verb combines with a verb or verb complement with a proper VFORM value.

Consider the following example with more than one auxiliary verb:

(67)

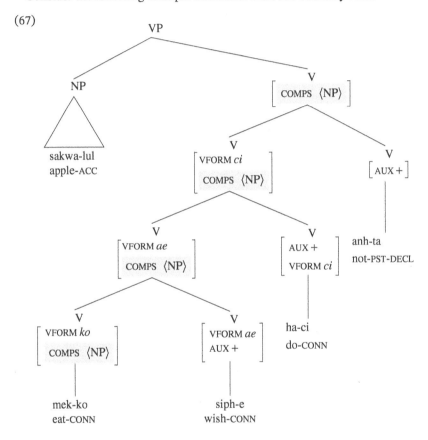

The bottom structure indicates that the auxiliary verb *siph-e* 'wish-CONN' forms a complex predicate by combining with the main verb *mek-ko* 'eat-CONN.' This complex predicate, which is still a LEX expression, inherits the main verb's COMPS value as well as the *ae* VFORM head feature from the auxiliary. Meanwhile, the auxiliary verb *ha-ci* also requires a LEX level expression with the VFORM value *ae*, legitimately combining with the preceding complex predicate. This combination again inherits the COMPS value. The final negative auxiliary then combines this complex predicate, yielding a final complex predicate that can combine with the object. Each combination makes a well-formed complex predicate allowed by the lexical projection of each auxiliary verb and the Head-LEX Rule.

7.3.4 Auxiliaries and Negation

The usual way to express sentence negation in Korean is to introduce the negative marker *an* or *mos* in the preverbal position and the negative auxiliary *anh-* in the postverbal position:

(68) SFN (short form negation)

    a. Kim-un an   ttena-ss-ta
       Kim-TOP not leave-PST-DECL
       'Kim did not leave.'

    b. Kim-un mos ttena-ss-ta
       Kim-TOP not   leave-PST-DECL
       'Kim could not leave.'

(69) LFN (long form negation)
    Kim-un   ttena-ci   anh-ass-ta
    Kim-TOP   leave-CONN not-PST-DECL
    'Kim did not leave.'

The SFN *an* and *mos* in (68) occurs in the preverbal position, and the LFN *anh-* follows the main verb marked with *-ci*, as given in (69). The position of the negator distinguishes the two forms, although they are essentially synonymous.

    The SFN *an* can be considered a special adverb or a prefix. But it has prefix-like properties, as seen in its inseparability from the verb root:

(70) a. cal   an ka-ss-ta
       well not go-PST-DECL

    b. *an cal   ka-ss-ta
       not well go-PST-DECL

If we accept the view that the true adverb *cal* and the negator *an* are both adverbs, we must account for why they have ordering restrictions with respect to each other, or we need to introduce a specific linear ordering constraint. The SFN thus has the following simple structure, where the negator plus the verb forms a verb:

(71)

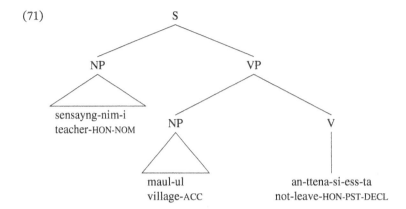

The LFN *anh-* is an auxiliary verb combining with a main verb, and the result is a complex predicate.

(72)

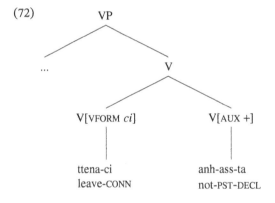

As given in this structure, the main verb must be marked with the connective marker *-ci*. The verb then combines with the auxiliary verb, forming a complex predicate.

7.4 Contrastive Notes

As we have seen, there are several main differences between English and Korean in describing when and how an event or situation occurs. The two languages have limited – and completely different – sets of auxiliary verbs. Auxiliary verbs in both languages contribute to the noncore sentential meaning but have different syntactic and semantic properties.

7.4.1 Syntactic Similarities and Differences

Auxiliary verbs in both languages have no independent syntactic status. English auxiliary verbs combine with a VP, but Korean auxiliary verbs combine with a main verb to form a complex predicate:

(73) a. Students [must [read the textbook]].
   b. 학생들은   교과서를   [읽어야   한다].
      haksayng-tul-un kyokwase-lul ilk-eya   ha-n-ta
      student-PL-TOP textbook-ACC read-CONN do-PRES-DECL
      'Students must read the textbook.'

In both languages, auxiliaries combine with a complement with a specific VFORM. The difference comes from the complement type. As given here, *must* combines with the VP *read the textbook*, whereas the auxiliary *ha-n-ta* in Korean combines with the main verb to form a complex predicate.

This structural difference leads to a visible difference between the two languages with respect to the behavior of auxiliary verbs. As noted, English auxiliary verbs allow the VP complement to be elided:

(74) a. Mimi can sing the song, and Momo can __.
   b. Mimi want to leave early, but Momo didn't want to __.

This kind of VP ellipsis or deletion thus allows auxiliary verbs to stand alone. However, Korean does not allow the auxiliary verb to stand alone:

(75) *미미가   사과를   먹고   싶었고,   모모도   싶었다.
   Mimi-ka   sakwa-lul mek-ko siph-ess-ko,   Momo-to   siph-ess-ta
   Mimi-NOM apple-ACC eat-CONN would.like-PST-and Momo-also like-PST-DECL
   '(int.) Mimi would like to eat apples, and Momo would, too.'

Korean does not allow the English-style VP ellipsis. Instead, it employs a VP-anaphor expression, similar to *do so* in English:

(76) 미미가   사과를   먹고
   Mimi-ka   sakwa-lul mek-ko
   Mimi-NOM apple-ACC eat-CONN

   싶었고,   모모도   그랬다.
   siph-ess-ko, Momo-to   kulay-ss-ta
   like-PST-and Momo-also do.so-PST-DECL
   'Mimi would like to eat apples, and Momo would also like to do so.'

The impossibility of the VP ellipsis in Korean is expected because the Korean auxiliary verb combines with its main verb, forming a verb-complex expression, as seen from the following:

(77) 모모도   사과를   [먹고   싶었다].
     Momo-to   sakwa-lul mek-ko   siph-ess-ta
     Momo-also apple-ACC eat-CONN would.like-PST-DECL
     'Momo would like to eat apples, too.'

7.4.2   Number of Auxiliary Verbs

We have noted that the number of auxiliary verbs allowed in English is limited. Because of the complement properties, the maximum number of auxiliary verbs in one sentence is four:

(78) a. Kim might have been being chased by the animal.
      b. Kim could have been being promoted.

This property is due to the restriction on the complement of each auxiliary verb. Modals are always finite and thus need to be first in the verb:

(79) a. *Kim had might left.
      b. *Kim has been could left alone.

The modals require a base VP, so only *have* and *be* can follow them.

(80) a. Kim could have left early.
      b. Kim could be left alone.
      c. *Kim could do leave the town.

The finite *do* or nonfinite *do* cannot follow a modal. Such restrictions on the complement form thus allow only four auxiliary verbs in one sentence.

However, in Korean, the number of auxiliary verbs is theoretically unlimited, as we have noted. Each auxiliary verb requires a main verb with a specific connected form. As long as this constraint is observed, we can have an unlimited number of auxiliary verbs in Korean.

7.4.3   Types of Auxiliary Verbs, and Expressing Modality

English auxiliary verbs are classified into four main categories: modal, *have/be, do*, and *to*. However, Korean auxiliary verbs have no such classification: there are 12 auxiliary types, depending on the meaning, or 5 types, depending on the connected form of the main verb they combine with.

We have seen that English auxiliaries include modals like *shall, can, will, may*, and *must*, expressing possibility, necessity, ability, obligation, and so forth. Korean auxiliary verbs include modals like *V-ya ha-ta* 'must' and *V-n po-ta* 'seem.' In Korean, modality is often expressed by a bound noun construction. For instance, possibility is expressed by the bound noun *swu*:

(81) 모모가　　책을　　읽을　　수　있다.
　　　Momo-ka　chayk-ul　ilk-ul　　swu　iss-ta
　　　Momo-NOM　book-ACC read-MOD BN　exist-DECL
　　　'Momo could read books.'

The English auxiliary verbs *have* and *be* often express aspectual information. Korean has an auxiliary verb *iss-ta* 'exist-DECL' to express an ongoing aspect, but it does not have any that correspond to *have* to express completion:

(82) 모모가　　책을　　읽고　　있다.
　　　Momo-ka　chayk-ul　ilk-ko　　iss-ta
　　　Momo-NOM　book-ACC read-CONN　exist-DECL
　　　'Momo is reading books.'

(83) a. Momo has read the book.
　　　b. 모모가　　책을　　읽었다.
　　　　 Momo-ka　chayk-ul　ilk-ess-ta
　　　　 Momo-NOM book-ACC read-PST-DECL
　　　　 'Momo has read the book.'

As illustrated here and noted earlier, the perfect situation in Korean is simply expressed by the past tense suffix *ess*.

7.5 Conclusion

This chapter has discussed the grammatical properties of auxiliary constructions in English and Korean, one of the main complex predicate constructions. The chapter first focused on the morphosyntactic properties of English auxiliary verbs. We showed that their distributional, ordering, and combinatorial properties follow from their lexical groupings and modals, *have/be, do*, and *to*. The chapter then discussed the properties of Korean auxiliary verbs. A key difference is that Korean auxiliary verbs have complex-predicate properties, calling for the introduction of a new combinatorial rule. This Head-LEX Rule allows an auxiliary verb to combine with a main verb. The system places no upper limit on the number of auxiliary verbs in a sentence.

Exercises

1 Draw syntactic trees for the following sentences, and provide the COMPS value of all the auxiliary verbs.

(i) a. You should buy a new car.
   b. I am writing a letter.
   c. I have written a letter.
   d. Mimi will soon leave the party.
   e. You might have told me about it!
   f. He must take his medicine three times a day.
   g. I can't lift that suitcase by myself.
   h. Kim has finished the project.
   i. Kim is singing the song.
   j. Kim is found by the student.
   k. Kim must have been being interrogated by the police.

2 Do the NICE-Tag tests for *need* and *dare* in the following, and decide whether each is an auxiliary verb or not.

(i) a. He needs to come with us.
   b. He need not come with us.
(ii) a. She dare not tell her to choose.
   b. She dared not return home.

3 Give syntactic trees for the following sentences. In doing so, give the COMPS value of the auxiliary verb as well as that of the complex predicate.

(i) a. 학생들이   문제를   하나씩   풀어   간다.
      haksayng-tul-i mwuncey-lul hana ssik phwul-e   ka-n-ta
      student-PL-TOP problem-ACC one.by.one solve-CONN go-PRES-DECL
      'The students are solving the problems one by one.'
   b. 경찰이   물건을   찾아   냈다.
      kyengchal-i mwulken-ul   chac-a   nay-ess-ta
      police-NOM   items-ACC   find-CONN   finish-PST-DECL
      'The police found the lost item.'
   c. 그 친구가   사과를   모두   먹어   버렸다.
      ku chinkwu-ka sakwa-lul   motwu   mek-e   pely-ess-ta
      the friend-NOM   apple-ACC   all   eat-CONN   finish-PST-DECL
      'The friend finished eating the apples.'
   d. 친구에게   무슨   일이   있나   보다.
      chinkwu-eykey mwusun   il-i   iss-na   po-ta
      friend-DAT   what   thing-NOM   exist-CONN maybe-DECL
      'Something might have happened to my friend.'

e. 학생들이   웃어   댄다.
   haksayng-tul-i   wus-e   tay-n-ta
   student-PL-NOM smile-CONN   on-PRES-DECL
   'The students continuously laughed.'

f. 미미가   빵을   먹곤   했다.
   Mimi-ka   ppang-ul   mek-kon   ha-yess-ta
   Mimi-NOM   bread-ACC   eat-CONN   used.to-PST-DECL
   'Mimi used to eat bread.'

g. 미미가   학교에   가야   한다.
   Mimi-ka   hakkyo-ey   ka-ya   ha-n-ta
   Mimi-NOM   school-to   go-CONN   must-PRES-DECL
   'Mimi has to go to school.'

4 Translate the following sentences into Korean. For the translated Korean sentences, give the glosses for each word. Then discuss the differences in expression modality in the two languages.

(i) a. I will get an A in this class.
   b. She should call you and give you another chance.
   c. He might arrive a bit later than I'd anticipated.
   d. This trip can take hours more than one expects.
   e. Would you like to have breakfast in bed?

5 We have seen that the Korean auxiliary verb forms a complex predicate with the preceding verb. This combination accompanies the process of argument composition, which inherits the main verb's argument structure – more precisely, the main verb's COMPS value. Consider the following data focusing on the case-marking value (NOM and ACC) of the object complement:

(i) a. 미미가   사과*가/를   먹었다.
   Mimi-ka   sakwa-*ka/lul   mek-ess-ta
   Mimi-NOM   apple-NOM/ACC   eat-PST-DECL
   'Mimi ate an apple.'

   b. 미미가   사과가/를   먹고   싶었다.
   Mimi-ka   sakwa-ka/lul   mek-ko   siph-ess-ta
   Mimi-NOM   apple-NOM/ACC   eat-CONN   wish-PST-DECL
   'Mimi would like to eat apples.'

Draw tree structures of these two sentences, providing the COMPS value for the main and auxiliary verbs. In addition, give any observations you can make. Can your observations also be applied to the following? State why or why not.

(ii) a. 미미가　　모모-가/*를　　좋다.
     Mimi-ka　　Momo-ka/*lul　　coh-ta
     Mimi-NOM　Momo-NOM/ACC　fond-DECL
     'Mimi likes Momo.'

  b. 미미가　　모모-를/*가　　좋아　　한다.
     Mimi-ka　　Momo-lul/*ka　　coh-a　　ha-n-ta
     Mimi-NOM　Momo-ACC/NOM　fond-CONN　do-CONN　do-PST-DECL
     'Mimi likes Momo.'

6 Try to figure out two different meanings of the negation *not* in English and *anh-* in Korean in the following sentences. For English, test the two readings with the formation of a tag question. For Korean, test the two readings by adding one or more sentences describing what would happen after eating the apples.

  (i) a. The president could not veto the bill.
    b. 미미가　　사과를　　모두　　먹지　　않았다.
       Mimi-ka　　sakwa-lul　motwu　mek-ci　anh-ass-ta
       Mimi-NOM　apple-ACC　all　　　eat-CONN　not-PST-DECL

7 Unlike in English, modality in Korean can be represented by a bound noun like 수 'swu,' as illustrated in the following. Discuss grammatical modality in these constructions and any grammatical properties you can observe in these three sentences. In addition, construct three more Korean sentences that express modality.

  (i) a. 미미가　　사과를　　　　먹을　　수　　있다.
      Mimi-ka　　sakwa-lul　　　mek-ul　swu　iss-ta
      Mimi-NOM　apple-NOM/ACC　eat-CONN　BN　　exist-DECL
      'Mimi can eat an apple.'

    b. 미미가　　사과를　　　　먹는　　듯　　하다.
      Mimi-ka　　sakwa-lul　　　mek-nun　tus　ha-ta
      Mimi-NOM　apple-NOM/ACC　eat-MOD　　BN　do-DECL
      'Mimi seems to eat an apple.'

    c. 미미가　　사과를　　　　먹을　　것　이다.
      Mimi-ka　　sakwa-lul　　　mek-ul　kes　i-ta
      Mimi-NOM　apple-NOM/ACC　eat-MOD　KES-COP-DECL
      'Mimi may eat an apple.'

8

Passive: Performing an Action or Being Acted Upon

8.1 Introduction

As we saw in the previous chapters, main and auxiliary verbs can express tense, aspect, and mood information. In addition, they can express a "voice" that describes the relationship between the situation described by the main verb and the participants (arguments) in the situation. Compare the following two sentences:

(1) a. Pat changed the flat tire.
    b. The flat tire was changed by Pat.

In both sentences, we have two participants (Pat and the flat tire) referred to by the subject and object (arguments) of the main verb *change*. The difference comes from the semantic role of the subject: in (1a), the subject is Pat, who functions as an agent or doer of the action; in (1b), the subject is a patient or undergoer of the action. The former is said to be in active voice, and the latter is in passive voice.

Korean verbs can also express active and passive voices:

(2) a. 경찰이   도둑을   잡았다.
       kyengchal-i totwuk-ul cap-ass-ta
       police-NOM thief-ACC catch-PST-DECL
       'The police caught the thief.'
    b. 도둑이   경찰에   잡히었다.
       totwuk-i   kyengchal-ey cap-hi-ess-ta
       thief-NOM police-by   catch-PASS-PST-DECL
       'The thief was caught by the police.'

The subject *the police* in (2a) performs the action, but the subject in (2b) is affected by the action. This active and passive distinction is marked by the verb: there is no specific active voice marker, but the *-hi* suffix in (2b) represents the passive marker.

English and Korean in Contrast: A Linguistic Introduction, First Edition. Jong-Bok Kim.
© 2024 John Wiley & Sons, Inc. Published 2024 by John Wiley & Sons, Inc.

In this chapter, we will discuss how English and Korean express active and passive voices and the two languages' grammatical similarities and differences.

8.2 English Passive Constructions

8.2.1 Canonical Passive

Promoting the Active Object as the Passive Subject

Let us consider two typical examples of active and passive voice in English.

(3) a. Kim threw the ball.
    b. The ball was thrown (by Kim).

In (3a), the verb *threw* is a transitive verb with *Kim* as its subject and *the ball* as its direct object. If we recast the verb in the passive voice (*was thrown*), *the ball* becomes the subject (it is "promoted" to the subject position) and *Kim* can be removed; the original "demoted" subject can be optionally expressed with the preposition *by*. The canonical use of passive is thus to map a clause with a direct object to a corresponding clause where the direct object is promoted to the subject.

"Be" + Passive Verb Form

In addition to promoting the direct object to the subject in passive, there is an important change in the verb form. The verb is in the passive (*-en*) form and combines with the auxiliary verb *be*. When there is another auxiliary verb, this auxiliary verb remains intact, although its form can be changed:

(4) a. Kim will finish the project.
    b. The project will be finished (by Kim).

(5) a. Kim will have finished the project.
    b. The project will have been finished (by Kim).

Other Intact Complements

Verbs can have other complements in addition to an object. For instance, the PP in the following is an oblique complement selected by the verb:

(6) a. Mimi taught English to the students. → English was taught to the students (by Mimi).
    b. Mimi blamed her friends for the failure. → Her friends were blamed for the failure.

In each case, the active object is promoted to the passive subject, but the PP complement is intact. This means complement(s) other than the object remain intact in passive.

In sum, passive has the following basic properties:

- Passive turns the active object into the passive subject.
- Passive leaves other aspects of the complement (COMPS) value of the active verb unchanged.
- Passive optionally allows the active subject to be the object of a PP headed by *by*.
- Passive makes the appropriate morphological change in the form of the main verb and requires that this verb be the complement of the auxiliary verb *be*.

Traditionally, these rules for the formation of passive are presented in terms of structural description (SD) and structural change (SC):

(7) Passive Formation Rule (approximation):

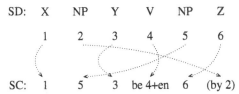

$$\begin{array}{ccccccc} \text{SD:} & \text{X} & \text{NP} & \text{Y} & \text{V} & \text{NP} & \text{Z} \\ & 1 & 2 & 3 & 4 & 5 & 6 \\ \\ \text{SC:} & 1 & 5 & 3 & \text{be 4+en} & 6 & \text{(by 2)} \end{array}$$

This rule means if anything fits the SD in (7), it will be changed into the given SC: that is, if we have any string in the order "X – NP – Y – V – NP – Z" (where X, Y, and Z are variables), the order can be changed to "X – NP – Y – be – V+en – Z – by NP'." For example, consider the following example:

(8) Luckily, Kim has thrown the ball to the friend. →
    Luckily, the ball has been thrown to the friend (by Kim).

The active object *the ball* is promoted to the subject in passive, and the active subject *Kim* is demoted to the optional PP. This change accompanies the change of the verb *thrown* into *been thrown*. All the remaining expressions are intact.

Note that it is possible to promote even a CP that serves as a direct object. In this case, however, the clause typically appears not to change its position in the sentence, and an expletive *it* takes the normal subject position. This is due to the process of extraposing the clause to the final sentence position:

(9) a. They say that he left. → That he left is said.
    b. That he left is said. → It is said that he left.

This means we need to allow not only an NP object but also a sentential object (CP) to be promoted to the subject in passive.

Another point to note is that not all transitive verbs can undergo passivization.

(10) a. The woman resembled Jackie.
   b. *Jackie was resembled by the woman.

The verb *resembled* is a transitive taking a subject and an object, but it has no passive form. The main reason is that the object NP does not bear the semantic role of patient or undergoer. That is, the promoted subject of a passive needs to be affected by the action denoted by the verb. There are also cases where verbs are used only in the passive voice:

(11) a. He was rumored to be a war veteran. → *[Someone] rumored him to be a war veteran.
   b. It was rumored that he was a war veteran. → *[Someone] rumored that he was a war veteran.

As noted, the verb *rumor* is used only in the passive voice, with its active counterpart falling out of use possibly because it has only a passive meaning.

These facts indicate that we may not refer to the structural descriptions but instead refer to lexical properties in figuring out when to have passive counterparts. That is, the formation of passive can be better treated by a lexical rule:

(12) Passive Rule:
   The object of an active transitive verb is promoted as the subject of a passive verb (whose VFORM value is *pass*), and its agent subject is demoted to an optional PP[*by*] complement. All the other arguments remain intact.

For instance, consider the active verb *send*. This verb has three arguments, participants in the situation of *sending*: agent, patient, and goal. This is represented with the so-called argument structure:

(13) Argument structure of the active verb *send*
   send: <NP[*agt*], NP[*pt*], PP[*goal*]> (agt=agent, pt=patient)

This allows sentences like *They send her to Seoul*, where the subject *they* is an "agent" performing the action, and the object *her* is a "patient" affected by this action. We can apply the passive rule in (12) to this active verb, yielding the following:

(14) Argument structure of the passive verb *send*
   sent: <NP[*pt*], PP[*goal*], (PP[*by*]) >

This passive verb, morphologically marked with the *-en* suffix, now has a patient subject (promoted from the active object), a goal PP complement, and an optional PP complement (demoted from the active subject).

This output lexical entry can then be embedded as shown in the following structure:

(15)

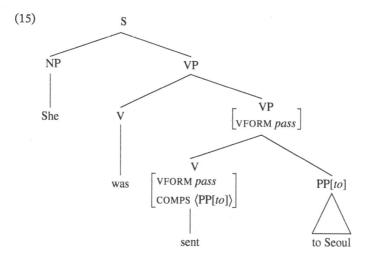

As shown in (15), the passive *sent* combines with its PP[*to*] complement. This VP functions as the complement of the auxiliary verb *was*. The active subject is demoted as an optional PP complement, so it need not appear.

Note that the analysis does not allow verbs like *resemble* or *remain* to be passive:

(16) a. Mimi resembled Momo.
     b. Mimi remained a good friend of many.

These verbs seem to combine with an NP, but the NP *Momo* and *a good friend of many* cannot be promoted as the passive subject because they do not bear the semantic role of "patient."

8.2.2 Prepositional Passive

English allows prepositional verbs to be passivized, as illustrated in the following:

(17) a. You can *rely on* Ben.
     b. Ben can be *relied on*.

(18) a. They *talked about* the scandal for days.
     b. The scandal was *talked about* for days.

As noted here, the prepositional object *Ben* and *the scandal* in the active sentence can function as the subject of the passive sentence. Notice that such pseudo-passives (often called prepositional passives) are possible with the verbs selecting a PP:

(19) a. The plan was *approved of* by my mother. (My mother approved of the plan.)

   b. The issue was *dealt with* promptly. (They dealt with the issue promptly.)
   c. That's not what's being *asked for*. (That's not what they are asking for.)

(20) a. *Boston was *flown to*. (They flew to/near/by Boston.)
   b. *The capital was *gathered near* by a crowd of people. (A crowd of people gathered near/at the capital.)
   c. *The hot sun was *played under* by the children. (The children played under/near the hot sun.)

The prepositions in (19) are all selected by the main verbs (no other prepositions can replace them). Meanwhile, the prepositions in (20) are not selected by the main verb, as attested to by the possibility of being replaced by another preposition in the active.

   The issues become more complicated when considering cases where the prepositional object of the unspecified PP can be promoted as the subject of a passive sentence:

(21) a. This bed was slept in. (He slept in this bed.)
   b. My hat has been sat on. (He has sat on my hat.)
   c. The bridge has already been flown under. (He has already flown under the bridge.)

Verbs like *sleep, sit* and *fly* require no specified PP, as can be observed from the possibility of replacing the following preposition with another one:

(22) a. Kim slept in/under/beside the bed.
   b. Kim sat on/under/behind the hat.
   c. The airplane flew under/over/beside the bridge.

   We could assume that the PP here is not selected by the verb, but the promoted subject of the passive bears the semantic role of patient. This is why examples like (21) are licensed.

   In terms of the structure for prepositional passive, we can assume that the intransitive forms a unit with the following preposition, similar to complex predicate formation in Korean:

(23)

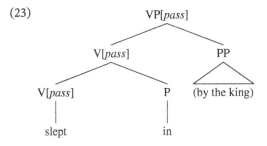

This structure differs from (22) in that the passive verb and the preposition form a constituent (the "reanalysis"). Both (22) and (23) capture the coherence between the prepositional verb and the preposition. This combination is allowed by the Head-LEX Rule we saw in Chapter 7:

(24) Head-LEX Rule:
    V → V, X[LEX +]

The only specifications are that the verb is a passive verb with the *en* suffix and the second expression is a preposition with the feature LEX (LEX assigned to the sentential negation *not*, preposition, and particle). An advantage of this grammar rule is for the pseudo-passive with a particle. We have seen that *off* in the following two examples functions as a particle:

(25) a. He took his shoes off.
     b. He took off his shoes.

The passive of these two active sentences would be something like the following:

(26) His shoes were taken off.

The following would be its partial structure:

(27)

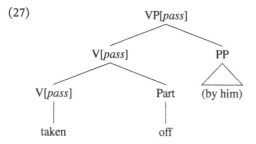

The passive verb *taken* and the particle *off* are combined based on the Head-LEX Rule.

8.2.3 Semantic and Pragmatic Constraints

As noted, for an active object to be promoted to the passive subject, it needs to function as a patient that is affected by the action described by the main verb. This kind of semantic/pragmatic constraint holds in many cases. Consider the following contrast:

(28) a. *Six inches were grown by the boy.
     b. *A pound was weighed by the book.

(29) a. The beans were grown by the gardener.
     b. The plums were weighed by the greengrocer.

The main difference between the possible and impossible examples here is that the individual referred to by the passive subject is acted on by an agent. That is, the passive subject is physically or psychologically affected by the action performed by the agent. For example, six inches cannot be affected by the action performed by the agent; but beans are under the direct influence of the action denoted by the gardener.

Thus, in forming passive voice, the promoted subject needs to be affected by the action represented by an (overt or unexpressed) agent. We can also observe that this "affectedness" condition is also a major constraint in the pseudo-passive:

(30) a. *San Francisco has been lived in by my brother.
    b. The house has been lived in by several famous personages.

(31) a. *Seoul was slept in by the businessman last night.
    b. This bed was surely slept in by a huge guy last night.

In (30a), San Francisco is just a location that cannot be affected by a person's living there. On the other hand, the house in (30b) can be affected by the action of "several famous personages" living there. In addition, it is hard to imagine that Seoul in (31a) is affected by the action of sleeping in it, but the bed in (31b) can be considered affected by the sleeping action.

8.2.4 Adjectivals and *Get*-Passive

Consider the following example:

(32) She was relieved to find her car undamaged.

Here, *relieved* is an ordinary adjective, although it derives from the past participle of *relieve*, and that past participle may be used in canonical passives:

(33) a. He was relieved of duty.
    b. He was very satisfied with the outcome.

Adjectival passives typically have no optional agent PP:

(34) a. I am satisfied with the service at my bank.
    b. She was worried about what people would think.

An adjectival passive can be distinguished from a true passive because the past participial adjective can be modified by a degree adverb or adverbial like *very* or *pretty*:

(35) a. She was very worried about her job review.
    b. I am pretty disgusted with my internet service provider.

Unlike adjectival passives with a stative meaning, there is another type of passive introduced by the verb *get*. Consider the following pair:

(36) a. You must come back in spring to see them. The man did; he was fired.
    b. He got fired by the liberals and rehired by Fox.

The *be* passive in (36a) and *get*-passive in (36b) both describe a situation in which an employer fired someone. Note that *be* and *get* passives are not always interchangeable, as illustrated in the following (Huddleston and Pullum 2002):

(37) a. Kim was/*got seen to leave the lab with Dr. Smith.
    b. He saw Kim get/*be mauled by my brother's dog.

In (37a), the head verb must be *be*, whereas in (37b) the head verb can only be *get*.

The *get*-passive typically focuses on what happened as the result of the action described by the participial complement predicate, and the subject referent of the *get*-passive is necessarily understood to have been affected by the action. This could account for the fact that the *get*-passive is often found with dynamic verbs describing the action in question. The predicates typically used in the *get*-passive are nonstative verbs like *caught, paid, done, dressed, fired, tested, picked, thrown, killed*, and *asked*. It is not natural for the complement of *get* to be a stative participle:

(38) a. It was/*got believed that the letter was a forgery.
    b. He is/*got feared by most of the staff.
    c. The teacher was/*got liked by everybody.

Perception verbs like *believe, fear* and *like* are difficult to construe as change-of-state verbs. Note that the effect conveyed by a *get*-passive sentence need not be negative:

(39) a. He got promoted multiple times.
    b. The story got published and won some recognition.

As shown by such examples, the *get*-passive is characteristically used in clauses involving adversity, but it can also describe a beneficial situation.

There is another key morphosyntactic difference between the status of *be* and *get*. Whereas the verb *be* is a typical auxiliary, *get* is not. This can be observed from the NICE properties discussed in Chapter 8:

(40) a. He was not fired by the company.
    b. Was he fired by the company?
    c. He wasn't fired by the company.
    d. John was fired by the company, and Bill was too.

(41) a. *He got not fired by the company.
    b. *Got he fired by the company?
    c. *He gotn't fired by the company.
    d. *John was fired by the company, and Bill got too.

As seen from the contrast here, the passive verb *got* fails every test for auxiliary status: the verb cannot have sentential negation following (41a), cannot undergo auxiliary inversion (41b), has no contracted form (41c), and cannot elide the following VP (41d). The possible alternatives are those in which the verb *get* is used as a lexical verb:

(42) a. He didn't get fired by the company.
    b. Did he get fired by the company?
    c. He didn't get fired by the company.
    d. John got fired by the company, and Bill did too.

These data indicate that the passive *get* is not an auxiliary verb. The *get*-passive verb thus does not bear the feature AUX but requires a passive VP as its complement. The following is a simple structure with the passive verb *get*:

(43)

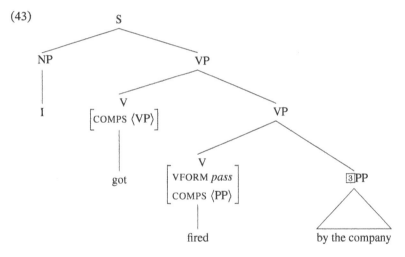

As seen in (43), *got* combines with the passive VP headed by the verb *fired*.

8.3 Korean Passive Constructions

8.3.1 Lexical and Syntactic Passives

Unlike English, Korean has two main types of passive, lexical and syntactic:

(44) Lexical passive
    a. 경찰이   범인을   잡았다.
       kyengchal-i pemin-ul   cap-ass-ta
       police-NOM criminal-ACC arrest-PST-DECL
       'The police arrested the criminal.'

b. 범인이　　　　경찰에게　　　　잡혔다.
pemin-i　　　　kyengchal-eykey　cap-hi-ess-ta
criminal-NOM　police-DAT　　　　catch-PASS-PST-DECL
'The criminal was arrested by the police.'

(45) Syntactic passive

a. 아이가　　　옷을　　　　심하게　　　찢었다.
ai-ka　　　　os-ul　　　　simhakey　ccic-ess-ta
child-NOM　clothes-ACC　severely　tear-PST-DECL
'The child tore the clothes severely.'

b. 옷이　　　　　심하게　　　찢어　　　지었다.
os-i　　　　　simhakey　　ccic-e　　　ci-ess-ta
clothes-NOM　severely　　tear-CONN　become-PST-DECL
'The clothes were severely torn.'

In lexical passive (44b), the addition of the passive morpheme -히 -*hi* to the predicate promotes the active object into the passive subject and also demotes the active subject into the passive oblique argument. Meanwhile, in syntactic passive (45b), the promotion and demotion of the arguments are triggered by the passive auxiliary 지다 *ci-ta*. The active main verb 찢- *ccic-* 'tear' is intact, other than the attachment of the connective marker -어 -*e*.

Lexical passive is realized with one of the passive morphemes, -이 -*i*, -히 -*hi*, 리 -*li*, and -기 -*ki*. The following are some of the lexical passive verbs:

(46) a. 이 -*i*:
보다 po-ta 'see-DECL'/보이다 po-i-ta 'see-PASS-DECL,' 차다 cha-ta 'kick-DECL'/차이다 cha-i-ta 'kick-PASS-DECL,' 바꾸다 pakku-ta 'change-DECL'/바꿔다 pakku-i-ta 'change-PASS-DECL'

b. 히 -*hi*:
잡다 cap-ta 'catch-DECL'/잡히다 cap-hi-ta 'catch-PASS-DECL,' 꼬집다 kkocip-ta 'pinch-DECL' /꼬집히다 kkocip-hi-ta 'pinch-PASS-DECL,' 뒤집다 twicip-ta 'turn.over-DECL'/뒤집히다 twichip-hi-ta 'turn.over-PASS-DECL'

c. 리 -*li*:
밀다 mil-ta 'push-DECL'/밀리다 mil-li-ta 'push-PASS-DECL,' 흔들다 huntul-ta 'shake-DECL'/흔들리다 huntul-li-ta 'shake-PASS-DECL,' 팔다 phal-ta 'sell-DECL'/팔리다 phal-li-ta 'sell-PASS-DECL'

d. 기 -*ki*:
감다 kam-ta 'wind-DECL'/감기다 kam-ki-ta 'wind-PASS-DECL,' 씻다 ssis-ta 'wash-DEL'/씻기다 ssis-ki-ta 'wash-PASS-DECL,' 안다 an-ta 'hug-DECL'/안기다 an-ki-ta 'hug-PASS-DECL'

These lexical passive verbs allow examples like the following:

(47) a. 글씨가   잘   보인다.
     kulssi-ka cal po-i-n-ta
     letter-NOM well see-PASS-PRES-DECL
     '(lit.) The letters are seen well.'

  b. 범인이   경찰에게   잡혔다.
     pemin-i   kyengchal-eykey cap-hi-ess-ta
     criminal-NOM police-DAT   catch-PASS-PST-DECL
     'The criminal was arrested by the police.'

  c. 차가   많이   밀린다.
     cha-ka   manhi mil-li-n-ta
     car-NOM a.lot push-PASS-PRES-DECL
     '(lit.) Cars are pushed a lot.' (There is a heavy traffic.)

Note that lexical passive is quite restricted and unproductive because not all transitive verbs can have lexical passive. For instance, the following transitive verbs have no lexical passive verbs:

(48) a. ditransitive: 주- *cwu-* 'give,' 드리- *tuli-* 'give,' 바치- *pachi-* 'give,' 넣- *neh-* 'put,' ...

  b. benefactive: 얻- *et-* 'obtain,' 만들- *mantul-* 'make,' 잃- *ilh-* 'lose,' 돕- *top-* 'help,' ...

  c. experience: 알- *al-* 'know,' 배우- *paywu-* 'learn,' 바라- *pala-* 'wish,' ...

  d. symmetric: 만나- *manna-* 'meet,' 닮- *talm-* 'resemble,' ...

Also notice that some words do not have lexical passive, unlike their synonyms. For example, the verb *tam-ta* 'fill-DECL' has the lexical passive *tam-ki-ta* 'put-PASS-DECL,' but its synonymous verb *neh-ta* 'put' does not have a lexical passive. There are even lexical passive verbs with no corresponding active verbs:

(49) a. 날씨가   풀렸다.
     nalssi-ka   phul-li-ess-ta
     weather-NOM   dissolve-PASS-PST-DECL
     '(lit.) The weather was dissolved.'

  b. *kupwun-inalssi-lul   phul-ess-ta
     the man   weather-ACCdissolve-PST-DECL

In Korean, there are about 300 lexically passivized verbs. Even though it is linguistically reasonable to develop a system that can link or derive lexically passive verbs from their active counterparts, their lexical idiosyncrasies and complex constraints offset the advantages: a more feasible way is to list these idiosyncratic lexical passives in the lexicon. However, syntactic passives formed with an auxiliary verb like *ci-ta* 'become-DECL' are productive, calling for an analysis that can systematically generate or link syntactic passives to their active counterparts.

Since even in the lexical passive, the subject is promoted from the active object, we can have a rule similar to the English one in (50), leaving aside other constraints to select the proper passive suffix:

(50) Passive Rule in Korean:
The object of an active transitive verb is promoted as the patient subject of a passive verb (marked with a suffixed *i/hi/li/ki*), and its subject is demoted to an optional NP[*eykey/uyhay*] complement. All the other arguments remain intact.

For instance, the active verb of 잡-다 *cap-ta* 'catch-DECL' undergoes this process:

(51) Argument structure of the active verb *cap-ta* 'catch'
cap- 'catch': <NP[*agt*], NP[*pt*] >

(52) Argument structure of the passive verb
cap-hi 'catch-PASS': <NP[*pt*], (NP[*eykey/uyhay*])>

The active verb *cap-ta* 'catch' has an agent subject and a patient object. Its passive verb then has a patient subject (promoted from the object) and an optional NP complement marked with either *eykey* or *uyhay*. This passive verb allows a structure like the following:

(53)

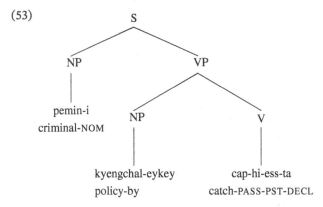

The passive verb *cap-hi-ess-ta* first combines with the optional complement NP *kyengchal-eykey*, and the resulting VP combines with the patient subject *pemin-i* 'criminal-NOM.'

8.3.2 Typical Syntactic Passives

As just discussed, the lexical verb involves only the passive suffix. In addition to this lexica passive, Korean allows syntactic passive with the auxiliary verb

지 다 *ci-ta*, similar to the auxiliary verb *be* in English. Consider the following active/passive pairs:

(54) a. 학생들이   바지를   찢었다.
　　　haksayng-tul-i   paci-lul   ccic-ess-ta
　　　student-PL-NOM   pants-ACC   tear-PST-DECL
　　　'Students tore trousers.'
　　b. 바지가   찢어   졌다
　　　paci-ka   ccic-e   ci-ess-ta
　　　pants-NOM tear-CONN become-PST-DECL
　　　'The trousers were torn.'

(55) a. 현대가   그 자동차를   미국에서   만들었다.
　　　Hyundai-ka   ku catongcha-lul mikwuk-eyse mantul-ess-ta
　　　Hyundai-NOM the car-ACC   America-LOC   make-PST-DECL
　　　'Hyundai made the car in America.'
　　b. 그 자동차가   미국에서   만들어   졌다.
　　　ku catongcha-ka   mikwuk-eyse mantul-e   ci-ess-ta
　　　the car-NOM   America-LOC make-CONN become-PST-DECL
　　　'The car was made in America.'

(56) a. 선생님이   학생들에게   숙제를   주었다.
　　　sensayng-nim-i   haksayng-tul-eykey swukcey-lul   cwu-ess-ta
　　　teacher-HON-NOM student-PL-DAT   homework-ACC give-PST-DECL
　　　'The teacher gave homework to the students.'
　　b. 학생들에게   숙제가   주어   졌다.
　　　haksayng-tul-eykey swukcey-ka   cwu-e   ci-ess-ta
　　　student-PL-DAT   homework-NOM give-CONN become-PST-DECL
　　　'Homework was given to the students.'

In terms of the propositional meaning, the active in (a) and its corresponding passive examples in (b) here are identical. One main difference is how the arguments are realized in the syntax: the active object is the passive subject, and the active subject is optionally unrealized. As seen from (55b) and (56b), the remaining locative or dative argument in the active are unchanged in the passive. These are similar to English passive.

In English, we have seen that the passive verb must be in a specific verb form (VFORM). Korean has a similar requirement. The passive auxiliary *ci-ta*, counterpart to the English *be*, requires its main verb to be marked with the connective marker -아/어 *-a/e* ([VFORM *ae*]).

(57) 바지가   찢어/*고/*야 졌다
　　　paci-ka   ccic-e/*ko/*ya ci-ess-ta
　　　pants-NOM tear-CONN   become-PST-DECL
　　　'The trousers were torn.'

Because the passive verb *ci-ta* is also an auxiliary verb, we expect the same situation, as given in the following lexical information:

(58) Lexical information of the passive auxiliary *ci-ta*:

$$\begin{bmatrix} \text{AUX} + \\ \text{COMPS} \left\langle \text{V[VFORM } ae] \right\rangle \end{bmatrix}$$

This lexical information ensures that the passive auxiliary verb *ci-ta* combines with a main verb bearing the [VFORM *ae*] feature:

(59)

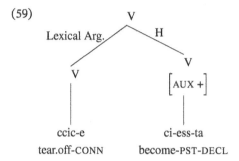

The structure allows the auxiliary verb 겼다 *ci-ess-ta* to combine with its lexical complement, the main verb 찢어 *ccic-e* 'tear-CONN.' This combination is allowed by the Head-LEX Rule, forming a complex predicate.

(60)

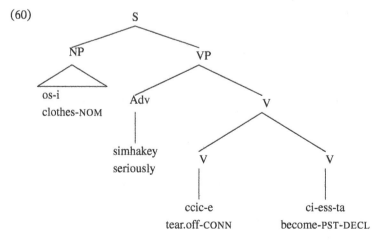

As given in the structure, the main verb and the passive auxiliary verb form a verbal complex. This is modified by the adverb, forming a head-modifier phrase. The resulting VP becomes a full sentence when combined with the subject *os-i* 'clothes-NOM.' This complex-predicate treatment gives us a simple way to capture the syntactic cohesion between the main verb and the passive auxiliary. The intervention of an adverb between the two is disallowed:

(61) *바지들이   [찢어   [많이   졌다]].
     *paci-tul-i   [ccic-e   [manhi   ci-ess-ta]]
     pants-PL-NOM tear-CONN much   become-PST-DECL
     'The trousers were torn a lot.'

The analysis also explains the changes in the main verb's subcategorization requirement even though it is in the same active form. Our analysis will not generate examples like (62b):

(62) a. 아이가   병을   깼다.
        ai-ka   pyeng-ul   kkay-ess-ta
        child-NOM bottle-ACC break-PST-DECL
        'The child broke the bottle.'

   b. *아이가   병을   깨어   졌다.
      *ai-ka   pyeng-ul   kkay-e   ci-ess-ta
      child-NOM bottle-ACC break-CONN become-PST-DECL

   c. 병이   깨어   졌다.
      pyeng-i   kkay-e   ci-ess-ta
      bottle-NOM break-CONN   become-PST-DECL
      'The bottle was broken.'

   d. 아이가   병을   깨어   버렸다.
      ai-ka   pyeng-ul   kkay-e   peli-ess-ta
      child-NOM bottle-ACC break-CONN happen-PST-DECL
      'The child happened to break the bottle.'

The active sentence (62a) can be linked to its auxiliary passive (62c): the active object functions as the passive subject in the latter, enforced by the passive auxiliary *ci-ess-ta*. This explains why (62b) is ungrammatical: the auxiliary verb indicates that the sentence involved is passive, but it still has the active subject and object. However, a nonpassive auxiliary verb like *peli-ess-ta* 'happen-PST-DECL' in (62d) does not trigger such a change in the subcategorization requirement.

8.3.3 Light-Verb Pseudo-Syntactic Passive

In addition to the syntactic passive with the auxiliary verb *ci-*, Korean also allows the formation of passive-like constructions with light verbs such as 되- *toy-*

'become,' 당하- *tangha-* 'suffer,' and 받- *pat-* 'receive' when they combine with a verbal noun (VN). Consider the following active examples with a VN (the case marking on the VN is optional):

(63) a. 친구들이   모모를   모욕(을)   했다.
    chinkwu-tul-i   Momo-lul   moyok-(ul)   ha-yess-ta
    friend-PL-NOM   Momo-ACC   insult-ACC   do-PST-DECL
    '(His) friends insulted Momo.'

    b. 친구들이   모모를   존경(을)   했다.
    chinkwu-tul-i   Momo-lul   conkyeng-(ul)   ha-yess-ta
    friend-PL-NOM   Momo-ACC   respect-ACC   do-PST-DECL
    'Friends respected Momo.'

    c. 경찰이   모모를   체포(를)   했다.
    kyengchal-i   Momo-lul   cheypho-(lul)   ha-yess-ta
    police-NOM   Momo-ACC   arrest-ACC   do-PST-DECL
    'The police arrested Momo.'

These examples include the VNs 모욕 *moyok* 'insult,' 존경 *conkyeng* 'respect,' and 체포 *cheypho* 'arrest,' each of which combines with the light verb 하다 *ha-ta* 'do-DECL.' The VNs here have the object 모모 Momo, implying that the sentences can be passivized. However, in such cases, the language uses a different passive structure, as given in the following:

(64) a. 모모가   친구들에게   모욕(을)   당했다.
    Momo-ka   chinkwu-tul-eykey   moyok-(ul)   tangha-yess-ta
    Momo-NOM   friend-PL-DAT   insult-ACC   suffer-PST-DECL
    'Momo was insulted by his friends.'

    b. 모모가   친구들에게   존경(을)   받았다.
    Momo-ka   chinkwu-tul-eykey   conkyeng-(ul)   pat-ass-ta
    Momo-NOM   friend-PL-DAT   respect-ACC   receive-PST-DECL
    'Momo received respect from his friends.'

    c. 모모가   경찰에게   체포(가)   되었다.
    Momo-ka   kyengchal-eykey   cheypho-(ka)   toy-ess-ta
    Momo-NOM   police-DAT   arrest-NOM   become-PST-DECL
    'Momo was arrested by the police.'

The passive examples here have the promoted subject from the active object in (63), whereas the active subject is demoted as an oblique argument (friends and police). In addition to this promotion and demotion of the active object and subject, the light verb includes 당하다 tangha-ta 'suffer-DECL,' 받다 pat-ta 'receive-DECL,' 되다 toy-ta 'become-DECL.'

There remain issues with treating these as canonical passive, but they have passive properties. For example, in this type of pseudo-VN-passive, we cannot have the agent subject:

(65) a. *친구들이   김을   모욕(을)   당했다.
　　　 chinkwu-tul-i Kim-ul   moyok-(ul) tangha-yess-ta
　　　 friend-PL-NOM Kim-ACC insult-ACC   suffer-PST-DECL

　　 b. *친구들이   김을   존경(을)   받았다.
　　　 chinkwu-tul-i Kim-ul   conkyeng-(ul) pat-ass-ta
　　　 friend-PL-NOM Kim-ACC respect-ACC   receive-PST-DECL

　　 c. *경찰이   김을   체포(를)   되었다.
　　　 kyengchal-i Kim-ul   cheypho-(lul) toy-ess-ta
　　　 police-NOM Kim-ACC arrest-ACC   become-PST-DECL

This implies that in the pseudo-passive, like the auxiliary passive verb 지다 ci-ta, these light verbs change the subcategorization requirement of the VNs so that they can select a patient subject and an optional agentive oblique argument.

Note that there are semantic constraints on the kinds of VNs the light verbs *toy-* 'become,' *pat-* 'receive,' and *tangha-* 'suffer' can combine with. Although we cannot do justice to all semantic and pragmatic constraints here, the major constraints have to do with the properties of the subject of each light verb. The subject of *tangha-* 'suffer' tends to undergo adversity:

(66) a. *물리학이   연구   당했다.
　　　 mullihak-i   yenkwu   tangha-yess-ta
　　　 physics-NOM study   suffer-PST-DECL
　　　 'Physics was studied.'

　　 b. *김이   사장에게   용서   당했다.
　　　 Kim-i   sacang-eykey yongse   tangha-yess-ta
　　　 Kim-NOM   president-DAT forgiveness suffer-PST-DECL
　　　 'Kim was forgiven by the president.'

(67) a. 도시가   폭격을   당했다.
　　　 tosi-ka   phokkyek-ul tangha-yess-ta
　　　 city-NOM   bomb-ACC   suffer-PST-DECL
　　　 'The city was bombed.'

b. 사무실이   검색을   당했다.
   samwusil-i   kemsayk-ul   tangha-yess-ta
   office-NOM   check-ACC   suffer-PST-DECL
   'The office was searched.'

Studying physics or forgiving somebody will bring benefits, not adversity. However, destroying a city or searching for an office can adversely affect the target.

On the other hand, the subject of 받- *pat-* 'receive' needs to function as a goal rather than a patient argument:

(68) a. *김이   체포   받았다.
        Kim-i   chepho   pat-ass-ta
        Kim-NOM   arrest   receive-PST-DECL
        'Kim was arrested.'
     b. *김이   배신   받았다.
        Kim-i   paysin   pat-ass-ta
        Kim-NOM   betrayal receive-PST-DECL
        'Kim was betrayed.'

(69) a. 김이   처벌을   받았다.
        Kim-i   chepel-ul   pat-ass-ta
        Kim-NOM   punishment-ACC   receive-PST-DECL
        'Kim was punished.'
     b. 김이   용서를   받았다.
        Kim-i   yongse-lul   pat-ass-ta
        Kim-NOM   forgiveness-ACC   receive-PST-DECL
        'Kim was forgiven.'

The person arrested or betrayed can be a patient but not a goal. However, the individual who is punished or forgiven can be a goal of the action.

The light verb *toy-* 'become' combines with a VN whose object functions as a patient undergoing non-adversity effects, as seen in the following contrast:

(70) a. 김이   승진   되었다.
        Kim-i   sungcin   toy-ess-ta
        Kim-NOM   promotion   become-PST-DECL
        '(lit.) Kim became promoted.'
     b. *김이   배신   되었다.
        Kim-i   paysin   toy-ess-ta
        Kim-NOM   betrayal become-PST-DECL
        'Kim became betrayed.'

This means we need to develop a finer-grained semantic analysis that reflects the semantic role of the arguments these light verbs require. Once again, notice what happens to the resulting complex predicate:[1]

(71)

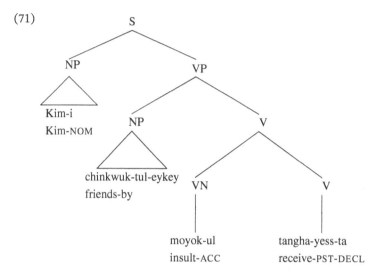

The combination of the VN and the light verb forms a complex predicate. This combines with the optional complement, which combines with the subject.

8.3.4 Inchoative and Stative Pseudo-Syntactic Passive

We have seen that English has adjectival passives. Korean has similar passives with an intransitive adjectival predicate as the main verb:

(72) a. 메리가   정말   아름다워   졌다.
　　　Mary-ka   cengmal   alumta-we   ci-ess-ta
　　　Mary-NOM really   pretty-CONN become-PST-DECL
　　　'Mary became really pretty.'

　　b. 강물이   맑아   졌다.
　　　kangmwul-i   malk-a   ci-ess-ta
　　　river.water-NOM clean-CONN become-PST-DECL
　　　'The river became clean.'

---

1 See the exercises for a discussion of examples where an adverbial expression intervenes between the VN and the light verb.

However, notice that an unergative verb (with an agent subject) cannot appear in such a construction:

(73) a. *메리가   달려   졌다.
       *Mary-ka   talli-e   ci-ess-ta
       Mary-NOM   run-CONN   become-PST-DECL

    b. *김이   놀아   졌다.
       *Kim-i   nol-a   ci-ess-ta
       Kim-NOM   play-CONN become-PST-DECL

This observation indicates that passives in (72) differ from canonical passives. Such passives are often considered inchoative or adjectival, describing the beginning of an event or the change of a state into a certain other state. Such passives have the following structure:

(74)

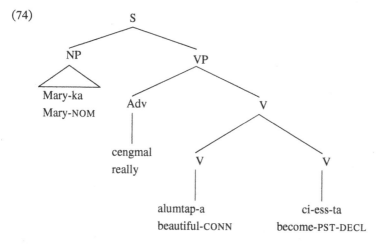

The inchoative verb *ci-ess-ta* now combines not with a transitive verb but with an adjectival unaccusative verb.

The possibility of having a stative verb as the main verb implies that this stative verb can be replaced by a passive lexical verb that can have a stative meaning. This prediction is born out. Examples like (75) are typical passives:

(75) a. 슬픈   사건은   잘   안   잊어   진다.
       sulphu-n saken-un cal an ic-e   ci-n-ta
       sad-MOD event-TOP well not forget-CONN become-PRES-DECL
       'The sad event isn't easily forgotten.'

b. 이　종이는　잘　찢어　진다.
i　congi-nun　cal　ccic-e　ci-n-ta
this　paper-TOP　well　tear-CONN　become-PRES-DECL
'This paper is easily torn.'

Note that the main verb is active, and the auxiliary verb *ci-* combines with it. This active main verb can be replaced by its lexical passive word:

(76) a. 슬픈　사건은　잘　안　잊혀　진다.
sulphu-n saken-un cal an ic-hi-e　ci-n-ta
sad-MOD　event-TOP well not forget-PASS-CONN become-PRES-DECL
'The sad event isn't easily forgotten.'

b. 이　종이는　잘　찢겨　진다.
i　congi-nun　cal　ccic-ki-e　ci-n-ta
this　paper-TOP　well　tear-PASS-CONN　become-PRES-DECL
'This paper is easily torn.'

These examples have two passive markings: one by the passive morpheme -히 *-hi* and -기 *-ki* in the main verb and the other by the auxiliary passive.

8.4　Contrastive Notes

Both English and Korean verbs can represent active and passive voice. The main properties are summarized in this section.

8.4.1　Similarities

In both languages, a passive sentence promotes the active object to its subject and demotes the active subject to an optional complement. The subject of the passive functions as the patient of the verb, and its optional complement plays the agent role. All the other arguments are intact. The following examples illustrate these points again:

(77) a. Mimi had sent an expensive gift to Momo.
b. An expensive gift had been sent to Momo.

(78) a. 미미가　모모에게　비싼　선물을　보냈다.
Mimi-ka　Momo-eykey pissa-n　senmwul-ul ponay-ss-ta
Mimi-NOM Momo-DAT　expensive-MOD gift-ACC　send-PST-DECL
'Mimi sent an expensive gift to Momo.'

b. 비싼   선물이   모모에게   보내   졌다.
   pissa-n   senmwul-i Momo-eykey ponay-e   ci-ess-ta
   expensive-MOD gift-NOM   Momo-DAT   send-CONN become-PST-DECL
   'An expensive gift was sent to Momo.'

8.4.2 Structural Differences

A canonical passive sentence in English introduces the form *be* + VP[*en*], whereas the passive in Korean introduces the form V[*ae*] + ci-ta:

(79) a. This movie was [secretly [made by the director].

    b. 이 영화는   그 감독에
      i   yenghwa-nun ku kamtok-ey
      this movie-TOP   the director-LOC

      의해 몰래   [만들어   졌다].
      uyhay mollay mantul-e   ci-ess-ta
      by   secretly make-CONN become-PST-DECL
      'This movie was secretly made by the director.'

As represented by the brackets, the copula auxiliary *is* in (79a) combines with the VP, whereas the Korean auxiliary *ci-ess-ta* combines with the main verb, yielding a complex predicate. A supporting argument for this structural difference comes from syntactic cohesion. An adverb like *secretly* can intervene between *is* and its passive VP in English. However, no expression can intervene between the main verb and the passive auxiliary in Korean, as discussed earlier:

(80) *이 영화는   그 감독에
      i   yenghwa-nun ku kamtok-ey
      this movie-TOP   the director-LOC

      의해 [만들어   몰래   졌다].
      uyhay mantul-e   mollay ci-ess-ta
      by   make-CONN secretly become-PST-DECL

8.4.3 Non-Canonical Passives

In addition to the canonical passive, English also allows prepositional passive, adjectival passive, and *get*-passive, each of which has its own grammatical properties.

(81) a. The store was broken into.
     b. They were very worried.
     c. They got involved in the accident.

Korean also has non-canonical passive constructions introduced by the light verbs 되- *toy-* 'become,' 당하- *tangha-* 'suffer,' and 받- *pat-* 'receive' when they combine with a verbal noun (VN). These light-verb passives have their own semantic and pragmatic constraints.

(82) a. 미미가   해고 되었다.
       Mimi-ka   hayko toy-ess-ta
       Mimi-NOM lay.off become-PST-DECL
       'Mimi was laid off.'
   b. 미미가   모욕을   당했다.
       Mimi-ka   moyok-ul tangha-yess-ta
       Mimi-NOM insult-ACC receive-PST-DECL
       'Mimi was insulted.'
   c. 미미가   오해를   받았다.
       Mimi-ka   ohay-lul   pat-ass-ta
       Mimi-ka   misunderstanding-ACC receive-PST-DECL
       'Mimi was misunderstood.'

8.5 Conclusion

This chapter has offered a description of passive constructions in English and Korean. Passive sentences are systematically related to active sentences.

For English passive, we first discussed *be-passive* and then prepositional as well as *get* passive. We have seen the grammatical properties of these passive types, including those related to grammatical categories, grammatical functions, and semantic/pragmatic constraints. For Korean, we have discussed the canonical passive types: lexical passive and syntactic passive. We have also seen that similar to English, Korean has adjectival passive. Even though the two languages have similar properties in the formation of passive, each has its own language-particular properties that any grammar must account for.

Exercises

1   Give the passive form of the following active English sentences:

   (i) a. They stopped me.
       b. They will stop me.
       c. They have stopped me.
       d. They would have stopped me.
       e. They are stopping me.
       f. They have been stopping me.
       g. They will have been stopping me.

2 Give the passive of the following active sentences:

(i) a. 온실을   유리로   만들었다.
   onsil-ul   yuli-lo   mantul-ess-ta
   greenhouse-ACC glass-with make-PST-DECL
   '(They) made the greenhouse with glass.'

   b. 피자를   여덟   조각으로 나누었다.
   phica-lul yetelp cokak-ulo nanwu-ess-ta
   pizza-ACC eight piece-as   divide-PST-DECL
   '(We) divided the pizza into eight pieces.'

   c. 초대장을   그녀에게   보냈다
   chotaycang-ul   kunye-eykey ponay-ess-ta
   invitation.letter-ACC she-DAT   send-PST-DECL
   '(We) sent the invitation letter to her.'

   d. 콘서트   도중에   바지를   찢었다.
   khonsethu tocwungey paci-ka   ccic-ess-ta
   concert   during   pants-ACC tear-PST-DECL
   '(Someone) tore my pants in the middle of the concert.'

   e. 누군가가   홈페이지를   해킹했다.
   nwukwunka-ka   hompheyici-lul   haykhingha-yess-ta
   somebody-NOM   homepage-ACC   hacking.do-PST-DECL
   'Somebody hacked our homepage.'

   f. 미미를   부모님이   사랑한다.
   Mimi-lul pwumonim-i salangha-n-ta
   Mimi-ACC parents-NOM love-PRES-DECL
   '(Her) parents love Mimi.'

3 Give the counterpart voice of the following sentences (active into passive and passive into active):

(i) a. They often speak of King's Canterbury.
   b. They looked up to the professor.
   c. The students paid attention to the teacher.
   d. Mary reminded him of her old sister.
   e. The police blamed the accident on the weather.

(ii) a. The scandal was talked about for days.
   b. Good use was made of the extra time.
   c. The fields look like they've been marched through by an army.
   d. Everything is being paid for by the company.
   e. Your books needed to be gone over by an accountant.

4 Give the passive lexical word for the following using one of the suffixes 이 i, 히 hi, 리 li, or 기 ki. In addition, find an example with the lexical word from a newspaper or article:

(i) a. 보다 po-ta 'see'
    b. 입다 ip-ta 'wear'
    c. 물다 mwul-ta 'bite'
    d. 남다 nam-ta 'leave'

5 Identify the grammatical error in each of the following sentences, and explain the nature of the error.

(i) a. *A black Mercedes wagon is had by mother.
    b. *John was arrived late at night.
    c. *Seoul Hotel was slept in by the businessman last night.
    d. *The store was run by Emma's granddaughter.
    e. *The problem has been talked a lot on TV.
    f. *The fork was eaten pasta with.

(ii) a. *그 분이   날씨를   풀었다.
         ku pwun-i   nalssi-lul   phul-ess-ta
         the person.HON-NOM weather-ACC dissolve-PST-DECL
         'He dissolved the weather.'
      b. *내가   편견을   깨졌다.
         nay-ka   phyenkyen-ul kkay-ci-ess-ta
         nay-NOM prejudice-ACC break-PASS-PST-DECL
         (lit.) 'I was broken my prejudice.'
      c. *피자는 여덟 조각으로 나누어   잘 졌다.
         phica-nun yetelp cokak-ulo nanwu-e   cal ci-ess-ta
         pizza-TOP eight piece-as divide-CONN well become-PST-DECL
         'The pizza was well divided into eight pieces.'
      d. *김 교수님은   학생들에게   존경   당한다.
         Kim kyoswu-nim-un   haksayng-tul-eykey conkyeng tangha-n-ta
         Kim professor-HON-TOP student-PL-DAT   respect   suffer-PRES-DECL
         'Professor Kim is respected by students.'

6 As noted in the chapter, phrasal verbs consist of a transitive verb and a particle, which can occur either after the object or right after the verb. These phrasal verbs also can be used as passive. Provide the argument structure of the active and passive verbs, and then draw tree structures for them.

(i)   a. They cut water and electricity supplies off.
      b. They cut off water and electricity supplies.
(ii) a. Brian asked Judy out to dinner.
      b. Brian asked out Judy to dinner.
(iii) a. Water and electricity supplies were cut off.
      b. Judy was asked out to dinner.

9

Interrogative Constructions: Asking a Question

9.1 Clausal Types and Interrogatives

As noted in Chapter 6, languages have a set of clause types characteristically used to indicate different speech acts or moods. Consider the following examples in English:

(1) a. Declarative: John is clever.
  b. Interrogative: Is John clever? Who is clever?
  c. Exclamative: How clever you are!
  d. Imperative: Be very clever.

Each sentence form here has its own typical function to represent a speech act. For example, the declarative makes a statement, the interrogative asks a question, the exclamative represents an exclamatory statement, and the imperative issues a directive. However, these correspondences are not always one-to-one. For example, the declarative in (2a) represents not a statement but a question, and the interrogative in (2b) indicates a directive:

(2) a. I ask you if this is what you want.
  b. Would you mind taking out the garbage?

Korean is no different. But as noted earlier, it marks the sentence mood or type with the verb-final suffix:

(3) a. Declarative
  사과를   먹었다.
  sakwa-lul mek-ess-ta
  apple-ACC eat-PST-DECL
  '(He) ate an apple.'

English and Korean in Contrast: A Linguistic Introduction, First Edition. Jong-Bok Kim.
© 2024 John Wiley & Sons, Inc. Published 2024 by John Wiley & Sons, Inc.

b. Interrogative

사과를   먹었니?

sakwa-lul   mek-ees-ni?

apple-ACC   eat-PST-QUE

'Did you eat the apple?'

c. Imperative

사과를   먹어라!

sakwa-lul   mek-ela!

apple-ACC   eat-IMP

'Eat an apple!'

d. Exclamative

사과를   맛있게   먹는구나!

sakwa-lul   masisskey   mek-nun-kwuna

apple-ACC   deliciously   eat-PRES-EXCL

'(lit.) How deliciously you are eating the apple!'

The declarative, interrogative, imperative, and suggestive here is marked by the final verbal suffix, and linked to a typical speech act. That is, (3a) makes a statement, (3b) asks a question, (3c) gives a command, and (3d) makes a suggestion. Similar to English, this general mapping relation can be overridden:

(4) a. 책을   읽었는지   물었다.

chayk-ul   ilk-ess-nunci   mwul-ess-ta

book-ACC   read-PST-QUE   ask-PST-DECL

'(I) asked (her) if she read the book.'

b. 창문을   열   수   있을까?

changmwun-ul   yel   swu   iss-ulkka?

window-ACC   open   BN   exist-QUE?

'Can you open a window?'

(4a) is a declarative sentence but asks a question, and (4b) is an interrogative but makes a request.

This chapter focuses on interrogatives in English and Korean, setting aside the mismatched mapping relationships between form and function. It discusses various types of interrogative sentence moods in the two languages and their usages.

9.2 English Interrogatives

9.2.1 Yes-No Questions and Answering System

Polar or *yes-no* questions in English are usually formed by placing a finite auxiliary before the subject:

(5) a. Has the boat left?

b. Is Ann writing a paper?
c. Could he have broken his leg?
d. Will she be waiting outside?

These polar questions can be considered related to the following declarative sentences:

(6) a. The boat has left.
b. Ann is writing a paper.
c. He could have broken his leg.
d. She will be waiting outside.

A key syntactic difference between (5) and (6) is the position of the finite auxiliary: the polar questions in (5) has the auxiliary in front of the subject or can be taken as inverting the auxiliary in front of the subject. This property has given such polar questions the name of SAI (subject-auxiliary inversion) construction.

In terms of syntactic structure, there could thus be two options. One is to assume that the auxiliary is moved to the front of the sentence, as in the following (t=trace):

(7)

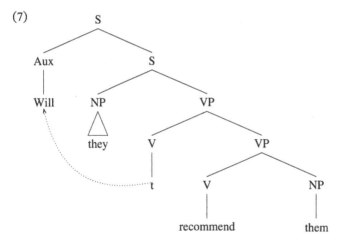

This movement-style analysis accounts for the connectivity between the inverted auxiliary and the VP:

(8) a. Kim is happy to meet the students.
b. Kim has been happy to study.
c.*Kim has being happy to study.

(9) a. Is Kim happy to meet the students?
b. Has Kim been happy to study?
c.*Has Kim being happy to study?

There are also sentences with no auxiliary:

(10) a. They lived in Sydney.
     b. Her efforts proved successful.
     c. He likes driving.

For such sentences, the dummy auxiliary *do* is introduced to form polar questions:

(11) a. Did they live in Sydney?
     b. Did her efforts prove successful?
     c. Does he like driving?

In addition, not all auxiliary verbs can be inverted:

(12) a. You better not leave.
     b.*Better you not leave.

Further, the auxiliary verb *aren't* is unique in that in the polar SAI question, it replaces *am not*:

(13) a. Aren't you lucky to have such a great family?
     b. Aren't I lucky to have such a great family?

These peculiarities in forming polar questions imply that the inversion is lexically sensitive, supporting a non-movement approach. That is, instead of assuming the auxiliary verb is inverted in polar questions, it is more reasonable to assume that an "invertible" auxiliary verb combines with a nonfinite S, as in the following:

(14)

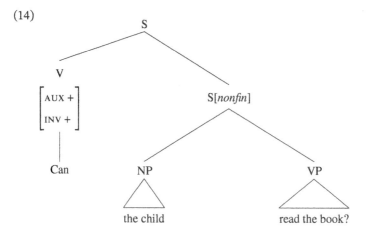

As represented in the tree structure, the auxiliary *can* is invertable (INV) and combines with the nonfinite S. This nofinite sentence is a head-subject construction whose VP *read the book* is nonfinite.

As noted, polar questions ask the hearer if the proposition evoked by the questions is true or not, and the hearer needs to provide a proper response. As a way of answering positive or negative polar questions, English can use response particles like *yes* and *no*:

(15) Q: Can you speak Korean?
       A1: Yes, I can.
       A2: No, I can't.

(16) Q: Can't you speak Korean?
       A1: Yes, I can.
       A2: No, I can't.

The response particles are followed by an optional statement. The positive answering particle *yes* in both cases confirms the positive statement *I can speak Korean*, whereas the negative particle *no* disconfirms the positive statement. This kind of answering system is called *polarity-based* because the positive and negative particles agree with the polarity of the elliptical (or non-elliptical) proposition of the answer. This is why the following is not a possible answer to the polar question:

(17) Q: Can't you speak Korean?
       A1: *Yes, I can't.
       A2: *No, I can.

9.2.2 Tag Questions

The tag question construction can be considered a subtype of *yes-no* questions. An observable property of the tag question construction is that a tag question is appended to a sentence:

(18) a. The boat hasn't left, *has it*?
       b. Joan recognized you, *didn't she*?

The form of the tag question depends on that of the statement/sentence. The formation observes the following rules: (i) the subject of the tag question is a pronominal copy of the subject of the sentence, (ii) the auxiliary verb of the tag question is a copy of the finite auxiliary of the sentence (if there is one), and (iii) the polarity of the tag question is the opposite of the polarity of the sentence. These are all demonstrated in (18). When constraint (i) or (ii) is violated, the sentence as a whole is ruled out.

(19) a.*Mary is here, isn't he?
       b.*Mary is here, wasn't she?

The negative polarity of the sentence can be expressed not only by *not* but also by other negative elements.

(20) a. She *rarely* calls, does she?
   b. She *hardly* ever called, did she?
   c. She has *scarcely* arrived, has she?

The tag questions cannot contain any additional elements except the auxiliary verb and the subject corresponding to those of the sentence.

(21) a. Mary will leave on Tuesday, won't she?
   b.*Mary will go to New York, won't she on Tuesday?
   c.*Mary will go to New York, won't she reluctantly?

There are also cases in which tag questions are appended to the embedded clause, not to the main clause.

(22) a. I suppose he saw her, didn't he?
   b. I suppose he didn't see her, did he?
   c. I don't suppose he saw her, did he?

An interesting property of such tag questions is that the negative polarity in the main clause has an effect on the embedded clause.

9.2.3 Alternative Questions

An alternative question is a question that presents two or more possible answers and presupposes that only one is true. It can be a simple alternative, as in (23a), or a polar alternative, as in (23b):

(23) a. Will he be found guilty or innocent?
   b. Can we afford it or not?

The simple particles *yes* and *no* alone cannot be proper answers to such alternative questions. Answers need to select one of the alternatives or accept/reject all of them. That is, *yes* or *no* cannot be a proper answer to an alternative, but selecting one or both alternatives given by the question could be a good choice:

(24) a.*Yes/No.
   b. Neither/Either.
   c. I think he can afford it.
   d. I don't think he can afford it.

Alternative questions can also be embedded:

(25) a. I wonder whether it is alive or dead.
   b. I'm marrying her whether you like her or hate her.

(26) a. I wonder whether it is alive or not.
   b. I'm marrying her whether you like her or not.

9.2.4 Direct *Wh*-Questions and Syntactic Structures

Unlike polar questions, *wh*-questions ask for a value for the *wh*-expression:

(27) a. What can the child play?
     b. What did the child like?
     c. Which (book) did the child read?
     d. When can the child come home?
     e. Why did the child come home?
     f. How did the child come home?

These *wh*-questions involve the inversion of a finite auxiliary (SAI) and also place a *wh*-phrase in the clause initial position. If there is no auxiliary verb, *do*-insertion occurs.

The *wh*-question requests a possible value for a variable linked to the *wh*-expression. For instance, the speaker expects the hearer to provide a value for *what* in (27a). The response to the *wh*-question in (27a) could be either a full sentence or a fragment:

(28) a. The child can play soccer.
     b. Soccer.

These answers thus offer a possible value for the variable "x" linked to *what*. The response particles *yes* and *no* cannot serve as answers to a *wh*-question because they simply affirm or disaffirm the statement.

Observe that a *wh*-phrase can be realized as a diverse grammatical function in the given clause:

(29) a. [Who] called the police? (subject)
     b. [Which version] did they recommend? (direct object)
     c. [Whose beautiful antiques] are these? (subject predicative complement)
     d. [How wide] did they make the bookcase? (object predicative complement)
     e. [On which table] did he put the apple? (oblique complement)
     f. [Why] did he eat the apple? (adjunct)

Wh-phrases can also have a variety of syntactic categories:

(30) a. [$_{NP}$ Which man] [did you talk to __]?
     b. [$_{PP}$ To which man] [did you talk? __]
     c. [$_{AP}$ How ill] [has Hobbs been __]?
     d. [$_{AdvP}$ How frequently] [did Hobbs see Rhodes __]?

As shown here, *wh*-questions consist of two parts: a *wh*-phrase and an inverted S with a missing element marked with an underline in (30). All the wh-questions would have the following template where XP is a missing element (marked with the slash symbol):

(31) Wh-interrogative sentences: Wh-XP + S/XP

Having a complete sentence with a fronted *wh*-phrase makes the sentence unacceptable:

(32) a.*Which man [$_S$ did you talk to Pat]?
     b.*To which man [$_S$ did you talk to Pat]?

The bracketed sentence here has no missing gap here, violating the schema in (31). An important property of *wh*-questions is that the *wh*-phrase (filler) must correspond to the missing element (gap) in terms of syntactic category.

(33) a.*[$_{NP}$ Which man] [did you talk [$_{PP}$ __]]?
     b.*[$_{PP}$ To which man] [did you talk to [$_{NP}$ __]]?

In addition, the distance between the filler and the gap can be long or unbounded.

(34) a. [[Whom] do you think [Mimi saw __]]?
     b. [[Whom] do you think [Mary said [Mimi saw __]]]?
     c. [[Whom] do you think [[Hobbs imagined [Mary said [Mimi saw __]]]]]?

There have traditionally been two means of representing the link between the filler *wh*-phrase and its corresponding gap (the missing element). One strategy is to assume that the filler *wh*-phrase is moved to the sentence-initial position by movement operations, as represented in (35):

(35)

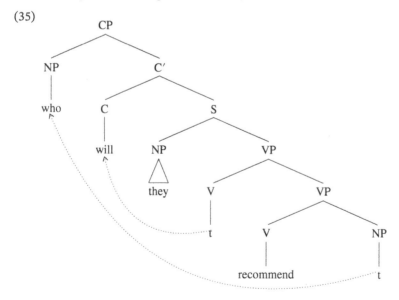

The *wh*-phrase *who* originates in the object position of *recommend* and is then moved to the specifier position of the intermediate phrase C′ (C-bar). The auxiliary verb *will* is also moved from the V position to the C. This kind of movement operation at first glance seems reasonable to capture the linkage between the filler and the gap. However, the movement analysis becomes less plausible when we consider examples like the following:

(36) a. Whom did Kim work for ___ and Sandy rely on ___?
    b.*Whom did Kim work for ___ and Sandy rely ___?
    c.*Whom did Kim work for ___ and Sandy rely on Mary?

If we adopt a movement analysis for (36a), there must be an operation in which the two NP gaps (marked by underscores) are collapsed into one NP and become *who*. We cannot simply move one NP, because doing so will generate an ill-formed example like (36c).

An alternative, feasible analysis is to assume that there is no movement process and posit a mechanism of communication through the tree, known as *feature percolation*, to allow such *wh*-questions. For example, the information that an NP is missing or that is gapped can be shared within the tree so the gap and its filler have the same specifications for the relevant features, such as syntactic category (t=trace).

(37)

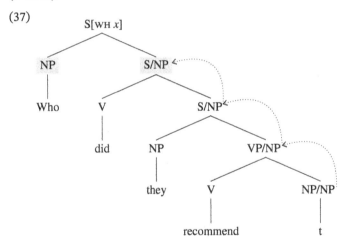

Notations like NP/NP (read as "NP slash NP") or S/NP ("S slash NP") here mean the category to the left of the slash is incomplete: it is missing one NP. This missing information percolates up to the point where the slash category is combined with the filler *who*. Instead of movement operations, this strategy has successive applications of a phrase-structure rule that creates a local tree in which a constituent with a gap feature is combined with another constituent, and the mother phrase has the same value for the gap feature as the gapped daughter. Note that every combination in the tree is licensed by the grammar rules, Head-Complement and Head-Subject, but no rule licenses the combination of the filler *who* and the incomplete S. This combination is licensed by the following grammar rule:

(38) Head-Filler Rule:
S → XP, S/XP

This rule says the S missing an XP combines with the filler XP. In other words, the filler is allowed to combine with a sentence containing the same XP as its gap.

It is also easy to verify that this feature percolation system accounts for examples like (39), in which the gap is a non-NP:

(39) a. [In which box] did John place the book __?
b. [How happy] has John been __?

The Head-Filler Rule in (38) ensures that the categorial status of the filler is identical to that of the gap. The structure of (39a) can be represented as follows:

(40)

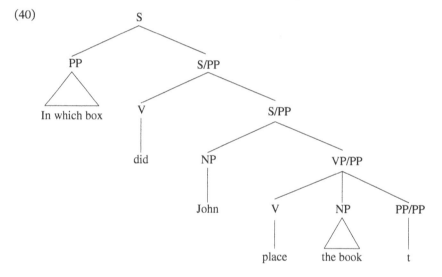

In this structure, the missing phrase is a PP encoded as the slash (or gapped) value. This value percolate up to the lower S and is discharged by the filler *in which box* based on the Head-Filler Rule.

We have seen the structure of *wh*-questions where an argument (subject or complement) is gapped. There are also adverbial *wh*-questions like the following examples, with a possible answer to each:

(41) a. Where did he buy the ingredients? At the store.
b. When is Lee arriving? In an hour.

c. Why is he making pasta? Because Lee loves it.

d. How did he do it? In a very elegant way.

One key difference from the *wh*-questions with *what* or *who* is that there is no missing element in the sentence following the *wh*-expression. The answers here denote a temporal point, a location, a reason, and a manner, all of which typically function as adverbial expressions. These adverbial expressions are optional and can even occur in the sentence-initial position:

(42) a. At the store, he bought the ingredients.

b. In an hour, Lee is arriving.

c. Because Lee loves it, he is making pasta.

d. In a very elegant way, he did it.

This means we can assume that the *wh*-word in (41) is modifying the following sentence:

(43)

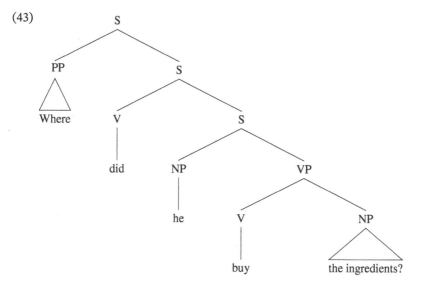

9.2.5 Indirect *Wh*-Questions

A certain class of verbs selects interrogative questions S[QUE +] as their complements. Compare the following set of data:

(44) a. Kim asks [whose book his son likes __].

b. Kim has forgotten [which player his son shouted at __].

c. He told me [how many employees Karen introduced __ to the visitors].

(45) a. Mimi denied [(that) she had spent five thousand dollars].
　　 b.*Mimi denied [which book she had been reading].
　　 c. Mimi claimed [(that) she had spent five thousand dollars].
　　 d.*Mimi claimed [how much money she had spent].

(46) a.*Kim inquired [(that) he should read it].
　　 b. Kim inquired [which book he should read].
　　 c.*Peter will decide [(that) we should review the book].
　　 d. Peter will decide [which book we should review].

(47) a. Kim told us that we should review the book.
　　 b. Kim told us [which book we should review].

As given in (44), verbs like *asks, forgotten,* and *told* combine with a bracketed sentence. The bracketed *wh*-constituents are called indirect *wh*-questions in that they are similar to direct *wh*-questions with respect to the interrogative force. An interesting property of the indirect *wh*-question construction is that the SAI does not occur, as seen here. Examples in (46) illustrate that verbs like *deny* or *claim* do not select an indirect question, but combine only with a CP. This contrasts with verbs like *inquire* and *decide* as given in (47). Verbs like *tell*, however, allow either an indirect question or a CP, as given in (48).

An indirect question, S[QUE +], can also appear in the subject position or be selected as a complement of a verb or another category such as an adjective, a preposition, or a noun.

(48) a. [How the book will sell] depends on the reviewers. (subject)
　　 b. The problem is [who will water my plants when I am away]. (subject predicative complement)
　　 c. I am not sure [which she prefers]. (complement of the adjective)
　　 d. They did not consult us on [whose names should be put forward]. (complement of the preposition)
　　 e. We solved the problem [who was at fault]. (complement of the noun)

Thus, at least three types of verbs take clausal complements with a different internal property. Lexical entries for three representative verbs are as follows:

(49) a. wonder-type: [COMPS <S[QUE +]>]
　　 b. deny-type: [COMPS <S[QUE −]>]
　　 c. tell-type: [COMPS <S[QUE ±]>]

The QUE feature flags the presence of a clause-initial *wh*-word like *who* or *which*; it is used to distinguish between indirect questions and declarative clauses. The QUE value of the verb's complement ensures that each verb combines with an appropriate clausal complement. For example, the verb *wonder*, requiring a [QUE +] clausal complement, is allowed in a structure like the following:

(50)

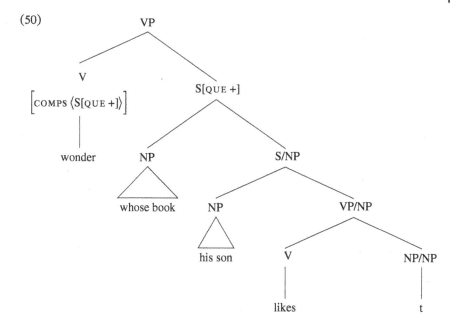

The slash value of *likes* is passed up to the lower S and discharged by the filler *whose book*. The *wh*-word *whose* carries the [QUE +] feature, which is passed up to the embedded S, where it is "visible" to the verb selecting its complement or the highest position needed to indicate that the particular sentence is a question.

9.2.6 Infinitival *Wh*-Questions

English not only allows finite indirect questions but also has infinitival ones.

(51) a. Fred knows [which politician to support].
　　b. Karen asked [where to put the chairs].
　　c. Wulfe is considering [whether to bring an emergency clinic to a property].

A syntactic constraint imposed on the infinitival *wh*-questions is that the subject of the infinitival VP cannot be overtly realized.

(52) a.*Fred knows [which politician for Karen/her/him(self) to vote for].
　　b.*Karen asked [where for Jerry/him/her(self) to put the chairs].
　　c.*Wulfe is considering whether for Fred/her/him(self) to bring an emergency clinic to a property.

Infinitival *wh*-questions also appear in positions other than the verb's complement.

(53) a. [Where to put the ever-increasing garbage] has become an important issue at all governmental levels.
  b. They had no clue [what to do].
  c. The first question was [whom to help], and it took weeks to answer.
  d. He's not quite sure [who to talk to].
  e. In most cases, the final decision on [whom to invite] still rests with the president.

9.2.7 Multiple *Wh*-Questions

English allows more than one element to be *wh*-questioned.

(54) a. Who gave what to whom?
  b. Which present did you give to whom?

However, we cannot have more than one *wh*-phrase in the clause's initial position.

(55) a.*Who what gave to whom?
  b.*Which present whom did you give?

If one of the *wh*-elements originates from the subject, it should be in the initial position.

(56) a. Who gave what to whom?
  b.*What did who give to whom?
  c.*To whom did who give what?

The observed constraint is that the likange between the front *wh*-expression and the missing expression cannot cross another *wh*-expression. For example, in (57c), *what* is intervening between *who* and the missing gap:

(57) a. What did you give to whom?
  b.*To whom did you give what?
  c.*Who did you give what to?

9.3 Korean Interrogatives

9.3.1 Yes-No Question and Response Particles

The interrogative sentence is used to make a question. There is no change in the word order, as in English; simply changing the declarative suffix form to the interrogative form at the final verb (or descriptive verb) is the only thing required.

The interrogative form of the speech level is done the same way as the declarative form, but exchanging the final -다 -ta to -니 -ni or 습니까 -supnikka:

(58) a. 미아가   미미를   만났다
     Mia-ka   Mimi-lul   manna-ss-ta
     Mia-NOM   Mimi-ACC   meet-PST-DECL
     'Mia met Mimi.'

   b. 미아가   미미를   만났니?
     Mia-ka   Mimi-lul   manna-ss-ni
     Mia-NOM   Mimi-ACC   meet-PST-QUE
     'Did Mia meet Mimi?'

   c. 미아가   미미를   만났습니까?
     Mia-ka   Mimi-lul   manna-ss-supnikka?
     Mia-NOM   Mimi-ACC   meet-PST-QUE
     'Did Mia meet Mimi?'

The syntactic structure of polar questions is thus similar to declaratives. The only difference is that the sentence bears the feature QUE which originated from the verb ending marking:

(59)

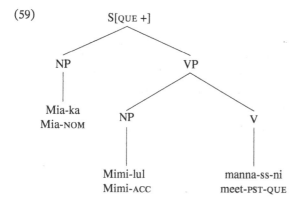

We have noted in English that among various possible ways to answer yes-no polar questions, *yes* and *no* are simple means to affirm or reject the proposition evoked from the question, as again illustrated in the following dialogue:

(60) Q: Are you tired?
    A: Yes. (=I am tired.)
    A': No. (=I am not tired.)

The answer particle *yes* here confirms the speaker's being tired, whereas the particle *no* disconfirms the proposition. Korean has a similar system:

(61) Q: 피곤해?
        phikonha-y
        tire-QUE
        'Are you tired?'
      A: 응 Ung. 'Yes.'
      A': 아니 Ani. 'No.'

The positive response particle *ung* confirms the proposition that the speaker is tired, whereas the negative one *ani* disconfirms the proposition. However, when these response particles function as answers to the negative yes-no question, Korean and English interpret them differently. Consider the following:

(62) Q: Isn't Mimi diligent?
      A: Yes. (=she is diligent.)

(63) Q: 미미   부지런하지   않아?
        Mimi   pwucilenha-ci   anh-a?
        Mimi   diligent-CONN   not-QUE
        'Isn't Mimi diligent?'

      A: Ung. 'Yes.' (=she is not diligent.)

In (62), the positive response particle *yes* means the positive proposition, whereas in (63), *ung* 'yes' means the negative proposition. This is because English has a polarity-based answering system, but Korean has a truth-based system. In the polarity-based system of English, the positive or negative particle agrees with the polarity of the proposition of the answer. In the truth-based system (e.g. Korean), the affirmative answer indicates agreement with the speaker, and the negative answer indicates disagreement with the speaker.

9.3.2 *Wh*-Questions

As is well known, languages differ in the formation of *wh*-questions. *Wh*-phrases metaphorically move or remain in situ. For example, English *wh*-phrases move to their scope position, and Korean *wh*-phrases remain in situ:

(64) a. What did Mimi read ___?
      b. 미미가   무엇을   읽었니?
          Mimi-ka   mwues-ul   ilk-ess-ni?
          Mimi-TOP   what-ACC   read-PST-QUE
          'What did Mimi read?'

In English, we could assume that *what* is moved to the initial position of the sentence. In Korean, the corresponding *wh*-expression *mwues-ul* 'what,' asking about a possible value for the variable "x" introduced by the *wh*, is in situ. That is, the *wh*-phrase is in the original place. In English, the sentence type is marked by the word of the *wh*-expression (WH), but in Korean, it is marked by the verb ending suffix (*-ni* here). Korean thus has a simpler syntactic structure, no different from the declarative:

(65)

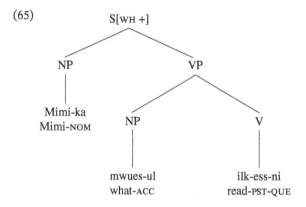

As an object NP can be scrambled in typical declarative sentences, the *wh*-object can also be positioned in the initial position:

(66)

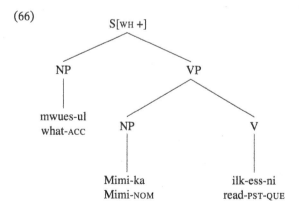

What we can observe here is that unlike in English, there is no movement or filler-gap dependency. The *wh*-phrase is either in situ or scrambled like other expressions in the declarative sentence. This is one key difference between English and Korean *wh*-constructions.

Korean employs a variety of *wh*-words: nominal, adnominal, adverbial, and predicative. Consider these *wh*-expressions used as nominals, and the corresponding examples:

(67) Nominal *wh*-words:

누구 nwukwu 'who' 무엇 mwues 'what' 얼마 elma 'which amount,' 몇 myech 'how many,' 언제 encey 'when,' 어디 eti 'where'

(68) a. 누가 왔니?
nwu-ka o-ass-ni?
who-NOM come-PST-QUE
'Who came?'

b. 무엇을 읽었니?
mwues-ul ilk-ess-ni?
what-ACC read-PST-QUE
'What did you read?'

c. 얼마가 모자라니?
elma-ka mocala-ni?
how.much-NOM lack-QUE
'How much do we lack?'

d. 학생 몇 명이 왔니?
haksayng myech myeng-i o-ass-ni?
sudent how.many person-NOM come-PST-QUE
'How many students came?'

e. 언제가 졸업이니?
encey-ka colep-i-ni?
when-NOM graduation-COP-QUE
'When is your graduation?'

f. 어디가 좋으니?
eti-ka coh-uni?
where-NOM like-QUE
'Which place do you prefer?'

All these examples include a *wh*-expression functioning as a nominal expression. Some of them can be used in the adnominal position:

(69) a. 무슨 음식을 좋아하니?
mwusun umsik-ul cohaha-ni?
what food-ACC like-QUE
'What food do you like?'

b. 어떤 사람이   오니?
  etten salam-i   o-ni?
  what person-NOM come-QUE
  'What kinds of people come?'

There are also adverbial *wh*-expressions, just like in English:

(70) a. 이   차는   어떻게   가니?
    i   cha-nun   ettehkey ka-ni?
    this car-TOP   how   go-QUE
    'How does this car move?'

  b. 왜   울고   있니?
    way wul-ko   iss-ni?
    why cry-CONN   exist-QUE
    'Why are you crying?'

  c. 언제   가니?
    encey ka-ni?
    when go-QUE
    'When do you go?'

  d. 어디로 가니?
    etilo   ka-ni?
    where go-QUE
    'Where are you going?'

Unlike English, Korean also has predicative *wh*-words:

(71) a. 어찌하다 eccihata 'how':

    아이들이   어찌하고   있니?
    ai-tul-i   ecciha-ko iss-ni?
    child-PL-NOM   how-CONN   exist-QUE
    'How are the children doing?'

  b. 어떠하다/어떻다 ettehata/ettehta 'how':

    이   색깔은   어떠하니?
    i   saykkkal-un   etteha-ni?
    this color-TOP   how-QUE
    'How about this color?'

These show that Korean has much richer types of *wh*-expressions than English.
    Another intriguing, complicated property comes from the fact that Korean
wh-expressions are ambiguous between an interrogative reading and a quantifier

reading (e.g. something or someone), depending on the environment in which they appear:

(72) a. 누가   왔다.
       nwu-ka   o-ass-ta.
       someone-NOM came-DECL
       'Someone came.'

     b. 누가   왔니?
       nwu-ka   o-ass-ni?
       who-NOM   came-PST-QUE
       'Who came?' or 'Did someone come?'

     c. 누구든지   와라.
       nwukwu-tunchi   wa-la
       someone-any   come-IMP
       'Come, anyone!' or 'Everyone can come.'

In (72a), the *wh*-expression is interpreted as an existential quantifier (there is someone "x"), whereas in (72b), it can have both an interrogative reading (what is the value of "x") and an existential quantifier reading. In (72c), it is interpreted as a universal quantifier (everyone) or may have a negative polarity reading (anyone).

A similar fact can be observed in the following. Note that the intonation disambiguates the readings:

(73) a. 누가   영희를   사랑하니?
       nwu-ka   Younghee-lul   salangha-ni? (with a rising tone)
       someone-NOM Younghee-ACC love-QUE
       'Does anyone love Younghee?'

     b. 누가   영희를   사랑하니?
       nwu-ka   Younghee-lul   salangha-ni? (with a falling tone)
       who-NOM Younghee-ACC love-QUE
       'Who loves Younghee?'

(74) a. 미아가   누구를   사랑하니?
       Mia-ka   nwukwu-lul   salangha-ni? (with a rising tone)
       Mia-NOM someone-ACC love-QUE
       'Does Mia love anyone?'

     b. 미아가   누구를   사랑하니?
       Mia-ka   nwukwu-lul salangha-ni? (with a falling tone)
       Mia-NOM who-ACC   love-QUE
       'Who does Mia love?'

The questions with a rising tone have only the [QUE +] feature value, whereas those with a falling tone also have the [WH +] feature, requesting a possible value for the variable. This means that depending on the tone, we could interpret the *wh*-expression in Korean either as an interrogative *wh*-expression (*who* or *what*) or an existential expression (*someone* or *something*) in English.

The adverbial *wh*-expression can also have two possible readings: a *wh*-reading or an indefinite reading.

(75) a. 미아가   언제   갔니?
      Mia-ka   encey   ka-ss-ni?
      Mia-NOM   when   go-PST-QUE
      'When did Mia go?' or 'Did Mia go at any time?'

    b. 미아가   어디   갔니?
      Mia-ka   eti   ka-ss-ni?
      Mia-NOM   where   go-PST-QUE
      'Where did Mia go?' or 'Did Mia go to some place?'

However, the adverbial expressions 어떻게 *ettehkey* 'how' and 왜 *way* 'why' do not have ambiguous readings. These expressions have only a *wh*-reading:

(76) a. 미아가   왜   화가   났니?
      Mia-ka   way   hwa-ka   na-ss-ni?
      Mia-NOM   why   anger-NOM   occur-PST-QUE
      'Why did Mia get angry?' #'Did Mia get angry for any reason?'

    b. 미아가   이   문제를   어떻게   풀었니?
      Mia-ka   i   mwuncey-lul   ettehkey   phwul-ess-ni?
      Mia-NOM   this   problem-ACC   how   solve-PST-QUE
      'How did Mia solve this problem?' #'Did Mia solve this problem anyhow?'

This implies that such questions must carry both the QUE (with the positive value) and WH features.

9.3.3 Indirect Questions

Similar to English, Korean allows embedded questions, in which the embedded clause has the main verb marked with the question ending is -은지/는지 *-(n)unci*, but -는가 *-nunka* or -나 *-na*:

(77) a. 미아가   떠났는지   몰랐다.
      Mia-ka   ttena-ss-nunci   moll-ass-ta
      Mia-NOM   leave-PST-QUE   not.know-PST-DECL
      'I didn't know that Mia left.'

b. 미아가   떠났는가   궁금하다.
Mia-ka   ttena-ss-nunka kwungkumha-ta
Mia-NOM   leave-PST-QUE   wonder-DECL
'I wonder if Mia left.'

The embedded verb here is marked with the question connective -*nunci* and
-*nunka*. These question markers are central in determining *wh*-scope. Compare
the following pair:

(78) a. 미아는 [누가   떠났다고]   믿니?
Mia-nun [nwu-ka ttena-ss-ta-ko]   mit-ni?
Mia-TOP who-NOM leave-PST-DECL-COMP believe-QUE
'Who does Mia believe left?' or 'Does Mia believe that someone left?'
b. 미아는 [누가   떠났는지]   아니?
Mia-nun [nwu-ka ttena-ss-nunci]   a-ni?
Mia-TOP who-NOM leave-PST-QUE   know-QUE
'Does Mia know who left?' but not 'Who does Mia know left?'

The key difference between the two has to do with the main verb in the embedded clause: the one 떠났다고 ttena-ss-ta-ko in (78a) has the connective complementizer suffix -*ko*, whereas the one 떠났는지 ttena-ss-nunci in (78b) has the
interrogative suffix -*nunci*. This makes the key difference how to interpret the
wh-expression *nwu-ka* 'who-NOM' in the embedded clause. In (78a), the verb 믿
mit- 'believe' combines with a declarative clause as its complement; the *wh*-phrase
here has only the matrix reading. Meanwhile, (78b) induces an indirect question
reading because of the Q-marked embedded verb. This implies that the WH feature
originated from a *wh*-word and is interpreted when it meets the QUE feature. This
difference can be represented in tree structures:

(79) a.

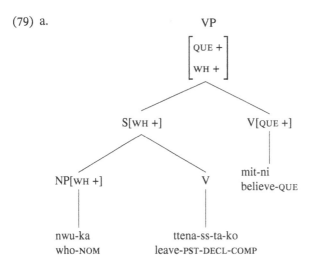

b.

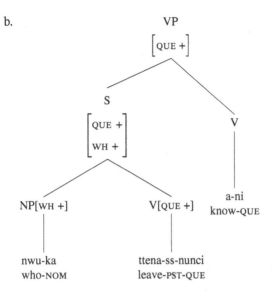

In (79a), the embedded clause is not an indirect question but a simple declarative clause because its verb is marked with the complementizer-like suffix -*ko*. This is why the WH feature introduced by *nwu-ka* is passed up to the matrix clause and then interpreted as a *wh*-question. In (79b), the embedded clause is QUE-marked by the suffix -*nunci*, rendering it an embedded question. This allows the WH feature of *nwu-ka* to be interpreted within this embedded clause.

Such a difference can be clearly observed by comparing with the English counterparts:

(80) a. Do you wonder who Kim met?
  b. Do you wonder why Kim was late?

(81) a. Who do you think Kim met?
  b. Why do you think Kim was late?

In (80), the scope of the *wh*-expressions *who* and *why* is within the embedded clause, whereas in (81), the scope is in the matrix clause. These sentences have the following Korean counterparts:

(82) a. 너는 [김이   누구를   만났는지]   궁금하니?
  ne-nun [Kim-i nwukwu-lul manna-ss-nunci] kwungkumha-ni?
  you-TOP Kim-NOM who-ACC   meet-PST-QUE   wonder-QUE
  'Do you wonder who Kim met?'

b. 너는 [김이 왜 늦었는지] 궁금하니?
ne-nun [Kim-i way nuc-ess-nunci] kwungkumha-ni?
you-TOP Kim-NOM why late-PST-QUE wonder-QUE
'Do you wonder why Kim was late?'

(83) a. 너는 [김이 누구를 만났다고] 생각하니?
ne-nun [Kim-i nwukwu-lul manna-ss-ta-ko] sayngkakha-ni?
you-TOP Kim-NOM who-ACC meet-PST-DECL-COMP think-QUE
'Who do you think Kim met?' or 'Do you think that Kim met someone?'

b. 너는 [김이 왜 늦었다고] 생각하니?
ne-nun [Kim-i way nuc-ess-ta-ko] sayngkakha-ni?
you-TOP Kim-NOM why late-PST-DECL-COMP think-QUE
'Why do you think Kim was late?'

Note that the only difference between (82) and (83) is the question marking on the embedded clause. That is, only (82) has the embedded clause whose verb ends with the question marking *-nunci*. The *wh*-expression is interpreted within the clause whose verb is marked with a question morpheme determining its scope.

9.3.4 Multiple *Wh*-Questions

Korean is a *wh*-in-situ language, but *wh*-phrases can optionally be scrambled. The example in (84a) has canonical word order: scrambling has not occurred. The sentence in (84b) illustrates the scrambling of the *wh*-phrase 무엇을 *mwues-ul* 'what-ACC' out of the position before a verb and into sentence-initial position.

(84) a. 미아가 무엇을 샀니?
Mia-ka mwues-ul sa-ss-ni?
Mia-NOM what-ACC buy-PST-QUE
'What did Mia buy?'

b. 무엇을 미아가 샀니?
mwues-ul Mia-ka sa-ss-ni?
what-ACC Mia-NOM buy-PST-QUE
'What did Mia buy?'

However, in multiple *wh*-words, Korean scrambling behaves differently than its English counterpart. In English, scrambling the two *wh*-expressions is not allowed; but in Korean, this is possible:

(85) a. Who bought what?
b. *What did who buy?

(86) a. 누가　　무엇을　샀니?
　　　 nwu-ka　　mwues-ul　sa-ss-ni?
　　　 who-NOM　what-ACC　buy-PST-QUE
　　　 'Who bought what?'
　　b. 무엇을　　누가　　샀니?
　　　 mwues-ul　nwu-ka　　sa-ss-ni?
　　　 what-ACC　who-NOM　buy-PST-QUE
　　　 'Who bought what?'

In (86b), the object *wh*-expression *mwues-ul* 'what-ACC' is scrambled to the sentence-initial position, which is not possible in English. Considering that the *wh*-interrogative is formed by fronting a *wh*-expression, the English limitation is unexpected.

9.3.5 Questions with Different Illocutionary Force

The typical yes-no question or *wh*-question in English as well as in Korean asks the truth of the statement in a question or the value of a variable indicated by a *wh* expression. But when it accompanies a special expression or atypical intonation or pitch, it can have a different illocutionary force or speech act. The following are some illustrative examples in Korean:

- Confirming interrogative: Checks how much the hearer knows about a given situation, or confirms the situation to the hearer.

　(87) a. 미아가　　진아를　　좋아하지?　그렇지?
　　　　 Mia-ka　　Jina-ul　　cohaha-ci?　kuleh-ci?
　　　　 Mia-NOM　Jina-ACC　like-QUE　　SO-QUE
　　　　 'Mia is fond of Jina, isn't it?'
　　　b. 담배를　　　피웠지?　　　그렇지?
　　　　 tampay-lul　phiwu-ess-ci?　kuleh-ci?
　　　　 cigarette-ACC　smoke-PST-QUE　SO-QUE
　　　　 '(You) smoked, isn't it?'

The expression 그렇지 *kuleh-ci* 'so-QUE' serves as a kind of tagging question, confirming the preceding yes-no question.

- Rhetoric interrogative: With a special pitch (indicated by capitals), we can express a strong statement against the proposition evoked by the question.

　(88) a. 그　사람이　　거짓말을　　하니?
　　　　 KU　SALAM-I　kecismal-ul　ha-ni?
　　　　 the　man-NOM　lie-ACC　　do-QUE
　　　　 'Is HE lying?' (He is not the kind of person to lie.)

b. 누가　　그　것을　　아니?
NWU-KA　ku　kes-ul　al-ni?
who-NOM　the　thing-ACC　know-QUE
'Who knows the answer?' (Nobody knows the answer.)

- Imperative interrogative: Interrogatives can be used as a kind of order or command.

(89) a. 여기　잠깐　　기다리겠니?
yeki　camkkan　kitali-keyss-ni?
here　shortly　wait-FUT-QUE
'Can you wait here for a while?' (Please wait here.)
b. 왜　이　약을　　안먹니?
way　i　yak-ul　an-mek-ni?
why　this　pill-ACC　not-eat-QUE
'Why aren't you taking this pill?' (How about taking this pill?)

- Exclamative: With an adverb like 정말 *cengmal* 'really,' we can use interrogatives to express surprise.

(90) a. 미아가　그　것을　　정말　　만들었니?
Mia-ka　ku　kes-ul　cengmal　mantul-ess-ni?
Mia-NOM　the　thing-ACC　really　make-PST-QUE
'Did Mia really make this?'
b. 저　그림　　정말　　멋지지?
ce　kulim　cengmal　mesiss-ci?
the　drawing　really　gorgeous-QUE
'Isn't this drawing really gorgeous?'

9.4　Contrastive Notes

Korean and English have distinctive ways of forming polar and *wh* interrogative sentences.

9.4.1　Polar Questions and Response Particles

To form polar or yes-no questions, English requires SAI (subject-auxiliary inversion), and Korean requires the matrix verb to have a question verbal ending.

(91) a. We could drink this water.
b. Could we drink this water?

(92) a. 이　물을　　마실　　수　있다.
　　　 i　 mwul-ul　masi-l　　swu　iss-ta.
　　　 this　water-ACC　drink-MOD　BN　exist-DECL
　　　 'We can drink this water.'

　　 b. 이　물을　　마실　　수　있니?
　　　 i　 mwul-ul　masi-l　　swu　iss-ni?
　　　 this　water-ACC　drink-MOD　BN　exist-QUE
　　　 'We can drink this water.'

As observed here, in English, the finite auxiliary *could* is inverted to the sentence-initial position. However, in Korean the polar question is marked by the verbal ending.

Like other languages, English and Korean have mono-syllable response particles, *yes*/응 and *no*/아니. When these are used as responses to positive polar questions, they all have the same function; but when they respond to negative polar questions, they have different meanings:

(93) Q: Don't you like this drink?
　　 A: Yes.
　　 A′: 응 ung. 'Yes.'

English has a polarity-based answering system, whereas Korean has a truth-based system. The English particle *yes* here means agreement with the positive proposition "I like this drink," but the Korean particle means agreement with the negative proposition "I don't like this drink."

9.4.2 *Wh*-Questions: In Situ or Not

As we have seen, to form a *wh*-interrogative, English requires a *wh*-expression to be fronted to the sentence's initial position, but Korean leaves the expression in situ. This can again be observed from the following pair:

(94) a. What can we drink?

　　 b. 우리가　무엇을　　마실　　수　있니?
　　　 wuli-ka　mwues-ul　masi-l　　swu　iss-ni?
　　　 we-NOM　what-ACC　drink-MOD　BN　exist-QUE
　　　 'What can we drink?'

9.4.3 Interpreting *Wh*-Expressions

A distinctive property of Korean *wh*-expressions is that they can be interpreted as indefinite pronouns like *someone* or *something*. Observe the following:

(95) a. Someone came.
   b. Who came?

(96) a. 누가   왔네.
   nwu-ka   o-ass-ney
   who-NOM come-PST-DECL
   'Someone came.'

   b. 누가   왔니?
   nwu-ka   o-ass-ni
   who-NOM   come-PST-QUE
   'Who came?' or 'Did someone come?'

In English, the indefinite pronoun *someone* and the *wh*-expression *who* are employed to express a statement and a question, respectively. However, in Korean, the same word *nwu-ka* can be used for both, and its interpretation depends on the sentence ending or context. This is why even the *wh*-expression in (96b) could be interpreted as an indefinite pronoun *someone*, together with an appropriate pitch tone.

9.5 Conclusion

This chapter discussed interrogative sentences in English and Korean. We have seen that the two languages behave differently in yes-no questions and *wh*-interrogatives.

For English interrogatives, we first discussed yes-no questions that require an inverted auxiliary in the sentence-initial position. *Wh*-questions also require inversion of the subject and auxiliary in addition to fronting the *wh*-expression in the question. English questions have two main parts: a *wh*-marked filler XP phrase and a sentence missing a gap XP. The dependency between the gap and its filler is captured by the percolation of the slash feature rather than by a movement. In addition to these two types of interrogative constructions, we have seen key properties of tag questions, indirect questions, infinitival questions, and multiple *wh*-questions.

For Korean interrogatives, we first discussed yes-no questions that require only a final question-marked verb ending. The key difference from English yes-no questions comes from interpreting a response particle that functions as the answer to a negative question. For *wh*-questions, we noted that there is no need to front the *wh*-phrase in the question: it stays in situ. We also discussed multiple *wh*-questions and questions with speech acts.

Exercises

1 Draw tree structures for the following sentences, and identify all the grammar rules that allow the combination in each phrase:

   (i) a. Did the girls get to school on time?
       b. Was the movie enjoyable?
       c. Is Mimi a student?
       d. Have you been to Seoul?
       e. Can you sing the song?
   (ii) a. What can we do in this unexpected situation?
       b. To whom shall I give the test results?
       c. They wonder which wildebeest the lions will devour.
       d. What did Kim believe Lee forgot?
       e. Why did he leave so early?

2 The expression *whether* or *if* can be used either as a complementizer or as a subordinating clause marker. Identify their uses in the following with tree structures, and give evidence for your structures.

   (i) a. I don't know [whether/if I should agree].
       b. She gets upset [whether/if I exclude her from anything].
       c. I wonder [whether/if you'd be kind enough to give us information].
       d. I am going whether you like it or not.

In addition, note in (ii) that *whether* indirect questions and *if* indirect questions behave differently in terms of the possibility of serving as a prepositional object. Account for this difference as much as you can:

   (ii) a. I am not certain about [when he will come].
       b. I am not certain about [whether he will go or not].
       c.*I am not certain about [if he will come (or not)].

3 Draw tree structures for the following sentences, and identify all the grammar rules:

   (i) a. 미아가 서울로 갔니?
         Mia-ka   Seoul-lo ka-ss-ni
         Mia-NOM Seoul-to go-PST-QUE
         'Did Mia go to Seoul?'
       b. 미아가 어제   무엇을   먹었습니까?
         Mia-ka   ecey   mwues-ul mek-ess-supnikka?
         Mia-NOM yesterday what-ACC eat-PST-QUE-formal
         'What did Mia eat yesterday?'

c. 너는   샌디가   무엇을   먹었다고   생각하니?
ne-nun   Sandy-ka   mwues-ul   mek-ess-ta-ko   sayngkakha-ni?
you-TOP Sandy-NOM what-ACC   eat-PST-DECL-CONN think-QUE
'What do you think Sandy ate?'

d. 너는   샌디가   무엇을   먹었는지   알았니?
ne-nun   Sandy-ka   mwues-ul   mek-ess-nunci al-ass-ni?
you-TOP Sandy-NOM what-ACC   eat-PST-QUE   know-PST-QUE
'Did you know what Mimi ate?'

4 Explain why the following English examples are ungrammatical.

   (i) a. *On whom does Mary believe Chris knows Sandy trusts?
      b. *What city will John say that Mary thinks that Fred lives?
      c. *John was wondering to whom he was referring to?
      d. *I wonder what city that Romans destroyed.
      e. *Kim denied which house his friend lived in.

5 Explain why the following Korean examples are ungrammatical.

   (i) a. *미아가   왜   철수를   만났다
      *Mia-ka way Chelswu-lul   manna-ass-ta
      Mia-NOM why Chelswu-ACC   meet-PST-DECL
      '(int.) Why did Mia meet Chelswu?'

      b. *미미가   왜   미아를   좋아한다
      Mimi-ka   way   Mia-lul   cohaha-n-ta
      Mimi-NOM why   Mia-ACC   like-PRES-DECL
      '(int.) Does Mimi like Mia for some reason?'

      c. *미아는   남자친구가   왜
      Mia-nun   namcachinkwu-ka   way
      Mia-TOP   boyfriend-NOM   why

      준   꽃을   버렸니?
      cwu-n   kkoch-ul   peli-ess-ni?
      give-MOD flower-ACC throw.away-PST-DECL
      '(int.) What is the reason x such that Mia threw away the flowers that her boyfriend gave to her for x?'

      d. *미미는   동생이   왜   보낸   책을   찢었니?
      *Miminun tongsayng-i   way ponay-n chayk-ul ccic-ess-ni?
      Mimi-TOP younger.sibling-NOM   why send-MOD book-ACC tear-PST-QUE
      '(int.) What is the reason x such that Mimi tore the book that her younger sibling sent to her for x?'

6 Discuss the differences between each of the following English and Korean pairs.

(i) a. What do you think Sandy ate?

b. 너는 　샌디가 　무엇을 　먹었다고 　생각하니?
ne-nun　Sandy-ka　mwues-ul　mek-ess-ta-ko　sayngkakha-ni?
you-TOP　Sandy-NOM　what-ACC　eat-PST-DECL-CONN　think-QUE
'What do you think Sandy ate?'

(ii) a. Why do you think Sandy came here?

b. 너는 　샌디가 　왜 　여기에 　왔다고 　생각하니?
ne-nun　Sandy-ka　way　yekiey　oa-ss-ta-ko　sayngkakha-ni?
you-TOP　Sandy-NOM　why　here　come-PST-DECL-CONN　think-QUE
'Why do you think Sandy came here?'

7 Draw tree structures for the following sentences, and then identify the element that determines each sentence's interrogative type.

(i) a. 미미가 　그 책을 　읽었니?
Mimi-ka　ku　chayk-ul　ilk-ess-ni?
Mimi-NOM　the　book-ACC　read-PST-QUE
'Did Mimi read the book?'

b. 해태는 　어떻게 　다시 　강팀이 　되었나?
Haythay-nun　ettehkey　tasi　kangthim-i　toy-ess-na?
Haythay-TOP　how　again　strong.team-NOM　become-PST-QUE
'How has Haythay become a strong team again?'

c. 너는 　주말에 　어디에서 　남자친구를 　만났니?
ne-nun　cwumal-ey　eti-eyse　namcachinkwu-lul　manna-ss-ni?
you-TOP　weekend-on　where-LOC　boyfriend-ACC　meet-PST-que
'Where did you meet your boyfriend on the weekend?'

d. 눈을 　감고 　무슨 　생각을 　하고 　있니?
nwun-ul　kam-ko　mwusun　sayngkak-ul　hako　iss-ni?
eye-ACC　close-and　what　thought-ACC　do-CONN　be-QUE
'What are you thinking about with your eyes closed?'

e. 어느 　별에서 　왔니?
enu　pyel-eyse　wa-ss-ni?
which　planet-from　come-PST-QUE
'Which planet did you come from?'

f. 어제 　몇 　점 　받았나요?
ecey　myech　cem　pat-ass-nayo?
yesterday　how.much　score　receive-PST-QUE
'What score did you receive yesterday?'

10

Relative Clauses: Building Bigger Nominal Expressions

10.1 Modifying an NP in the Postnominal Position

There are two main ways to have a complex NP in English: with a prenominal or postnominal modifier:

(1) a. He is a [theoretical] linguist.
 b. He is a linguist [studying English and Korean].

The adjective *theoretical* functions as a prenominal modifier, whereas *studying English and Korean* is a postnominal modifier. Postnominal modifiers are the same as prenominal modifiers with respect to what they modify. The only difference is that they follow the expression they modify. Various phrases can function as postnominal modifiers not a simple but complex expression:

(2) a. [The boy [$_{PP}$ in the doorway]] waved to his father.
 b. [The man [$_{AP}$ eager to start the meeting]] is John's sister.
 c. [The man [$_{VP}$ holding the bottle]] disappeared.
 d. [The papers [$_{VP}$ removed from the safe]] have not been found.

Relative clauses can also function as postnominal modifiers:

(3) a. [The boy [who stood in the doorway]] waved to me.
 b. [The money [that you gave me]] disappeared last night.

The bracketed relative clauses are introduced by a special class of pronouns called relative pronouns, such as *who* and *that*. In other languages, relative clauses may

English and Korean in Contrast: A Linguistic Introduction, First Edition. Jong-Bok Kim.
© 2024 John Wiley & Sons, Inc. Published 2024 by John Wiley & Sons, Inc.

be marked in different ways: they could be introduced by a suffixal marker called a relativizer. That is, the main verb of the relative clause may appear in a special morphological variant as in Korean and Mandarin Chinese:

(4) a. [[내가 좋아하는] 옷은] 비싸다
    nay-ka cohaha-nun os-un pissa-ta
    I-NOM like-MOD clothing-MOD expensive-DECL
    'The clothes I like are expensive.'

  b. [[Wo xihuan de] yifu] hen gui
    I like PRT clothing very expensive
    'The clothes I like are expensive.'

There are also languages like Japanese where a relative clause is marked by word order alone, with no morphological marking on the verb:

(5) Hanako-ga [[Taroo-ga _ tukutta] susi-o] tabeta
    Hanako-NOM Taroo-NOM made sushi-ACC ate
    'Hanako ate the sushi that Taroo made.'

In this chapter, we discuss relative clauses in English and Korean and see how they behave alike and differently.

10.2 Relative Clauses in English

10.2.1 *Wh*-Relative Clauses

As noted, a relative clause is a type of subordinate clause that modifies a nominal expression. The relative clause includes an expression or device to indicate that one of the complements or modifiers within the clause has the same referent as the antecedent NP. For example, consider the following:

(6) I like [the student [who has a grit mindset to reach their long-term goals]].

In this sentence, the bracketed expression is a relative clause and modifies the antecedent NP *the student*. The relative pronoun *who* indicates that it refers to the same individual as the antecedent *the student*.

The combination of a relative clause with its antecedent NP is allowed by the Head-Modifier Rule. The relative clause functions as a modifier of the antecedent *the student*. The antecedent is typically the closest possible constituent to the relative pronoun. There are two possible structures for English relative clauses (Rel.S):

(7) a. NP-Rel.S structure

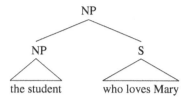

b. CNP-Rel.S structure

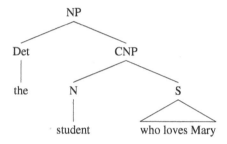

The key difference lies in the semantics. In (7a), the relative clause modifies the whole NP; but in (7b), the clause modifies only the CNP (common noun phrase, which lacks a determiner), and the determiner specifies the resulting value.[1] The semantic reason strongly favors the CNP-Rel.S given in (7b). Consider the following two sentences from the NP-Rel.S analysis:

(8) a. John ate [[every fish] [that/which he caught]].
b. John ate [[no fish] [that/which he caught]].

The NP-S analysis indicated by the brackets incorrectly implies that John either caught 'x' ('every fish') and ate every fish, and John caught 'x' (no fish) and ate no fish, respectively. However, these sentences mean John caught some fish and ate all of them, and John caught some fish but ate none of them, respectively. These meanings are best represented by the CNP-Rel.S analysis, as follows:

(9) a. John ate [every [fish [that/which he caught]]].
b. John ate [no [fish that/which he caught]].

---

1 The CNP is thus a nominal expression that can combine with a determiner. This is often called an intermediate N-bar (N ') phrase, which is bigger than a word but smaller than a full NP.

The structures here indicate that the relative clause combines with the CNP *fish*, which can then refer to all the individual 'fish' John caught. The determiners *every* and *no* then can refer to all or none of them, respectively, yielding the desired meanings.

An important property of relative clauses is that just like *wh*-interrogatives, the relative clause consists of two parts: a relative pronoun and an incomplete sentence missing an expression (marked with an underscore), as illustrated in these examples:

(10) a. the person [[whom] [the police are looking for __]].
b. the person [[on whom] [we all rely __]].

The ungrammaticality of the following indicates that the relative clause obligatorily contains one missing element:

(11) a. *The police are looking for.
b. *We all rely.

(12) a. *the person [[whom] [the police are looking for the thief]].
b. *the person [[on whom] [we all rely on the man]].

As with *wh*-interrogatives, the missing element is linked to the relative pronoun and the antecedent, as seen from the propositional meaning of the relative clauses:

(13) a. The police are looking for the man.
b. We all rely on Kim.

The data gives us the following observations for English relative clauses:

- The English relative clause is introduced by a relative pronoun (marked with the feature REL (relativizer).
- The relative clause modifies a preceding antecedent CNP.
- The relative clause is an incomplete sentence with one missing element (marked as /XP).
- The slashed gap is discharged by the filler *wh*-relative phrase.

Reflecting these properties, we can have a structure like the following for a relative clause such as *the person whom Fred met*:

(14)

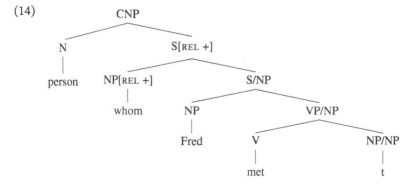

As shown in the structure, the object of the verb *met* is slashed (realized as a gap). The slashed NP metaphorically percolates up until it is discharged by the filler, *who*. The relative pronoun, which has the REL feature, ensures that the relative clause introduced by the pronoun modifies a proper antecedent. This incomplete S containing the slashed NP combines with its filler based on the Head-Filler Rule, forming a complete S. This complete S[REL +] relative clause then modifies the head noun *person*, whose resulting phrase forms a CNP that can combine with a determiner like *nor* or *every*, as in the following:

(15) a. [No [person [whom Fred met]]] came to the party.
  b. [Every [person [whom Fred met]]] came to the party.

Because the relative clause is a type of the head-filler construction (refer to Chapter 9), there must be a total syntactic identity between the gap and the filler:

(16) a. Jack is the person [[$_{NP}$ whom] [Jenny fell in love with [$_{NP}$ __]]].
  b. Jack is the person [[$_{PP}$ with whom] [Jenny fell in love [$_{PP}$ __]]].

(17) a. *Jack is the person [[$_{NP}$ whom] [Jenny fell in love [$_{PP}$ __]]].
  b. *Jack is the person [[$_{PP}$ with whom] [Jenny fell in love with [$_{NP}$ __]]].

In (16a) and (16b), the gap and the filler are in the same category, whereas those in (17) are not. The putative gap in (17a) is a PP and that in (17b) an NP, but the fillers are the nonmatching categories NP and PP, respectively.

In addition, the gap relative clauses, as the one in interrogative clauses, can be embedded in a deeper position, provided that it finds an appropriate filler. This is possible because the slash feature can percolate up to the point where it is discharged:

(18)

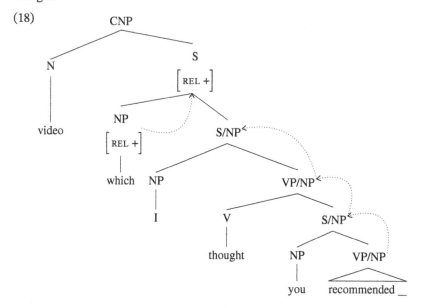

In (18), the slash value starts from the verb of the embedded clause and percolates up to the top S. The value is discharged by the filler *wh*-phrase *which*.

Just like the QUE feature which we discussed in the previous chapter, the non-local REL feature can come from a deeper position within the nonhead daughter of the relative clause:

(19) a. I met the critic [whose remarks [I wanted to object to ___]].
   b. This is the friend [for whose mother [Kim gave a party ___]].
   c. The teacher set us a problem, [the answer to which [we can find ___ in the textbook]].

A simplified structure for (19b) serves to illustrate this point:

(20)

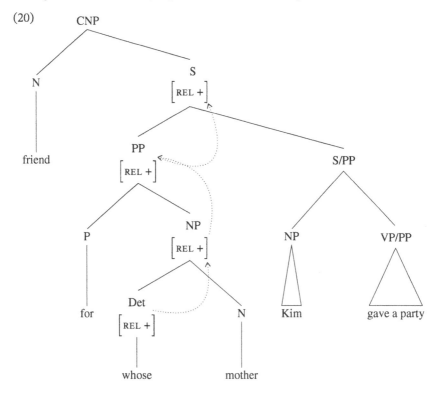

The REL feature is embedded in the specifier of the inner NP *whose mother*, and this value percolates up to the top S so that it can function as a modifier of the head noun *friend*.

The gapped element in the relative clause can be any argument, including the subject. Subject relative clauses must have a *wh*-relative pronoun including *that*:

(21) a. The senators *(who) met Fred were all delighted.
    b. Do not eat the apple *(that) fell on the ground.

A possessive noun can also be relativized:

(22) The senator whose son was arrested by the police announced his resignation.

A finite VP is not allowed to function as a postnominal modifier in subject relative clauses:

(23) a. *The student [met Kim] came.
    b. *The problem [intrigued us] bothered me.

The relative clauses we have discussed so far include *wh*-phrases that function as arguments (subject or complement). The relative clause can also be introduced by an adverbial *wh*-phrase:

(24) a. That's the restaurant where we met. (where = in which)
    b. I remember the day when we first met. (when = on which)
    c. Tell me the reason why you came home. (why = for which)

The adverbial relative pronoun can be replaced by a preposition and a relative pronoun, as given in parentheses. This implies that there are two interpretations for such adverbial relative clauses. One is to assume that there is no gap within the relative clause, the adverbial relative pronoun combines with the clause, and the result modifies the antecedent:

(25)

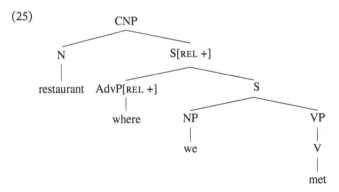

The other possible analysis is to assume that there is a missing adverbial in the clause, denoting place, time, or reason:

(26)

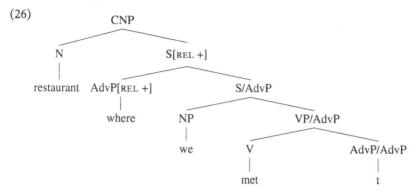

10.2.2 *Wh-* vs. *That-*Relative Clauses

Most relative pronouns are *wh-*pronouns, but we can also have *that* as a relative pronoun. The following coordination data tell us that *that* behaves just like *which*:

(27) a. Every essay [which] she's written and [that] I've read is on that pile.
 b. Every essay [that] she's written and [which] I've read is on that pile.

The only real obstacle facing the treatment of relative *that* as a pronominal is the fact that it disallows pied-piping, the relative pronoun dragging the preposition together to the front position. As seen from (28), the relative pronouns *which*, *whose*, and *whom* can be fronted with the preposition:

(28) a. The company [in which] we placed our trust …
 b. The people [in whose house] we stayed …
 c. The person [with whom] we were talking …

However, this kind of pied-piping is not possible with the relative pronoun *that*:

(29) a. *The city [in that] they were living …
 b. *The person [with that] we were talking …

10.2.3 Reduced Relative Clauses

The examples in the following include a postnominal expression, but each of the postnomincal expression can be taken as a reduced relative clause with the string '*wh-*phrase + *be*' is omitted.

(30) a. the person [standing on my foot]
 b. the prophet [descended from heaven]
 c. the people [in Rome]
 d. the people [happy with the proposal]

    e. the people [passed by the House yesterday]
    f. the person [to finish the project by tomorrow]

The bracketted VP, PP, or AP here modifies the preceding antecedent. This then implies that each can be interpreted as the elided form of a *wh*-phrase and the copula verb:

(31) a. the person [who is] standing on my foot
      b. the prophet [who is] descended from heaven
      c. the people [who are] in Rome

The difference between the reduced relative clause and the full relative clause is what modifies the noun, as shown in the following:

(32)

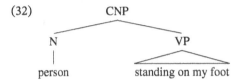

As given in the structure, the VP[*ing*], not a relative clause, modifies the preceding head noun. Of course, not all VP phrases can function as postmodifiers. A base VP or finite VP cannot function as a postnominal modifier:

(33) a. *the person [stand on my foot]
      b. *the person [stood on my foot]
      c. *the person [stands on my foot]

10.2.4 Finite vs. Infinitival Relative Clauses

We can also classify relative clauses by the finiteness of the verb in the relative clause:

(34) a. I found a book [which you can read].
      b. I found a book [for you to read].

    These two types are identical in terms of meaning, but infinitival clauses have additional constraints. Consider these infinitival examples:

(35) a. He is the kind of person with whom to consult.
      b. There is not a whole lot with which to disagree.
      c. We will invite volunteers with whom to work.

Interestingly, the *wh*-infinitival relative clause, just like the wh-infinitival interrogative clause we discussed in the previous chapter, does not allow the missing expression (gap) to be an NP; it must be a PP, as exemplified in (36) and (37):

(36) a. *a person whom to give the book to
      b. a person to whom to give the book

(37) a. *a bench which to sit on
  b. a bench on which to sit

Infinitival relative clauses never allow an overt subject:

(38) a. *the baker in whom for you to place your trust
  b. the baker in whom to place your trust

Another intriguing property concerns that infinitival relatives cannot follow a *wh*-relative clause, as illustrated in (39):

(39) a. The only person [(for us) to visit] [whose kids Dana is willing to put up with] is Pat.
  b. *The only person [whose kids Dana is willing to put up with] [(for us) to visit] is Pat.

10.2.5 Restrictive vs. Nonrestrictive Relative Clauses

An important property of English relative clauses is the distinction between restrictive and nonrestrictive (or supplementary) relative clauses:

(40) a. The builder who erects very fine houses will make a large profit. (restrictive)
  b. The builder, who erects very fine houses, will make a large profit. (nonrestrictive)

As given here, the distinction between the two types is made by punctuation (pause in speech) and contributes to a significant meaning difference. A restrictive relative clause limits the thing it refers to. The meaning of the sentence would change if the clause were deleted. Meanwhile, a supplementary (nonrestrictive) relative clause adds extra or additional information to a sentence. The sentence's meaning would not change if the clause were omitted. This optionality in a sense makes nonrestrictive or suppplementary relative claues to be set off by commas. With this difference, we could observe that (40a) refers not to a single builder but to a set of builders who meet a particular qualification (being able to erect fine houses). Meanwhile, (40b) refers to only one individual builder, and this individual builds 'very fine' houses and will make a large profit.

To understand more detailed properties of these two types of relative clauses, let us first consider typical examples of restrictive relative clauses:

(41) a. [The person] who Kim asked for help thinks Kim is foolish.
  b. Kim has [two sisters] who became lawyers.

The relative clauses in (41) semantically restrict the denotation of *person* and *two sisters*. Indefinite pronouns such as *everyone* and *nothing*, or indefinite determiners like *every* and *no*, can be modified by the restrictive relative clause. As noted earlier, unlike the restrictive relative clause, the supplementary relative clause semantically provides extra information, with a *wh*-phrase separated from the noun by a comma or comma intonation:

(42) a. [The person], who Kim asked for help, thinks Kim is foolish.
    b. Kim has [two sisters], who became lawyers.

The phrase *two sisters, who became lawyers* means there are two sisters, and they both became lawyers. In addition, only a supplementary relative clause can modify a proper noun:

(43) a. [Reagan], whom the Republicans nominated in 1980, now lives in California.
    b. *[Reagan] whom the Republicans nominated in 1980 now lives in California.

Certain quantified NPs do not allow supplementary relative clauses:

(44) a. No child who was examined by the doctor received a lollipop.
    b. *[No child], who was examined by the doctor received a lollipop.

The reason for the unacceptability of (44b) is attributed to the meaning of *no child*. To add additional information, we need to identify the reference of *no child*, but it is not possible. However, as we have seen, we could interpret [child who was examined by the doctor] first and then select none of the individuals referred by the CNP.

One way to account for these differences between restrictive and supplementary relative clauses is to adopt different syntactic structures. That is, the syntactic and meaning difference has given rise to the idea that the RRC modifies the meaning of CNP – a noun phrase without a determiner – whereas the SRC modifies a fully determined NP:

(45) Restrictive relative clause (RRC)

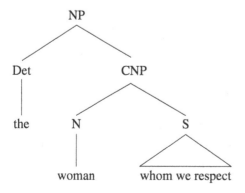

(46) Supplementary relative clause (SRC)

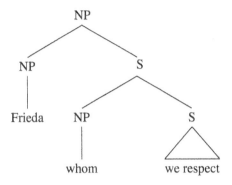

These representational differences are intended to reflect the fact that the RRC is interpreted as restricting the set of women under consideration to a particular subset (those whom we respect), whereas the SRC simply adds information about the antecedent 'Frieda.'

10.3 Relative Clauses in Korean

10.3.1 Complex NPs

Similar to English, Korean can have a prenominal modifier. In Chapter 4, we saw that an adjectival expression (stative VP), a possessive NP, or a relative clause can function as a prenominal modifier:

(47) a. 부지런한   [(그) 학생]
        pwucilenha-n ku   haksayng
        diligent-MOD the   student
        'the diligent student'

   b. [미미의] 학생
        Mimi-uy haksayng
        Mimi-GEN student
        'Mimi's student'

   c. [미미가   만난]   [부지런한]   [(그) 학생]
        Mimi-ka   manna-n pwucilenha-n ku   haksayng
        Mimi-NOM meet-MOD diligent-MOD the   student
        'the diligent student whom Mimi met'

Unlike English, however, Korean does not allow a postnominal modifier:

(48) a. *그 학생　　부지런한
　　　ku　haksayng　pwucilenha-n
　　　the　student　　diligent-MOD
　　　'(intended) the diligent student'

　　b. *그 학생　미미가　만난　부지런한
　　　ku haksayng Mimi-ka　manna-n pwucilenha-n
　　　the student　Mimi-NOM meet-MOD diligent-MOD
　　　'the diligent student whom Mimi met'

Korean, similar to English, has several different types of complex NPs with a clause, including appositive and relative clauses. Compare the following two:

(49) a. Appositive
　　　미미가　　사건을　　보고한　　사실
　　　Mimi-ka　saken-ul　pokoha-n　sasil
　　　Mimi-NOM accident-ACC report-MOD fact
　　　'the fact that Mimi reported the accident'

　　b. Relative
　　　미미가　＿＿　보고한　사실
　　　Mimi-ka　　pokoha-n　sasil
　　　Mimi-NOM　report-MOD fact
　　　'the fact that Mimi reported ＿'

The difference is that the appositive clause contains no gap, whereas the relative clause has the object gapped. That is, the prenominal clause has no syntactic gap but functions as the complement of the appositive noun:

(50) a. Appositive clause

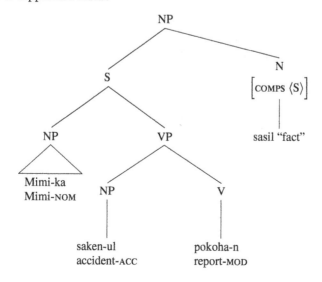

b. Relative clause

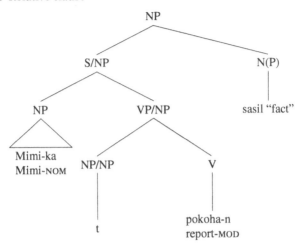

As represented in the structure, the noun *sasil* 'fact' in (50a) has an appositive clause as its complement, whereas in (50b), the noun 'fact' is modified by a relative clause (S) missing a slashed NP. In this section, we will see the structural difference between appositive and relative clauses.

10.3.2 Canonical Relative Clauses

The starting point of Korean relatives is their morphology. The predicate (stative or nonstative verb) of a relative clause preceding the head noun is marked with a morphological marker that varies with tense information. Observe the following data set:

(51) a. [미미가 읽는] 책
    [Mimi-ka ___$_i$ ilk-nun] chayk $_i$
    Mimi-NOM read-PRES.MOD book
    'the book that Mimi reads'

  b. [미미가 읽은 책]
    [Mimi-ka ___$_i$ ilk-un] chayk $_i$
    Mimi-NOM read-PST.MOD book
    'the book that Mimi read'

  c. [미미가 읽을 책]
    [Mimi-ka ___$_i$ ilk-ul] chayk
    Mimi-NOM read FUT.REL book
    'the book that Mimi will read'

Like mood suffixes, the prenominal relative clause has a verb marked with a modifying (MOD) suffix carrying its own tense information. These three basic tense-sensitive markers can also be extended to denote aspects when combined with tense suffixes. Thus, the other possible prenominal verb forms of the lexeme 읽- *ilk-* 'read' are 읽 던 *ilk-ten* 'read-progressive,' 읽 었 던 *ilk-essten* 'read-past progressive,' 읽 었 을 *ilk-essul* 'read-past conjecture,' 읽 었 었 을 *ilk-essessul* 'read-past perfective conjecture,' 읽고 있던 *ilk-ko issten*, and 'read-past perfective progressive.' Let us consider the structure of (51b):

(52)

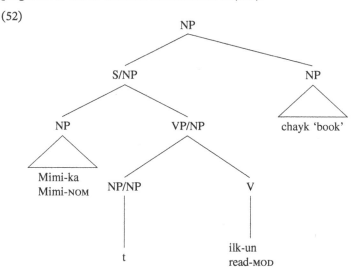

As represented here, the object NP is slashed (/). This slash value percolates up to the S level, whereas *ilk-un* indicates that the sentence (or clause) projected from this modifies an N(P). Note that unlike English relative clauses with a relative pronoun, there is no relative pronoun with which the incomplete S can combine (e.g. *which Mimi read*). The key reason is that the MOD suffix already tells us that the incomplete S with a MOD V will modify the nominal that follows the clause. This implies that unlike in English, an incomplete S with a missing element projected from the MOD marked verb functions as a prenominal clausal modifier, as stated in the following:

(53) Head-Rel Modifier Rule in Korean:
    NP → S/NP[MOD <NP>], N(P)

This rule tells us that relative clause formation is a subtype of the Head-Modifier Rule. The relative clause, similar to English bare relative clauses (e.g. *the student Mimi met*), has no relative pronoun and is an incomplete sentence. However, the incomplete sentence must be marked with a MOD value. This MOD value comes from the verb ending, blocking examples like the following:

(54) # 미미가   읽어   모모
    [Mimi-ka   __   ilk-e]   Momo
    Mimi-NOM   read-CONN   Momo

The analysis can account for more complex cases. Even in complex sentences, the prenominal morphological marker appears on the highest verb, as in (55):

(55) [모두가   [미미가   __   읽었다고]]   생각하는   책
    motwu-ka   Mimi-ka   __$_i$ ilk-ess-ta-ko   sayngkakha-nun chayk $_i$
    everyone-NOM Mimi-NOM   read-PST-DECL-COMP think-MOD   book
    'the book that everyone thinks Mimi read.'

The following structure illustrates this point:

(56)

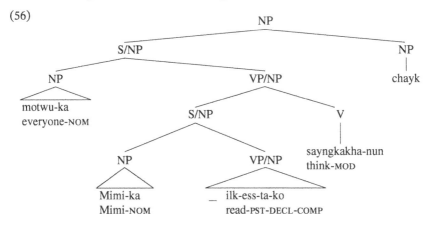

This structure tells us that the verb *sayngkakha-nun* 'think-MOD' ensures that the clause headed by the verb modifies an NP. The object of the verb *ilk-ess-ta-ko* 'read-PST-DECL-COMP' is gapped, and this value percolates up to the top S. This percolated, gapped NP is linked to the antecedent NP *chayk*, giving us a proper meaning relation between the relative clause and the antecedent NP.

Most of the syntactic properties of a relative clause are determined by the morphology of its main verb. Korean relative clauses, one of whose distinctive properties is the absence of any relative pronouns in English, allow the relativization of the subject as well as complements:

(57) a. Subject
    [메리에게   책을   준]   김
    [__ Mary-eykey chayk-ul cwu-n]   Kim (Subject Relative)
        Mary-DAT   book-ACC give-MOD Kim
    'Kim who gave the book to Mary'

   b. Object

      [김이   메리에게 준]   책

      [Kim-i   __ Mary-eykey cwu-n] chayk (Object Relative)

      Kim-NOM   Mary-DAT   give-MOD book

      'the book that Kim gave Mary'

   c. Indirect Object

      [김이   책을   준]   메리

      [Kim-i   chayk-ul __ cwu-n] Mary (IO Relative)

      Kim-NOM book-ACC   give-MOD Mary

      'Mary to whom Kim gave the book'

In terms of relativization, there is no distinction between complements and adjuncts. In addition to source or instrument arguments, adverbials such as time, place, manner, degree, process, and reason can be easily relativized. We can analyze such examples as having no gap or as having a gap value in the clause, as shown in (58):

(58) a. [그 학생이   __ 노래를 부른]   시간

      [ku haksayng-i   __ nolay-lul pwulu-n] sikan

      the student-NOM   song-ACC sing-MOD time

      'the time when the student sang a song'

   b. [그 학생이   __ 노래를 부른]   장소

      [ku haksayng-i   __ nolay-lul pwulu-n] cangso

      the student-NOM   song-ACC sing-MOD place

      'the place where the student sang a song'

   c. [그 학생이   __ 노래를 부른]   이유

      [ku haksayng-i   __ nolay-lul pwulu-n] iyu

      the student-NOM   song-ACC sing-MOD reason

      'the reason why the student sang a song'

As represented here, we could assume that there is an adverbial gap (temporal, location, reason) in each of these examples. This gapped element, like an argument gap, is linked to the antecedent adverbial NP.

10.3.3 Internally Headed Relative Clauses

Some relative clauses do not contain a gap in Korean. Examples in the following include the so called *internally headed relative clauses*:

(59) a. [[도둑이 보석을 훔쳐 도망가는] 것을] 잡았다.
   totwuk-i posek-ul hwumchi-e tomangka-nun kes-ul cap-ass-ta
   thief-NOM jewel-ACC steal-CONN run.away-MOD KES-ACC catch-PST-DECL
   '(They) caught the thief who stole a jewel and ran away.'

   b. 미미는 [[사과가 쟁반 위에 있는] 것을] 먹었다.
   Mimi-nun sakwa-ka cayngpan wi-ey iss-nun kes-ul mek-ess-ta
   Mimi-TOP apple-NOM tray on-LOC COP-MOD KES-ACC eat-PST-DECL
   'Mimi ate the apple that was on a tray.'

The semantic object of *cap-ass-ta* 'catch-PST-DECL' in (59a) is not *kes-ul* 'thing-ACC' but *totwuk-i* 'thief-NOM', which is inside the embedded clause. The sentence means what Mimi ate is the apple that was on the tray, not the thing. The head noun ('apple') that the relative clause modifies is inside the relative clause.

These IHRCs clearly differ from the typical EHRCs (externally headed relative clauses) that we have discussed. Consider the corresponding EHRCs in the following:

(60) a. [[보석을 훔쳐 도망가는] 도둑을] 잡았다.
   posek-ul hwumchi-e tomangka-nun totwuk-ul cap-ass-ta
   jewel-ACC steal-CONN run.away-MOD thief-ACC catch-PST-DECL
   '(They) caught the thief who stole a jewel and ran away.'

   b. 미미는 [[쟁반 위에 있는] 사과를] 먹었다.
   Mimi-nun cayngpan wi-ey iss-nun sakwa-lul mek-ess-ta
   Mimi-TOP tray on-LOC COP-MOD sakwa-ACC eat-PST-DECL
   'Mimi ate the apple that was on a tray.'

In these examples, the semantic objects (*totwuk* and *sakwa*) of the verbs *cap-ass-ta* 'caught' and *mek-ess-ta* 'eat' are not in the clause but outside the clause. The head is thus in the external position, not in the internal position of the relative clause.

In addition to this internally and externally headed difference, there are three others. First, the internally headed relative clause in (59) is a complete sentence, whereas the externally headed relative clause in (60) is an incomplete sentence with a syntactic gap (slashed value), as we saw earlier. Second, the head noun that the IHRC modifies is the so-called bound noun 것 *kes*, whereas the head noun the EHRC modifies is a regular nominal expression. This bound noun, unlike common nouns, must have a specifier (determiner or a clause) as in (61):

(61) a. *(이/저/그) 것
   i/ce/ku kes
   this/that/the thing

b. *(미미가   책을   읽은)   것이   자랑스럽다.
  Mimi-ka   chayk-ul ilk-un   kes-i   calangslep-ta
  Mimi-NOM book-ACC read-PRES thing-NOM proud-DECL
  'I am proud of Mimi's reading the book.'

The IHRC combining with *kes* is thus an obligatory expression, whereas the EHRC modifying a head noun is optional. This serves as the third difference between IHRCs and EHRCs: in IHRCs, the bound noun *kes* is not modified by a clause, as in EHRCs, but syntactically combines with its sentential complement, as illustrated in the following:

(62)

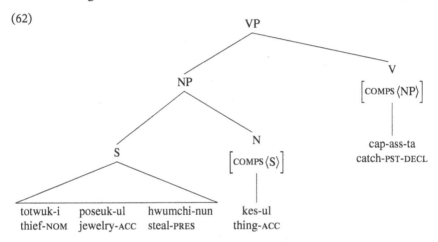

It is clear that the relative clause includes no syntactic gap, but its head verb is still marked with the present-tense modifier suffix:

(63) 도둑이   보석을   훔치는/*훔쳤던   것을   잡았다.
    totwuk-i posek-ul   hwumchi-nun/*humchi-ess-ten kes-ul cap-ass-ta
    thief-NOM jewelry-ACC steal-MOD/steal-PST-MOD   KES-ACC catch-PST-DECL
    '(They) caught the thief stole who stole a jewel.'

There is an issue in the interpretation: how to link the antecedent head noun *kes* with the internal head within the clause, given that the matrix verb selects the NP headed by this bound noun as in (62). Not only the subject but also the object can serve as the internal head:

(64) a. 책이   책상   위에   있던   것이   사라졌다.
      chayk-i chayksang wi-ey   iss-ten kes-i   salaci-ess-ta
      book-NOM desk   on-LOC COP-MOD KES-NOM disappear-PST-DECL
      'The book which was on the desk disappeared.'

b. 소년이 공을 던진 것이 멀리 날아갔다.
sonyen-i kong-ul tenci-n kes-i melli nalaka-ss-ta
boy-NOM ball-ACC throw-MOD KES-NOM far.away fly-PST-DECL
'The ball that the boy threw flew far away.'

What disappeared in (64a) is the subject 'the book', and what flew far away is not the subject 'boy' but the object 'ball' in (64b). We have seen that in the canonical relative clause with no relative pronoun, the index value of a gap in the clause is identified with the head noun. But in the IHRC, the head noun 것이 kes-i is identified with either the subject or the object within its complement clause. We could thus have the following generalization:

(65) Antecedent Constraint in the IHRC:
In the IHRC, the head noun *kes* is identified with the most prominent argument (usually the subject or object) of its complement clause.

The complement clause of *kes* in (64) describes the situation where the book is on the desk, and the most prominent argument is the subject *chayk-i* 'book-NOM,' not the oblique argument *chayksang* 'desk.' This constraint thus identifies *kes* with the subject, and hence what disappeared is the book. This kind of constraint blocks examples like the following, where the bound noun *kes* is linked to the oblique complement *chayksayng wi-ey* 'desk on-at':

(66) *책이 책상 위에 있던 것이 부서졌다.
chayk-i chayksang wi-ey iss-ten kes-i pwuse-ci-ess-ta
book-NOM desk on-LOC COP-MOD KES-NOM break-PASS-PST-DECL
'(int.) The desk on which a book was located broke.'

10.3.4 Pseudo-Relative Clauses

Korean has one more type of relatives that is controlled by discourse. Consider the following so-called pseudo-relative clauses:

(67) a. 태풍이 지나간 흔적
thayphwung-i cinaka-n huncek
typhoon-NOM pass-MOD trace
'the trace from a typhoon's passing by'
b. 생선이 타는 냄새
sayngsen-i tha-nun naymsay
fish-NOM burn-MOD smell
'the smell from a fish's burning'

At first glance, such examples resemble typical relative clauses (EHRCs). But they behave differently from relative clauses and so are called pseudo-RCs. The key distinctive property of the relative clause here is that it contains no syntactic gap but modifies the head nominal.

The following examples indicate that the prenominal clause is a complete clause with no missing expression:

(68) a. 태풍이　　　지나갔다.
　　　thayphwung-i　cinaka-ss-ta
　　　typhoon-NOM　pass.by-PST-DECL
　　　'The typhoon passed by.'
　　b. 생선이　　　탔다.
　　　sayngsen-i tha-ss-ta
　　　fish-NOM　burn-PST-DECL
　　　'The fish burned.'

The modification by the complete clause describes a situation caused by the relative clause. That is, (67a) refers to the trace left from a typhoon, whereas (67b) denotes the smell caused by the fish's burning. If the head noun cannot build such a cause-effect relation, we have illegitimate examples:

(69) a. 태풍이　　　지나간　흔적/*모양/*냄새
　　　thayphwung-i　cinaka-n　huncek/moyang/naymsay
　　　typhoon-NOM　pass-MOD　trace/posture/smell
　　　'(lit.) the trace/posture/smell from a typhoon's passing by'
　　b. 생선이　　　타는　　　냄새/*모양/*흔적
　　　sayngsen-i tha-nun　naymsay/moyang/huncek
　　　fish-NOM　burn-MOD smell/posture/trace
　　　'(lit.) the smell/posture/trace from the fish's burning'

A posture or smell cannot directly cause a typhoon; neither can a trace be a cause of cooking a fish.

An additional property of the pseudo-RC, similar to the IHRC, is that the clause allows only present-tense information:

(70) 생선이　　　타는/*탈/*탔던　　　　　냄새
　　sayngsen-i tha-nun/tha-l/tha-asstun　　naymsay
　　fish-NOM　burn-MOD.PRES/MOD.FUT/MOD-PST smell
　　'the smell from a fish's burning/*having burned/*being burned in future'

The IHRC and pseudo-RC are also alike in that they both denote a positive situation (the situation that happens or happened):

(71) *고무가　　타지　　　않는　냄새
　　*komwu-ka tha-ci　　anh-nun naymsay
　　rubber-NOM burn-CONN not-MOD　smell
　　'the smell from synthetic rubber's not being burned'

Observing these examples, we can state the following constraint:

(72) Cause-effect constraint on the pseudo-RC:
A pseudo-RC with no syntactic gap modifies a head noun when the two are in a cause-effect relation observed in the present situation.

This pragmatic constraint accounts for why the pseudo-RC must describe a current situation that we can see. The cause-effect constraint in pseudo-RCs allows examples like the following:

(73) a. 잠이   오는   음악
cam-i   o-nun   umak
sleep-NOM come-MOD   music
'the music that makes you sleep'

b. 머리가   아픈   주사
meli-ka   aphu-n   cwusa
head-NOM   sick-MOD   shot
'(lit.) the shot that makes you head sick'

Similar to the other pseudo-RC examples, there is a cause-effect relation between the music and the situation of making one sleep.

The pseudo-RC has a simple syntactic structure:

(74)

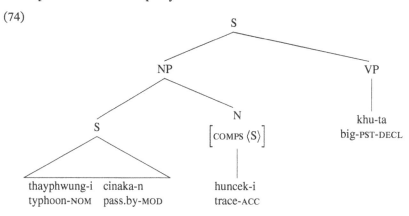

The relative clause modifies the head nominal *huncek-i* 'trace-NOM.' They have a cause-effect relationship. When there is no such relation, we have an appositive construction:

(75) 태풍이   지나간   사실
thayphwung-i cinaka-n   sasil
typhoon-NOM   pass.by-MOD   fact
'the fact that a typhoon passed by'

In such a case, there is an identity semantic relation between the head noun 'fact' and the clause 'a typhoon passed by.' The noun *fact* that has an appositive clause thus selects a sentential complement, resulting in an identity semantic relation.

10.4 Contrastive Notes

10.4.1 Relative Pronoun or Not

An obvious difference between English and Korean comes from relative pronouns: unlike English, Korean does not employ relative pronouns like *who, which, why, how,* and *that.* Korean makes the relative clause using the word order and the prenominal ending on the verb. We have observed that the MOD feature of a relative clause originates from a relative pronoun in English and from a MOD-marked verb in Korean. This contrast can again be seen in the following pair:

(76) a. Mimi met [the boy [who read the book]].
 b. 미미는   책을   읽은   아이를 만났다.
   Mimi-nun chayk-ul ilk-un   ai-ul   manna-ss-ta
   Mimi-TOP book-ACC read-MOD boy-ACC meet-PST-DECL
   'Mimi met the boy who read the book.'

10.4.2 Types of Relative Clauses

Typical relative clauses in English and Korean have a syntactic gap: the incomplete relative clause modifies a head noun. Depending on the type of this gap, both languages have argument-gapped relative clauses and adjunct (-gapped) relative clauses.

Other than this similarity, English and Korean have different subtypes of relative clauses. A key classification of English relative clauses is between restrictive and nonrestrictive (supplementary) RCs, but Korean has no such classification. As we have noted, the differences between restrictive and supplementary clauses yield distinctive differences in meaning:

(77) a. The student who missed class was behind on her homework.
  b. The student, who missed class, was behind on her homework.

The restrictive clause in (77a) talks about a specific student who missed class. The student is the one behind on her homework and not any of the other students. On the other hand, the supplementary nonrestrictive clause in (77a) tells us the extra information about the student that the interlocutors are aware of. This student missed class, and she was behind on her homework. Such a distinction is important in English.

In Korean, subject relative clauses with intransitive stative or nonstative verbs are possible:

(78) a. 달리고   있는   기차
      talli-ko   iss-nun   kicha
      run-CONN exist-MOD train
      'the train that is running'
    b. 더러운   강아지
      telewu-un kangaci
      dirty-MOD dog
      'dirty dog'

In these examples, the relative clause includes only a nonstative verb complex or a simple stative predicate. The latter superficially behaves like an adjective in English.

Unlike English, Korean does not allow postposition stranding or pied-piping simply because the counterpart expression is attached to the host NP. The contrast can be observed from the following:

(79) a. the kettle which I boiled water in
    b. the kettle in which I boiled water

(80) a. 물을   주전자에   끓였다.
      mwul-ul   cwucenca-ey kkulhi-ess-ta
      water-ACC kettle-in   boil-PST-DECL
      'I boiled water in the kettle.'
    b. 물을   끓인 주전자를   버렸다.
      mwul-ul ___ kkulhi-n cwucenca-lul peli-ess-ta
      water-ACC   boil-MOD kettle-ACC   discard-PST-DECL
      'I discarded the kettle I boiled water in.'
    c. *물을   에 끓인   주전자
      *mwul-ul ey kkulhi-n cwucenca
      water-ACC in boil-MOD kettle

As given in (80c), the postposition expression 에 cannot occur alone but must be attached a nominal expression, as we have discussed in Chapter 3.

The link between the antecedent head noun and a missing element in the relative clause depends on context. This sometimes causes ambiguous readings in adverbial relative clauses:

(81) 내가   기사를   쓴   식당
     nay-ka kisa-lul   ssu-n   siktang
     I-NOM   article-ACC write-MOD restaurant

This can mean either of the following, depending on the semantic role of the missing expression:

(82) a. a restaurant about which I wrote an article
  b. a restaurant in which I wrote an article

10.4.3 Context-Sensitive Relative Clauses

Korean has special relative clauses – IHRCs and pseudo-RCs – that are not found in English. These two types of relative clauses are context-sensitive. The distinctive properties of pseudo-RCs can again be seen from the following:

(83) a. 머리가　　좋아　　　지는　　　약
  meli-ka　coh-a　　ci-nun　　yak
  head-NOM　good-CONN　become-MOD　pill
  'the pill that makes our brain smarter'

 b. *약이　　머리가　　좋아　　진다.
  *yak-i　meli-ka　coh-a　ci-n-ta
  pill-NOM　brain-NOM　good-CONN　become-MOD-DECL

 c. 약이　　머리를　　좋게　　한다.
  yak-i　meli-lul　coh-key　ha-n-ta
  pill-NOM　brain-ACC　smart-CONN　do-MOD-DECL
  'The pill makes our brain smarter.'

Example (83a) involves a pseudo-RC with no syntactic gap. (83b) could be a putative source of the relative clause, but it is not acceptable. (83c) is what (83a) is describing, but it cannot serve as its source, as seen from the different grammatical functions of *meli* 'brain.' As we discussed earlier, there is a cause-effect relation between the relative clause and the head nominal in pseudo RCs.

10.5 Conclusion

In this chapter, we have reviewed the grammatical properties of relative clauses in English and Korean. Like *wh*-interrogatives, in both languages, canonical relative clauses have a missing gap in the clause linked to the head noun. The slash feature is linked to the antecedent through the relative pronoun in English and the verb morphology in Korean.

We have also noted that English and Korean have many subtypes of relative clauses. In addition to canonical relative clauses, English has infinitival and reduced relative clauses. Korean has IHRCs and pseudo-relative clauses, neither of which can be found in English. The differences in relative clauses in the two languages have to do with the fact that English relies on structure, whereas Korean often resorts to contextual information.

Exercises

1   Identify the type of each relative clause (e.g. restrictive, nonrestrictive, supplementary, reduced, adverbial, etc.), and mark where the missing element is located in the clause. In addition, give tree structures for the examples. In doing so, use a triangle for the relative clause and an underline for the gap location.

   (i) a. This is the book which I need to read.
       b. The person whom they intended to speak with agreed to reimburse us.
       c. The man on whose lap the puppet is sitting is a ventriloquist.
       d. Valerie looked for a windowsill on which to sit.
       e. She has two teenage children born in the United States.
       f. I work with the people writing those algorithms and the people building the systems.
       g. My friend has two children, whom she loves very much.
       h. I am looking for a person who confesses to me.
       i. The seat where we sat last Saturday is still free.
       j. I can remember a time when I could eat four hamburgers.
       k. We do not know the reason why he left.

2   Give tree structures for the following Korean relative clauses. When there is a missing gap (expression), identify it within the structure with a slash value. When the gap is an adverbial expression, indicate no gap or an adverbial gap.

   (i) a. 내 피자를   먹은   친구
          nay phica-lul mek-un chinkwu
          my pizza-ACC eat-MOD friend
          'the friend who ate my pizza'
       b. 도둑을   잡은   경찰
          totwuk-ul cap-un   kyengchal
          thief-ACC catch-MOD police
          'the police who caught the thief'
       c. 미미가   그 영화를   본   이유
          Mimi-ka   ku yenghwa-lul po-n   iyu
          Mimi-NOM the movie-ACC watch-MOD reason
          'the reason that Mimi watched the movie'

d. 전등이 　바람에 　떨어지는 　것을 　잡았다.
centung-i palam-ey tteleci-nun kes-ul cap-ass-ta
lamp-NOM wind-by fall-MOD KES-ACC catch-PST-DECL
'(I) caught the lamp that was falling because of wind.'

e. 미미는 　모모가 　읽었다고
Mimi-nun Momo-ka ilk-ess-ta-ko
Mimi-TOP Momo-NOM read-PST-DECL-COMP

생각한 　　책을 　　버렸다.
sayngkakha-n chayk-ul peli-ess-ta
think-MOD book-ACC throw.away-PST-DECL
'Mimi threw away the book that she thought Momo read.'

f. 머리가 　타는 　　냄새
meli-ka tha-nun naymsay
hair-NOM burn-MOD smell
'the smell that comes from burning hair'

g. 꽃이 　　꽃병에 　　있던 　　것이 　사라졌다.
kkoch-i kkochpyeng-ey iss-ten kes-i salaci-ess-ta
flower-NOM vase-at exist-MOD KES-NOM disappear-PST-DECL
'The flower which used to be in the vase disappeared.'

3　Draw structures for the following English relative clauses. Also translate each of them into Korean sentences and give glosses. For your Korean translations, give tree structures and briefly note the differences between English and Korean relative clauses.

(i) a. The builder, who erects very fine houses, will make a large profit.
b. The builder who erects very fine houses will make a large profit.

4　Find a grammatical error in each of the following English and Korean sentences, and then explain the nature of the error.

(i) English
a. *They said they are still grateful to the U.S. for removing Saddam Hussein who persecuted the Shia.
b. *Each woman, who thought she was to attend a fashion program, has a friend or relative as coach.
c. *A mentor provides support, encouragement, friendship, and is a person whom to share joys, frustrations, and feelings with.
d. *He had seen a woman resemble Erin get into another car at the scene.
e. *Obama who is expected to make a formal nomination in the fall made clear he had no favored candidate at this point.

    f. *He blasts the media and individual reporters with that he disagrees.

    g. *I looked at Bob quickly who shrugged.

    h. *There are many other artists whom to learn the craft of poetry composition.

    i. *Both young and old people have friends with whom John to drink, discuss, or play games.

(ii) Korean

    a. *김이　　메리에게　책을　　준　　소설
    Kim-i　　Mary-eykey chayk-ul cwu-n　　sosel
    Kim-NOM Mary-DAT　book-ACC give-MOD novel
    '(int.) the novel that Kim gave to Mary'

    b. *식당에서　　　스파게티를　　먹은　　것이　　이층이다.
    siktang-eyse　　suphakeythi-lul mek-un kes-i　　ichung-ita
    restaurant-LOC spaghetti-ACC　　eat-MOD KES-NOM second.floor-be-DECL
    '(int.) That (we) ate spaghetti in the restaurant was on second-floor.'

    c. *생선이　　썩지　　않는　　냄새
    sayngsen-i ssek-ci　　anh-nun naymsay
    fish-NOM　　rot-CONN not-DECL smell
    '(lit.) smell that fish does not rot'

    d. *그 학생이　　대학에　　간　　장소
    ku haksayng-i tayhak-ey ka-n　　cangso
    the student-NOM college-to go-MOD place
    '(int.) the place where the student attended university'

5 The following have structural ambiguities allowing more than one tree structure. Identify these ambiguities with tree structures.

    (i) a. the fact that Momo reported to the headquarters

      b. 모모가　　본부에　　　보고한　　사실
      Momo-ka　　ponpwu-ey　　pokoha-n sasil
      Momo-NOM headquarter-to report-MOD fact

6 We have seen that Korean allows not only EHRCs (externally headed relative clauses) but also IHRCs (internally head relatives) and pseudo-RCs (pseudo-relative clauses). Give at least three confirmed examples for each of these three types, along with their syntactic structures.

11

Topic and Focus: Specifying Given and New Information

11.1 Introduction

We have seen that we can refer to at least three different dimensions when analyzing a given sentence: syntactic category or form, grammatical functions, and semantic roles. For instance, consider this simple sentence:

(1) The monkey chased a weasel in the wood.

The sentence can be analyzed in terms of syntactic categories (e.g. NP, VP, PP), grammatical functions (e.g. subject, complement, modifier), or semantic roles (e.g. agent, patient, location):

(2) a. By syntactic categories or forms:
   $[_S [_{NP}$ The monkey] $[_{VP}$ chased $[_{NP}$ a weasel] $[_{PP}$ in the wood]]].
   b. By grammatical functions:
   $[_S [_{SUBJ}$ The monkey] $[_{PRED}$ chased $[_{OBJ}$ a weasel] $[_{MOD}$ in the wood]]].
   c. By semantic roles:
   $[_S [_{agt}$ The monkey] $[_{pred}$ chased $[_{pat}$ a weasel] $[_{loc}$ in the wood]]].

The syntactic forms are the projections of lexical categories, the grammatical functions indicate the syntactic function of each phrase in the given sentence, and the semantic roles represent each participant's role in the given situation denoted by the main verb.

In addition to these three criteria, we can analyze a sentence based on what role each constituent plays in terms of information structure: that is, old or new information. In (1), the subject NP *the monkey* represents what the sentence is about and is called the *topic*. The VP *chased a weasel* is what is being said about the topic and is called a *comment*. Part of the comment structure includes the *focus*, representing new information. The focus expression typically serves as an answer to a *wh*-question:

English and Korean in Contrast: A Linguistic Introduction, First Edition. Jong-Bok Kim.
© 2024 John Wiley & Sons, Inc. Published 2024 by John Wiley & Sons, Inc.

(3) Q: What did the monkey chase in the wood?
    A: The monkey chased a weasel in the wood.
    A′: A weasel.

The question requests a value for what the monkey chased in the wood. The answer consists of a topic and a comment: the subject *the monkey*, representing old information, is the topic, and the NP *a weasel* tells us new information. The object NP *a weasel* thus gives us the value for *what*.

(4) [$_S$ [$_{Top}$ The monkey] [$_{Comment}$ chased [$_{Foc}$ the weasel] in the wood]].

The focus alone can be an appropriate fragment answer to the *wh*-question, as seen from the A ′ answer in (3).

Korean is no different. All Korean sentences can be analyzed based on syntactic categories (form), grammatical functions, semantic roles, or information structure. In discourse-oriented and topic-oriented languages like Korean, the information structure (topic, comment, focus) plays an important role in sentence formation. Consider the following:

(5) Q: 이   책을   누가   읽었니?
       i   chayk-ul nwu-ka   ilk-ess-ni?
       this book-ACC who-NOM read-PST-QUE
       'Who read this book?'
    A: 그 책은   미미가   읽었어.
       ku chayk-un Mimi-ka   ilk-ess-e
       the book-TOP Mimi-NOM read-PST-DECL
       'Mimi read the book.'

The *wh*-question asks who read the book, and the answer gives us the value for *who*. This means *ku chayk-un* 'the book-TOP' functions as the topic of the answer, and *Mimi-ka* is a focus giving us new information. Since the topic is old or given information, we could not answer to this question with the nomaitive NP ku chayk-i 'the book-NOM'.

In this chapter, we discuss topics and focus in English and Korean and see how they are marked in sentences and their roles in a given sentence.

11.2 Topic Constructions in English

As we have seen, the topic of a sentence is what is being talked about, and a comment is what is being said about the topic. In English, the definite subject in the sentence-initial position typically functions as the topic:

(6) a. The window is opened.

    b. A window is opened.

The definite NP in (6a) represents old or shared information, whereas the indefinite NP *a window* in (6b) denotes new information. In this respect, the NP *the window* is the topic of the sentence, but *a window* is not. In English, the subject is often used as the topic of a sentence with no specific grammatical marking. The property of placing the subject in the sentence-initial position or making it the most prominent item leads to English being classified as a subject-prominent language. On the other hand, Korean, as we will see, is considered a topic-prominent language: it places the topic first in a given sentence.

The topic in English is not marked by any grammatical form, but there are three types of topic-marking constructions, as illustrated in the following examples:

(7) a. As for your other objections, I will return to them next week.

    b. My father, he's Armenian, (and my mother, she's Greek).

    c. Fido, Kim likes ___.

In these examples, the sentence topic is not the subject but is placed in the sentence-initial position. Each has a different syntactic structure. In (7a), the topic is marked by the *as for* phrase. In (7b), the topic is *my father*, which combines with a complete sentence. The pronoun *he* also is correferential with the topic *my father*. And in (7c), the topic is the NP *Fido*, which functions as the filler of the gap in the incomplete sentence that follows it.

Let us consider the structure of these three types of topic constructions in English. In terms of syntactic structure, the *as for* PP topic in (7a) functions as a modifier to the structure that follows it, as shown in the following:

(8)

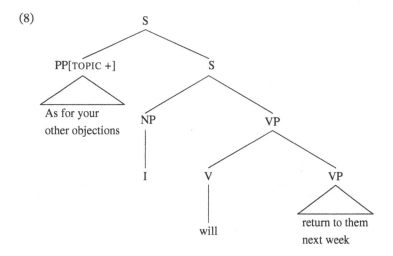

The topic here, introduced by the *as for* PP, is followed by a complete comment-representing sentence.

The structure of (7b) differs somewhat. The topic NP *my father* is linked to the pronoun *he* in the following main clause. These two NPs refer to the same individual. The meaning of this sentence is identical to *His father is Armenian*. Such a topic sentence is often called *left dislocation*, which dislocates the topic to the left of a given sentence while leaving behind its coreferential pronoun. The sentence has a structure like the following:

(9)

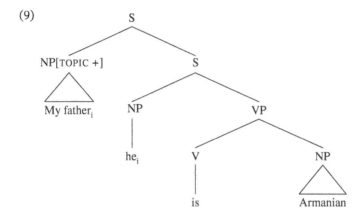

We can see here that the topic and subject have the same index value "i," indicating that they refer to the same individual. This topic-like dislocation can be applied not only to the subject but also to an object or even a specifier:

(10) a. That book$_i$ you borrowed, are you finished reading it$_i$ yet?
     b. The window$_i$, it$_i$ is still open.
     c. My sister$_i$, her$_i$ eyes were popping out.

The left-dislocated NP is linked to the pronoun in the matrix clause; further, it must be given information functioning as a topic. This accounts for the oddness of having an indefinite NP as a left-dislocated expression.

(11) a. *A book you borrowed, are you finished reading it yet?
     b. *A window, it's still open.

Now let's consider the third type given in (7c). Here we can see that the NP *Fido* is the topic and linked to the object gap in the following incomplete sentence *Kim likes*. This missing expression is linked to the initial topic, as in the following structure:

(12)

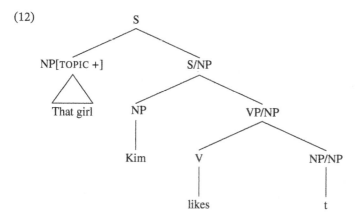

The object NP of *likes* is gapped (slashed) and is discharged by the filler topic *that girl*, in accordance with the Head-Filler grammar rule that we have discussed in Chapters 9 and 10. This kind of topic construction is a subtype of long-distance dependency construction, just like wh-interrogatives and relatives.

(13) a. That girl, I think Kim likes ___.
    b. That girl, I think that Lee believes that Kim likes ___.
    c. That girl, I think Mary assumes that Lee believes that Kim likes ___.

In each case, the fronted NP *that girl* functions as a topic. This topic is linked to the gap in the main clause and functions as its filler. Topic sentences are thus similar to *wh*-interrogatives and relative clauses, all of which also display a long-distance dependency relation between a gap and its filler.

Note that not all sentences need a topic. When the whole sentence represents new information, it contains no topic but just a focus (or comment). For instance, consider the following:

(14) a. It is raining.
    b. There is some room in this house.

The subjects here are *it* and *there*, called *expletives* or *dummies*. These subject NPs have no meaning but are syntactically required. This means they cannot represent any information and thus cannot be the topic of the sentence. The remaining part is a comment that represents new information.

11.3 Topic Constructions in Korean

11.3.1 General Properties

Korean is well known for its topic-prominent properties: it places the topic in the sentence-initial position as the most prominent element. Most Korean sentences thus start with a topic, which we do not find in subject-prominent Indo-European languages. As in English, Korean topic constructions represent what the sentence is about, typically marked by the sentential initial expression with the -은/는 -(n)un marker in Korean. The following are some typical examples:

(15) a. 미미는   항상   그 책을   읽는다.
Mimi-nun hangsang ku chayk-ul ilk-nun-ta
Mimi-TOP always   the book-ACC read-PRES-DECL
'As for Mimi, she always reads the book.'

b. 그 책은   미미가   항상   읽는다.
ku chayk-un Mimi-ka   hangsang ilk-nun-ta
the book-TOP Mimi-NOM always   read-PRES-DECL
'As for the book, Mimi always reads it.'

Both sentences, consisting of a topic in the initial position and a comment clause (the remainder of the sentence), identically describe the truth-conditional meaning that Mimi always reads the book, but they package the information differently. Sentence (15a) talks about the topic expression *Mimi*, but (15b) is about *the book*. Each topic expression describes old and definite information, stating that the individual it refers to is familiar in discourse.

Note that for a speaker to say something about an individual or entity, they must assume that the hearer can identify the individual, too. This explains why the topic needs to be "old" information already mentioned in the discourse. Consider the following:

(16) a. 한   학생이/#은   집에   갔다.
han haksayng-i/#un cip-ey   ka-ss-ta
one student-NOM/TOP home-to go-PST-DECL
'One student went home.'

b. 태양은/#이   밤에도   빛난다.
thayyang-un/#i pam-ey-to   pichna-n-ta
sun-TOP/NOM   night-at-also shine-PRES-DECL
'The sun shines at night, too.'

In (16a), the indefinite NP 한 학생 *han haksayng* 'one student' refers to an individual whose information is not shared by the interlocutors. This is why the topic marker on the indefinite NP makes the sentence degraded in such a context. The topic also represents shared knowledge. In (16b), both the speaker and the hearer have knowledge about the sun, so it is more natural to have the topic marker rather than the nominative marker. It is unnatural to have the nominative marker -이/가 -i/ka here because the indefinite subject is typically associated with new or unshared knowledge.

11.3.2 Semantic/Pragmatic Classifications: Aboutness, Contrastive, and Scene-Setting

The literature identifies three types of topic constructions: aboutness, contrastive, and scene-setting. The aboutness topic, which is the most typical, represents familiar and identifiable information, as illustrated by the following dialogue:

(17) A: (How is Mimi doing?)

B: 미미는 　　　친구들과　　　　　주말마다　　　　자전거를　　탄다.
　　Mimi-nun chinkwu-tul-kwa cwumal-mata　cacenke-lul tha-n-ta
　　Mimi-TOP　friend-PL-with　　weekend-every bike-ACC　ride-PRES-DECL
　　'As for Mimi, she is biking with friends every weekend.'

The expression 미미는 *Mimi-nun* 'Mimi-TOP' in the sentence-initial position represents what this sentence is about. The topic refers to the individual familiar to both interlocutors, which we can conjecture from the dialogue.

The contrastive topic, unlike the aboutness topic, describes a contrast between the topic constituent and a previously mentioned referent:

(18) a. 사과는　　　아이들이　　먹지만,　　배는　　　먹지　　않는다.
　　　sakwa-nun ai-tul-i　　mek-ciman, pay-nun mek-ci　anh-nun-ta
　　　apple-TOP　child-PL-NOM eat-but　　pear-TOP eat-CONN not-PRES-DECL
　　　'Children eat apples but do not eat pears.'

　　b. 내가　　이　책들은　　　읽었지만,
　　　nay-ka i　chayk-tul-un　ilk-ess-ciman,
　　　I-NOM this book-PL-TOP　read-PST-but

　　　저　　책들은　　　읽지　　못했다.
　　　ce　chayk-tul-un ilk-ci　mos-ha-yess-ta
　　　that book-PL-TOP　read-CONN not-do-PST-DECL
　　　'I read these books but did not read those books.'

The -은/는 *(n)un*-marked object expression occurs in the initial position in (18a), whereas that in (18b) is in the non-initial position. In these sentences, the -은/는 *(n)un*-marked expressions 사과는 *sakwa-nun* 'apple-TOP' and 이 책들은 *i chayk-tul-un* 'this book-PL-TOP' represent contrastive information. For example, 'apples' contrasts with 'pears,' and 'these books' contrasts with 'those books.' Note that even in the initial position with no scrambling, an expression may carry contrastive information:

(19) 미미는   그 책을   읽었다.
    Mimi-nun ku chayk-ul ilk-ess-ta.
    Mimi-TOP the book-ACC read-PST-DECL

    (그러나   유미는   읽지   않았다.)
    (kulena Yumi-nun   ilk-ci   anh-ass-ta.)
    but   Yumi-TOP   read-CONN   not-PST-DECL
    'Mimi read the book. (But Yumi didn't read it.)'

Unlike the aboutness topic, the topic here carries an additional implicature that the -은/는 -(n)un-marked constituent is in opposition to a set of alternatives: say, other people like 'Yumi.' This meaning implicature allows even an indefinite NP to function as a contrastive topic, as illustrated in the following example:[1]

(20) a. 많은   남자들은   모임에   갔다.
        manhun namca-tul-un moim-ey   ka-ss-ta.
        many   male-PL-TOP   meeting-at go-PST-DECL
        'Many men attended the meeting.'

    b. 많은   남자들은   모임에   갔지만,
        manhun namca-tul-un moim-ey   ka-ss-ciman,
        many   male-PL-TOP   meeting-at go-PST-but

       여자들은   안   갔다.
       yeca-tul-un   an   ka-ss-ta
       female-PL-TOP not go-PST-DECL
       'Many men attended the meeting, but women didn't.'

In (20a), the indefinite NP 많은 남자 *manhun namca* 'many men,' with no proper context, cannot be a topic because of its newness. However, the same indefinite NP can function as a contrastive topic with a proper context, as in (20b), even if it does not refer to familiar information. This is possible because the contrastive topic requires an alternative set.

Unlike these two types of topic constructions, a scene-setting topic provides a spatial, temporal, or individual framework within which the main predication holds. Unlike the aboutness topic, the scene-setting topic need not be discourse-familiar or old because it only offers a scene for the comment clause:

---

1 The contrastive topic can thus occur in any location as long as the topic is phonologically prominent and semantically proper. This also means there is no syntactic constraint in allowing a contrastive topic.

(21) a. 오늘은 내가 낼   차례이다.
　　　onul-un nay-ka nay-l chalyey-i-ta
　　　today-TOP I-NOM pay-FUT turn-COP-DECL
　　　'As for today, it is my turn to treat.'

　　b. 여름은   맥주가   맛있다.
　　　yelum-un   maykcwu-ka masiss-ta
　　　summer-TOP beer-NOM   tasty-DECL
　　　'As for summer, beer tastes good.'

As given in these examples, scene-setting topics, located in the clausal-initial position, are typically expressed by an adverbial phrase and set up a scene for the proposition of the main clause.

11.3.3 Syntactic Classifications and Structures

Unlike the semantic/pragmatic distinctions, we can classify topic constructions in terms of their syntactic properties, such as how they are integrated into the comment clause that follows. As we have seen, in English, a significant type of topic construction has a gap (slash) in the comment clause linked to the topic. Korean is no different. Let us consider some typical Korean topic constructions in which an argument is topicalized:

(22) a. 학생들은   [그 책을   읽었다].
　　　haksayng-tul-un [$_S$ __ ku chayk-ul ilk-ess-ta]
　　　student-PL-TOP   __ the book-ACC read-PST-DECL
　　　'As for the students, they read the book.'

　　b. 그 책은   [학생들이   __ 읽었다].
　　　ku chayk-un [$_S$ haksayng-tul-i __ ilk-ess-ta]
　　　the book-TOP student-PL-NOM   __ read-PST-DECL
　　　'As for the book, the students read it.'

In these examples, the subject and object of the sentences are topicalized, respectively. This means there is a syntactic dependency or connectivity between the topic and a putative gap in the comment clause. To account for such sentences, we can accept a movement or derivational view that introduces a trace together with movement operations. For example, (22b) has a structure like the following:

(23)

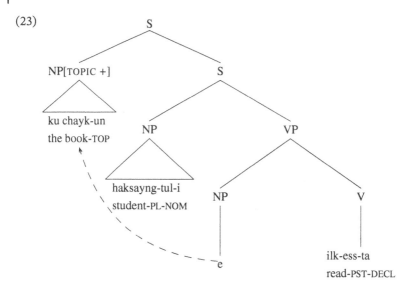

The object moves to the sentence-initial position, leaving its trace behind. The movement operations and empty element are thus key points in the derivational and movement view.

Unlike this movement analysis, we can adopt a nonderivational view that posits neither an empty expression "t(race)" nor movement operations. For example, the empty expression in the object position introduces a slashed value that percolates up to the higher node until it is discharged:

(24)

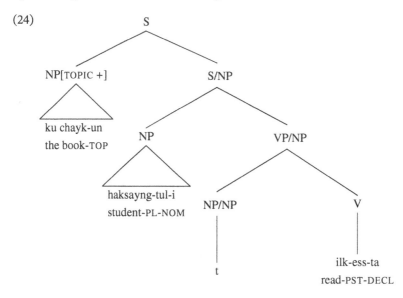

As shown in this structure, the object of the verb 읽었다 *ilk-ess-ta* 'read-PST-DECL' is gapped, and its slashed (or gapped) value percolates up until it meets its filler topic.[2] As seen earlier for relative clauses and interrogatives, the combination of a gapped or slashed sentence with its filler is allowed by the Head-Filler Rule:

(25) Head-Filler Rule:
   $S \rightarrow XP, \quad S/XP$

This construction rule means a sentence with a missing (slashed) XP combines with its filler, yielding a well-formed, complete S.

The syntactic dependency of a topic and its putative gap can be over a long distance:

(26) a. 그 책은 　　[미미가 [유미도 ＿ 읽었다고] 　　믿었다].
   ku chayk-un [Mimi-ka [Yumi-to ＿ ilk-ess-ta-ko] mit-ess-ta]
   the book-TOP Mimi-NOM Yumi-also read-PST-DECL-COMP believe-PST-DECL
   'As for the book, Mimi believed Yumi also read it.'

b. *그 책은 　　미미가 [유미도 영화를 보았다고]
   *ku chayk-un Mimi-ka Yumi-to yenghwa-lul po-ass-ta-ko
   the book-TOP Mimi-NOM Yumi-also movie-ACC see-PST-DECL-COMP
   믿었다.
   mit-ess-ta
   believe-PST-DECL
   '(int.) As for the book, Mimi believed Yumi also saw the movie.'

In (26), the topic expression 그 책은 *ku chayk-un* 'the book-TOP' is in a dependency relation with the object gap in the embedded clause. When there is no such a dependency relation, as in (26b), the sentence is ungrammatical.

Not only an argument but also an adverbial expression can be topicalized:

(27) a. 오늘은 날씨가 참 좋다.
   onul-un nalssi-ka cham coh-ta
   today-TOP weather-NOM very good-DECL
   'As for today, the weather is really good.'

b. 이 도시에는 안개가 많이 낀다.
   i tosi-ey-nun ankay-ka manhi kki-n-ta
   the city-at-TOP fog-NOM much rise-PRES-DECL
   'As for the city, the fog rises a lot.'

---

2 In the present system, this sentence can be interpreted with no movement. That is, the verb first combines with the subject, and the resulting phrase combines with *ku chayk-un* 'this book-TOP.' This assigns no sentential topic reading to this topic-marked expression.

In these examples, the temporal expression 오늘 *onul* 'today' and the locative expression 이 도시 *i tosi* 'this city' function as topics of the sentences headed by the intransitive verbal predicates 좋다 *coh-ta* 'good-DECL' and 낀다 *kki-n-ta* 'rise-PRES-DECL.' Thus there is no gap or slashed value in the matrix clause; the topic expression simply modifies the following sentence. This implies that examples with adverbial topicalization can be considered head-modifier constructions, as in the following:

(28)

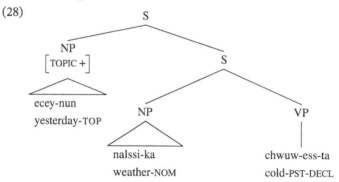

The topicalized adverbial expression *ecey* 'yesterday' is not moved but base-generated. It just modifies the sentence that follows based on the Head-Modifier Rule. At the same time, the adverbial also functions as a topic of the sentence, being in the sentence-initial position.

Korean has another intriguing type of topic construction: a topic expression serving as a type of scene-setting can be neither an argument nor an adjunct of the comment clause in question:

(29) a. 꽃은   [ₛ 장미가   아름답다].
       kkoch-un [ₛ cangmi-ka alumtap-ta]
       flowers-TOP rose-NOM   pretty-DECL
       'As for flowers, roses are pretty.'
     b. 생선은   [ₛ 고등어가   맛있다].
       sayngsen-un [ₛ kotunge-ka masiss-ta]
       fish-TOP   mackerel-NOM tasteful-DECL
       'As for fish, mackerel is tasty.'

In these examples, 꽃 *kkoch* 'flower' and 생선 *sayngsen* 'fish' are neither arguments of the matrix verb nor modifiers. In each case, the matrix sentence headed by the pure intransitive verb is fully saturated, even without the topic expression. The grammatical function of the nominal topic expression is thus adverbial, interpreted as "as for talking about flowers" or "as for talking about fish." Such topics are often called syntactically *dangling topics*. Such dangling topic constructions have a structure like the following:

(30)

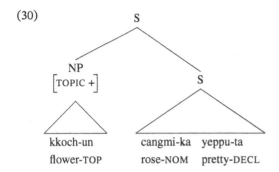

There is no gap or missing value in the matrix sentence, but the sentence is modified by the nominal topic. Note that even though the topic expression here is a nominal, it functions as an adverbial. The present base-generation system allows such a construction as long as there is an *about relation* between the topic and the head S:

(31) Aboutness condition in topic constructions:
The topic of a given sentence and the comment clause that follows must be in an "about" relation.

This semantic/pragmatic construction blocks examples like the following:

(32) *자동차는   장미가   예쁘다.
*catongcha-nun [cangmi-ka yeppu-ta]
car-TOP   rose-NOM   pretty-DECL
'*As for cars, roses are pretty.'

There is no *about*-relation between the topic *catongcha-nun* 'car-TOP' and the sentence that follows.

The remaining type of topic construction involves the topicalization of a possessor:

(33) a. 코끼리는   코가   길다.
khokkili-nun kho-ka   kil-ta
elephant-TOP nose-NOM long-DECL
'As for the elephant, its nose is long.'
b. 그   아이는   눈이   예쁘다.
ku ai-nun   nwun-i   yeppu-ta
the child-TOP eyes-NOM pretty-DECL
'As for the child, his eyes are pretty.'

Here, the elephant owns the nose, and the child owns the eyes. The first NOM phrase is introduced as a specifier (typically the determiner of a noun phrase and the subject of a VP) with a possessive relation with the second NOM. In the present system, the topicalization of the specifier is allowed by letting the specifier be introduced as a sentential specifier when the specifier and the remaining head noun (subject) are in a possessive relation:

(34)

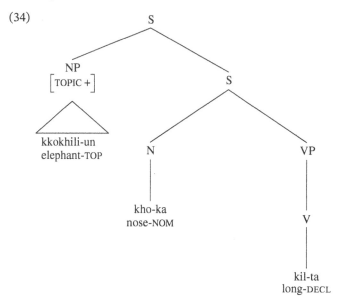

The verb *kil-ta* 'long-DECL' is an intransitive stative verb requiring a subject. The subject and the topic are in a possessive relation, which allows the topic to be in an about relation with the lower sentence.

11.4 Focus Constructions in English

11.4.1 General Properties

Information structure interacts with various grammatical components in specific ways and structures sentences by syntactic, prosodic, or morphological means to meet the communicative demands of a particular context. In other words, information structure indicates how linguistically conveyed information fits into the hearer's information state at the time of utterance. Thus no proper information structuring results in infelicitous answers.

As noted earlier, the *wh*-phrase in the *wh*-question typically represents a focus of the question, and an answer needs to be linked to this *wh*-phrase:

(35) Q: What did you give to Mary?
    A: A book.
    B: *To Mimi.

The focused expression is *what*, and a proper answer needs to be something about this *wh*-phrase.

The focus value can also be marked with a phonological marking, as shown in (36) and (37):

(36) A: What does he hate?
      B: He hates CHOCOLATES.
      B: #He HATES chocolates.

(37) A: Does John LIKE rugby?
      B: No, he HATES rugby.
      B: #No, he hates RUGBY.

In addition to such a phonological marking, English employs several syntactic constructions to mark a focus expression. In this section, we consider cleft constructions, which are also employed to place a focus on a designated syntactic position.

11.4.2   Cleft Constructions in English and Their Syntactic Structures

The examples in (38) represent the three canonical types of cleft constructions in English – *it*-cleft, *wh*-cleft, and inverted *wh*-cleft:

(38) a. It's their teaching material that we're using. (*it*-cleft)
      b. What we're using is their teaching material. (*wh*-cleft)
      c. Their teaching material is what we are using. (inverted *wh*-cleft)

All the English cleft constructions involve the copula verb *be*, which has at least three different functions:

(39) a. Specificational
         The director of this movie is Steven Spielberg.
      b. Predicational
         The doctor is gentle.
      c. Identificational
         The evening star is the morning star.

In sentence (39a), the subject NP asks who the movie's director is, and the post-copular NP "specifies" a value, which is Spielberg. Sentence (39b) just tells us the property of the subject NP *the doctor*. In this sense, the postcopular NP is predicated on the subject. In (39c), the two NPs are identificational.

These three types of clefts, as given in (38), also all denote the same proposition as the following simple declarative sentence:

(40) We are using their teaching material.

The immediate question that follows is, what is the extra function of the cleft structure instead of the simple sentence (40)? It is commonly accepted that clefts share the information-structure properties given in (41), for the example in question:

(41) a. Presupposition (background): We are using X.
   b. Highlighted (foreground or focus): their teaching material
   c. Assertion: X is their teaching material.

In terms of structure, the three types of clefts all consist of a matrix clause headed by a copula and a relative-like cleft clause whose relativized argument is coindexed with the predicative argument of the copula. The only difference is where the highlighted (focused) expression is placed.

Wh-Clefts

The *wh*-cleft construction places a cleft clause in the subject position followed by the highlighted XP in the postcopular position. This gives a wide range of phrases. As shown in (42), almost all the phrasal types can serve as the highlighted XP:

(42) a. What you want is [NP a little greenhouse].
   b. What's actually happening in London at the moment is [AP immensely exciting].
   c. What is to come is [PP in this document].
   d. What I've always tended to do is [VP to do my own stretches at home].
   e. What I meant was [CP that you have done it really well].

The *wh*-cleft allows the AP, base VP, and clause (CP, simple S, and *wh*-clause) to serve as the highlighted XP:

(43) a. What you do is [VP wear it like that].
   b. What happened is [S they caught her without a license].
   c. What the gentleman seemed to be asking is [S how policy would have differed].

In terms of the syntactic structure, notice that the expression *what* is a "fused" NP interpreted as "the thing that." Given this, we can assign the following structure to (42a):

(44)

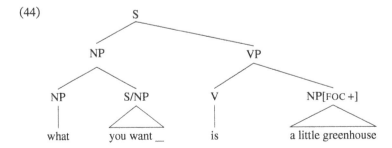

As shown here, *what* combines with the cleft clause, which includes an object gap. A peculiar property of this fused relative clause is that the combination of *what* and the incomplete sentence yields not an S (as does the Head-Filler Rule) but an NP. The resulting expression is thus an NP, which can be interpreted as "the thing that you want." This is allowed by the following independent rule in English:

(45) Free Relative Clause Rule
NP → NP[*what*] S/NP

This analysis implies that the first clause needs to be an NP, blocking examples like the following as a *wh*-cleft:

(46) a. *[To whom I gave the cake] is Kim.
b. *[That brought the letter] is Bill.

The subjects here are not headed by NPs.

Inverted *Wh*-Clefts
Although the inverted *wh*-cleft construction is similar to the *wh*-cleft, the possible types of phrases are different:

(47) a. [$_{NP}$ That] is what they're trying to do.
b. [$_{AP}$ Insensitive] is how I would describe him.
c. [$_{PP}$ In the early morning] is when I do my best research.

(48) a. *[$_{VP}$ Wear it like that] is what you do.
b. *[$_{S}$ They caught her without a license] is what happened.
c. *[$_{CP}$ That you have done it really well] is what I meant.

In general, all *wh*-words except *which* can be used in inverted *wh*-clefts:

(49) a. That's [when] I read.
b. That was [why] she looked so nice.
c. That's [how] they do it.
d. That's [who] I played with over Christmas.

The inverted *wh*-cleft is motivated by a different information structure perspective. In particular, the postcopular clause is more prominent than the subject:

(50)

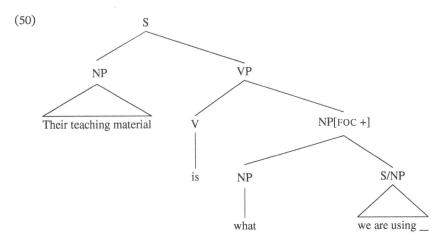

The subject position of a *wh*-cleft is restricted to NPs, but the postcopular *wh*-phrase can be introduced by almost any *wh*-expression except *which*:

(51) *That was [which] I decided to buy.

It-Clefts

The *it*-cleft construction consists of the pronoun *it* as the subject of the matrix verb *be*, the highlighted (or focused) phrase XP, and the remaining cleft clause. The pronoun *it* here functions as an anticipatory pronoun linked to the cleft clause:

(52) A: I share your view, but I just wonder why you think that's good.
     B: Well, I suppose it's the writer [that/who gets you so involved].

Regarding the type of the highlighted XPs, only certain types of phrases can be used:

(53) a. It was [NP the man] who bought the articles from him.
     b. It was [AdvP then] that he felt a sharp pain.
     c. It was [PP to the student] that the teacher gave the best advice.
     d. It was [S because it rained] that we came home.

Phrases such as an infinitival VP, AP, or CP cannot function as the XP:

(54) a. *It was [VP to finish the homework] that Kim tried.
     b. *It is [AP fond of Bill] that Kim seems to be.
     c. *It is [CP that Bill is honest] that Kim believes.

Also notice that in addition to *that*, *wh*-words like *who* and *which* can also introduce a cleft clause:

(55) a. It's the second Monday [that] we get back from the Easter holiday.

    b. It was the girl [who] kicked the ball.

    c. It's mainly his attitude [which] convinced the teacher.

Another key property of the *it*-cleft is that the focused expression is linked to the gap (slash) in the cleft clause, as seen in the following:

(56) a. It is John whom we're looking for __.

     b. It is money that I love __.

     c. It was from John that she heard the news __.

The focused expression of an *it*-cleft is the nominal head introduced by a relative pronoun *that*, *which*, or *who*. If we look closely, however, we find that this is not the right analysis for an *it*-cleft. As we saw in the previous chapter, a pronoun or proper noun cannot be the antecedent of a restrictive relative clause. However, unlike relatives, *it*-clefts allow a pronoun or proper noun to be in the putative head position:

(57) a. It is Pat that we are looking for __.

     b. *Pat that we are looking for showed up.

This contrast suggests that the focused element (*Pat* in (57a)) and the relative clause that follows do not form a syntactic unit as a restrictive relative clause does with its nominal head.

These observations lead us to the following informal generalization for the structure of *it*-clefts in English:

(58) *It*-Cleft Formation Rule:

    The copula verb can introduce the anticipatory subject *it* and a focused expression XP, whereas the subject is linked to the extraposed cleft clause with a missing phrase. The focus thus provides a value for the variable evoked from the missing phrase.

The following structure reflects this generalization:

(59)

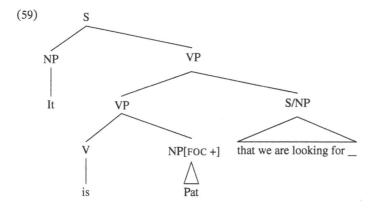

The structure means the copula verb *be* has two arguments: the subject *it* and the focused expression *Pat*. Note that this focused expression is linked to the gapped expression in the extraposed clause. The sentence thus tells us the follwoing three at least:

(60) a. the variable "x" evoked from the cleft clause: we are looking for "x"
   b. The provided value: Pat
   c. The equation: x is Pat

An advantage of this analysis is that there is no need to introduce an additional type of copula *be*. Here, the copula *be*, just as in the other uses of *be*, has two syntactic arguments: the first is a clausal subject, and the second can be any nominal-type expression that functions as a focus. Such variations can be seen in examples like the following:

(61) a. It was your sister that I met.
   b. It is August that you are going on holiday.
   c. It's the parents who were protesting most.
   d. It is Kim on whom we rely.

This analysis also leads us to expect examples like (62), in which a parenthetical expression intervenes between the focused phrase and the extraposed cleft clause.

(62) a. It was the boy, I believe, who bought the book.
   b. It was in the attic, the police believed, where Ann had been hiding.

11.5 Focus Constructions in Korean

11.5.1 General Properties

Like English, Korean uses phonological means, morphological markers, word order, and syntactic constructions to encode old and new information. Let us consider each approach in more detail.

As in English, accented constituents in Korean are interpreted as foci. The constituents with bold-faced letters in (63) indicate accent or phonological prominence, and the interpretations provided in (63) illustrate the focus assignment of these elements:

(63) a. 미미가   맥주를   마셨어.
       MIMI-ka   maykcwu-lul masi-ess-e
       Mimi-NOM beer-ACC   drink-PST-DECL
       'It is Mimi who drank beer.'

b. 미미가　　　**맥주를**　　　마셨어.
Mimi-ka　　　MAYKCWU-LUL　masi-ess-e
Mimi-NOM　beer-ACC　　　　drink-PST-DECL
'It is beer that Mimi drank.'

c. 미미가　　　맥주를　　　**마셨어.**
Mimi-ka　　　maykcwu-lul　MASI-ESS-E
Mimi-NOM　beer-ACC　　　drink-PST-DECL
'What Mimi did with beer was drink it.'

The phrase with the subject case marking -*i/ka* can denote various discourse functions depending on its syntactic position, as we will discuss later. The phrase with the subject marker -이/가 -*i/ka* generally either registers a narrow-focus reading (identification focus), as in (64a), or projects a presentational reading (information focus), as in (64b).

(64) a. [$_{Foc}$ 미미가]　사과를　　먹었다.
[$_{Foc}$ Mimi-ka]　sakwa-lul　mek-ess-ta
Mimi-NOM　　　apple-ACC　eat-PST-DECL
'It is Mimi who ate apples.'

b. [$_{Foc}$ [$_{Foc}$ 미미가]　사과를　　먹고　　있다].
[$_{Foc}$ [$_{Foc}$ Mimi-ka]　sakwa-lul　mek-ko　iss-ta]
Mimi-NOM　　　apple-ACC　eat-CONN　be-DECL
'There is Mimi eating apples.'

Korean also employs various syntactic constructions in encoding information structure, including clefts and multiple-nominative constructions. The following pair illustrates:

(65) a. 사과를　　먹은　　것은　　[$_{Foc}$ 미미]이다.
sakwa-lul　mek-un　kes-un　[$_{Foc}$ Mimi]-i-ta
apple-ACC　eat-MOD　thing-TOP　Mimi-COP-DECL
'It is Mimi who ate apples'

b. [$_{Foc}$ 미미가]　어머니가　미인이시다.
[$_{Foc}$ Mimi-ka]　emeni-ka　miin-i-si-ta
Mimi-NOM　　　mother-NOM　pretty.person-COP-HON-DECL
'As for Mimi, her mother is pretty.'

Sentence (65a) is a typical cleft sentence: the cleft clause is introduced by the bound noun *kes*, and the focus expression combines with the copula verb *i-ta*. In the multiple-nominative sentence (65b), the first nominative marked NP *Mimi-ka* is an encoder of focus, and the second nominative NP functions as the subject. This element provides an exhaustive reading, a canonical property of focus.

11.5.2 Cleft Constructions in Korean

As in English, cleft constructions mark a certain constituent as a prominent discourse element. We have seen that English has at least three different uses of the copula verb *be* and the cleft constructions linked to these copula uses. Korean cleft constructions can be classified similarly. The language has at least the following three types of clefts:

(66) a. Specificational

[미미가 ___$_i$ 읽은 것은] [이 책]$_i$이다.
[Mimi-ka ___$_i$ ilk-un kes-un] [i chayk]$_i$-i-ta
Mimi-NOM read-MOD KES-TOP this.book-COP-DECL
'What Mimi read is this book.'

b. Predicational

[미미가 ___$_i$ 읽은 것은] [가짜]$_i$이다.
[Mimi-ka ___$_i$ ilk-un kes-un] [kacca]$_i$-i-ta
Mimi-NOM read-MOD KES-TOP fake-COP-DECL
'What Mimi read is fake.'

c. Identificational

[이 책]$_i$이 바로 [미미가 ___$_i$ 읽은 것이다].
[i chayk]$_i$-i palo [Mimi-ka ___$_i$ ilk-un kes-i-ta]
this book-NOM very Mimi-NOM read-MOD KES-COP-DECL
'This book is what Mimi read.'

These types of clefts primarily consist of a cleft clause, a pivot XP, and the copula verb. The specificational cleft in (60a) is the most typical type of cleft. The cleft clause has a missing object and combines with *kes*, forming an NP structure, as follows:

(67)

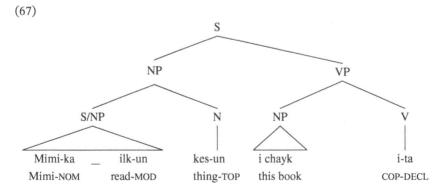

The structure behaves like a relative clause in which an incomplete S combines with the bound noun 것 kes-un. This NP subject is a type of topic evoking a variable. The variable's value is provided by the postcopular NP *i chayk*, which functions as a focus or a value for this variable evoked from "what Mimi read."

The predicational cleft in (66b) has a similar structure. The only difference from the specificational cleft is that the postcopular NP is adjectival and denotes the property of the subject "the thing that Mimi read." That is, the subject has the property of being fake. Its structure is thus similar to the specificational one:

(68)

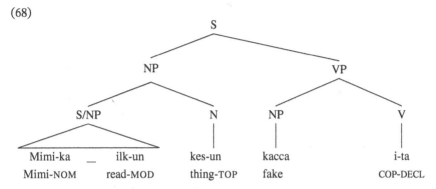

The cleft clause, representing old information, contains an object gap. This gap is linked to the head noun *kes*. The predicative expression "fake" describes this nominal expression.

The identificational cleft in (66c) is similar to the inverted pseudo-cleft in English. The nominative phrase 이 책 *i chayk* 'this book' serves as the subject. This reference is the same as the individual the missing object refers to in the cleft clause, which now functions as the focus. The first NP and this individual are in an identity relation.

(69)

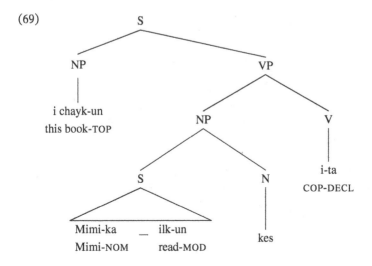

In addition to these three types, Korean has one more type of cleft. Compare the following typical declarative with an eventual cleft:

(70) a. Typical declarative

그 때   미미가   집에   왔다.
ku ttay   [Mimi-ka   cip-ey   o-ass-ta
the moment Mimi-NOM home-LOC come-PST-DECL
'At that moment, Mimi came home.'

    b. Eventual:

그 때   [미미가   집에   온]   것이었다.
ku ttay   [Mimi-ka   cip-ey   o-n]   kes-i-ess-ta
the moment Mimi-NOM home-LOC come-MOD KES-COP-PST-DECL
'(lit.) It is at the very moment that Mimi came home.'

The eventual cleft here differs from the declarative cleft only in that it ends with *kes-i-*. This makes the whole event the focus. That is, the situation of Mimi's coming home is new information that happened at the moment. In the eventual cleft, the whole clause preceding the *kes* expression is clefted, functioning as the pivot focus phrase. Consider these similar examples:

(71) a. [그 때]   [사고가   난]   것이야.
[ku ttay]   [sako-ka   na-n]   kes-i-ya
that moment accident-NOM happen-MOD KES-COP-DECL
'It is at that moment that [an accident happened].'

    b. [그 여자가   김을   만난]   것이야.
[ku yeca-ka   Kim-ul   manna-n] kes-i-ya
the woman-NOM Kim-ACC meet-MOD KES-COP-DECL
'The fact is that [that woman met Kim].'

Such an event cleft cannot be used initially in discourse:

(72) 잘   있었어?   내가   돌아   왔어/*온 거야.
cal   iss-ess-e?   nay-ka tola   o-ass-e/*o-n ke-ya
well exist-PST-QUE I-NOM   return come-PST-DECL/*come-MOD-KES-COP-DECL
'How have you been? I came back.'

This kind of eventual-cleft construction thus conveys a meaning of "cause, reason, explanation, or consequence" for the previously evoked situation.

As for the syntactic structure of such an eventual cleft, (71a) would have the following structure:

(73)

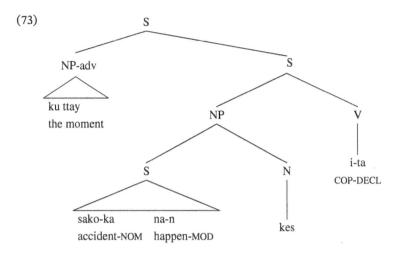

The structure shows that the temporal nominal, modifying the following S, introduces it as a presentational focus sentence, roughly paraphrased as "What happened at the moment was that an accident happened." Also note that the focused phrase is a complete phrase with no syntactic gap. The eventual cleft thus allows *kes* to nominalize the entire preceding S, highlighting an event.

Regarding the possible type of pivot or focus phrase, the focused XP can be either an argument or an adjunct. The postposition or semantic marker of the focused expression is optional:

(74) a. 김이 　　메리를 　만난 　　것은 　[공원(에서)]이다.
　　　Kim-i 　　Mary-lul manna-n 　kes-un 　[kongwen-(eyse)]-i-ta
　　　[Kim-NOM Mary-ACC meet-MOD KES]-TOP park-at-COP-DECL
　　　'It was at the park that Kim met Mary.'

　　b. 김이 　　메리를 　만난 　　것은 　[도서관(에서)]이다.
　　　Kim-i 　　Mary-lul manna-n 　kes-un 　[tosekwan-(eyse)]-i-ta
　　　Kim-NOM Mary-ACC meet-MOD KES-TOP library-at-COP-DECL
　　　'Where Kim met Mary was (at) the library.'

In a typical cleft, an adverbial element also can be focused as long as it is categorically nominal:

(75) 김이 　　메리를 　만난 　　것은 　[어제]이다.
　　Kim-i 　　Mary-lul manna-n 　kes-un 　[ecey]-i-ta
　　Kim-NOM Mary-ACC meet-MOD KES-TOP yesterday-COP-DECL
　　'It was yesterday when Kim met Mary.'

However, true adverbs cannot be focused:

(76) a. *김이   달린   것은   [천천히]이다.
　　　*Kim-i   talli-n   kes-un   [chenchenhi]-i-ta
　　　Kim-NOM   run-MOD   KES-TOP   slowly-COP-DECL
　　　'(lit.) The way Kim ran was slowly.'

　　b. *[천천히]가   김이   달린   것이다.
　　　*[chenchenhi]-ka Kim-i   talli-n   kes-i-ta
　　　slowly-NOM   Kim-NOM run-MOD KES-COP-DECL

As noted here, neither the predicational nor identificational cleft allows a true adverb to be focused.

The gapped element in the cleft clause can be in the embedded clause, allowing a long dependency relationship between the gap and the linked XP:

(77) a. [김이   [메리가   __ 좋아한다고]   생각하는   것]은
　　　[Kim-i   [Mary-ka   __ cohaha-n-ta-ko]   sayngkakha-nun kes]-un
　　　Kim-NOM   Mary-NOM   like-PRES-DECL-CONN think-MOD   KES-TOP

　　　이   그림이다.
　　　i   kulim-i-ta
　　　this   picture-COP-DECL
　　　'What Kim thought Mary likes is this picture.'

　　b. 이   그림이   [김이   [메리가   __ 좋아한다고]
　　　i   kulim-i   [Kim-i   [Mary-ka   __ cohaha-n-ta-ko]
　　　this picture-NOM Kim-NOM   Mary-NOM   like-PRES-DECL-CONN

　　　생각하는   것]이다.
　　　sayngkakha-nun   kes]-i-ta
　　　think-MOD   KES-COP-DECL
　　　'This picture is what Kim thought Mary likes.'

In both clefts, the pivot phrase 이 그림 *i kulim* 'this picture' is linked to the object of the embedded clause. However, this pivot XP cannot be an adjunct in the embedded clause. This is again similar to relative clauses:

(78) a. [김이   [메리가   책을
　　　[Kim-i   [Mary-ka   chak-ul
　　　Kim-NOM   Mary-NOM   book-ACC

　　　읽었다고]]   생각한   어제
　　　ilk-ess-ta-ko]]   sayngkakha-n   ecey
　　　read-PST-DECL-CONN think-MOD   yesterday
　　　'the time (yesterday) when Kim thought Mary read the book'

b. [김이   [메리가   읽었다고]
   [Kim-i   [Mary-ka chak-ul   ilk-ess-ta-ko]
   Kim-NOM Mary-NOM book-ACC read-PST-DECL-CONN

   생각하는   것]은   어제이다.
   sayngkakha-nun kes]-un ecey-i-ta
   think-MOD   KES-TOP yesterday-COP-DECL
   'The time when Kim thought Mary read the book was yesterday.'

In these relative and cleft examples, the relativized and cleft adjunct is linked to the higher main clause, not to the embedded clause.

11.5.3 Multiple-Nominative Focus Constructions

Focus constructions representing new information are also closely related to the information structure. In representing the focus or new information in a given sentence, we can adopt a mechanism such as prosodic prominence or special syntactic constructions like the well-known cleft constructions. Korean has another peculiar focus construction called a multiple-nominative construction. Multiple-nominative constructions (MNCs) like those in (79a) and (79b) are a puzzling phenomenon in topic-prominent languages like Korean, Japanese, and Chinese:

(79) a. 김이   손이   크다.
        Kim-i   son-i   khu-ta
        Kim-NOM hand-NOM big-DECL
        'It is Kim whose hand is big.'

    b. 여름이/에   맥주가   최고이다
       yelum-i/-ey   maykcwu-ka choyko-i-ta
       summer-NOM/-LOC beer-NOM   best-COP-DECL
       'It is summer when beer tastes best.'

Both examples have two nominative phrases. The first introduces a focus phrase, and the second is the subject. Note that the first nominative NPs *Kim* and *summer* are not direct arguments of the matrix predicate. Given that a clause usually contains at most one subject, expressed as a NOM phrase, the function of the first NOM is a puzzle. In terms of pragmatic conditions, the first NOM phrase characterizes the remaining part (often called the *sentential predicate*). For example, in (79a), having a big hand is a characterizing property of Kim, whereas in (79b), tasty beer is a characteristic of summer.

At first glance, the MNC seems similar to a genitive construction. However, we can immediately see that not all MNCs have genitive counterparts. Compare the following:

(80) a. 김의   손이   크다.
     Kim-uy   son-i   khu-ta
     Kim-GEN   hand-NOM   big-DECL
     'It is Kim whose hand is big.'

    b. *여름의   맥주가   최고이다.
     yelum-uy   maykcwu-ka   choyko-i-ta
     summer-GEN   beer-NOM   best-COP-DECL
     'It is summer when beer tastes best.'

Because the adjunct NP *yelum* 'summer' and the subject NP *maykcwu* 'beer' cannot be in a possessive relation, the summer cannot be realized as a genitive NP. This implies that the MNC has two subtypes – argument MNCs and adjunct MNCs – and only the first can have a possessive counterpart.

Another clear difference between MNCs and genitive constructions comes from the possibility of invoking an idiomatic reading. Only the MNC allows an idiomatic reading, as illustrated in (81):

(81) a. 김이   발이   넓다.
     Kim-i   pal-i   nelp-ta
     Kim-NOM   feet-NOM   wide-DECL
     'Kim's feet are wide.' or 'Kim has more contacts (idiomatic).'

    b. 김이   가방   끈이   제일   길다.
     Kim-i   kapang   kkun-i   ceyil   kil-ta
     Kim-NOM   bag   strap-NOM   most   long-DECL
     'The straps of Kim's bag are longest.' or 'Kim is the most highly educated (idiomatic).'

The genitive construction has no such an idiomatic meaning, as seen from the possible English translation in the following:

(82) 김의   발이   넓다.
   Kim-uy   pal-i   nelp-ta
   Kim-GEN   feet-NOM   wide-DECL
   'Kim's feet are wide.'

MNCs like (81a) have the following syntactic structure:

(83)

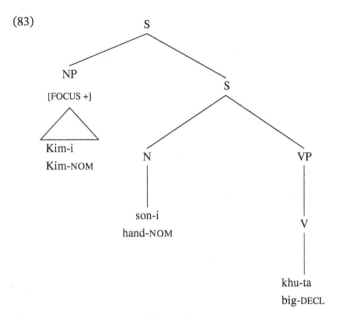

The first nominative NP *Kim-i* 'Kim-NOM' has focus properties, and it combines with the full sentence S 'hand is big.' These two are in a characterizing relation: Kim has a characterizing property of his hand's bigness.

Note that the first focused nominative NP can be the topic of the sentence:

(84) a. 김은   손이   크다.
    Kim-un   son-i   khu-ta
    Kim-TOP   hand-NOM   big-DECL
    'As for Kim, his hand is big.'

    b. 김은   발이   넓다.
    Kim-un   pal-i   nelp-ta
    Kim-TOP   feet-NOM   wide-DECL
    'As for Kim, Kim's foot is wide.'

Unlike the MNCs, these topic sentences assign topic properties to the first nominal expressions.

11.6 Contrastive Notes

11.6.1 Subject-Prominent vs. Topic-Prominent

Both English and Korean sentences can be analyzed using information structures, including topic and focus. In English, the subject typically functions as the most prominent expression and is placed in the sentence-first position. It often functions as the topic of the sentence as well. Unlike this subject-prominent language, Korean makes the topic the most prominent expression. The topic is also clearly marked with the marker *-nun*. Thus Korean is often said to be a topic-oriented language; most sentences start with a topic. This is why English sentence (85a) has (85b) as its more proper corresponding sentence, which starts with the "topic"-marked subject rather than the "nominative"-marked one:

(85) a. My friend drank coffee.
  b. 친구는   커피를   마셨어.
    chinkwu-nun   khephi-lul   misi-ess-e
    friend-TOP   coffee-ACC   drink-PST-DECL
    'My friend drank coffee.'

11.6.2 Types of Topics

English has a few subtypes of topic constructions, including gapped topic constructions, *as-for*, and left dislocation. Considering that English is subject-prominent rather than topic-prominent, we expect its topic sentences to be less developed.

(86) a. These students are clever.
  b. As for these students, they are clever.
  c. These students, they are the cleverest.
  d. These students, the teacher likes a lot.

The first example is a typical declarative sentence, but the initial definite NP functions as the topic of the sentence. The second sentence introduces the *as-for* PP as the topic; and the third dislocates the definite NP to the left of the sentence, leaving behind the coreferential NP. The final sentence introduces the filler NP as the topic.

Meanwhile, topic-oriented Korean has a variety of topic constructions. In terms of semantic/pragmatics, it has aboutness, contrastive, and scene-setting topic constructions. In terms of syntactic classification, the sentence topic can be a filler, an adverbial, or a dangling expression. All these topic expressions have a semantic/pragmatic function. The variations in Korean topic constructions can be again seen in examples like the following:

(87) a. 이 학생들은   똑똑하다.
    i   haksayng-tul-un   ttokttokha-ta
    this student-PL-TOP   smart-DECL
    'These students are smart.'

b. 이 학생들은 미미가 똑똑하다고 추천했다.

i haksayng-tul-un Mimi-ka ttokttokha-ta-ko chwuchenha-yess-ta

the student-PL-TOP Mimi-NOM smart-DECL-COMP recommmend-PST-DECL

'As for these students, Mimi recommends them because they are smart.'

c. 김치는 한국이 최고이다.

kimchi-nun hankwuk-i choyko-i-ta

Kimchi-TOP Korea-NOM best-COP-DECL

'As for Kimchi, Korea's is the best.'

d. 서울은 날씨가 점점 더워진다.

Seoul-un nalssi-ka cemcem tewue-ci-n-ta

Seoul-TOP weather-NOM gradually hot-become-PRES-DECL

'As for Seoul, the weather is becoming hotter.'

11.6.3 Focus Constructions: Clefts and Multiple Nominatives

Unlike the topic, the focus represents new information. In both languages, the focus can be marked by phonological prominence or syntactic constructions. Cleft constructions are used in both languages to mark focus expressions. English has three main types of clefts: *it*-cleft, *wh*-cleft, and inverted *wh*-cleft, as again illustrated in the following. These syntactically marked constructions are fully developed in English:

(88) a. It is this class that Mimi can't miss.

b. What Mimi cannot miss is this class.

c. This class is what Mimi can't miss.

Korean also has cleft constructions, introduced by *kes*. They can be classified as specificational, predicational, and identificational in terms of the semantic function of the focused expression. Korean also has an additional type of cleft called the eventual cleft, which makes the whole sentence the focus:

(89) 이제 기후 변화가 심각해진 것이다.

icey kihwu pyenhwa-ka simkakhayci-n kes-i-ta

now climate change-NOM serious.become-MOD kes-COP-DECL

'Now it is that climate change becomes serious.'

In addition, Korean has a language-particular focus construction called the multiple-nominative construction (MNC):

(90) 모든 수업이 후반부가 어렵고 중요하다.

moten swuep-i hwupanpwu-ka elyep-ko cwungyoha-ta

all classes-NOM latter-NOM difficult-and important-DECL

'(lit.) As for all classes, the latter is difficult and important.'

11.7 Conclusion

This chapter discussed how a given sentence can be analyzed using the concept of information structure. The two key notions are topic and focus. The topic tells us what the sentence is about and typically denotes old information. The focus, as part of the comment clause that tells about the topic, represents new information.

English and Korean have their own ways of marking topic and focus constructions. English does not employ topic constructions as often as Korean does. Korean, a topic-oriented language, uses the topic marker -(n)un to indicate what the utterance of the sentence is about, and most sentences start with this topic marker. The most visible focus construction is the cleft construction. We have seen subtypes of cleft constructions in the two languages and their syntactic structures.

Exercises

1 Identify the uses of the copula verb (specificational, predicational, and identificational) in the following:

   (i) a. The hat is big.
        b. The thing I bought for Harvey is big.
        c. What I bought for Harvey is big.
        d. The director of *Anatomy of a Murder* is Otto Preminger.
        e. The only director/person/one I met was Otto Preminger.
        f. Whom I met was Otto Preminger.
        g. That woman is Sylvia.
   (ii) a. 이 식당이 고급이다.
        b. 미미를 위해 구입한 것이 진짜이다.
        c. 영문과 학과장이 미미이다.
        d. 내가 만난 유일한 배우는 윤여정이다.
        e. 저 분이 바로 윤여정이다.
        f. 바로 그 순간 바람이 분 것이다.

2 Identify the type of topic in the following, and give a tree structure for each:

   (i) a. My sister, Pet likes.
        b. As for my sister, Pet likes her.
        c. My sister, she's a high school teacher.

3 Identify the semantic/pragmatic type of the topic in the following sentences, and give a tree structure for each:

(i) a. 이 책은   모두가   읽었다.
    i chayk-un   motwu-ka   ilk-ess-ta
    this book-TOP   all-NOM   read-PST-DECL
    'As for this book, everyone read it.'

b. 여름은   맥주가   최고다.
   yelum-un   maykcwu-ka   choiko-i-ta
   summer-TOP   beer-NOM   best-COP-DECL
   'As for summer, beer is the best.'

c. 생선은   고등어가   맛있다.
   sayngsen-un   kotunge-ka   masiss-ta
   fish-TOP   mackerel-NOM   delicious-DECL
   'As for fish, mackerel is delicious.'

d. 그   집은   창문이   크다.
   ku   cip-NOM   changmwu-i   khu-ta
   the   house-NOM   window-NOM   big-DECL
   'It is the house whose window is big.'

4 Identify the focus in the following, and give tree structures. In addition, translate each sentence into Korean. For the translated Korean sentences, also give their syntactic structures.

(i) a. It is the book that Pat wants to read.
   b. What Pat wants to read is the book.
   c. The book is what Pat wants to read.

5 Identify the focus in the following, and give tree structures.

(i) a. 우리가 구입한   것은   바로 이 책이다.
    wuli-ka kwuipha-n kes-un   palo i chayk-i-ta
    we-NOM buy-MOD   thing-TOP very this book-COP-DECL
    'What we bought is too expensive.'

b. 우리가 구입한   것은   너무   비싸다.
   wuli-ka kwuipha-n kes-un   nemwu pissa-ta
   we-NOM buy-MOD   thing-TOP too   expensive-DECL
   'What we bought is too expensive.'

c. 이 책이   선생님이   추천한   것이다.
   i   chayk-un sensayngnim-i chwuchenha-n   kes-i-ta
   this book-TOP teacher-NOM   recommend-MOD thing-COP-DECL
   'This book is what the teacher recommended.'

d. 그 때   경찰이   나타난   것이다.
   ku ttay   kyengchal-i nathana-n kes-i-ta
   the moment police-NOM appear-MOD thing-COP-DECL
   'At that very moment, the police came up.'

6 Provide at least three multiple-nominative sentences in Korean where the first nominative phrase has a different grammatical function (e.g. possessor or adjunct). In doing so, also give glosses and English translations. In addition, draw their syntactic structures.

12

Comparative Constructions: Comparing Two Things or Situations

12.1 Introduction

Every language has a way to establish orderings among individuals or entities but has its own way of expressing comparison of the gradable properties of two entities or events on a single scale. The following are prototypical English comparative examples:

(1) a. This book is more interesting than that one.
    b. Words are more powerful than a sword.

There are five parameters in the comparative construction. The main elements are the two participants (in the first example, *this book* and *that one*) being compared and the property in terms of which they are compared. The two participants are the target of comparison, *this book*, which is being compared, and the "standard of comparison," *that one*, which the target is being compared against. The property is the parameter of comparison represented as a gradable predicate like *interesting* here. The canonical comparative also includes the index of comparison, which is expressed by the comparative morpheme *-er* or word *more*, and the marker for the standard of comparison, for which English employs *than*.

Korean comparatives have similar parameters:

(2) 수필보다   소설이   더   재미있다.
    swuphil-pota sosel-i   te   caymiiss-ta
    essay-than   novel-NOM   more   interesting-DECL
    'The novel is more interesting than the essay.'

In this Korean sentence, the targets of comparison are two individuals: an essay and a novel. The compared property is which is more interesting. The comparative

English and Korean in Contrast: A Linguistic Introduction, First Edition. Jong-Bok Kim.
© 2024 John Wiley & Sons, Inc. Published 2024 by John Wiley & Sons, Inc.

morpheme is the optional adverb *te* 'more,' and the comparative standard marker is *pota* 'than,' which is attached to the standard of comparison *swuphil* 'essay.'

Even though the structure of comparative constructions is straightforward in both languages, its complexity is well known, as reflected by Hoeksema's (1983) remarks:

> "If the realm of language is seen as a cosmos, vast, largely, unexplored and sometimes bewildering, then the comparative construction must be a microcosm, reflecting all the complexity of the whole."

This chapter reviews some basic grammatical facts in English and Korean comparatives. To better understand the complex systems, we will also do a contrastive study between English and Korean comparative constructions.

12.2   English Comparatives

12.2.1   Clausal and Phrasal Comparatives

There are two different types of comparatives, phrasal and clausal:

(3) Phrasal comparatives
   a. There are far more similarities than differences.
   b. They can cause more harm than good.
   c. The company now builds more vehicles in Asia than in Europe.

(4) Clausal comparatives
   a. Pat met more students than Bill met.
   b. More people live in Russia than live in the United States.
   c. In the 2000 presidential election in Florida, more people thought they voted for Gore than thought they voted for Bush.

The phrasal comparatives in (3) contain a single phrase following the standard marker *than*. The standard of comparison, functioning as the complement of the standard marker *than*, thus has phrasal syntax. The clausal comparatives in (4) all have a clausal expression as the standard of comparison, functioning as the complement of the standard marker *than*. The clause is incomplete and missing an expression; having a complete sentence as the standard of comparison is unacceptable:

(5) a. *Pat met more students than Bill met [students].
   b. *More people live in Russia than [more people] live in the United States.

12.2.2 Coordination vs. Subordination Properties

Comparatives, in particular phrasal comparatives, display coordination properties: they behave like coordination in terms of syntax. Compare the following pairs:

(6) a. [The boys] and [the girls] sent flowers to him today.
   b. More [boys] than [girls] sent flowers to him today.

(7) a. [The boys sent] and [the girls dropped off] flowers for him today.
   b. [More boys sent] than [girls dropped off] flowers for him today.

(8) a. The boys sent [flowers to him] and [chocolates to her] today.
   b. More boys sent [flowers to him] than [chocolates to her] today.

(9) a. The boys sent [flowers to him today] and [chocolates to her yesterday].
   b. More boys sent [flowers to him today] than [chocolates to her yesterday].

The structure of the comparatives in the (b) sentences is similar to that of coordination in the (a) sentences. This similarity supports treating the comparative marker *than just* like the coordinator *and*. The coordination treatment results in a simple structure like the following for (6b):

(10)

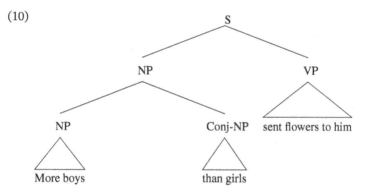

This structure takes *than* as a conjunction: *than girls* forms the second conjunct combining with the first conjunct *more boys*. Another possible analysis is to take *than* as a preposition, considering that it can host an accusative pronoun as in *I love Kim more than him*. This preposition analysis, however, misses the coordination-like properties of phrasal comparatives.

Note that there are many cases where such a parallel structure is not required in clausal comparatives:

(11) a. We invited more people [than wanted to come].
   b. A better striker was playing for them [than we have].

    c. More passengers [than the airline had issued tickets] tried to board the plane.

    d. More guests [than we had chairs] showed up.

There are no parallel structures between the two. This implies that the *than*-clause is not a coordination but a clause that may function as a subordination clause.

(12)

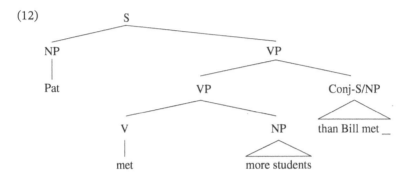

The structure says that the comparative standard clause (Bill met) is an incomplete sentence that structually modifies the preceding VP (met more students). The semantic constraint ensures that this clause is in comparison with the modifying clause headed by the VP. The optionality of the standard clause supports this modifying structure when the context provides the information:

(13) a. I just wanted more information.

    b. These guiding ideals have never been more important.

    c. The factory spends its fuel much more quickly.

12.2.3 Comparative Deletion and Ellipsis

A key property of the clausal comparatives is that there is a missing element in the standard expression. Consider the standard clause in (4).

(14) a.*Kim believed that Pat met.

    b. Kim believed that Pat met boys.

(15) a.*Pat met more boys than Bill met boys.

    b. Pat met more boys than Bill met.

As seen in the contrast between (14a) and (14b), in a regular declarative clause, the verb *met* lexically requires an object. However, such a subcategorization requirement does not exist in the comparative construction, as in (15a).

The missing element in the standard clause is obligatory. It is often assumed that clausal comparatives like (4a) are derived from structures like (16) in which the compared expression is interpreted as a quantified NP with the degree element:

(16) Pat met [[*d*-many] students] than Bill met ~~[[*d'*-many] students]~~ (*d* = degree)

As the structure indicates, the sentence tries to compare two different degrees, *d* and *d'*. In this process, the Comparative Deletion (CD, marked with double strike-out lines) deletes the lexical material in the comparative clause when it is identical to the material in the compared constituent. The CD is an obligatory process. Observe the following contrast:

(17) a. Fred reads more books than Susan reads __.
   b. *Fred reads more books than Susan reads books.

(18) a. We invited more people than __ came.
   b. *We invited more people than people came.

(19) a. She was happier than I was __.
   b. *She was happier than I was happy.

All the (b) sentences are unacceptable because they have no CD process.

In addition to this CD Rule, the grammar must posit a Comparative Ellipsis (CE) to generate examples like (20a) from (20b):

(20) a. Kim will meet more students than Mary will.
   b. Kim will meet [[*d*-many] students] than Mary will ~~meet [[*d'*-many] students]~~

Whereas the CD deletes what is compared, the CE elides the remaining constituents in the comparison under identity.

Using these two rules (CD and CE), we can see that various syntactic elements can undergo CD and CE, as illustrated in the following:

(21) a. Adjectival comparison (CD)
      Kim is taller than Mary is ~~[*d'*-tall]~~.
   b. Adverbial comparison (CD)
      Few people ran faster than Mary ran ~~[*d'*-fast]~~.
   c. Comparison on PP (CD and CE)
      Kim was happier in New York than Mary ~~was [*d'*-happy]~~ in London.
   d. Determiner comparison (CD)
      Kim bought more books than Mary has ~~[*d'*-many] books.~~
   e. S-operator comparison (CD and CE)
      Mary had more friends than Kim thought ~~Mary had [*d'*-many] friends.~~.

As seen here, the CD and CE can be applied to various syntactic categories. Most comparatives can be linked to clausal sources. Note that even phrasal comparatives can be considered derived from clausal sources with the application of the CD and CE Rules. For instance, (22a) can be derived from (22b):

(22) a. Pat met more students than Bill.
　　 b. Pat met [[*d*-many] students] than Bill ~~met [[*d'*-many] students]~~

Most of the phrasal comparatives have clausal counterparts, but there are many cases where we cannot link phrasal comparatives to clausal sources: Consider the following contrast.

(23) a. Mary ran faster than the world record.
　　 b. *Mary ran faster than the world record ran.

(24) a. To be taller than Kim would be quite amazing.
　　 b. *To be taller than Kim to be would be quite amazing.

The putative source sentences for (23a) and (24a) would be the ungrammatical ones in (23b) and (24b), respectively. In addition, some putative underlying sources cannot be reduced to well-formed phrasal comparatives, either:

(25) a. There couldn't have been any more people than there were.
　　 b. *There couldn't have been any more people than there.

The clausal comparative in (25a) is acceptable, but its corresponding phrasal comparative does not exist, as in (25b). The data thus tells us that we cannot derive phrasal comparatives from clausal sources.

12.3　Korean Comparatives

12.3.1　General Properties

Just like English, Korean has two main types of comparatives: phrasal and clausal. Phrasal comparatives involve two nominals, and clausal comparatives have core clausal properties, as exemplified in (26):

(26) a. [비행기보다]　열차가　　더　　편리하다.
　　　 pihayngki-pota yelcha-ka (te)　 phyenliha-ta
　　　 airplane-than　train-NOM　more convenient-DECL
　　　 'The train is more convenient than the airplane.'
　　 b. 미미가　 [모모가　　__ 읽은　　 것보다] 더　 많이　읽었다.
　　　 Mimi-ka　Momo-ka　__ ilk-un　 kes-pota (te)　more many read-ess-ta
　　　 Mimi-NOM Momo-NOM　　read-MOD KES-than　more many read–PST-DECL
　　　 'Mimi read more books than Momo read.'

In the phrasal comparative (26a), the standard of comparison expression 비행기 *pihayngki* 'airplane' combines with the standard marker 보다 *pota* 'than.' The target of comparison 열차 *yelcha* 'train' functions as the subject, whereas the comparative morpheme is realized as the optional adverb 더 *te* 'more' modifying the gradable predicate 편리하다 *phyenliha-ta* 'convenient-DECL.' Unlike this phrasal comparative, the standard of comparison in (26b) is clausal in the sense that it has a gapped clause. The gapped element in the clause functions as the object of *read* and is followed by the noun *kes* which can be replaced by a canonical noun like *chayk* 'book.'

The standard marker *pota* 'than' in both cases is postpositional because it is attached to an NP or a clause headed by the bound noun *kes*. The attachment to a clause-like property can also be seen with the -*ki* nominalized standard clause or the gapless clause with *kes*:

(27) a. 그는   욕심이   많다기보다   부지런하다.
        ku-nun yoksim-i   manh-ta-ki-pota   pwucilenha-ta
        he-TOP greed-NOM many-DECL-NMLZ-than diligent-DECL
        'He is diligent rather than greedy.'

    b. 우리가   가는   것이   학생들이
        wuli-ka ka-nun   kes-i   haksayng-tul-i
        we-NOM   go-MOD   KES-NOM student-PL-NOM DECL

        오는   것보다   편하다.
        o-nun   kes-pota phyenha-ta
        come-MOD   KES-than convenient-DECL
        'For us to go is more convenient than for students to come.'

Unlike the clausal comparative in (26b), in which the object is gapped, the clause with the pure nominalizer -*ki* here is complete, with no syntactic gap.

The standard -*pota* phrase can modify a variety of syntactic phrases:

(28) a. 엄마가   아버지보다 바쁘다.
        emma-ka   apeci-pota   [pappu-ta] (AP)
        mom-NOM dad-than   busy-DECL
        'Mom is busier than dad.'

    b. 동생이   형보다   부자이다.
        tongsayng-i   hyeng-pota   [pwuca]-i-ta (NP)
        younger.brother-NOM elder.brother-than rich-COP-DECL
        'The younger brother is richer than the elder.'

c. 평균보다 　　　많이 　　높았다
pyengkyun-pota [manhi] noph-assta (AdvP)
average-than 　　many 　　high–PST-DECL
'(It) is much higher than the average.'

Even though the category type of the XP in the XP-*pota* can only be nominal (unlike English), the language can express complex comparisons in terms of semantics:

(29) a. 이　　옷은 　　　백화점에서보다 　　　시장에서
i 　　os-un 　　　paykhwacem-eyse-pota sicang-eyse
the clothes-TOP department-LOC-than 　　market-LOC

더 　　잘 　　팔린다.
te 　　cal 　　phalli-n-ta
more well sell-PRES-DECL
'The clothes sell better in the market than in the department store.'

b. 인터뷰는 　　　우리가 생각하는 　　　것보다 　　　적게 걸렸다.
inthepju-nun wuli-ka sangkakha-n kes-pota 　　cekkey kelli-ess-ta
interview-TOP we-NOM think-MOD 　　thing-than less 　　take–PST-DECL
'The interview took fewer hours than we thought.'

Sentence (29a) expresses a comparison of two locations with respect to the degrees to which the same object (the clothes) possesses different properties (selling proportions). Meanwhile, (29b) relates the actual degree that an object (interview) possesses a property to the degree we expected.

As hinted earlier, the comparative expression *te* 'more' is optional in both phrasal and clausal comparatives, but there are cases where its existence is obligatory:

(30) a. 평소보다 　　　삼십 　　　분이 　　*(더) 　　　걸렸다.
phyengso-pota samsip 　　pwun-i *(te) 　　kelli-ess-ta
normal-than 　30 minutes-NOM more take–PST-DECL
'It took 30 more minutes than usual.'

b. 남보다 　　*(더) 먹었다.
nam-pota *(te) mek-ess-ta
others-than more eat–PST-DECL
'(He) ate more than others.'

Such a constraint concerns the lexical properties of the predicate modified by the comparative expression. Consider these copular examples where the nominals are predicative:

(31) a. 동생보다　　　　　　더　　부자이다.
　　　tongsayng-pota　　　　te　　pwuca-i-ta
　　　younger.brother-than　more　rich.person-COP-DECL
　　　'(He) is richer than the young brother.'

　　b. *동생보다　　　　　　더　　학생이다.
　　　tongsayng-pota　　　　te　　haksayng-i-ta
　　　younger.brother-than　more　student-COP-DECL
　　　'*(He) is a more student than the younger brother.'

The main difference between *pwuca* 'rich.person' and *haksayng* 'student' is that the former, not the latter, is inherently gradable, so it can occur in comparatives. The semantic constraint thus requires the inherently nongradable predicate to have the comparative marker *te* 'more' as an obligatory element for it to be gradable.

Another intriguing property of comparative constructions in Korean is that the standard marker *-pota* can also be used as a comparative expression, meaning *more*:

(32) a. 보다　많은　　　학생들이　　그　수업을　　들었다.
　　　pota　manhun　haksayng-tul-i　ku　swuep-ul　tul-ess-ta
　　　more　many　　student-PL-NOM　the　class-ACC　listen–PST-DECL
　　　'More students took the class.'

　　b. 사람들은　　　보다 안전한　　곳으로　　갔다.
　　　salamtul-un　pota　ancenha-n　kos-eulo　ka-ass-ta
　　　people　　　more　safe-MOD　place-to　go–PST-DECL
　　　'People went to a safer place.'

The multiple functions of the expression *pota* allow it to be used in different ways in the same sentence:

(33) a. 자린고비보다 (보다) 더　　현명하게　　　소비한다.
　　　calinkopi-pota　pota　te　hyenmyonghakey　sopiha-n-ta
　　　miser-than　　more　more　wisely　　　　consume-PRES-DECL
　　　'(He) consumes more wisely than a miser.'

　　b. 우리가　생각하였던　　　것보다 (보다) 재미있다.
　　　wuli-ka　sayngkakha-yess-ten　kes-pota　pota　caymi-iss-ta
　　　we-NOM　think–PST-MOD　　KES-than　more　interesting-exist-DECL
　　　'It was more interesting than we thought.'

These two uses of *pota* are different. The use of the first *pota* in (33a) and (33b) is a postpositional marker of standard, whereas the second in both is the comparative morpheme. A clear piece of evidence for these two different grammatical properties comes from the optionality. The postpositional use of the standard marker *pota* cannot be deleted, whereas the comparative adverb *pota* is optional.

The optional comparative expression *pota*, functioning as an adverb, can also modify various syntactic categories as long as they are gradable. In such environments, the expression can be replaced by the comparative adverb *te* 'more':

(34) a. 방을   보다/더 아름답게   바꾸었다.
pang-ul   pota/te   alumtap-key pakkwu-ess-ta (AdvP)
room-ACC more   pretty-CONN change–PST-DECL
'(We) made the room more beautiful.'

b. 보다/더 넓은 은   의미로   사용된다.
pota/te nelp-un   uymi-lo   sayong.toy-n-ta (AP)
more   wider-MOD meaning-with use.become-PRES-DECL
'(It) is used with a wider meaning.'

c. 그   일은   보다/더 전문가
ku   il-un   pota/te   cenmwunka
the work-TOP more   expert
중심으로   진행되었다
cwungsim-ulo cinhayng.toy-ess-ta (NP)
center-with   progress.become-PST-DECL
'The work was pursed by those with more expertise.'

As we have seen, Korean comparatives are different from English comparatives in many respects, even though semantically they behave alike in comparing two objects.

12.3.2   Structure of Phrasal Comparatives

As in English, phrasal comparatives in Korean behave like nominal coordination. The XP-*pota* displays the same distributional properties as nominal conjunction. Let's compare the two:

(35) a. 소설보다   수필이   재미있다.
sosel-pota   swuphil-i   caymi-iss-ta
novel-than   essay-NOM   interesting-exist-DECL
'Essays are more interesting than novels.'

b. 소설과   수필이   재미있다.
sosel-kwa   swuphil-i   caymi-iss-ta
novel-and   essay-NOM   interesting-exist-DECL
'Novels and essays are interesting.'

As the XP-*(k)wa* nominal conjunct, the XP-*pota*, as well as its compared XP, must be nominal. Non-nominal elements cannot function as an XP in both coordination and comparative phrases:

(36) a. *미미가 예쁘게보다 신나게 노래했다.
      Mimi-ka yeppukey-pota sinnakey nolayhay-ess-ta
      Mimi-NOM beautifully-than joyfully sing–PST-DECL
      '(intended) Mimi sang joyfully rather than beautifully.'

   b. *미미가 예쁘게와 신나게 노래하였다.
      Mimi-ka yeppukey-wa sinnakey nolayhay-ess-ta
      Mimi-NOM beautifully-and joyfully sing–PST-DECL

The use of *-pota* as a conjunction marker can be further supported with examples like the following:

(37) 미미는 미국보다 캐나다에 가기로 결정하였다.
    Mimi-nun mikwuk-pota khaynata-ey ka-kilo kyelcengha-yess-ta
    Mimi-TOP America-than Canada-to go-CONN decide–PST-DECL
    'Mimi decided to go Canada rather than to America.'

The phrase *mikwuk-pota* is directly linked to Canada rather than the whole sentence.

The possibility of having more than one XP-*pota* phrase, just like the nominal coordination conjunct XP-*wa*, also indicates that the XP-*pota* functions like a coordination conjunct:[1]

(38) a. 영어보다 중국어보다 한국어가 어렵다.
    yenge-pota cwungkwuke-pota hankwuke-ka elyepta
    English-than Chinese-than Korean-NOM difficult-DECL
    '(lit.) Korean is more difficult than English and Chinese.'

   b. 영어와 중국어와 한국어가 어렵다.
    yenge-wa cwungkwue-wa hankwuke-ka elyepta
    English-and Chinese-and Korean-NOM difficult-DECL
    'English, Chinese, and Korean are difficult.'

Reflecting these properties, we consider the standard marker *-pota* a nominal affix with a simple coordination-like meaning. Taking the NP-*pota* preceding the standard phrase to be a conjunction, we can generate the following structure:

(39)

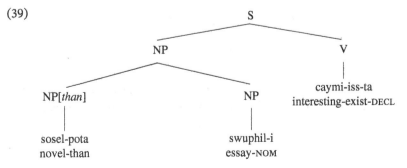

---

1 English does not allow more than one *than* standard clause.

This analysis, assuming the existence of base-generated phrasal comparatives, treats the "standard" and compared phrase as a closed constituent with a semantic interpretation that does not involve the rest of the sentence.

However, as noted earlier, the XP-*pota* has another use: as a verbal modifier, as seen from its flexible distributional position.

(40) a. 한국어가   정말   영어보다   어렵다.
hakwuke-ka cengmal yenge-pota elyep-ta
Korean-NOM really   English-than difficult-DECL
'Korean is really more difficult than English and Chinese.'

b. 열차가   정말   비행기보다   더   편리하다.
yelcha-ka cengmal pihayngki-pota (te) phyenliha-ta
train-NOM really   airplane-than more convenient-DECL
'The train is really more convenient than the airplane.'

There is no strong positional constraint on the distributional possibilities for the standard of comparison XP-*pota* expression: it can appear in almost any position. To deal with these core properties, we accept that -*pota* is a nominal affix, generating a word that can syntactically modify a verbal element. We assume that the XP-*pota* syntactically functions as a modifier of a verbal element and semantically serves as an argument to the given comparative relation with the modifying element. This analysis allows a structure like the following:

(41)

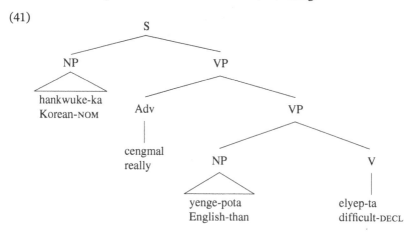

The XP-*pota* modifies the verbal element *difficult*, which serves as a semantic argument of the *than* relation. In this structure, the comparative phrase "English-than" can function only as a modifier to the predicate "difficult."

12.3.3 Structure of Clausal Comparatives

As noted earlier, the canonical clausal comparative clause with a syntactic gap behaves like a relative clause in many ways. The clausal comparative clause consists of the standard of comparison clause with a gap and the nominal expression *kes*. First, note that, as have been noted earlier, the *kes* expression has at least three uses in the language:

(42) a. 내 것이 너 것만큼 크다.
    nay kes-i ne kes-mankhum khu-ta
    my thing-NOM your thing-as big-DECL
    '(Lit.) My thing is as big as yours.'

  b. 미미가 먹은 것을 먹었다.
    Mimi-ka __ mek-un kes-ul mek-ess-ta
    Mimi-NOM eat-MOD thing-ACC eat–PST-DECL
    '(We) ate the thing that John ate.'

  c. 미미가 달리는 것을 몰랐다.
    Mimi-ka talli-nun kes-ul moll-ass-ta
    Mimi-NOM run-MOD thing-ACC not.know-PST-DECL
    '(We) didn't know that Mimi was running.'

As noted here, *kes* in (42a) combines with a determiner specifier, whereas the one in (42b) combines with the relative clause with a missing argument. In both of these examples, *kes* refers to a 'thing.' Meanwhile, *kes* in (42c) combines with a complete sentence, referring to the event denoted by the clause.

In clausal comparatives, the "standard" clause must have a syntactic gap like a relative clause, as in (43a). The putative gap cannot be replaced by a canonical NP as in (43b):

(43) a. 이 책상은 내가 만든 것보다 더 크다.
    i chayksang-un nay-ka __ mantu-n kes-pota (te) khu-ta
    this desk-TOP I-NOM make-MOD thing-than more big-DECL
    'This desk is bigger than the one I made.'

  b. *i chayksang-un [[nay-ka chayksang-ul mantu-n] kes-pota] khu-ta

In addition, both comparative and canonical relative clauses allow the head noun *kes* to be replaced by a content noun like *book*:

(44) a. 형이 읽은 것보다/책보다
    hyong-i __ ilk-un kes-pota/chayk-pota
    brother-NOM read-MOD thing-than/book-than

책을   더   많이   읽었다.
chayk-ul te   manhi ilk-ess-ta
book-ACC more many   read–PST-DECL
'(He) read more books than his older brother did.'

b. 형이   읽은   것을/책을   또   읽었다.
   hyeong-i   __   ilk-un   kes-ul/chayk-ul   tto   ilk-ess-ta
   brother-NOM   read-MOD   thing-ACC/book-ACC   again   read–PST-DECL
   '(He) again read the books that his older brother read.'

The clausal comparative also has the salient feature of a relative clause, allowing a long-distance relationship:

(45) 형이   읽었다고   생각한   것-보다
     hyeong-i   __   ilk-ess-ta-ko   sayngkakha-n   kes-pota
     brother-NOM   read–PST-DECL-COMP   think-MOD   KES-than

     책을   더   많이   읽었다.
     chayk-ul   te   manhi ilk-ess-ta
     book-ACC   more many   read–PST-DECL
     '(He) read more books than we thought his older brother did.'

As shown in this example, the standard clause consists of a gapped clause with the noun *kes* to which the standard marker *pota* is attached.

Let us consider the structure of (43a):

(46)

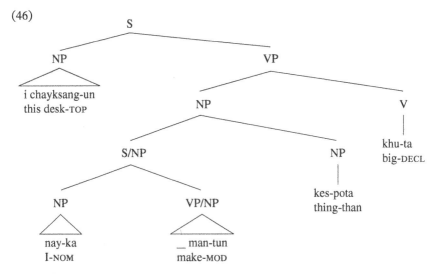

The comparative marker *pota* is attached to the noun *kes* forming the head of the NP. This head combines with the relative clause whose object is realized as a gap (slashed). That is, *kes* has the effect of turning a relative clause into an NP. Semantically, the noun *kes* is a common noun referring to an individual, which is coindexed with the gapped object of *mantu-n* 'make-MOD.' Because the verb *mantu-n* 'make' also requires its object to be a referential individual, there is no mismatch between these two requirements.

As noted earlier, in some cases, the standard comparative clause does not contain an argument (subject or object) gap even though it is nominalized with the noun *kes* or *ki*. Let us consider these similar examples:

(47) a. 존은   톰이   달린   것보다 빨리 달렸다.
     John-un Tom-i   talli-n   kes-pota ppalli tali-ess-ta
     John-TOP Tom-NOM run-MOD KES-than fast   run–PST-DECL
     'John ran faster than Tom did.'

   b. 우리가 가는   것이   학생들이   오는   것보다 편하다.
     wuli-ka ka-nun KES-i   haksayng-tul-i o-nun   kes-pota phyenha-ta
     we-NOM go-MOD KES-NOM student-PL-NOM come-MOD KES-than convenient-
                                        DECL
     'For us to go is more convenient than for students to come.'

The treatment of (47b) is simple: *-ki* is a pure nominalizer suffix with no substantial meaning. The present analysis, in which *kes* can be linked to either an individual or an event, also allows examples like (47a) with no syntactic gap. Consider the structure the present analysis generates:

(48)

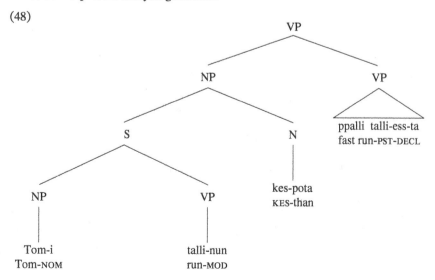

Unlike the common noun *kes* the expression *kes* here is a bound noun selecting a sentence and is linked to its eventual meaning of Tom's running. This noun forms an NP with its sentential complement, the result of which modifies the VP *ran fast*.

12.3.4 Context-Dependent Comparatives

As in English, phrasal and clausal comparatives in Korean are often regarded as the same type because most phrasal comparatives can be re-paraphrased as clausal types:

(49) a. 김은   메리보다 사과를   더   많이   먹었다.
      Kim-un Mary-pota sakwa-lul te   manhi mek-ess-ta
      Kim-TOP Mary-than apple-ACC more many eat-PST-DECL
      'Kim ate more apples than Mary.'

    b. 김은   [메리가   먹은   것]보다 사과를   더   많이 먹었다.
      Kim-un [Mary-ka __ mek-un kes]-pota sakwa-lul te   manhi mek-ess-ta
      Kim-TOP Mary-NOM   eat-MOD KES-than apple-ACC more many eat-PST-DECL
      'Kim ate more apples than Mary ate.'

Based on such semantic similarities between the two, phrasal comparatives are often assumed to have a clausal source, as in English. However, in many cases, phrasal comparatives cannot be linked to clausal counterparts:

(50) a. 김은   나이보다 어리게   보인다.
      Kim-un nai-pota eli-key   poi-n-ta
      Kim-TOP age-than young-CONN look-PRES-DECL
      'Kim looks younger than his age.'

    b. 고집은   철수가   영희보다   더   하다.
      kocip-un   Chelswu-ka Yenghuy-pota te   ha-ta
      stubborn-TOP Chelswu-NOM Yenghuy-than more do-DECL
      'As for stubbornness, Chelswu is more stubborn than Yenghuy.'

There doesn't appear to be a plausible clausal counterpart for (50a) because age cannot be "young."

Attested data show us another peculiar example for which it is hard to assume any clausal-like source sentences:

(51) a. 철수의   성적이   친구보다   뒤쳐졌다.
      Chelswu-uy sengcek-i chinkwu-pota twichyeci-ess-ta
      Chelswu-GEN grade-NOM friend-than low-PST-DECL
      'Chelswu's grade was lower than his friend's.'

b. 올   해   입시가   작년보다   어렵다.
ol   hay   ipsi-ka   caknyen-pota   elyep-ta
this year   entrance.exam-NOM   last year-than   difficult-DECL
'This year's entrance exam is more difficult than last year's.'

Such examples are intriguing because there is a mismatch between the associate and the standard expression. That is, what is compared is Chelswu's grade and his friend in (51a) and this year's entrance exam and last year in (51b). Such mismatched comparisons are not allowed in English:

(52) a. *Chelswu's grade was lower than his friend.
     b. *This year's entrance exam is more difficult than last.

In a CD- and CE-based analysis, such examples would mean deleting the head noun of the standard expression, as represented in the following semantic representation:

(53) [Chelswu's grade-NOM [his friend's grade NOM low]-than low]

Under traditional assumptions, such a deletion is illegitimate because both the deletion and ellipsis processes apply only to a syntactic constituent.

12.4 Contrastive Notes

12.4.1 Types of Comparatives

We have seen that there are at least two main types of comparatives, phrasal and clausal, in English and Korean. Consider the following phrasal comparatives in the two languages:

(54) a. The star is more massive than the sun.
     b. 그 별은   태양보다   더   크다.
        ku   pyeol-un   thayyang-pota   te   khu-ta
        the star-TOP   sun-than   more big-DECL
        'The star is bigger than the sun.'

In both examples, two NPs are compared with respect to the gradable expressions "massive" and "big." The comparative markers *than* and 보다 pota 'than' behave like coordination conjunctions. Clausal comparatives are a bit different:

(55) a. Momo read more books than Mimi did.

b. 미미가   읽은   것보다 모모가   (더)   많이   읽었다.
Mimi-ka __ ilk-un   kes-pota Momo-ka (te) manhi ilk-ess-ta
Mimi-NOM   read-MOD KES-than Momo-NOM more many read-PST-DECL
'Momo read more than Mimi read.'

In English, the standard expression introduced by *than* is an incomplete sentence; but in Korean, the standard clause is a relative clause headed by *kes*.

12.4.2 Comparative Morphemes and Standard Markers

English adopts a comparative morpheme *-er* or the word *more* as the comparative morpheme and *than* as a standard marker. The comparative morpheme or word is obligatory, whereas *than*-XP can be optional in certain contexts.

(56) a. I want to have more information (than this).
b. It is much more complicated (than I expected).

In Korean, this optional standard of comparison is obligatory, but the comparative morpheme or word is optional:

(57) 이   것보다   정보를   (더) 많이   원한다.
i   kes-pota cengpo-lul   te   manhi wonha-n-ta
this thing-pota information-ACC more many want-PRES-DECL
'I want more information than this.'

12.4.3 Comparative Deletion and Comparative Ellipsis

The two suggested rules, CD (comparative deletion) and CE (comparative ellipsis), can account for the variations in English clausal comparatives:

(58) a. Lucas will become more powerful than you'll ever be.
b. Lucas will become [*d*-much powerful] than you'll ~~become [[d'-much power]~~.

In Korean, we apply CD (deleting the identical compared constituent), not CE (eliding other identical expressions in the clause). For instance, in (55b), we cannot delete the verb 읽은 ilk-un 'read-MOD' in the comparative clause even if it is identical to the main verb.

12.4.4 Context Dependency

A significant difference between the two languages is shown by examples where the comparison is highly dependent on context:

(59) a. 그는　　나이보다　젊어　　　보인다.
　　　ku-nun　nai-pota　celm-e　　poi-n-ta
　　　he-TOP　age-than　young-CONN　look-PRES-DECL
　　　'(lit.) He looks younger than age.'

　　b. 그의　　키는　　나보다　크다.
　　　ku-uy　khi-nun　na-pota　khu-ta
　　　he-GEN　height-TOP　I-than　tall-DECL
　　　'(lit.) His height is taller than I.'

There is no explicit comparison between the standard expression and the target. For example, we cannot compare "he" and "age," as in (59a), or "his height" and "I," as in (59b). In (59a), the standard expression 나이보다 *nai-pota* is similar to "compared to" in English. In (59b), the compared targets are induced from context: his height and my height. In terms of semantics, as we have seen, the interpretation of English comparatives is compositional (semantic-based), whereas that of Korean comparatives hinges on context. Issues remain concerning what these language differences imply for the cognition systems of the comparative constructions in these individual languages as well as in universal languages.

12.5　Conclusion

Comparative constructions have the most intriguing properties in natural languages, in that they interact with various syntactic, semantic, and pragmatic phenomena. In this chapter, we examined the comparative constructions of Korean and English. The two languages are similar in that each employs its own morphological and syntactic ways of expressing gradable concepts and comparing properties of two objects. However, the languages are also different in many respects. A primary difference between English and Korean is that Korean clausal-like comparatives are relative clauses headed by the formal noun *kes*. In addition, in terms of semantics, the interpretation of English comparatives is compositional, whereas that of Korean comparatives hinges on context.

Exercises

1　Construct two compared sentences in each example, and identify what is being compared. In addition, identify the CD (comparative deletion) and CE (comparative ellipsis) rule applied, if any.

　　(i) a. I think the conference is tougher than people think.

    b. I was about a foot taller than the man.

    c. I enjoy my food much more than most people do.

    d. They are more youthful than their parents were at this age.

    e. Diving in shallow water is riskier than many people think.

    f. Kansas also now has more restrictions on abortion than any state in the United States.

    g. The capital city of Caracas is cleaner than in past years.

    h. Technology is changing faster than the law.

    i. The shapes seem to be longer than they are thick.

2 Give the source sentences of the following Korean comparatives, and discuss what is compared. In addition, identify the CD (comparative deletion) and CE (comparative ellipsis) rule applied, if any.

(i) a. 당신보다   제가   훨씬   더   오래   그를   만났다.
        tangsin-pota cey-ka hwelssin te   olay   ku-lul manna-ass-ta
        you-than   I-NOM much   more longtime he-ACC meet-PST-DECL
        'I have known him much longer than you.'

    b. 저는   커피보다   홍차를   더   좋아해요.
        ce-nun khephi-pota hongcha-lul te   cohahay-yo
        I-TOP   coffee-than black.tea-ACC more like-DECL
        'I like black tea more than coffee.'

    c. 미미가   정수보다   영수에게   더
        Mimi-ka   Jungsoo-pota Youngsoo-eykey te
        Mimi-NOM Jungsoo-than Youngsoo-DAT   more
        많은   음식을   줬어요.
        manhun umsik-ul cwu-ess-eyo
        many   food-ACC give-PST-DECL
        'Mimi gave more food to Youngsoo than to Jungsoo.'

    d. 스마트   와치가   스위스 시계보다   더   많이   팔렸다.
        sumathu wachi-ka   suwisu sikyey-pota te   manhi phalli-ess-ta
        smart   watch-NOM Swiss   watch-than more many sell-PST-DECL
        'More smart watches have been sold than Swiss watches.'

    e. 과거보다   미래가   더   중요하다
        kwake-pota milay-ka   te   cwungyoha-ta
        past-than   future-NOM more important-DECL
        'The future is more important than the past.'

    f. 당신은   어제보다   더   아름답습니다.
        tangsin-un ecey-pota   te   alumtap-supni-ta
        you-TOP   yesterday-than more beautiful-FRML-DECL
        'You are more beautiful than yesterday.'

3 Give a tree structure for each of the following sentences, and discuss the degree properties that are compared.

(i) a. This car costs more than your last car cost you.
b. Ralph is more qualified than Jason is.
c. Ralph has more books than Jason has manuscripts.
d. Brenda is more enthusiastic now than she used to be.
e. I'm more of a man than you are.

4 Give a simple tree structure for each of the following, and discuss the degree properties that are compared.

(i) a. 나쁜   언론은   나쁜   정부보다   더   나쁘다.
nappun enlon-un nappun cengpwu-pota   te   nappu-ta
bad   press-TOP bad   government-than more bad-DECL
'A bad press is worse than a bad government.'

b. 저는   커피보다   홍차를   더   좋아해요.
ce-nun khephi-pota hongcha-lul   te   cohahay-yo
I-TOP   coffee-than black.tea-ACC more like-DECL
'I like black tea more than coffee.'

c. 도서관에서보다   커피숍에서   더
tosekwan-eyse-pota khephisyop-eyse te
library-LOC-than   coffee.shop-LOC more

집중을   잘   한다.
cipswung-ul cal   ha-n-ta
focus-ACC   well do-PRES-DECL
'I can be more focused in a coffee shop than in a library.'

d. 나는   어제보다   오늘 더   많이   먹었다.
na-nun ecey-pota   onul te   manhi mek-ess-ta
I-TOP   yesterday-than today more much eat-PST-DECL
'I ate more today than yesterday.'

e. 한국을   여행하는   것이   일본을   여행하는
hankwuk-ul yehanyngha-nun kes-i   ilpon-ul   yehayngha-nun
Korea-ACC   travel-MOD   KES-NOM Japan-ACC travel-MOD

것보다 더   저렴하다.
kes-pota te   celyemha-ta
kes-than more economical-DECL
'It is more economical to travel in Korea than to travel in Japan.'

5 Discuss the function(s) of the comparative marker -보다 -*pota* in the following Korean sentences.

(i) a. 많은   사람들이   보다 어려
     manhun   salam-tul-i   pota   elye
     many   person-PL-NOM   more   young

     보이는   피부를   원한다.
     poi-nun   phipwu-lul   wenha-n-ta
     look-MOD   skin-ACC   want-PRES-DECL
     'Many people want skin that looks younger for their age.'

   b. 때론   여자보다   남자가   더   힘들   수도   있다.
     ttaylon   yeca-pota   namca-ka   te   himtul   swu-to   iss-ta
     sometimes   woman-than   man-NOM   more   distressed   can-also   be-DECL
     'Sometimes men may feel more distressed than women.'

   c. 보다   나은   미래를   만드는
     pota   naun   milay-lul   mantu-nun
     more   good   future-ACC   make-MOD

     힘은   현재   순간에   있다.
     him-un   hyencay   swunkan-ey   iss-ta
     power-   present   moment-LOC   be-DECL
     'The power of making a better future is in the current moment.'

   d. 수채화보다   더   수채화같은   사진이다.
     swuchayhwa-pota   te   swuchayhwa-kathun   sacin-i-ta
     watercolor.painting-than   more   watercolor.painting-like   picture-be-DECL
     'It is a picture like a watercolor painting that looks more like a
     watercolor painting.'

6 Find three English phrasal and clausal comparatives from authentic sources like newspapers or web pages (give the source of each sentence), and give their syntactic (tree) structures. Translate them into Korean, and discuss the differences between English and Korean comparatives.

7 Find three Korean phrasal and clausal comparatives from authentic sources like newspapers or web pages (give the source of each sentence), and give their syntasctic (tree) structures. Translate them into English, and discuss the differences between English and Korean comparatives.

13

Agreement: Harmonizing Together

13.1 Introduction

Agreement is a phenomenon where the form of one expression covaries with that of another in the given sentence. For instance, in English, the verb agrees with its subject in person and number:

(1) a. The book is/*are in the drawer.
     b. The books *is/are in the drawer.

The verb *is* is conditioned by the singular number feature of the subject *the book* and *are* by the plural number feature of *the books*. Korean has a similar agreement phenomenon:

(2) a. 선생님이   왜   전화하시나요?
        sensayng-nim-i   way cenhwaha-si-nayo?
        teacher-HON-NOM why phone-HON-QUE?
        'Why is the teacher calling (me)?'

     b. *학생이   왜   전화하시나요?
        haksayng-i   way cenhwaha-si-nayo?
        student-NOM   why phone-HON-QUE?
        '(int.) Why is the student calling (me)?'

The honored subject 선생님 sensayng-nim 'teacher-HON' in (2a) must agree with the honored verb, but in (2b), the nonhonored subject 학생이 haksayng-i 'student-NOM' is in disagreement with the honored verb.

This chapter discusses such agreement phenomena in English and Korean, where the two expressions are in concordance with the value of grammatical features like person, number, gender, and honorification.

English and Korean in Contrast: A Linguistic Introduction, First Edition. Jong-Bok Kim.
© 2024 John Wiley & Sons, Inc. Published 2024 by John Wiley & Sons, Inc.

13.2 Agreement in English

13.2.1 Agreement Features in English

As noted, agreement phenomena have to do with matching the value of grammatical features in the two relevant expressions. In English, three agreement features are relevant: person, number, and gender.

(3) a. I am in love with this book.
    b. You are in love with this book, aren't you?
    c. She is in love with this book.

Each subject pronoun here requires a different copula verb, depending on its person value: first, second, or third. This kind of person agreement can also be found in examples like the following:

(4) President Lincoln delivered his/*my/*your Gettysburg Address in 1863.

The pronoun *his* and its antecedent *President Lincoln* are in concord with respect to its third-person value. This is also true in examples like the following:

(5) The students did their/*his/*her job.

The gender feature also plays a role in this type of pronoun-antecedent agreement:

(6) a. The man reached his/*her/*its destination.
    b. The ship reached her/its/*his destination.

The antecedent *the man* linked to the pronoun *his* is masculine, whereas *the ship* is either feminine or neutral. As seen in these examples, violating the gender agreement between the pronoun and the antecedent renders the sentences ungrammatical.

    In English agreement, the number feature is also important:

(7) a. a/this book/*books
    b. these/those books/*book

(8) a. The student sings/*sing.
    b. The students sing/*sings.

In (7), the number value of the article and that of the head noun need to agree; in (8), the number feature of the subject agrees with that of the verb.

    As we have just seen, the relevant agreement features in English include person, number, and gender. In this section, we will consider how these three agreement features play key roles in English agreement phenomena.

13.2.2 Determiner-Head Agreement

All countable nouns are used as either singular or plural. When they combine with a determiner, there must be a number agreement relationship between the two:

(9) a. this book/that book
 b. *this books/*that books/these books/those books
 c. *few dog/few dogs

However, nothing prevents a singular noun from combining with a determiner with no number information (singular or plural):

(10) a. *those book, *these book, …
 b. no book/books, the book/books, my book/books, …

13.2.3 Pronoun-Antecedent Agreement

The second type of agreement is pronoun-antecedent agreement, as shown in (11).

(11) a. If <u>Kim</u> wants to succeed in corporate life, he/*she has to know the rules of the game.
 b. The <u>critique</u> of Plato's *Republic* was written from a contemporary point of view. It was an in-depth analysis of Plato's opinions about possible governmental forms.

The pronoun *he* or *it* here must agree with its antecedent not only with respect to the number value but also with respect to the person (first, second, third) and gender (masculine, feminine, neuter) values.

A singular pronoun like *each* or *someone* takes a singular pronoun, and a plural pronoun like *both* is linked to a plural pronoun:

(12) a. Each of the clerks does a good deal of work around his or her office.
 b. Both did a good job in their office.

For collective nouns, we expect index-based agreement. Depending on what they refer to in the given context, they can be linked to either a singular or plural pronoun:

(13) a. The jury read its verdict.
 b. The jury gave their individual opinions.

In (13a), *The jury* has a unit reference, whereas *the jury* in (13b) refers to the members.

13.2.4 Subject-Verb Agreement as Morphosyntactic Agreement

The third type of agreement is subject-verb agreement, which is one of the most important phenomena in English syntax. Let us look at some slightly complex examples:

(14) a. The <u>characters</u> in Shakespeare's *Twelfth Night* *lives/live in a world that has been turned upside-down.

    b. <u>Students</u> studying English read/*reads Conrad's *Heart of Darkness* while at university.

As observed here, the subject and the verb must have identical number values. In addition, the person value is involved in agreement relations, in particular when the subject is a personal pronoun:

(15) a. <u>You</u> are/*is the only person that I can rely on.

    b. <u>He</u> is/*are the only person that I can rely on.

These facts show us that a verb lexically specifies information about both the number and person values of the subject it requires.

    Note the importance of identifying the head of the subject for agreement:

(16) a. The list of items is/*are on the desk.

    b. The woman with all the dogs walks/*walk down my street.

In these examples, the head of the subject is *list* and *woman*, respectively, not the nouns closer to the verb. This head, not the closer noun, agrees with the verb in each case. No intervening expression can affect the agreement relations, either:

(17) a. The politician, along with the reporters, is expected shortly.

    b. Excitement, as well as nervousness, is the cause of her shaking.

    c. The book, including all the chapters in the first section, is boring.

13.2.5 Subject-Verb Agreement as Index Agreement

At first glance, subject-verb agreement in English seems to be morphosyntactic, but there are many cases where the index (semantic) value of the subject plays a key role in determining agreement:

(18) a. The committee hasn't yet made up its mind.

    b. The committee haven't yet made up their mind/minds.

The morphosyntactic value of the subject is the same in these two examples, but the verb is singular or plural. This implies that what matters is what the subject refers to. Collectives nouns like *committee, family, government, jury, audience,* and so forth often display such index-based agreement. In the following examples, either the singular or plural verb is acceptable, depending on what *my family* and *the jury* refer to:

(19) a. All of my family has/have arrived.

    b. Most of the jury is/are here.

When a collective noun refers to a group as a whole, the singular verb is used. When it refers to individuals in the group, the plural verb is adopted.

English agreement is thus not purely morphosyntactic, but context-dependent in various ways via the index value that tells us what the NP refers to in the given context. Index agreement involves sharing referential indexes, closely related to the semantics of a nominal and somewhat separate from the morphosyntactic agreement features. Such agreement patterns can also be found in examples like the following, where the underlined parts have singular agreement with *four pounds*, which is morphosyntactically plural:

(20) [Four pounds] <u>was</u> quite a bit of money in 1950, and <u>it</u> was not easy to come by.

Given the separation of the morphological agreement features and the semantic index values, nothing blocks mismatches between the two as long as all the other constraints are satisfied. Following are some further examples:

(21) a. [Five pounds] is/*are a lot of money.

    b. [Two drops] deodorizes/*deodorize anything in your house.

    c. [Fifteen dollars] in a week is/*are not much.

    d. [Fifteen years] represents/*represent a long period of his life.

    e. [Two miles] is/*are as far as they can walk.

In all of these examples with measure nouns, the plural subject combines with a singular verb. An apparent conflict arises from the agreement features of the head noun. For proper agreement in the noun phrase, the head noun must be plural; but for subject-verb agreement, the noun must be singular. For instance, the nouns *pounds* and *drops* here are morphologically plural and thus must have a plural determiner, to observe the noun-determiner agreement. But when these nouns are anchored to the group as a whole – that is, conceptualized as referring to a single measure – the index value must be singular to observe the subject-verb index agreement in English. The present analysis takes determiner-head agreement to be morphosyntactic agreement, so the head *pounds* must refer to only the feature value. This way of looking at English agreement enables us to explain the following:

(22) a. *These dollars are what I want to donate to the institute.

    b. *These pounds is a lot of money.

There is nothing wrong in forming *these dollars* or *these pounds*, because *dollars* and *pounds* can combine with a plural Det (determiner). The issue is the agreement between the subject *these dollars* and the verb *is*. Unlike *five dollars* or *five pounds*, *these dollars* and *these pounds* are semantically not taken to refer to a single unit: they always refer to plural entities. Thus no mismatch is allowed in these examples.

A similar mismatch between subject and verb is found in cases involving collective nouns for social organizations or collections, as in the following authentic examples:

(23) a. The government have been more transparent in the way they have dealt with public finances than any previous government.
b. In preparation for the return game, this team have trained more efficiently than they had in recent months.

The head noun *government* or *team* is singular, so it can combine with the singular determiner *this*. But the conflicting fact is that the singular noun phrase can combine with the plural verb *have* as well as with the singular verb *has*, depending on what the nouns refer to.

13.3 Agreement in Korean

13.3.1 Subject-Verb Agreement as Honorific Agreement

Honorification, a primary feature of spoken language in Korean, plays a key role in proper and successful verbal communication. The Korean honorific system requires that when the subject is in the honorific form (usually with the marker -님 *-nim* and marked as [HON +]), the predicate must also be inflected with the honorific form -(으)시 *-(u)si*, as in (24):

(24) a. 선생님이   웃으셨어.
     sensayng-nim-i wus-usi-ess-e
     teacher-HON-NOM laugh-HON-PST-DECL
     'The teacher laughed.'
b. #선생님이   웃었어.
     #sensayng-nim-i wus-ess-e
     teacher-HON-NOM laugh-PST-DECL
     'The teacher laughed.'

This type of agreement is often assumed to be purely pragmatic, mainly because context can allow cases where the subject and verb disagree: the sentence in (24b) is acceptable when the speaker does not honor the referent of the subject (marked by #). The possibility of such disagreement has often led work in the literature to assume that using the -님 *-nim* and -시 *-si* verb forms is a matter of gradience and appropriateness rather than grammaticality.

However, an often-neglected fact is that this agreement constraint must be observed when the subject is nonhuman, as in (25)

(25) a. 차가   오(*시)었어.
     cha-ka   o-(*si)-ess-e
     cha-NOM come-HON-PST-DECL
     'The car came.'

   b. 국회가   그 법안을 심의하(*시)었어.
     kwukhoy-ka ku pepan-ul simuy-ha-(*si)-ess-e
     congress-NOM the bill-ACC review-do-HON-PST-DECL
     'The congress reviewed the bill.'

If we rely only on pragmatic information, we will have difficulty understanding why, unlike the disagreement in (24b), disagreements like (25) are rarely found in real language usages.

In addition, there are agreement-sensitive syntactic phenomena such as auxiliary verb constructions:

(26) a. 선생님이   노래를   부르(시)지   않(으시)었어.
     sensayng-nim-i nolay-lul pwulu-(si)-ci anh-(usi)-ess-e
     teacher-HON-NOM song-ACC sing-HON-CONN not-HON-PST-DECL
     'The teacher did not sing a song.'

   b. 선생님이   돈을   모(*시)어   두셨어.
     sensayngnim-i ton-ul   mo-(*si)-e   twu-si-ess-e
     teacher-NOM   money-ACC save-HON-CONN held-HON-PST-DECL
     'The teacher saved money (for rainy days).'

   c. 선생님이   노래를   부르시나   보(*시)어.
     sensayng-nim-i nolay-lul pwulu-si-na po-(*si)-e
     teacher-HON-NOM song-ACC sing-HON-CONN seem-HON-DECL
     'The teacher seems to sing a song.'

As noted here, even though the subject is honored in each case, the honorific marker on the main predicate in (26a) is optional, with the auxiliary 않- *anh-* 'not.' in (26b), the marker must appear only on the auxiliary verb 두- *twu-* 'hold.' And in (26c), the marker cannot appear on the auxiliary 보- *po-* 'seem.' We can hardly attribute these clear contrasts to pragmatic factors, but we could observe that the honorific suffix could occur either in the main or in the auxiliary verb with a honorific subject.

13.3.2 Addressee Agreement

Matters become more complicated when we consider agreement triggered by verbal endings. Korean has at least two different endings depending on the honoring relationship between speaker and addressee:

(27) a. 학생이　　　왔어/왔어요.
　　　haksayng-i　o-ass-e/o-ass-eyo
　　　student-NOM　come-PST-DECL/come-PST-DECL
　　　'The student came.'
　　b. 선생님이　　　오셨어/오셨어요.
　　　sensayng-nim-i　o-si-ess-e/o-si-ess-eyo
　　　teacher-HON-NOM　come-HON-PST-DECL/come-HON-PST-DECL
　　　'The teacher came.'

As noted here, the verbal endings -어 *-e* and -어요 *-eyo* are different with respect to addressee agreement. The 'respectful declarative' ending -어요 *-eyo* is used when the social status of the addressee is higher than that of the speaker. The data implies that not only the speaker but also the addressee plays a role in proper communication strategies with respect to the honorification system.

13.3.3　Multiple Honorification

It is possible to have cases with multiple honorifics in which subject agreement occurs together with the object:

(28) 아버님이　　　선생님을　　　뵈(시)었어.
　　　ape-nim-i　　　sensayng-nim-ul　poy-(usi)-ess-e
　　　father-HON-NOM　teacher-HON-ACC　HON.see-HON-PST-DECL
　　　'The father saw the teacher.'

The honorific suffix -시 *-si* on the verb here requires the subject to be [HON +], whereas the suppletive verb stem requires its object to be [HON +]. In such cases, the honorific marker on the verb is optional, and the verb can be replaced by the nonsuppletive form 보- *po-* 'see.' However, the grammar does not allow cases like the following:

(29) a. *미미가　　　선생님을　　　뵈셨어.
　　　*Mimi-ka　　sensayng-nim-ul　poy-usi-ess-e
　　　Mimi-NOM　teacher-HON-ACC　HON.see-HON-PST-DECL
　　　'Mimi saw the teacher.'
　　b. *아버님이　　　미미를　　뵈었어
　　　*ape-nim-i　　　Mimi-lul　poy-ess-e
　　　father-HON-NOM　Mimi-ACC　HON.see-HON-PST-DECL
　　　'The father saw Mimi.'

(29a) is ruled out because the HON form -(으)시 *-(u)si* requires the subject to be [HON +], and (29b) is now allowed because the suppletive form 뵙- *poy-* 'see' has an [HON +] object.

Oblique agreement can also occur together with subject agreement:

(30) a. 어머님이   선생님에게   선물을   드리셨어.
      eme-nim-i   sensayng-nim-eykey senmwul-ul tuli-si-ess-e
      mother-HON-NOM teacher-HON-DAT   present-ACC give.HON-PST-DECL
      'Mother gave the teacher a present.'

  b. # 어머님이   선생님에게   선물을   드렸어.
      eme-nim-i   sensayng-nim-eykey senmwul-ul tuli-ess-e
      mother-HON-NOM teacher-HON-DAT   present-ACC give.HON-PST-DECL

  c. #어머님이   선생님에게   선물을   주(시)었어.
      eme-nim-i   sensayng-nim-eykey senmwul-ul cwu-(si)-ess-e
      mother-HON-NOM teacher-HON-DAT   present-ACC give.HON-PST-DECL

  d. *미미가   선생님에게   선물을   드리셨어.
      *Mimi-ka sensayng-nim-eykey senmwul-ul tuli-si-ess-e
      Mimi-NOM teacher-HON-DAT   present-ACC give.HON-PST-DECL

  e. *어머님이   미미에게   선물을   드리셨어.
      *eme-nim-i   Mimi-eykey senmwul-ul tuli-si-ess-e
      mother-HON-NOM Mimi-DAT   present-ACC give.HON-PST-DECL

Because the nonhonorific verb does not restrict the subject, the grammar allows the disagreement in (30b) and (30c). However, (30d) and (30e) cannot be formed: the former violates subject agreement, and the latter violates object agreement.

13.3.4 Agreement in Auxiliary Constructions

The honorification system offers a streamlined way to explain the agreement in auxiliary verb constructions, as briefly noted earlier. There are three types of auxiliaries with respect to agreement:

Type I

In constructions with auxiliary verbs like 않- *anh-* 'not,' when the subject is in the honorific form, the honorific suffix -시 *-si* can optionally appear on the preceding main verb, the auxiliary verb, or both:

(31) a. 선생님이   오시지   않으셨어.
      sensayng-nim-i   o-si-ci   anh-usi-ess-e
      teacher-HON-NOM come-HON-CONN not-HON-PST-DECL
      'The teacher did not come.'

b. 선생님이   오시지   않았어.
   sensayng-nim-i   o-si-ci   anh-ess-e
   teacher-HON-NOM   come-HON-CONN   not-PST-DECL

c. 선생님이   오지   않으셨어.
   sensayng-nim-i   o-ci   anh-usi-ess-e
   teacher-HON-NOM   come-CONN   not-HON-PST-DECL

d. #선생님이   오지   않았어.
   #sensayng-nim-i   o-ci   anh-ess-e
   teacher-HON-NOM   come-CONN   not-PST-DECL

Type II

When the head auxiliary verb is something like 보- *po-* 'try,' 두- *twu-* 'hold,' or 지- *ci-* 'become,' subject honorification occurs only on the auxiliary verb. That is, the preceding main verb with the specific CONN suffix form -아/어 *-a/e* cannot have the honorific suffix -시 *-si*:

(32) a. *선생님이   미미를   잡으셔   두셨어.
     *sensayng-nim-i   Mimi-lul   cap-usi-e   twu-si-ess-e
     teacher-HON-NOM   Mimi-ACC   catch-HON-CONN   leave-HON-PST-DECL
     '(lit.) The teacher held Mimi for future.'

b. 선생님이   미미를   잡아   두셨어.
   sensayng-nim-i   Mimi-lul   cap-a   twu-si-ess-e
   teacher-HON-NOM   Mimi-ACC   catch-CONN   leave-HON-PST-DECL

c. *선생님이   미미를   잡으셔   두었어.
   *sensayng-nim-i   Mimi-lul   cap-usi-e   twu-ess-e
   teacher-HON-NOM   Mimi-ACC   catch-HON-CONN   leave-PST-DECL

d. #선생님이   미미를   잡아   두었어.
   #sensayng-nim-i   Mimi-lul   cap-a   twu-ess-e
   teacher-HON-NOM   Mimi-ACC   catch-CONN   leave-PST-DECL

Type III

Unlike Type II, auxiliary verbs like 보- *po-* 'see' and 같- *kath-* 'seem' cannot have the honorific suffix -시 *-si* even if the subject is in the honorific form:

(33) a. *선생님이   책을   읽나   보시다.
     *sensayng-nim-i   chayk-ul   ilk-na   po-si-ta
     teacher-HON-NOM   book-ACC   read-CONN   seem-HON-DECL
     'The teacher seems to be reading a book.'

b. 선생님이   책을   읽으시나   보다.
   sensayng-nim-i   chayk-ul   ilk-usi-na   po-ta
   teacher-HON-NOM   book-ACC   read-HON-CONN   seem-DECL

c. #선생님이   책을   읽나   보다.
   #sensayng-nim-i   chayk-ul   ilk-na   po-ta
   teacher-HON-NOM   book-ACC   read-CONN   seem-DECL

d. *선생님이   책을   읽으시나   보시다.
   *sensayng-nim-i   chayk-ul   ilk-usi-na   po-si-ta
   teacher-HON-NOM   book-ACC   read-HON-CONN   seem-HON-DECL

13.4   Contrastive Notes

13.4.1   Subject-Verb Agreement

English and Korean both have agreement phenomena but differ in several respects. A clear difference is that agreement in English is morphosyntactic and index-based, whereas agreement in Korean is context-dependent. This means the violation of agreement rules in English renders the sentence in question unacceptable:

(34) The teacher respects/*respect their opinion.

Korean, however, allows violations with a proper context. For instance, consider the following:

(35) 선생님은   그 의견을   존중하셨다/존중하였다.
    sensayng-nim-un ku uykyen-ul   concwungha-si-ess-ta/concwungha-yess-ta
    teacher-HON-TOP   the opinion-ACC respect-HON-PST-DECL/respect-PST-DECL
    'The teacher respected the opinion.'

The subject has an honorific marker *nim*, calling for an honorific verb. But as shown here, the verb's honorific suffix is optional.

13.4.2   Other Types of Agreement

English has determiner-noun and pronoun-antecedent agreement, as seen in the following example:

(36) a. The volunteers are offering their help to the victims.
     b. Every cow and cat lost its life in the fire.

The pronouns *their* and *its* agree with their antecedents *the volunteers* and *every* in terms of person, number, and gender. The determiner *every* also agrees with its head noun *cow* and *cat* in number values.

Korean does not have determiner-head agreement because the language assigns no number (singular or plural) feature to nouns and also requires no determiner, as we have seen:

(37) 책을   읽었다.
    chayk-ul   ilk-ess-ta
    book-ACC   read-PST-DECL
    '(I) read a book/the book/books.'

Unlike in English, the noun *book* requires no determiner. Its determiner depends on the context. However, Korean has pronoun-antecedent agreement in a certain context:

(38) 미미는   그를   만났다.
    Mimi-nun ku-ul   manna-ss-ta
    Mimi-TOP   he-ACC meet-PST-DECL
    'Mimi met him.'

The pronoun *he* here must be linked only to a masculine singular individual provided by the context.

13.5 Conclusion

Many languages employ agreement or concord phenomena in which two different expressions are in concord with respect to grammatical features. In English, there are three main agreement phenomena: determiner-noun, pronoun-antecedent, and subject-verb agreement. The key features involved in these phenomena in English are person, number, and gender. The key feature of agreement in Korean is honorific agreement. This honorific agreement has some syntactic features, but it can be violated depending on the context.

Exercises

1   Identify the agreement(s) types in the following sentences.

    (i) a. The committee finds itself unable to endorse the quantitative conclusions in the reports about projected highway fatalities and injuries.
        b. Once, after sailing into a quiet cove at dusk, the family woke to find themselves surrounded by big coral reefs.
        c. He sighed, longing momentarily for Vermont and what the family had built for themselves there.
        d. In truth, though, the family was shaping itself into a spider web and doing it through words.

e. I want the audience to enjoy themselves.

f. All I was doing was asking the question the audience was asking itself at that moment.

g. I think that the crew handled themselves in a very good manner.

h. After that, the crew divided itself into groups: work groups and social groups, which were not always the same.

2 Identify the agreement type in each of the following examples.

(i) a. 시간   되실   때   교수님을   찾아
    sikan   toysil   ttay   kyoswu-nim-ul   chac-a
    hour   available   time   professor-HON-ACC   look.for-CONN
    뵙겠습니다.
    poyp-kyess-supnita
    see-FUT-DECL
    'When available, I will visit you, professor.'

b. 이   것은   사장님께서   써주신   글입니다.
    i   kes-un   sacang-nim-kkeyse   ssecwu-si-n   kul-i-pnita
    this thing-TOP CEO-HON-HON   write-HON-MOD writing-COP-DECL
    'This is the writing that your CEO wrote for us.'

c. 나는   사장이   하라는   대로   했다.
    na-nun sacang-i   halanun taylo ha-yss-ta
    I-TOP   CEO-NOM   do-must follow do-PST-DECL
    'I just followed what the CEO told me to do.'

d. 미미가   대사님을   모시고   왔다.
    Mimi-ka   taysa-nim-ul   mosi-ko   o-ass-ta
    Mimi-NOM   ambassador-HON-ACC   attend.to-CONN   come-PST-DECL
    'Mimi came, accompanying the ambassador.'

3 Translate the following sentences into Korean using the main and auxiliary verbs in the parentheses. Assume that all the sentences are meant to be spoken to a person you need to honor.

(i) a. Will you try to learn Korean? (paywu-e po-ta 'learn-CONN try-DECL')

b. The teacher is waiting for you. (kitali-ko iss-ta 'wait-CONN is-DECL')

c. The grandfather has read the book up to the end. (ilk-e nay-ta 'read-CONN finish-DECL')

d. My father lost his wallet in the subway today. (ilh-e peli-ta 'lose-CONN ended-DECL')

e. Mom helped her friend to finish the repair. (to-a cwu-ta 'help-CONN in.favor-DECL')

f. Can you send this parcel to the teacher? (pona-y cwu-ta 'send-CONN in.favor-DECL')

g. The lady used to laugh a lot without any reason. (wus-kon ha-ta 'laugh-CONN do-DECL')

h. Put this book on the desk, please. (noh-a twu-ta 'put-CONN place-DECL')

i. The teacher wants to read this book. (ilk-ko siph-ta 'read-CONN want-DECL')

j. On Sunday, you don't have to come to my office. (o-ci anh-ato toy-ta 'come-CONN not-CONN become-DECL')

4   Consider the following two different types of agreement patterns in English. State any generalizations you can see from these two patterns.

(i)   Type I

a. Each of the suggestions is acceptable.

b. Neither of the cars has air conditioning.

c. None of these men wants to be president.

(ii) Type II

a. Most of the fruit is rotten.

b. Most of the children are here.

c. Some of the soup needs more salt.

d. Some of the diners need menus.

e. All of the land belongs to the government.

f. All of these cars belong to me.

5   Consider the following examples, and choose the correct verb form based on the generalizations you have seen in this chapter.

(i)   a. Some of the pies is/are missing.

b. Neither of these differences was/were statistically significant at high levels of confidence.

c. None of these problems is/were likely to disappear quickly.

d. Most of the damage was/were limited to the newest products.

e. Three miles is/are too far to walk.

f. Five years is/are the maximum sentence for that offense.

g. Ten dollars is/are a high price to pay.

h. One percent of students take/takes drugs.

i. The hammer and sickle was/were flying over the Kremlin.

j. More than half of the students is/are in noncredit programs, mainly citizenship courses.

6   Assume that you missed an important, scheduled interview with a professor because you were involved in a car accident. Write an apology letter to them in English, and translate it into Korean. Give appropriate glosses for the Korean sentences. Then compare any differences in the uses of agreement.

14

Figurative Languages and Metaphors: Those We Live By

14.1 Literal vs. Figurative Uses in English

In daily language, we use words based on their proper meanings. Unlike this literal language, we also use words that deviate from their literal definitions to achieve a better understanding or heightened effect. That is, literal language means exactly what it says, whereas figurative language uses different expressions to describe something, often through comparison with something different. Compare the following:

(1) a. I am really hungry.
   b. I am so hungry I could eat a cow.
(2) a. My pizza is cold.
   b. My pizza is as cold as ice.

The (a) examples here have literal uses, whereas the (b) examples are figurative. Using literal language, we simply state the facts as they are. But in figurative cases, we use the language more creatively and emotionally, trying to convey an intended message more clearly and vividly. There are several different types of figurative language, as illustrated in the following:

- *Personification*: This usage assigns the qualities of a person to something that isn't human or, in some cases, isn't even alive. Personification is often adopted to describe something abstract or inanimate so that others can understand. It can also be used to emphasize a point. Here are some examples:

(3) a. My teddy bear gave me a hug.
   b. The stars danced playfully in the moonlit sky.
   c. The run-down house appeared depressed and out of sorts.
   d. The first rays of morning tiptoed through the meadow.
   e. Opportunity knocks at the door but once.
   f. Her last chance was walking out the door.

English and Korean in Contrast: A Linguistic Introduction, First Edition. Jong-Bok Kim.
© 2024 John Wiley & Sons, Inc. Published 2024 by John Wiley & Sons, Inc.

    g. The bees played hide and seek with the flowers.

    h. The wind howled its mighty objection.

- *Alliteration*: This figurative use repeats the same initial letter, sound, or group of sounds in a series of words. In addition to tongue-twisters, alliteration is used in poems, song lyrics, and so forth:

  (4) a. Peter Piper picked a peck of pickled peppers.

      b. She sells seashells by the seashore.

      c. Alice's aunt ate apples and acorns around August.

      d. Carrie's cat clawed her couch, creating chaos.

      e. Hannah's home has heat, hopefully.

      f. Kim's kids kept kiting.

- *Onomatopoeia*: This use describes or imitates a natural sound or the sound made by an object or an action. Common onomatopoeias include animal noises such as *oink, meow, roar, chirp*. Note that onomatopoeias are not the same across all languages. For example, animal noises in Korean are 꿀꿀 *kkwulkwul* 'oink,' 으르렁 *ululung* 'roar,' and 푸드덕 *pwututek* 'chirp.' And the sound of a clock is 'tick tock' in English but 똑딱 *ttok ttak* 'tick tock' in Korean.

- *Hyperbole*: This employs exaggeration as a rhetorical device. Hyperbole typically evokes a strong feeling or creates a strong impression, resulting in an emphasized or highlighted effect.

  (5) a. The bag weighed a ton.

      b. He was so hungry, he ate that whole cornfield for lunch, stalks and all.

- *Irony*: This is a rhetorical device or literary technique that expresses a situation in the opposite way. It is often employed for humorous or emphatic effect.

  (6) a. Oh, that's beautiful. (after looking at an ugly picture)

      b. Oh, your room is so clean. (after seeing his son's messy room)

- *Metonymy*: This is a rhetorical usage in which a thing or concept is called not by its own name but instead by the name of something intimately associated with that thing or concept. The subject *hands, the ham sandwich*, and *Hollywood* in the following all refer to parts or properties of the referents each subject is describing.

  (7) a. All hands on deck!

      b. The ham sandwich left a big tip.

      c. Hollywood has been releasing a surprising amount of sci-fi movies lately.

- *Simile*: This use includes words like *like* or *as* to compare one object or idea with another.

  (8) a. She runs like a deer.

      b. He's as white as a sheet.

      c. He is as busy as a bee.

- *Metaphor*: A metaphor describes a subject by asserting that it is, on some point of comparison, the same as another otherwise unrelated object. Unlike a simile, a metaphor compares two objects or things without using the word *like* or *as*. Consider the following from *As You Like It*:

> (9) All the world's a stage,
> And all the men and women merely players;
> They have their exits and their entrances.

This quote is a metaphor because the world is not literally a stage. By figuratively asserting that the world is a stage, Shakespeare uses the points of comparison between the world and a stage to convey an understanding of the mechanics of the world and the lives of the people within it.

In this chapter, we will focus on metaphoric uses of language in English and Korean and see how the two languages use figurative language in daily life.

14.2 Metaphors in English

14.2.1 Conceptual Metaphors in English

As noted earlier, a metaphor describes a subject (individual) by asserting that it is the same as another otherwise unrelated object. Metaphor is pervasive in everyday life, not just in language but also in thought and action. Metaphoric expressions are traditionally defined to provide a mapping across two concepts, source and target concept, as represented in the followig Figure 14.1.

For instance, consider the following metaphoric expressions:

(10) a. Your claims are indefensible.
    b. She attacked every weak point in my argument.
    c. They had to surrender to the force of our arguments.
    d. I've never won an argument with him.

These examples show us the so-called conceptual metaphor ARGUMENT IS WAR. That is, the war is the *source concept* from which features are taken, and the argument is the *target concept* onto which features are mapped (see Table 14.1).

The source domain of a metaphor is typically concrete, whereas the target domain is abstract. Thus, the concrete features of the source domain help us

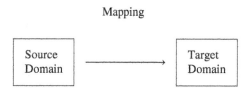

Mapping

Figure 14.1 Conceptual mapping.

Table 14.1 Mapping from war to argument.

War (source)		Argument (target)
Military conflict	→	Verbal conflict
Combat	→	Exchange of utterances
Military strategies	→	Discussion strategies
Actions: attack, defend	→	Actions: express a (pro/con) view
Participants: at least two	→	Participants: discussants
Results: win, lose	→	Results: presenting convincing points
Tools: weapons	→	Tools: expressions addressing specific aspects of the dispute

better understand the abstract target domain. Such metaphoric concepts underlie not only the way we talk but also the way we think. Such metaphoric uses are called conceptual metaphors.

Let us consider another conceptual metaphor, LIFE IS A JOURNEY:

(11) a. His life has taken a good course.
  b. I go where my path leads me.
  c. As I've traveled through life, I've made a lot of friends along the way.
  d. He has changed his direction in life and taken a more spiritual path.
  e. Difficulties in life are impediments to travel.

These examples show that the target domain is our life and the source domain is the journey. The source domain has properties such as travelers, journey, vehicle, path, obstacles, and so forth, whereas the target domain (life) has people who are alive, events in life, moving, and so on. With such metaphoric uses, we could understand the meaning of life as we experience journeys:

(12) a. Target domain: the conceptual domain that we try to understand (e.g. [life] is a journey).
  b. Source domain: the conceptual domain from which we draw metaphorical expressions (e.g. life is a [journey]).

As just illustrated, metaphors are cognitive processes that help us understand the complex issues around us. The conceptual structures of metaphor govern our everyday functioning, but we are not aware of them. Most of our conceptual system is metaphorical in nature. Our daily uses of language employ such conceptual metaphors often.

14.2.2 Structural, Ontological, and Orientational Metaphors in English

Conceptual metaphors have three main subcategories: structural, ontological, and orientational. The kind of conceptual metaphor we just have seen is called *structural conceptual metaphor* because abstract experiences are conceptualized based on the experience of more familiar, simple experiences. Structural metaphors, the most frequently used of the three categories, are those in which one concept is metaphorically structured in another.

Ontological metaphors are based on experience with physical objects. They conceptualize abstract things that normally do not have such a boundary. The following examples illustrate typical ontological metaphors we often use in our daily life.

- IDEAS ARE OBJECTS
  - (13) a. It is hard to get that idea across to him.
    - b. I gave you that idea.
    - c. Your reasons came through to us.
    - d. This sentence is without meaning.
    - e. The idea is buried in terribly dense paragraphs.
- UNDERSTANDING IS SEEING
  - (14) a. We have observed how he went wrong.
    - b. Notice that X does not follow from Y.
    - c. We now see the outline of the argument.

The abstract concepts of idea and understanding are objects with boundaries and can be in a container. This is because humans are containers with boundaries and an orientation of inside and outside. This orientation is also used for nonphysical objects like ideas and understanding. These metaphors thus help us view nonphysical or abstract entities (e.g. events, activities, emotions, ideas) as concrete physical entities and substances.

Orientational metaphors are based on orientation in space: a spatial relationship is made for a concept. Most of these metaphors have a basis in physical and cultural experiences and have to do with spatial orientation: up-down, in-out, front-back, on-off, deep-shallow, or central-peripheral. The following includes some typical examples of orientational metaphors in English.

- CONSCIOUS IS UP; UNCONSCIOUS IS DOWN

  - (15) a. Wake up.
    - b. He fell asleep.
- HEALTH AND LIFE ARE UP; SICKNESS AND DEATH ARE DOWN

  - (16) a. He's at the peak of health.
    - b. He came down with the flu.

- MORE QUANTITY IS UP; LESS QUANTITY IS DOWN

  (17) a. The number of books printed every year keeps going up.
       b. The number of errors he made is incredibly low.
- GOOD IS UP; BAD IS DOWN

  (18) a. Things are looking up.
       b. Things are at an all-time low.

As obdserved here, orientational metaphors map human posture: someone who is sad has a bowed posture, and a happy person is upright. When we are happy, we are up; when we are sad, we crouch and lie down.

As we have seen so far, our daily language uses employ a variety of conceptual metaphors, which we often unnotice. Such metaphors play a key role in communication because they show how we think and communicate. We make sense of the world by seeing how one part relates to and is reflected in another. It is important to understand the role of metaphor in human communication.

There are two important points to note about metaphor. First, metaphor is a tool of cognition: it helps us to conceptualize the world. Second, metaphor allows us to deal with abstractions by conceptualizing them in terms of something more concrete/basic/perceptual in our experience of the world. This implies that proper uses of metaphor in English and other languages are important parts of effective language use.

14.3 Figurative Speech in Korean

Just like English, Korean employs a variety of figures of speech.

- *Simile*: This is a figure of speech that makes a comparison, showing similarities between two different things. Unlike a metaphor, a simile draws resemblance with the help of the expression -처럼 -*chelum* 'like' or 같다 *kath-ta* 'as.' Therefore, it is a direct comparison.

  (19) a. 저   사람의   마음은   하늘처럼   넓다.
          ce   salam-uy   maum-un hanul-chelem nelp-ta
          that person-GEN mind-TOP sky-like   wide-DECL
          '(lit.) That person's mind is as wide as the sky.'
       b. 차기가   마치 얼음 같다.
          chaki-ka   machi elum kath-ta
          coldness-NOM as.if ice   seem-DECL
          '(lit.) The coldness is the same as ice.'

- *Personification*: This a figure of speech in which a thing, an idea, or an animal is given human attributes.

(20) a. 거울이   웃는다.
   kewul-i   wus-nun-ta
   mirror-NOM smile-PRES-DECL
   'The mirror is smiling.'

   b. 컴퓨터가   말을   잘 안 듣는다.
   khemphyuthe-ka mal-ul   cal an tut-nun-ta
   computer-NOM   word-ACC well not listen-PRES-DECL
   'The computer doesn't work well.'

- *Metonymy*: In this usage, the name of a thing replaces the name of something else with which it is closely associated.

   (21) a. 칼보다   펜이   강하다.
      khal-pota   phen-i   kangha-ta
      sword-than pen-NOM   strong-DECL
      '(lit.) The pen is stronger than the sword.'

      b. 오늘 청와대가   새   내각을   발표했다.
      onul chengwatay-ka say naykak-ul   palphyoha-yess-ta
      today blue.house-NOM new cabinet-ACC announce-PST-DECL
      'Today, the blue house announced new cabinet members.'

- *Hyperbole*: Hyperboles are exaggerations to make a point. We employ this figure of speech in our day-to-day speech.

   (22) a. 가방이   산만큼   무겁다.
      kapang-i san-mankhum mwukep-ta
      bag-NOM   mountain-like heavy-DECL
      'The suitcase is as heavy as a mountain.'

      b. 부끄러워   죽겠다.
      pwukkule-we   cwuk-keyss-ta
      shameful-CONN die-FUT-DECL
      'I am dying of shame.'

- *Metaphor*: This figure of speech makes an implicit, implied, or hidden comparison between two things that are unrelated but share common characteristics. In English, we have seen that metaphoric uses are everywhere. This is also true in Korean, as we will discuss in the next section.

   (23) a. 사랑은   위험한   게임이다.
      salang-un wihemha-n   keyim-i-ta
      love-TOP dangerous-MOD game-COP-DECL
      'Love is a dangerous game.'

b. 내 마음은   호수이다.
nay maum-un hoswu-i-ta
my mind-TOP lake-COP-DECL
'(lit.) My mind is a lake.'

14.4 Metaphors in Korean

14.4.1 Conceptual Metaphors in Korean

We have seen that English uses metaphors to understand a concept or thing in terms of another concept or thing. Korean is no different: people unconsciously or consciously use metaphors in everyday life. Consider the following:

(24) a. 화가   난다.
     hwa-ka   na-n-ta
     anger-NOM break.out-PRES-DECL
     'Anger broke out.'

    b. 화가   치민다.
     hwa-ka   chimi-n-ta
     anger-NOM push.up-PRES-DECL
     'Anger is alleviating.'

    c. 화를   부채질한다.
     hwa-lul   pwuchaycilha-n-ta
     anger-ACC boost.up-PRES-DECL
     'You make me more angry.'

    d. 화를   가라 앉힌다.
     haw-lul   kala anchi-n-ta
     anger-ACC down seat-PRES-DECL
     '(lit.) (That) caused anger calm down.'

These are examples of the conceptual metaphor ANGER IS FIRE. Many properties of fire are linked to those of anger. That is, the source domain of anger is mapped onto the target domain of fire. As such, metaphors offer an effective way of examining ideas and viewing the world. Metaphor is thus not just a linguistic ornament but also an important process of human thought and reasoning.

14.4.2 Structural, Ontological, and Orientational Metaphors in Korean

Just like English, Korean also employs a variety of conceptual metaphors. Let us examine the three main types of conceptual metaphors: structural, ontological, and orientational.

First, consider the conceptual metaphor TIME IS MONEY in Korean:

(25) a. 시간은 돈이다.
   sikan-un ton-i-ta
   time-TOP money-COP-DECL
   'Time is money.'

   b. 시간을 절약하자.
   sikan-ul celyakha-ca
   time-ACC save-SUG
   'Let's save time.'

   c. 할애할 시간이 없다.
   halayha-l sikan-i eps-ta
   share-MOD time not.exist-DECL
   'There is no time to spare.'

   d. 많은 시간을 투자했다.
   manh-un sikan-ul thwucaha-yess-ta
   much-MOD time-ACC invest-PST-DECL
   'A lot of time was invested.'

   e. 적지 않은 시간을 잃어 버렸다.
   cekci anh-un sikan-ul ilh-e peli-ess-ta
   little not-MOD time-ACC lose-CONN become-PST-DECL
   'Not a little time has been lost.'

Time and money are different concepts, but we understand the abstract notion of time from the conceptual domain of money. They both are understood as entities that we need to save for future uses, that we can give to others, that we can invest to make more, and that we can lose. We map the structure of money to the structures of time. As in English, we conceptualize the concept of time through the experience of saving money saving.

We also can conceptualize events and actions as substances or containers. Such ontological metaphors are not hard to find in Korean. Consider the ontological metaphor THE MIND IS BRITTLE:

(26) a. 마음이 약하다.
   maum-i yakha-ta
   mind-NOM weak-DECL
   'My mind is weak.'

   b. 마음이 쉽게 흔들린다.
   maum-i swipkey huntul-li-n-ta
   mind-NOM easily shake-PASS-PRES-DECL
   '(His mind) is easily shaken.'

c. 생각이　　잘　정리되었다.
　　sayngkak-i　　cal　cengli-toy-ess-ta
　　thought-NOM　well　arrange-become-PST-DECL
　　'(His) thoughts were well organized.'

d. 생각이　　많았다.
　　sayngkak-i　　manh-ass-ta
　　thought-NOM　many-PST-DECL
　　'(I) had many thoughts.'

e. 곤궁에서　　　　탈출하다.
　　konkwung-eyse　thalchwulha-ta
　　difficulty-at　　escape-DECL
　　'(He) escaped from the predicament.'

f. 절망에　　빠지다.
　　celmang-ey　ppaci-ta
　　despair-at　fall.in-DECL
　　'I was in despair.'

Events and actions are conceptualized as substances, states, and containers. The mind is considered a concrete object that is fragile. Difficulty and despair can be containers from which one can escape or into which one falls. The conceptual domain of concrete and tangible entities helps us understand abstract experiences and ideas. As in English, this kind of metaphor helps us understand abstract concepts through concrete, tangible concepts. Such conceptual metaphors are used so frequently that we often take them for granted.

The third main type of conceptual metaphor is the orientational metaphor. Such a metaphor organizes an abstract domain in the relation of space, such as up-down, inside-out, front-behind, shallow-deep, and so forth. The following includes some typical examples of orientational metaphor in Korean:

(27) a. HAPPY IS UP

　　기분이　　　날아갈　것　　같다.
　　kipwun-i　　nalaka-l kes　　kath-ta
　　feeling-NOM　fly-MOD　thing　seem-DECL
　　'(lit.) My feeling seems to be something that is flying.'

b. SAD IS DOWN

　　슬픔에　　　잠겨있다.
　　sulphum-ey　camkieiss-ta
　　sadness-at　be.soaked-DECL
　　'(lit.) He is soaked in sadness.'

c. CONSCIOUS IS UP

일찍　일어났다.
ilccik　ilena-ss-ta
early　rise-PST-DECL
'(I) woke up early.'

d. UP IS GOOD

월급이　올랐다.
wolkup-i　olla-ss-ta
salary-NOM　rise-PST-DECL
'My salary went up.'

e. DOWN IS BAD

바닥까지　추락하였다.
patak-kkaci　chwulakha-yess-ta
bottom-to　fall-PST-DECL
'(lit. He collapsed to the bottom.'

f. FUTURE IS FRONT

밝은　미래가　우리 앞에　있다.
palkun　milay-ka　wuli aph-ey　iss-ta
bright　future-NOM　we front-at exist-DECL
'A bright future is in front of us.'

g. PAST IS BACK

지난　일을　뒤로 하자.
cinan　il-ul　twilo ha-ca
past-MOD work-ACC back do-SUG
'Let's put the past behind.'

The conceptual metaphors HAPPY IS UP and SAD IS DOWN are derived from our body posture when we are happy or sad. When we are depressed or sad, we often lie down; but when we are happy, we raise our heads or jump. Such orientational metaphors are closely related to culture and experiences. For instance, consider the oriental metaphors RATIONAL IS UP and EMOTIONAL IS DOWN in English:

(28) a. The discussion fell to the emotional level, but I raised it back up to the rational plane.
  b. We put our feelings aside and had a high-level intellectual discussion.

These examples show that the ability to control is up, whereas an uncontrollable state is down. This may be linked to the fact that the rational brain is up and the emotional heart is down. However, what we often see in Korean is rather different:

(29) a. 감정의   롤러코스터를   탔다.
     kamaceng-uy lollekhosethe-lul tha-ss-ta
     emotion-GEN roller.coaster-ACC ride-PST-DECL
     'His emotion was up and down.'

   b. 이성이   제자리를   찾았다.
     iseng-i ceycali-lul   chac-ass-ta
     rational orginal.position-ACC find-PST-DECL
     '(lit.) The rational found its original position back.'

   c. 마음을   가라앉히고
     maum-ul kalaanchi-ko
     mind-ACC calm.down-and
     'calming down one's mind'

Emotion is in the air, whereas rationality is down on the ground.

14.5 Contrastive Notes

Both English and Korean often adopt figurative speech in daily uses of language. Rather than using literal senses, figurative language makes expressions more dramatic and attentive. English and Korean have rich systems of figurative uses but differ in the types of linguistic expressions.

(30) a. as light as a feather
   b. as cold as ice

(31) a. 날개처럼   가볍게
     nalkay-chelem kapyebkey
     feather-like light
     'as light as a feather'

   b. 얼음처럼   차갑게
     elum-chelem chakapkey
     ice-like   cold
     'as cold as ice'

The data shows the difference in linguistic expressions: English uses *as, …as*, whereas Korean uses the nominal suffix *chelem*.

In terms of conceptual metaphors, both languages have rich data on structural, orientational, and ontological metaphors. Because the way we view the world

Table 14.2 ME-FIRST vs. OUR-FIRST orientation.

ME-FIRST (English)	OUR-FIRST (Korean)
my house	wuli cip 'our house'
my parents	wuli pwumo 'our parents'
my wife	wuli cip salam 'our house person'

is similar for speakers of English and Korean, there are no major differences. However, for orientational metaphors, there are some differences depending on how we perceive our space. As noted in Chapter 1, Korean has an OUR-FIRST orientation, whereas English has a ME-FIRST orientation. Based on the ME-FIRST orientation, we put the word FIRST whose meaning is relatively nearest to "the properties of the prototypical person." This cultural orientation determines certain English word orders like "up and down," "here and there," and "now and then." But in Korean, the OUR-FIRST orientation determines the conceptual system. Table 14.2 shows some contrastive examples.

The OUR-FIRST orientation is related to the Korean metaphorical concept that ME-FIRST IS SELFISH AND IMPOLITE.

(32) a. 드러내지도　나서지도　　　　말아라.
     tulenay-cito　nase-cito　　　mala-la
     reveal-also　step.forward-also　not-IMP
     'Don't reveal yourself and step forward, either!'

   b. 겸손의　　　미덕.
     kyemson-uy　mitek
     modesty-GEN　virtue
     'virtue of being modest'

   c. 오른손이　　　하는　일　왼손이　　　모르게.
     olunson-i　　ha-nun　il　oynson-i　　molukey
     right.hand-NOM　do-MOD　work　left.hand-NOM　not.know
     '(lit.) Do the left hand not know what your right hand does.'

The expressions in (33) show that the Korean cultural context encourages people to put themselves behind the scenes. However, Western culture encourages people to "express yourself". This may be summarized from the following quote:

> The right to freedom of expression is justified first of all as the right of an individual purely in his capacity as an individual. It derives from the widely accepted premise of Western thought that the proper end of man is the realization of his character and potentialities as a human being (Thomas Emerson, 1963).

Western people are encouraged to express their feelings, whereas people in the East are educated to hold them in to be tactful and show good manners. Speech has particular importance in the Western cultural context as a primary means to express one's internal attributes, whereas silence is a virtue in the Eastern cultural context. These cultural differences emphasize the ME-FIRST orientation in Western culture and the OUR-FIRST orientation in Eastern culture and are reflected in the use of orientational metaphors in the two languages.

14.6 Conclusion

Figurative speech is a word or phrase used in a nonliteral sense to add rhetorical force to a spoken or written passage. Figures of speech are prevalent in daily language usage, providing emphasis, freshness of expression, or clarity.

We have seen that a metaphor expresses the unfamiliar or abstract in terms of the familiar or concrete. When Neil Young sings, "Love is a rose," we understand love in terms of the concrete object "rose." As such, metaphor helps us understand a concept. We live in a world of metaphor. Metaphors show us how we conceptualize the world around us, concrete or abstract, and how we act accordingly.

Exercises

1 Identify the types of figurative speech in the following English examples.

   (i) a. Alright, the sky misses the sun at night.
      b. I had a ton of chores to do.
      c. I move fast like a cheetah.
      d. Jane is three, as cute as a button!
      e. Her head was spinning from all the new information.
      f. The toast jumped out of the toaster.
      g. I'm so hungry I could eat a horse.
      h. Misfortune stalked my grandmother all her life.
      i. Nick's nephew needed new notebooks now.
      j. The Sea lashed out in anger at the ships, unwilling to tolerate another battle.
   (ii) a. 그는   여우처럼   교활하다.
      ku-nun yewu-chelem kyohwalha-ta
      he-TOP fox-like   sly-DECL
      'He is as sly as a fox.'

b. 인생은   마라톤이다.
insayng-un malathon-i-ta
life-TOP   marathon-COP-DECL
'Life is a marathon.'

c. 교실이   절간처럼   조용하다.
kyosil-i celkan-chelem coyongha-ta
classroom-NOM temple-like   quiet-DECL
'The classroom is as quiet as a temple.'

d. 해가   구름   속에서   나와   방긋   웃었다.
hay-ka kwulum sok-eyse na-wa pangkus wus-ess-ta
sun-NOM cloud   inside-from come-CONN beamingly smile-PST-DECL
'The sun came out from the clouds and beamed.'

e. 그녀의   얼굴이   홍당무처럼   빨개   졌다.
kunye-uy elkwul-i hongtangmwu-chelem ppalka-y ci-ess-ta
she-GEN face-NOM carrot-like   red-CONN become-PST-DECL
'Her face became as red as a carrot.'

f. 배고파   죽겠다.
paykophu-a cwuk-keyss-ta
hungry-CONN die-FUT-DECL
'I am hungry to death.'

2   Give at least one Korean and one English example for the following figures of speech.

(i) Simile, metaphor, hyperbole, personification, metonymy

3   As we have seen, language deeply affects the categorization of concepts and things, as reflected in metaphoric usage. Expressions using body parts (e.g. mouth, lips, tongue, ears) are no exception, as exemplified by the following:

(i) 미미는   입이   가볍다.
Mimi-nun ip-i kapyep-ta
Mimi-TOP mouth-NOM light-DECL
'Mimi is glib-tongued.'

Give at least three metaphoric uses of 입 *ip* 'mouth' in Korean and 'tongue' in English.

4   Consider the following three types of conceptual metaphors in English, and give at least three additional English examples for each exemplar metaphor. In addition, give Korean examples that match each metaphor.

(i) a. LOVE IS WAR: He won the love.

b. ARGUMENT IS A BUILDING: The evidence buttresses my statement.

c. ECONOMIC ACTIVITY IS WAR: Trade war is harming the American economy more than China's.

(ii) a. SEEING IS TOUCHING: I can pick out every detail.

b. INFLATION IS AN ENTITY: Inflation is lowering our standard of living.

c. IDEAS ARE OBJECTS: It's hard to get that idea across to him.

(iii) a. MORE IS UP; LESS IS DOWN: Speak up, please. Keep your voice down, please.

b. HEALTHY IS UP; SICK IS DOWN: Lazarus rose from the dead. He fell ill.

c. VIRTUE IS UP; LACK OF VIRTUE IS DOWN: She's an upstanding citizen. That was a low-down thing to do.

5 Identify the metaphors in the following English sentences, and discuss what kinds of metaphors are used. Also translate these into Korean (with glosses), and then discuss similarities and differences between the two languages in the uses of the metaphors in question.

(i) a. A good diet will help your body fight disease.

b. The virus attacks the immune system.

c. Jean died on Sunday after a long battle with cancer.

(ii) a. I have to bear the responsibility for this.

b. The responsibility was weighing on my mind.

c. I don't want to be a burden to you.

6 Consider the following examples, and discuss the metaphors adopted. In addition, find other metaphors for climate change, air pollution, and nuclear energy in English and Korean.

(i) a. Climate change threatens more than half the bird species in the United States.

b. Air pollution kills more than 600,000 people in India each year.

c. Nuclear energy frightens more governments into pursuing earth-friendlier options.

7 Eating food and drinking liquids represent universal practices among humans, and one can reasonably inquire about the linguistic expression of these concepts in any language, as illustrated in the following. Discuss any metaphorical differences between English and Korean with respect to the uses of *eat* and 먹다. In doing so, see what kinds of objects occur with these verbs in each language.

(i) a. Well, not this very one; I *ate the actual evidence. While I was chewing,* that phrase kept popping into my head.

b. Relentlessly, they *ate into* GM's market share.

(ii) a. 우리의   월급을   떼어   먹었다.
wuli-uy   welkup-ul   ttey-e   mek-ess-ta
we-GEN   salary-ACC   take.off-CONN   eat-PST-DECL
'They didn't pay for our salary.'

b. ATM이   내   카드를   먹었다.
ATM-i   nay   khatu-lul   mek-ess-ta
ATM-NOM   my   card-ACC   eat-PST-DECL
'The ATM ate my cash card.'

Bibliography

Aarts, B. (1997/2001). *English Syntax and Argumentation*. Basingstoke, Hampshire, and New York: Palgrave.

Aarts, B. (2007). *Syntactic Gradience: The Nature of Grammatical Indeterminacy*. Oxford: Oxford University Press.

Abney, S. (1987). The English noun phrase in its sentential aspect. Doctoral dissertation. MIT.

Ahn, H.-D. (1991). Light verbs, VP-movement, negation and clausal architecture in Korean and English. Doctoral dissertation. University of Wisconsin-Madison.

Ahn, H.-D. (1996). Preliminary remarks on Korean NP. In *Papers from the Sixth International Conference in Korean Linguistics* (ed. E.-J. Baek), 1–15. Seoul: Hanshin Publishing Co.

Aikhenvald, A. and Dixon, R.M.W. (2006). *Serial Verb Constructions: A Cross-linguistic Typology*. Oxford: Oxford University Press.

Alexiadou, A., Haegeman, L., and Stavrou, M. (2007). *Noun Phrase in the Generative Perspective*. New York: De Gruyter.

Antilla, A. and Kim, J.-B. (2011). On structural case in Finnish and Korean. *Lingua* 121 (1): 625–652.

Bratt, E. (1996). Argument composition and the lexicon: lexical and periphrastic causatives in Korean. Doctoral dissertation. Stanford University.

Bresnan, J. and Mchombo, S.A. (1995). The lexical integrity principle: evidence from Bantu. *Natural Language and Linguistic Theory* 13 (2): 181–254.

Büring, D. (2006). Focus projection and default prominence. In *The Architecture of Focus* (ed. V. Molnar and S. Winkler). Berlin/New York: Mouton De Gruyter.

Cha, J.-Y. (1997). Type-hierarchical analysis of gapless relative constructions in Korean. Paper presented at the 4th Conference on HPSG.

Chae, H.-R. (1996). Verbal nouns and light verbs in Korean. *Language Research* 33, 581–600.

Chae, H.-R. (2004). Passive light verb constructions in Korean. *Harvard Studies in Korean Linguistics X* 331–344.

English and Korean in Contrast: A Linguistic Introduction, First Edition. Jong-Bok Kim.
© 2024 John Wiley & Sons, Inc. Published 2024 by John Wiley & Sons, Inc.

Chae, H.-R. (2013). Myths in Korean morphology and their computational implications. In: *Papers from the 27th Pacific Asia Conference on Language, Information and Computation* 505–511. Taipei: National Chengchi University.

Chang, S.-J. (1996). *Korean*. John Benjamins.

Cho, S.-Y. (2005). Non-tensed VP coordination in Korean: structure and meaning. *Language and Information* 9: 35–49.

Cho, S.-Y. and Kim, J.-B. (2002). Echoed verb constructions in Korean: a construction-based HPSG analysis. *Ene (Korean Journal of Linguistics)* 27 (4): 661–681.

Cho, S. and Whitman, J. (2019). *Korean: A Linguistic Introduction*. Cambridge: Cambridge University Press.

Cho, Y.-M. and Sells, P. (1995). A lexical account of inflectional suffixes in Korean. *Journal of East Asian Linguistics* 4: 119–174.

Choe, H.S. (1995). Focus and topic movement in Korean and licensing. In: *Discourse Configurational Languages* (ed. E. Kiss), 269–334. New York: Oxford University Press.

Choe, J.-W. (2004). Obligatory honorification and the honorific feature. *Studies in Generative Grammar* 14: 545–560.

Choi, I.-C. (2003). Case and argument structure in Korean and English. Doctoral dissertation. University of Texas at Austin.

Choi, I.-C. and Wechsler, S. (2001). Verbal nouns and light verbs in Korean and Japanese. Online proceedings of HPSG 2001, 103–120.

Choi, K. (1991). A theory of syntactic X^0-subcategorization. Doctoral dissertation. University of Washington.

Choi, K. (2009). *Case Markings and Particles in Generative Grammar* (In Korean). Seoul: Hankwuk Publishing.

Choi, K. (2010). Subject honorification in Korean: in defense of agr and head-spec agreement. *Language Research* 46 (1): 59–82.

Chomsky, N. (1957). *Syntactic Structures*. The Hague: Mouton.

Chomsky, N. (1965). *Aspects of the Theory of Syntax*. Cambridge, MA: MIT Press.

Chomsky, N. (1970). Remarks on nominalization. In *Readings in English Transformational Grammar* (ed. R. Jacobs and P. Rosenbaum), 184–221. Waltham, MA: Ginn.

Chomsky, N. (1977). On *Wh*-movement. In: *Formal Syntax* (ed. P. Culicover, A. Akmajian, and T. Wasow), 71–132. New York: Academic Press.

Chomsky, N. (1981). *Lectures on Government and Binding*. Dordrecht: Foris.

Chomsky, N. (2000). Minimalist inquiries: the framework. In: *Step by Step: Essays on Minimalist Syntax in Honor of Howard Lasnik* (ed. R. Martin, D. Michaels, and J. Uriagereka), 89. Cambridge, MA: MIT Press.

Chomsky, N. and Lasnik, H. (1993). Principles and parameters theory. In: *Syntax: An International Handbook of Contemporary Research* (ed. J. Jacobs et al.), 506–565. Berlin: Mount de Gruyter.

Chung, C. (1995). A lexical approach to word order variation in Korean. Doctoral dissertation. Ohio State University.

Chung, C. (1998). Argument composition and long distance scrambling in Korean: an extension of the complex predicate analysis. In *Complex Predicates in Nonderivational Syntax* (ed. E. Hinrichs et al.), 159–220. New York: Academic Press.

Chung, C. and Kim, J.-B. (2002). Korean copula constructions: a construction and linearization perspective. *Ene (Korean Journal of Linguistics)* 27 (2): 171–193.

Chung, C. and Kim, J.-B. (2003). Differences between externally and internally headed relative clauses. In: *Proceedings of the Ninth International Conference on Head-Driven Phrase Structure Grammar* (ed. J. Kim and S. Wechsler), 43–65. Stanford: CSLI Publications.

Chung, C. and Kim, J.-B. (2008). Korean serial verb constructions: a construction-based approach. *Studies in Generative Grammar* 18 (4): 559–582.

Chung, D. (1996). On the structure of the so-called head internal relative construction. *Proceedings of the Pacific Asia Conference on Language, Information and Computation* 11: 393–402.

Chung, D. (2000). On the categorial status of interrogatives and some theoretical implications. *Ene* 25 (4): 723–747.

Chung, T. (1993). Argument structure and serial verbs in Korean. Doctoral dissertation. University of Texas at Austin. Copestake, A. (2002). *Implementing Typed Feature Structure Grammars*. CSLI Publications.

Culicover, P. and Jackendoff, R. (1997). Semantic subordination despite syntactic coordination. *Linguistic Inquiry* 28: 195–218.

Culicover, P. and Jackendoff, R. (2005). *Simpler Syntax*. Oxford: Oxford University Press.

Dahl, O. (1979). Typology of sentence negation. *Linguistics* 17: 79–106.

Di Sciullo, A.-M., and Williams, E. (1987). *On the Definition of Word*. Cambridge, MA: MIT Press.

Dowty, D. (1991). Thematic proto-roles and argument selection. *Language* 67: 547–619.

Ginzberg, J. and Sag, I.A. (2000). *English Interrogative Constructions*. Stanford: CSLI Publications.

Goldberg, A. (1995). *Constructions*. Chicago and London: University of Chicago Press.

Goldberg, A. (2003). Constructions: a new theoretical approach to language. *Trends in Cognitive Science* 7 (5): 219–224.

Goldberg, A. (2006). *Constructions at Work: Constructionist Approaches in Context*. New York: Oxford University Press.

Grimshaw, J. and Mester, A. (1988). Light verbs and (theta)-marking. *Linguistic Inquiry* 19: 205–232.

Hagstrom, P. (1997). Scope interactions and phrasal movement in Korean negation. In: *Harvard Studies in Korean Linguistics VII* (ed. S. Kuno et al.). Cambridge, MA: Harvard University Department of Linguistics.

Han, C., Lidz, J., and Musolino, J. (2007). Verb-raising and grammar competition in Korean: evidence from negation and quantifier scope. *Linguistic Inquiry* 38 (1): 1–47.

Han, C. and Kim, J.-B. (2001). Are there double relative clauses in Korean? *Linguistic Inquiry* 35 (2): 315–337.

Heycock, C. (1993). Syntactic predication in Japanese. *Journal of East Asian Linguistics* 2: 167–211.

Hilpert, M. (2014). *Construction Grammar and Its Application to English*. Edinburgh: Edinburgh University Press.

Hong, K.-S. (1991). Argument structure and case marking. Doctoral dissertation. Stanford University.

Hong, S.-H. (2005). Aspects of the syntax of wh-questions in English and Korean. Doctoral dissertation. University of Essex.

Hong, Y.-C. (2010). Peripheral nominal modifiers and noun phrase structure in Korean. *Studies in Generative Grammar* 20 (1): 27–50.

Huddleston, R. and Pullum, G. K. (2002). *The Cambridge Grammar of the English Language*. Cambridge: Cambridge University Press.

Jackendoff, R. (1977). *X'-Syntax*. Cambridge, MA: MIT Press.

Jackendoff, R. (2002). *Foundations of Language*. Oxford: Oxford University Press.

Jun, J.-S. (2006). Semantic constraints on the genitive complements of verbal nouns in Korean. *Language Research* 42: 357–397.

Kaiser, L. (1998). The morphosyntax of clausal nominalizations. Doctoral dissertation. Yale University.

Kang, M.-Y. (1988). Topics in Korean syntax: phrase structure, variable binding, movement. Doctoral dissertation. MIT.

Kay, P. and Fillmore, C. (1999). Grammatical constructions and linguistic generalizations: the what's X doing Y? Construction. *Language* 75: 1–33.

Kim, A.H.-O. (1985). The grammar of focus in Korean syntax and its typological implications. Doctoral dissertation. University of Southern California.

Kim, A.H.-O. (2011). Korean politeness. In: *Politeness in East Asia: Theory and Practice* (ed. S. Mills and D. Kadar), 176–207. Cambridge, UK: Cambridge University Press.

Kim, J.-B. (1995). On the existence of NegP in Korean. In: *Harvard Studies in Korean Linguistics VI*, 267–282. Cambridge, MA: Dept. of Linguistics, Harvard University.

Kim, J.-B. (1998a). Interface between morphology and syntax: a constraint-based and lexicalist approach. *Language and Information* 2: 177–233.

Kim, J.-B. (1998b). A head-driven and constraint-based analysis of Korean relative clause constructions: with a reference to English. *Language Research* 34 (4): 1–41.

Kim, J.-B. (1999). Korean short form negation and related phenomena: a lexicalist, constraint-based analysis. *Language and Information* 3 (2): 13–29.

Kim, J.-B. (2000). *The Grammar of Negation: A Constraint-Based Approach*. Stanford: CSLI Publications.

Kim, J.-B. (2004). *Korean Phrase Structure Grammar*. (In Korean). Hankwuk Publishing.

Kim, J.-B. (2005). A constraint-based approach to Korean passive constructions (in Korean). *Korean Linguistics* 26: 67–92.

Kim, J.-B. (2006). Minimal recursion semantics: an application into Korean. *Linguistics* 14 (2): 59–85.

Kim, J.-B. (2010a). On the NP structure and prenominal ordering in Korean. *Studies in Generative Grammar* 20 (4): 579–602.

Kim, J.-B. (2010b). Argument composition in Korean serial verb constructions. *Studies in Modern Grammar* 61: 1–24.

Kim, J.-B. (2013). Floated numeral classifiers in Korean: a non-derivational, functional account. *Lingua* 133: 189–212.

Kim, J.-B. (2015). Syntactic and semantic identity in Korean sluicing: a direct interpretation approach. *Lingua* 66: 260–293.

Kim, J.-B. (2016a). *The Syntactic Structure of Korean: A Construction-based Perspective*. Cambridge University Press.

Kim, J.-B. (2016b). Copular constructions and asymmetries in the specificational pseudocleft constructions in Korean. *Language and Linguistics* 17 (1): 89–112.

Kim, J.-B. (2019). Predicate topicalization in Korea: a construction-based HPSG approach. *Korean Journal of Linguistics* 44 (3): 395–423.

Kim, J.-B. (2020). Negated fragments: a direct interpretation approach. *Korean Journal of English Language and Linguistics* 20 (3): 427–449.

Kim, J.-B. and Choi, I. (2004). The Korean case system: a unified, constraint-based approach. *Language Research* 40 (4): 885–921.

Kim, J.-B. and Michaelis, L.A. (2020). *Syntactic Constructions in English*. Cambridge University Press.

Kim, J.-B. and Park, B.-S. (2000). The structure of LFN and argument composition. *Language Research* 36 (4): 715–733.

Kim, J.-B. and Sag, I. (2002). Negation without movement. *Natural Language and Linguistic Theory* 20 (2): 339–412.

Kim, J.-B. and Sells, P. (2007). Some remarks on information structure and 'kes'. *Studies in Generative Grammar* 17: 479–494.

Kim, J.-B. and Sells, P. (2008a). *English Syntax: An Introduction*. Stanford: CSLI Publications.

Kim, J.-B. and Sells, P. (2008b). Korean honorification: A kind of expressive meaning. *Journal of East Asian Linguistics* 16: 303–336.

Kim, J.-B. and Sells, P. (2010a). On the role of the eventuality in case assignment on adjuncts. *Language and Linguistics* 11 (3): 625–652.

Kim, J.-B. and Sells, P. (2010b). Oblique case marking on core arguments in Korean. *Studies in Language* 34 (3): 602–635.

Kim, J.-B. and Sells, P. (2011a). On the Korean inferential cleft construction. *Studies in Modern Grammar* 64: 45–72.

Kim, J.-B. and Sells, P. (2011b). The big mess construction: interactions between the lexicon and constructions. *English Language and Linguistics* 15: 335–362.

Kim, J.-B. and Yang, J. (2004a). Korean auxiliary system and a computational implementation (in Korean). *Language Research* 3: 195–226.

Kim, J.-B. and Yang, J. (2004b). Projections from morphology to syntax in the Korean resource grammar: implementing typed feature structures. In *Lecture Notes in Computer Science* 2945: 13–24.

Kim, J.-B. and Yang, J. (2005). Parsing mixed constructions in a typed feature structure grammar. *Lecture Notes in Artificial Intelligence* 3248: 42–51.

Kim, J.-B. and Yang, J. (2011). Symmetric and asymmetric properties in Korean verbal coordination: a computational implementation. *Language and Information* 15 (2): 1–21.

Kim, J.-B., Lim, K.-S., and Yang, J. (2007). Structural ambiguities in the light verb constructions: lexical relatedness and divergence. *Linguistics* 15 (2): 207–231.

Kim, J.-B., Yang, J., Song, S.-H., and Francis, B. (2011). Deep processing of Korean and the development of the Korean resource grammar. *Linguistic Research* 28 (3): 635–672.

Kim, M.-J. (2007). Formal linking in internally headed relatives. *Natural Language Semantics* 15 (4): 279–315.

Kim, Y.-J. (1990). The syntax and semantics of Korean case: the interaction between lexical and syntactic levels of representation. Doctoral dissertation. Harvard University.

Kim, Y.-K. (2012). A syntactic and pragmatic analysis of subject honorification. Paper presented at the 18th International Conference of Korean Linguistics (ICKL 2012).

Kim-Renaud, Y.-K. (2009). *Korean: An Essential Grammar*. New York: Routledge.

Kim-Renaud, Y.-K. and Pak, M. (2011). Agreement in Korean revisited. In: *Inquiries into Korean Linguistics IV* (ed. D. Silva), 209–222. Seoul: Thaehaksa.

Kiss, K. (1998). Identificational focus versus information focus. *Language* 74: 245–273.

Ko, H. (2005). Syntactic edges and linearization. Doctoral dissertation. MIT.

Ko, Y.-K. (1997). *A Contemporary Grammar of National Language*. (In Korean.) Seoul: Jipmundang.

Ko, Y.-K. (2012). A study on case-markers, adpositions, and particles, and in Korean and their typological implication. *Kuokak/Journal of Korean Linguistics* 65: 74–108.

Kroeger, P.R. (2004). *Analyzing Syntax: A Lexical-Functional Approach*. Cambridge: Cambridge University Press.

Kuno, S. (1973). *The Structure of the Japanese Language*. Cambridge: MIT Press.

Lakoff, G. and Johnson, M. (1980). *Metaphors We Live By*. Chicago: Chicago UP.

Lapointe, S. (1993). Dual lexical categories and the syntax of mixed category phrases. In: *Proceedings of ESCOL* (ed. A. Kathol and M. Bernstein), 199–210. Cornell University.

Lee, C. (1989). (In)definites, case markers, classifiers and quantifiers in Korean. In: *Harvard Studies in Korean Linguistics 3* (ed. S. Kuno et al.), 469–487. Cambridge, MA: Harvard University, Department of Linguistics.

Lee, C. (1994). Definite/specific and case marking. In: *Theoretical Issues in Korean Linguistics* (ed. Y. Kim-Renaud), 325–342. Stanford University.

Lee, C. (2006). Contrastive topic/focus and polarity in discourse. In: *Where Semantics Meets Pragmatics* (ed. K. von Heusinger and K. Turner), 381–420. Elsevier.

Lee, I. and Ramsey, R. (2000). *The Korean Language*. State University of New York Press.

Lee, K. (1993). *A Korean Grammar on Semantic-Pragmatics Principles*. Seoul: Hankuk Mwunhwasa.

Lee, K. (1999). *Computational Morphology*. Korea University Press.

Martin, S. (1992). *A REFERENCE GRAMMAR of Korean*. Rutland, VT: Charles Tuttle.

Müller, S. and Lipenkova, J. (2009). Serial verb constructions in Chinese: an HPSG account. In: *Proceedings of the International Conference on HPSG.* (ed. S. Müller). Stanford: CSLI Publications.

Na, Y. and Huck, G. (1993). On the status of certain island violations in Korean. *Linguistics and Philosophy* 16: 181–229.

Nam, K.-S. and Ko, Y.-K. (1993). *The Standard Grammar of Korean.* (In Korean.) Tower Press.

O'Grady, W. (1991). *Categories and Case: The Sentence Structure of Korean*. Philadelphia: Benjamins.

Park, C. (2013a). Nominal and clausal grounding of Korean verbal nouns. *Linguistics* 51 (6): 1361–1395.

Park, C. (2013b). Setting and location: case-marked adverbials in Korean. *Constructions and Frames* 5 (2): 190–222.

Park, C. (2010). (Inter)subjectification and Korean honorifics. *Journal of Historical Pragmatics* 11 (1): 122–147.

Park, M.-K. (1994). A morphosyntactic approach to Korean verbal inflections. Doctoral dissertation. University of Connecticut.

Pollard, C. and Yoo, E.J. (1998). A unified theory of scope for quantifiers and wh-phrases. *Journal of Linguistics* 34: 415–445.

Pollard, C. and Sag, I. (1994). *Head-Driven Phrase Structure Grammar*. University of Chicago Press and CSLI Publications.

Pollock, J.-Y. (1989). Verb movement, universal grammar, and the structure of IP. *LI* 20: 365–424.

Sag, I. (1997). English relative clause constructions. *Journal of Linguistics* 33: 431–484.

Sag, I. (2013). Sign-based construction grammar: an informal synopsis. In: *Sign-Based Construction Grammar* (ed. H. Boas and I. Sag). Stanford: CSLI Publications.

Sag, I., Wasow, T., and Bender, E. (2003). *Syntactic Theory: A Formal Approach*. Stanford: CSLI Publications.

Sells, P. (1994). Sub-phrasal syntax in Korean. *Language Research* (Journal of the Linguistic Society of Korea) 30: 351–386.

Sells, P. (1995a). Korean and Japanese morphology from a lexical perspective. *Linguistic Inquiry* 26: 277–325.

Sells, P. (1995b). The category and case marking properties of verbal nouns in Korean. In *Harvard Studies in Korean Linguistics VI*, 370–386. Harvard University Press.

Sohn, H.-M. (1994). *Korean*. London and New York, Routledge.

Sohn, H.-M. (1999). *The Korean Language*. The Cambridge University Press.

Song, J.-J. (1997). The so-called plural copy in Korean as a marker of distribution and focus. *Journal of Pragmatics* 27: 203–224.

Song, S. (2014). A grammar library for information structure. Doctoral dissertation. University of Washington.

Suh, C.-S. (1996). *Kwuke Mwunpob* (Korean Grammar). Seoul: Hanyang University Press.

Wechsler, S. and Lee, Y.-S. (1996). The domain of direct case assignment. *Natural Language and Linguistic Theory* 14: 629–64.

Yang, D.-W. (1999). Case features and case particles. In: *West Coast Conference on Formal Linguistics* 18: 626–639.

Yoo, E.-J. (1997). Quantifiers and wh-interrogatives in the syntax-semantics interface. PhD dissertation. Ohio State University.

Yoo, E.-J. (2002). Auxiliary Verbs and structural case assignment in Korean. *Language Research* 38 (4): 1009–1036.

Yoon, J.-H. (1994). Different semantics for different syntax: relative clauses in Korean. *Japanese and Korean Linguistics* 4: 413–428.

Yoon, J.H.S. (1989). A restrictive theory of morphosyntactic interaction and its consequences. Doctoral dissertation. University of Illinois, Urbana-Champaign.

Yoon, J.H.S. (1995). Nominal, verbal, and cross-categorial affixation in Korean. *Journal of East Asian Linguistics* 4: 325–356.

Yoon, J.H.S. (2009). The distribution of subject properties in multiple subject constructions. *Japanese/Korean Linguistics* 16: 64–83.

Yoon, J.-M. (1990). Verb movement and structure of IP in Korean. *Language Research* 26 (2): 343–371.

Zubizarreta, M.L. and Oh, E. (2007). *On the Syntactic Composition of Manner and Motion*. Cambridge, MA: MIT Press.

Zwicky, A.M. (1985). Heads. *Journal of Linguistics* 21: 1–29.

Zwicky, A.M. (1993). Heads, bases and functors. In: *Heads in Grammatical Theory* (ed. G. Corbett, N. Fraser, and S. McGlashan), 292–315. Cambridge: Cambridge University Press.

Index

English and Korean in Contrast: A Linguistic Introduction, First Edition. Jong-Bok Kim.
© 2024 John Wiley & Sons, Inc. Published 2024 by John Wiley & Sons, Inc.